FIREFIGHTERS

FIREFIGHTERS
Their Lives in Their Own Words

Dennis Smith

Broadway Books

New York

BROADWAY

PRINTED IN THE UNITED STATES OF AMERICA

Broadway Books titles may be purchased for business or promotional use or for
special sales. For information, please write to: Special Markets Department,
Random House, Inc., 1540 Broadway, New York, NY 10036.

BROADWAY BOOKS and its logo, a letter B bisected on the diagonal, are trademarks
of Broadway Books, a division of Random House, Inc.

First Broadway Books trade paperback edition published 2002

The Library of Congress has cataloged the hardcover edition as follows:

Smith, Dennis, 1940–
Firefighters: their lives in their own words.
1. Firefighters—United States—Interviews.
2. Firefighters—United States—Attitudes. I. Title.
TH9118.A1S65   1988   363.3'7'0922   88-11815

ISBN 0-7679-1307-8

5   7   9   10   8   6

To all those brave souls
who cannot any longer catch the rig

Acknowledgments

I'd like to thank Jane O'Connor for her coordination, Mimi Bright for her attention, and Harvey Eisner for his connections with fire departments all over the country.

Contents

Preface

SOMEONE HAS TO DEAL WITH FIRE. WHEN PEOPLE FIRST BANDED together in small societies, they realized that if fire were not dealt with, it would consume everything in its path.

In our highly developed, technological society, the same confrontation with fire exists, as it has for thousands of years. When a fire occurs, someone has to deal with it. Here in America, those men and women whose responsibility it is to deal with fire are those seemingly easygoing folks down at the local firehouse. When the alarm comes in at three in the morning on a cold winter night for a fire rushing through a tenement building in a poor section of a large city . . . or at one in the afternoon for a young child who has fallen into an abandoned water well . . . or at seven in the evening for a barn fire that is miles away from any kind of water supply . . . there is this particular group of people who put on their rubber boots and their specially treated fire coats and their fire helmets to respond to the call of others in need of help.

They may ride the engine, which is the squat vehicle with all the hose in it, or they may ride the truck, which is the long hook and ladder or the one with the aerial ladder. The truck firefighters' responsibility is to rescue trapped victims, to force entry, and to ventilate so that the heat and smoke have a way to escape the building. Or they may belong to the rescue squad, whose responsibility is to deal with all the special emergencies, such as building collapses, hazardous material situations, explosions, extrications from vehicles, trains, or planes, landslides, snowslides, and cave-ins.

It doesn't matter what group the firefighter is attached to. It matters only that he or she is out there in all weather and emergency conditions to give service to fellow human beings. Somebody has to do the job, and in the following pages you will read about the lives of these men and women, both paid and volunteer, who protect us from the ravages of fire and other emergencies, or die trying.

The firefighters in these pages are at once very special and not so special. They are very special because they represent a group of people who are different from other professional and working-class people. They represent a group of people who die in the line of duty more often, proportionately, than those in any other occupation, including police, construction workers, and miners. They are people who understand the dangers surrounding them, yet respond to each new alarm with newfound enthusiasm for the action ahead. These men and women like what they do, and they like themselves because of what they do. They are pleased that they have been given the opportunity and the calling to help others in a way that is at once meaningful and exciting. Like other Americans, they care about their homes, their families, their churches and organizations, yet they are the ones who answer the alarm at three in the morning, not knowing what awaits them. They are trained to meet any emergency, perhaps to give a fast wink to death and a pat on the butt to danger.

At the same time, they are very ordinary and not at all special, for they are just some of the one and a half million firefighters in all fifty states. About two hundred thousand of them are paid firefighters working in our metropolitan areas, military installations, large factories, and airports. The rest are volunteers serving their communities for no compensation and no pension, in that wonderful and important American tradition of voluntarism. Where would the country be without these volunteers? it might be asked. The question is only rhetorical, for the volunteers will always be with us, serving proudly just as they have since men got together to fight the first recorded American fire in the provision warehouse of Jamestown, Virginia, in 1609, and since Benjamin Franklin organized the first volunteer fire company in Philadelphia in 1735.

It takes a dedicated, committed, and courageous person to enter the blind, boiling darkness of a building on fire, to crawl through poisonous smoke, to confront the threat of the flames. These are the kind of people I met and talked with in the course of creating this book. Yet not one firefighter would refer to himself as any of these things but simply as a person trying to do his best in tough situations.

I have been reminded often in these interviews of how natural and graceful real humility can be, and how well humility fits within the true heart. I felt I was a small reporter being honored by people who are as close as we can get to royalty in America. I have been moved to tears, I have felt the blood pushing hard through my veins, I have felt empathy and deep admiration for these men and women who have done significant things in their lifetimes. I cherish my moments with these firefighting citizens.

To create a book is man's work, but to put one's life on the line to protect the life of another human being is the work of God. Although I have written many books and fought many more fires, I have never felt so accomplished as I feel in bringing the stories of these American firefighters to you.

Dennis Smith
New York City, 1988

Introduction

THE ECONOMIC BENEFITS OF BEING A FIREFIGHTER ARE NOT RE-
ally great. The time off is fairly decent. Work schedules vary widely from
place to place, but generally speaking firefighters have more time off in a
consecutive way than most people. At the same time, many of them work
forty-eight and fifty-two hours a week. New York firefighters work forty.
Volunteer firefighters don't enjoy this same benefit, but they do share in
the greater benefit of working with great guys. When you go to work, you
know you are going to sit in the firehouse kitchen with people who are
interesting, funny, and worthy of your attention.

Another benefit of being a firefighter is your sense of self-worth. You
go out on a job, you eat some smoke, you take a little heat, and you get the
great satisfaction of confronting the flames and defeating them. You know
you're doing a good job, and that's a very valuable benefit.

There's not much money for the paid firefighters. Only the bosses get
paid well. The fire commissioner of New York gets paid more than most
big-city mayors. But the ordinary firefighter is almost always paid less
than a schoolteacher, generally on a parity with policemen—and he works
more hours.

Paid vacation time is good, generally three or four weeks after four or
five years. The trouble is, your time off is seldom in sync with the rest of
the world. When your kids are starring in the school play, you're working.
If there's a rare family reunion at Thanksgiving, you're working. And
when you should be celebrating the baby's first Christmas, you're working.
That's a minus. And, that's the breaks.

What makes up for it in the long run is that you're not chained to an
assembly line putting caps on bottles for eight hours a day, at the end of
which you rush to the time clock to escape into the open air. Firefighters

like going to work, and there are few jobs at any level of pay about which this can be said with such certainty.

When I was first appointed to the fire department we had to go to training school for eight weeks. (Today the training period is generally twelve weeks.) At the time, I was driving a really old car that belonged to my then girlfriend and future wife. It was just a piece of junk, really. I parked it on Second Avenue, intending to drive it to the training school in the morning. Second Avenue is one of the most heavily traveled thoroughfares in Manhattan, and you can't leave a car parked there after seven o'clock in the morning. When I got to the car, however, just before seven, it was completely dead. I had no choice but to leave it there.

In order to avoid getting a ticket, I did something that was incredibly naive. I took my badge, which had just been issued to me, pinned it to the sun visor of the car, and put a note on the dashboard saying I was going to the fire training school and would be back for the car shortly. Your badge is something you must fiercely protect, and if you lose it, it's a two-day fine, plus all the trouble of changing your records in the department, where your badge number is your identifying number.

Incredibly, when I returned from school in the late afternoon, the car and the badge were still there, the car had not been towed away, and I had not gotten a ticket. Whatever cop had seen the badge hanging down from the sun visor must have shaken his head and said, "This guy's got no brains at all, and I won't add to his burden by giving him a ticket."

I loved those days out at the training school on Welfare Island, and I made a lot of friends. Few of us knew much about the fire department, and it was great listening to the old-time firefighters, who were assigned to light duty positions at the school because they had been injured on the job. They would tell you war stories and firehouse kitchen stories, and you'd sit around between classes, absolutely transfixed, as if watching a Eugene O'Neill drama.

It was rather like a Marine Corps boot camp, where the veterans tell the recruits what it was like in Korea and Vietnam. The difference was that the Marines were there to fight a war, whereas in our training school it was an opportunity to do something more constructive with your life.

But before we went out to live these stories ourselves, there was training that had to be done. There were building laws to be learned, and the different types of building construction—frame, brick, steel, and, in New

York, the old cast-iron ones. We had to learn about the different kinds of windows—regular windows, casement windows, and the nonopening ones in skyscrapers—and the different locks people use to secure themselves from the harsh realities of the outside world—standard bolt locks, police locks that lock on either side of the door, and fox locks, which have bars going down into the floor like flying buttresses. You had to learn the multitudinous knots used for moving equipment and people, and a whole communications system, the signals and alarms, the difference between "ten-four" and "ten–twenty-two."

We studied water hydraulics, the laws of physics that govern the movement of water rushing through a two-and-a-half-inch hose and coming out of a one-inch nozzle. Outdoors, we learned about tools, everything from how to swing an ax to how to pull a hook and how to use your weight on a battering ram. We learned about the motorized tools, the power saw, the pneumatic tools and jacks used in collapse situations. Then there was the practical work of fighting the fire itself in controlled situations, where we had to crawl into a room and pull out a 150-pound dummy and carry it down six flights of stairs after taking a beating from the smoke. Later in the afternoon we had to carry ladders from one side of the street to the other.

A wonderful old captain gave us the ladder lessons. He was a classy guy, very military in his white firefighter's shirt with the captain's bars and the razor-sharp creases in his pants. He was a real gentleman, considerate with time and giving extra assistance to anybody who needed it, while at the same time making sure the probationary firefighters were taught correctly, knowing that if they were not, they could get themselves and others in a lot of trouble.

Once he was giving us a lesson on carrying a twenty-foot ladder by ourselves, the single-man carry. It's a fairly heavy ladder, and you carry it by holding the third rung and putting your arm through in a kind of buttress position, and you walk carefully.

I was walking, and he was behind me. I lost my balance, and the ladder went right back over my shoulder. Somebody yelled, the captain held up his elbow, and the ladder caromed off it. In seconds, his elbow developed a lump the size of a softball. I went to him, saying, "Geez, I'm sorry, Cap, I'm sorry, Cap." A gentleman to the last, he just looked at me and didn't say a word. He went off to have the thing x-rayed. Fortunately, it wasn't broken. He was out of work for a few days. I saw him when he came back and again at our graduation ceremony, but nothing was ever said.

That captain got hurt not so much by my not paying attention as by my being inexperienced and inadequate to the particular job. So you can get hurt in training, and no matter how good you are at the job, you must remember you can't control the environment of a fire like you can in training.

In Engine Company 82, it was an honor to take the nozzle at a fire. In other locations, they call it the "tip" or the "pipe." This one day, I was the nozzle man. The fire was on the third floor of a tenement building, going really good. It had evidently been cooking for a long time, because by the time we got there the fire fully involved this apartment of five or six rooms. I had my boots up, coat closed, helmet on, and I was ready to go. Willie Knapp was behind me, and I said, "All right, guys, let's go."

There was this long hallway, and we ran in crouching positions into the fire with an inch-and-a-half hose. We got to the end of the hallway, I opened up the hose and led the way into the room there. Immediately, a large part of the ceiling came down on me, knocking my helmet off. Embers went down my neck and back, and I was burned pretty severely. So, with the nozzle still in my hand, I shut it off, made a complete U-turn, and started back out of the room. Willie Knapp said, "Hey, give us back the knob," another name for the nozzle.

So I gave Willie the nozzle and continued out of the room. When I got out into the hall, the embers had died out, and I had a lifetime three-inch burn down my neck from hairline to shoulder blade. Thereafter, every time Willie Knapp referred to that fire, he called it "Dennis Smith's great U-turn approach to firefighting."

The interesting thing is, you hardly mind getting hurt in a fire, as long as you don't get hurt too badly. A gash in your arm that takes twelve stitches, a burn on your neck, a broken wrist, or some injury like that is, in a sense, just another red badge of courage that reinforces the things you believe about firefighting and reinforces your confidence in yourself to do a tough, challenging, and dangerous job.

I once got hurt just pulling a hose over a barbed wire fence. I had to tug so hard I pulled a ganglion, or nerve center, in my back. It was one of the most painful things I've ever experienced. It was difficult to treat. I had to lie on my stomach in bed for three months, doing everything in that position, eating, reading, writing notes, watching television. Finally a doctor shot a whole bunch of cortisone into my back, which completely relieved the pain, and finally I was able to go back to work. The cortisone never disappeared, though, and still moves around. I still feel the pain from time to time, especially when I'm tired.

There is an overriding awareness of the possibility of getting badly hurt, because we see it around us all the time. We see guys getting disabled permanently, and you learn not to take even the smallest fire for granted.

I remember a job in a school right up the street from the firehouse, where there was a small fire in a closet on the fourth floor. There was a lot of smoke, but there seemed to be just a bunch of papers and rubbish in there. What no one knew was that it had purposely been set and that there was a lot of gasoline poured onto the closet floor and the floor of the nearby bathroom. Three guys from the engine company were in the room, but none of them smelled the gasoline because of the smoke.

The three guys started to extinguish the fire just as the heat got to the gasoline. The gasoline exploded, and the whole room went on fire. Two of the guys got to the door and were safe, but the fire expanded so rapidly, it cut the third guy off, and he ended up at the window. Unless you've had the experience, you will never believe how quickly a fire can move through a room, two rooms, three rooms.

This firefighter, Tom Kearney, was at the window yelling, and Ladder 31 began to put its tower ladder up. That's a long boom with a platform at the end of it, with room enough for four or five fighters to stand. There were two firefighters on the platform, raising it. As it reached the third floor, Kearney, now framed in the fourth-floor window, was on fire, and he couldn't wait the extra five seconds for the tower ladder to get to him. He was forced to jump.

He jumped into the bucket and hit one of the guys there, Lt. Bilcik, breaking his leg. But even with a broken leg, Bilcik was able to grab an extinguishing can and put out the flames on the burning firefighter. Tom Kearney had his fire-safe coat on, but it was the clothes beneath it, his pants and his shirt, that were on fire. All this happened from a very little fire in a closet in a school.

I visited this man in the New York Burn Center. He was terribly burned on his arms and shoulders, and on the bottom part of his body around his buttocks and the backs of his legs. He was very courageous. You would have to be in such a situation.

You really do muster up extraordinary strength in times of personal crisis. There's a spiritual part of us, and when we get hurt seriously we realize how fragile we are as human beings, and we rely on this spirituality to bring forth the dignity of our souls.

This guy was in great pain, but he was also very funny. He said his wife was concerned about his being in the burn center with all these beautiful nurses. But he reassured her. He said that a nurse who is tearing the burned layers of skin off your body, inch by painful inch, no matter how gorgeous she is, is never going to be thought of as anybody but a person who's tearing off the top layer of your skin, inch by painful inch.

Sometimes people get killed. Every firefighter has to deal with the death of a brother firefighter at some point in his life. In America, a firefighter dies in the line of duty every other day. I remember many, many funerals. I remember looking at the children of firefighters and thinking that they will live with the memory of their father giving his life in a job that cared about him. The only standing room you'll find at a firefighter's funeral is out in the street, down the block.

I remember when eleven firefighters died in the line of duty at Twenty-third Street in New York. I was at that terrible scene when we were searching for the bodies. I remember the bodies coming out, one by one. The hundreds of firefighters who were there took their helmets off, as if the bodies were passing in review. The floors of the building had collapsed, taking these firefighters down into the bowels of the fire. I remember the quiet in the immediate vicinity as their bodies came out.

I reconcile that memory with the memory of the funeral as the coffin-laden fire trucks moved down Fifth Avenue to the Methodist and Episcopal churches there and on to St. Patrick's Cathedral. The services at the different houses of worship were held simultaneously, attended by New York firefighters, ten thousand strong, and thousands of visiting firefighters from all over the country who had come to pay their respects to the profession of firefighting as well as to the men who had died in this tragic fire.

After the funeral, some of us went over to Engine 8 on Fifty-first Street and Third Avenue and had coffee and cake and sandwiches. And that was it. I was dismayed at how little the city had done to make those thousands of visiting firefighters welcome. The firehouses alone had opened their doors and taken them in, given them something to eat, and made them feel at home.

A couple of years later, in Boston, there was the tragic Vandome Building fire, in which nine firefighters were killed. A group of twenty of us from Engine 82 and Ladder 31 went to the funeral. We didn't think about it, it was just assumed that since firefighters had died, we would naturally go to the funeral. I hired the bus to come at three in the morning so we could get up there by nine for the Mass at the cathedral in Boston.

It was a dismal day in mid-June. The bus came, and the twenty of us were in our dress blue uniforms. We had a whole bunch of sandwiches and fifteen cases of beer. That was more beer than we could possibly drink, but firefighters like to be ready for all contingencies and unexpected guests. Shortly after we took off, a couple of the guys began opening the beer, saying they planned to sleep for a few hours on the trip. More beer was opened, cans were snapping, then somebody said, "Hey, Dennis, where's the bathroom on this bus?"

I looked around and realized they had sent a bus for twenty-odd firefighters to travel from the city of New York to the city of Boston, up the New England Thruway for six hours or so, and they had embezzled us out of the bathroom that was supposed to be on the bus.

We had a big pot with ice in it to chill the beer. The bus driver, after being somewhat verbally abused, was told to open the door. He said, "I have to stop the bus." We said, "Don't stop the bus, just open the door." He said, "I can't, it's against the law." Finally, as the bus was cruising along the Cross Bronx Expressway, we took the big pot and threw all the ice out onto the road to be pelted by the rain.

Then the pot was put on the entry step and, of course, became the bus's bathroom. I'll never forget the face of the driver every time one of the beer drinkers went forward and deposited digested beer into the pot. As the hours passed, every time the bus hit a bump, great yellow waves sloshed over the side of the pot.

When we reached Boston, we went directly to Florian Hall, where we were to congregate. There I saw what it was like when a city decided it was going to make itself host to the visiting firemen. Boston and its citizens opened themselves up, the hotels held free rooms for the visiting firefighters, and the firehouses, of course, welcomed their visitors. The city donated its buses for transport duty, and the bus drivers volunteered their time and their days off to drive them.

One of Boston's leading citizens donated five thousand pairs of white gloves, because he felt it would look nice for all the firefighters to be wearing white gloves. It was a terribly rainy day, and some other citizen donated thousands of little plastic rain covers for the firefighters to wear. And a huge luncheon was given in Florian Hall for the visitors.

It was a typical Irish-style wake and funeral reception, plenty to eat and drink, lots of funny stories to mitigate the tragedy that was the cause of our coming together. So it was an altogether wonderful experience, though set in tragedy, especially when juxtaposed with what I thought was the chintzy reception for the visiting firefighters in New York.

I have to say, however, that I have never seen a funeral procession as beautiful as the procession of flag-draped coffins down Fifth Avenue to the tune of a somber funeral march. I went home that evening, watched it on television, and collapsed in tears. The event was just too emotion-packed for me.

There is a great difference in style of management from fire department to fire department across the country. I have observed most of it firsthand, and I've always felt that the upper echelons in New York City are composed—with some notable exceptions—of extremely political people who never really remember the days when they were back-step firefighters. The working class is governed, they seem to think, by the divine right of rulers.

Of all the fire commissioners I have known in the city, the two black ones, Bob Lowry and Gus Beekman, were the most considerate and gentlemanly. Perhaps that came from their own experiences in the city fire department, which, at one point in its history, had "black beds." I guess that they themselves had slept in black beds in the firehouses but were big enough to transcend the insult and relate to the joy and the opportunity the fire department presented. One cannot rise in ranks through the fire department without the support and respect of a large group of people. Apparently neither man forgot what it was like to be a working man or a sensible manager responsible for a large city agency. They didn't let political opportunism interfere with the running of the fire department or the running of their lives.

The New York Fire Department has also had a great line of chiefs of department. The chief of department is the highest uniformed position, a competitive civil service position, and once a man makes it he is secure in the job and outside the authority of the mayor's office. He represents the safety of the city's public, not the interests of the mayor or the fire commissioner. In critical situations the chief of department is the man with the responsibility, not the fire commissioner. Most fire commissioners don't know the male end of the hose from the female. But we've had some of the finest men I've ever met as chiefs of department.

It should be remembered by all the politicians in America that the fire department is always better run and the public safer when the head of it has come up through the ranks. The fire commissioner, who is appointed by politicians, is, almost by definition, transient and cannot be responsible for preserving the tradition of the fire department and fighting for the future safety of the public. This job should be filled by a person whose life has been dedicated to firefighting.

There is something that happens to a man when he becomes a firefighter. I'm certain, too, it will happen to women now that they appear with greater frequency on the rolls of fire departments. That something is that he begins to care about what he is doing, about the people he works with, and about the department's reputation in a way that surprises, a depth of feeling that is entirely new. It is that feeling that enables people to enter burning buildings, and it is that feeling that will preserve the histories of fire departments throughout the land. It becomes a part of the man, and a part of every action.

Chapter One

I ALWAYS WANTED TO BE A FIREMAN

WHEN I WAS A KID, I HAD NO GREAT AWARENESS OF FIREMEN. I mean, I saw them as guys who were extremely tall and who came around once in a while and ambled down the long, dark hallways of the tenement buildings in New York City where I grew up. There were times when I ended up on a fire escape because there was smoke in the building and everyone got frightened. I remember my mother being frightened of fires, just as anyone who lived in an old tenement would have a natural fear of fire.

So I never knew a great deal about firemen. Few firemen lived in our neighborhood. The parents of the kids I went to school with were waiters, boiler workers, steamfitters, construction workers. No cops or firemen.

As I grew up, cops and firemen were kind of interchangeable. The same kind of people who became firefighters became cops. It's still true today. They are high school graduates for the most part, but the fire department gets the cream of the crop because there are more firefighters with college degrees. It's seldom a lifelong ambition. Most people who take the fireman's test also take the police test. They're civil service tests, and the results are published, so you have a pretty good idea of when you might be called. If you pass both tests and are on both lists, almost always you will take the fireman's job. You will take it because, quite frankly, it is the better job.

Any intelligent person can see that a fireman is on the street to help people. He is never caught in an ugly situation where he is an opponent, he is there in a positive way, whereas a cop, let's face it, there are times when nobody really likes a cop. You may step back a little and say, "Oh, yeah, cops are good people, it's a tough job, they do a good job." Which is all true. But cops are the ones who ticket the car when you double-park in

1

front of the drugstore to fill a prescription for the sick baby. Cops are the ones in negative situations, in ghettos for instance, where a man and a woman are fighting, and the cop has to cool the situation down by pushing someone around. Their whole job has an aura of internal distrust: the patrolman is afraid of the sergeant, the lieutenant, the captain, the commander, and the "shooflies," the guys who hide in the shadows to see what the cop is doing. I like cops, personally, because they almost always have a good sense of humor, but their profession suffers from bad P.R., no doubt about it.

A firefighter, on the other hand, is out there only to help people. In a car accident, if you pull the alarm the fire engines usually come faster than the ambulance. The firefighter will pull somebody out of the car, it doesn't matter what kind of a mess the victim is in. He is well trained in emergency situations. He knows how to deal with people. He knows when to move an injured person and when not to, when to put on a splint and when not to. He is trained to make a fast assessment of an emergency situation. When he arrives at a fire and sees people on the fire escape in the front of the building, he automatically knows there will be people on the back fire escape and in trouble inside the building. He knows to think about what isn't immediately seen. He is there only to help, and he is asked to help in all kinds of situations—not only fires but accidents, drug overdoses, shootings, knifings, injuries from whatever cause. So a young guy coming out of high school sees all this, and asks himself, "What is it that I really want to do?" And the fire department winds up getting the best people.

When that time came for me, I had just gotten out of the service. I needed a job, and I was drawn to the firefighters' and cops' jobs more strongly than to construction workers' jobs, for instance.

The reason is simple: there's this huge, Buddha-like symbol that makes you fall on your knees and say, "This is what is going to direct my life." It's called a pension.

The fire department has a twenty-year pension system. This is the American dream, the twenty-year pension. I think of the old relatives who came here from Ireland. They didn't know about the twenty-year pension. Too bad. The whole country would have come over, leaving cottages unswept and cows unmilked, to get to America and participate in this great idea called the twenty-year pension system.

That was the attraction for young folks like myself who wanted a job.
Dennis Smith

□

What really got me interested in the fire department was working on the new Chesapeake Bay Bridge. I had been in the Navy and gotten some firefighting training, but nothing that really interested me. Then, after I got out, we were putting in the foundation of the bridge, working in a hole sixty feet below sea level. The work was sporadic because it was wintertime and the rough seas prevented us from working.

So I hung around periodically on weekdays, and I had this friend who was always around in the daytime. I said to him, "It seems like you never work. You know, you're always home. Every time I come by, you're here, working on your car, or doing something. What do you do for a living?"

"Oh," he said, "I'm a fireman in the city." He was working nights, and I would see him during the day when he was off. So he was telling me about the job, and it sounded real interesting. So I put in an application and took the exam and came up in the top 5 percent. That was sixteen years ago.

I grew up in Brooklyn, Maryland. Not to be mixed up with Brooklyn, New York. It's sort of a suburb of Baltimore, yet it's in the city itself. Lower-middle-class family. One of eight children, three brothers and four sisters. My mother is still alive, but my father has passed away.

I'd seen a few house fires when I was younger, but it hadn't drawn me in. There were some people in my class at fire school who were from fire families. You know, their fathers and their grandfathers were in, and they had a working knowledge of the fire department. I didn't. I had no knowledge of the nomenclature or job description. It was all new to me.

My father lost an arm in World War II. He received a pension from the service. We were poor, but he always worked and he never accepted welfare. He worked at the post office during the Christmas rush, and in parking lots. This was besides his regular job of driving a florist truck. He worked to raise his family. Today, a lot of people are saying they need help, they need this, they want that. I'm thankful for everything I have, the opportunity to go to school and live the way I'm living now, the opportunity to work.

I finished high school and went into the service. I came out of the service, worked on the Chesapeake Bay Bridge, and came into the fire department. After I graduated from the fire academy I went to college part-time while I was in the fire department. I finished and got my AA in fire protection. I'm the only one in the family who has ever gone to college.

□

Now that I'm a full-time medical student, I miss firefighting a great deal. I started volunteer firefighting seven years ago in the Tri Village Fire Department in New York State. I'm still a member there.

I grew up on Long Island in Garden City. That's an affluent suburb. We were a block away from the firehouse. I think they had paid chauffeurs, while the rest of the fire company was volunteers. The horns were always blasting as I was growing up, and the blue lights of the volunteers were always rushing by the house to wherever they were going.

I remember very well going to the firehouse once when I was a little kid. One of the firemen showed me the remnants of a watch, a new kind of watch that had been melted down into a wad of black plastic. It had come out of a fatal fire caused by someone smoking in bed. That sticks in my mind.

I went to a private Catholic school on Long Island. My father died in 1968, and in 1970 my mother took a job at Ithaca College, and we lived there for two years. Then she was appointed by Governor Carey to run an agency in Albany, the New York State Higher Education Services Corporation. They administer loans and grants, all those things. I think it's from her I got this sense of public service. There was a great deal of freedom in my environment. I suspect that if she had been stricter and tried to push me along in a certain direction, I never would have taken the tangent off into the fire service.

Anyway, we moved out to where we are now in Brainard, south of Albany. We weren't sure where we were going to end up living, so I spent the last two years of high school at Concord Academy in Massachusetts. In Massachusetts, it's funny, towns are very small. In New York State they would have mostly volunteer firefighters, while in Massachusetts they were mostly paid firefighters but with very small crews in their companies. Before I left Ithaca, I think when I was sixteen, some of the kids who were eighteen were trying to get involved with the volunteer fire department. I remember looking at them with admiration. I knew it was something I wanted to do.

I matured a lot in prep school, and I wanted to be a lawyer. I thought that was the best way to share the talents God had given me with other people.

During my college years, at Colgate, in Hamilton, New York, I ran with the Hamilton Fire Department.

There is a certain amount of glamour to the fire service. A lot of little kids want to be firemen. There is also a sense of being able to do something, of being involved and doing something exciting.

Things change, though. My roommate in my freshman year at college was going to be a doctor. He just graduated from Columbia Law, and I'm here at medical school.

□

My dad has just retired from the Chicago Fire Department after thirty-three years on the job. My grandfather was a captain of an engine company in Chicago, and I had an uncle who was also a firefighter in a suburb. So I have always, as long as I can remember, been used to my dad going to work and being gone. I thought everybody's dad did that, and that they didn't come home until the next morning.

I used to have to wait for beatings. You know, "Wait until your father gets home." Most little kids have to wait at the most eight hours to get beaten. But firefighters' kids, if their fathers were working a twenty-four-hour shift, they would have to wait until the following morning and then maybe a whole other day of school to get beat. It was an important thing to me when I was younger.

When you're young you think your dad is great, and then when you get into your teens you think your old man is the dumbest guy in the whole world. I thought the same thing. It always takes hearing it from somebody else. I heard it from many people in positions where they didn't have to lie to me to know that my dad was, if not *the* best, one of the best firefighters in the city of Chicago. I mean, a dedicated man.

In those days certain civilians could ride the apparatus, especially a fireman's son. When I was around thirteen I was a big, tall, lanky kid, so I looked all right wearing firefighter's gear. I used to ride on the apparatus up through high school, actually going in fires. Every weekend, every chance I got, I would go to my dad's firehouse with my bedding and stay the twenty-four-hour shift. Those men treated my dad like a god because they looked up to him so much. He was a lieutenant at the time. Later, when he got old and his arthritis got too bad, he went out to O'Hare Airport, but I continued to go to the busy stations where he worked years ago.

Twice he was almost killed on the job. He is not a big storyteller. In fact, he never told me fire stories until I was older and said I wanted to enter the fire department. Then he tried to teach me things. He said, "Bill, you watch out for those truss roofs, because when one component fails the whole roof and parapet will come down, and they will kill you."

One time my dad was in a fire in a three-story building. It had a very high parapet which concealed the bowstring truss roof behind. He was operating the turntable of the ladder truck, and he had two guys in the basket. It was real smoky. He saw a crack developing in this parapet. Everybody else hauled ass to get away, because you could see what was going to happen. My dad stayed there and swung that snorkel boom away and got those two guys in the basket out of the way just as the wall came down. It buried my old man. Just buried him. One of the things that fell on him was an electrical transformer, and he had an electrical burn across his groin from a wire landing right there.

The wires were sparking, and the other guys were afraid to jump right in. Then some crusty old fire chief, who had a truckman's belt on, had them attach a rope to the belt, and he said, "I'm going to start digging the bricks off this guy. And if something happens to me, yank me back." Well, as soon as he took off the first couple of bricks, they could see that he wasn't going to be electrocuted, and they all jumped in, and they pulled all of the bricks off my dad. He was in bad, bad shape. In critical condition. They were just about ready to drill holes in his head.

My dad was one of the first guys to wear a helmet with a neckstrap. You know, there was all that talk against the strap, saying you will fall through the floor and it will strangle you, and all that business. My dad said that the first brick would have hit him on the head and the rest of them would have killed him. That helmet stayed on his head.

What I'm trying to say is that he isn't a storyteller. What he was trying to do was to give me as much information as he could, so I wouldn't get hurt on the job.

□

It seems like I've been firefighting my whole life. That is, my father was a volunteer firefighter when I was a young boy, and I used to go with him when he responded to alarms, and to most of his drill sessions. Then I was actually able to join the volunteer fire department in Little Silver, New Jersey, when I became twenty-one.

I think I got from my parents a legacy, a kind of social commitment to help out the community—in church or synagogue or promoting good government or becoming involved with the schools. My dad was involved with Little League baseball, as an example. He worked as a technical writer for the government, writing training manuals. I was expected to go to college, to make something of myself. And I think I picked up that commitment to one's fellowman from my religion. I think there are probably a good number of us who came on the job in the early seventies who had that kind of background.

It's a long way from a small town volunteer to a career firefighter. I really didn't envision myself doing that until I got word of fire protection engineering as a profession. My parents took me down to the University of Maryland, and one of the professors there convinced my folks that this was a legitimate profession. I saw that I could take my avocation and merge it with my vocation. I was going to be a fire protection engineer.

So I went to the Illinois Institute of Technology and got my degree.

My father became a volunteer firefighter relatively late in life. Frankly, the reason he had been discouraged from joining the local fire company years earlier was because he was Jewish. It was only after he happened to have a car fire, and he happened to know the fire chief from work, that this man said, "Well, sure you can join, and I'll sponsor you." He was accepted, and he played on the department ball team.

For myself, after graduation I went on the job in Northbrook, Illinois, and references to my being Jewish were made. When I went to Panama to work on the fire department there I had learned my lesson, and I didn't push it. Some people knew my religion, but I didn't advertise it. I have heard some snide remarks at various times, and I don't need that in my life. I am willing to overlook it. I guess sometimes that is the price one pays to be accepted in the fire department.

□

I grew up right here in Florida, about eighty miles north of here. I had no interest in firefighting. My father was an automobile mechanic, and he ran a garage that was located just south of the Florida Fire College. I remember being with my dad at his desk and watching the guys training in the smoke and fire. And I'd say, "God, that is a tough job. I don't know if I ever want to do that."

Amazingly enough, here I am today. But as far as having a desire to make a career of it, no, I don't think I did. It was just something I ended up doing.

□

I always wanted to be a fireman since I was a little kid. I never changed my mind. It's in my blood, I don't know. Every time a fire truck went down the street, I loved it. That was right here in Burbank.

I used to hang out at the fire stations a lot. I would go after school, and when I was able to drive I would go to the fires. My history in the fire department really goes back to when I could drive to the fires. I took up picture taking.

At the time I didn't know what a fire buff was. I had never heard of them, and there was never anybody else who was really like me. There was a fire buff club in Los Angeles that I wasn't aware of, because I really hadn't been around. Then as time went on I realized there were other people who liked doing what I did.

My earliest experience with a fire was when I was four or five years old. It was a fire in the neighborhood, and I was actually afraid of it. I can remember hiding in the house to get away from the sirens, the flames, and the smoke.

My dad was interested in fire. He was an optometrist. Any time he would see smoke or a large fire in the city, he would take me to it. He knew I was interested. Later, when I had my own car, I got a radio, and I'd listen to the calls. Then he would get into the car with me. I knew he enjoyed going to the big ones, anyway.

□

Yeah, I'm a Northern guy in a Southern town. I was raised in Ashland, New Jersey, outside of Camden and across from Philly. There was a volunteer firehouse right up the street. The fire trucks would go by every day, and at a very early age I was fortunate enough to know what I wanted to do.

When I was around ten, I was like a station mascot. I'd be up there on weekends, helping them clean the trucks and wash the hose. And whenever the siren would go, I'd get my bike and follow them. It was a neighborhood kind of thing.

They had a junior program then, and at sixteen I joined. It slowly became a combination fire department, and I was hired to work on the staff. I worked in the fire marshal's office. But the transformation to a paid department was slow in coming. So I applied here in Charlotte and was hired.

□

I first thought of becoming a firefighter when I was twenty-two years old, right out of the Army. Right out of Vietnam. It's just that when I came back to this country I didn't have any job. The only thing I knew how to do was to cut meat. I was a meat cutter before I went in, and I didn't want to do that again.

A friend of mine told me about the fire department. Back then, the fire department was hungry for people. Because times were pretty good then, back in '71, and because the fire department pay wasn't that good a lot of people were going into other professions. So I chose the fire department.

I didn't know anything about it. I didn't even know the truck had a pump in it. I took the civil service test, and I failed it. I didn't know what a hook was, I didn't know what certain types of nozzles were. So I came down to the firehouse and met with the chief, and he gave me a booklet to study, and then I went ahead.

I was kind of getting over Vietnam and getting back into life. Over there I was so inexperienced, I was like a kid, a nineteen-year-old kid. I was expected to be a man, I thought I was, but I really wasn't.

There were a lot of deaths, a lot of fire deaths, mainly from the white phosphorus. I never related that to firefighting at the time. I was a door gunner on a helicopter. I was transporting dead people who were burnt, just crisp. It was a horrible sight to see something like that. Transported a lot of live ones, too. Really a lot more wounded than anything. It wasn't normally our job, but we were called upon, especially if it was an American. We would try our best to go in and rescue them.

They say being in a helicopter was very dangerous, but I tell you, the people I felt the sorriest for were the soldiers on the ground. They called them the grunts, the ones that actually had to live and stay right on the ground. If somebody shot at us, if they didn't shoot us down, we could fly away and get out of range, we could circle back or call in air support. But those guys on the ground, they were right in the middle of it. So I thought they had the roughest job. Of course, a door gunner had a high possibility of getting killed. I did lose a lot of my friends. It was sad.

I learned nothing there. Maybe I was better prepared than other guys to handle emergency situations, that's about all. We had no medical training, but we did try to help the Medevac people out, to get some bandages or something on the wounded guys. Tried to help them out the best we could.

□

My first memory of firefighters goes back to when I was seven. We lived in Baltimore County, and my dad was in the volunteer fire department. I used to hang out at the firehouse as often as I could. With my dad I could slide down the poles or just hang around. Talk with the guys.

Our elementary school was maybe two or three blocks from the fire station. In those days they used to blow the siren to alert the members when there was a fire in the neighborhood. Myself and a couple of the other guys would make sure that we had to go to the little boys' room when the siren blew, so that we could be out front to see the fire trucks go by, and see the guys.

As we got older, it just developed into the place to go. Other guys hung out on the corner, and we hung out at the firehouse. And when it was time to help a neighbor, that's where we were. We weren't out there ripping somebody off or causing any problems. I think I have a much better outlook on life than most people out there. I enjoy life, I really do.

I remember the time of the True-Fit fire in Baltimore. It killed a half dozen firemen. That kind of thing had a big impact on me. I thought, "Well, this is all nice, but I really don't know how nice it is. You can go out there, and one minute you're here, and the next you're gone." Of course, that adds to it. Not the death part or getting injured, but there is a certain amount of excitement involved. When people think of the fire department, they think of somebody rushing into buildings and saving lives, but that's not the only thing in it by a long shot.

As a kid, I lived and breathed the fire department. I think in those days my ambition may have been to achieve a battalion chief's position.

I started going to fire schools through the University of Maryland when I was fifteen. I lied and told them I was sixteen, because in those days you had to be sixteen in order to participate. I was pretty big for my age. I joined the volunteer fire department, and I stayed there day and night when I wasn't in school. That was my second love. I didn't have a lot of girlfriends, I just had the fire department, and that was where I stayed.

□

My grandfather was a New York City fireman, and when I was a little kid I was exposed to the fire service through him. He used to take me to the firehouse where he worked, which wasn't far from where we lived in Jamaica, Queens. Then when I was five we moved to Freeport on Long Island. They had a volunteer fire department there, so we'd see the trucks once in a while.

I always wanted to be a fireman. But when I grew up and it was time to get a job, my dad, who was a telephone man, told me to take the telephone test. So I got involved with the phone company for a number of years, but in the back of my mind I was thinking about the fire department. So after getting married and moving back to Freeport, I got involved with the volunteers.

□

I didn't enter the fire department until I was thirty-five. I grew up in the Kensington section of Philadelphia. When I was ten years old, my father died. My mother died when I was fifteen, during my first year of high school. I had a multitude of brothers and sisters, six brothers and two sisters. My father's death was obviously a traumatic experience for me because I kind of block out a lot of my early childhood. I was aware of what was going on. I felt the loss, I did miss my father, and if it hadn't been for the fact that I had so many brothers and sisters, it probably would have been more devastating. But we had each other to take us through the loss.

My mother, she did the best she could with what she had, and she was really exemplary in raising a family. It was tough for her. We didn't have a lot of uncles and aunts to help out, so it was pretty much one look out for the other. When she died five years later, it was like, now what happens? Like I said, there were nine of us, and we scattered in every direction. My older brothers and sisters were pretty much set in their ways, but my two younger brothers and me, we really didn't know what was going to happen.

Well, a couple of my sisters took in a couple of my brothers, and other brothers went into the service. I was in a better way than most of my brothers. I went and lived with my aunt in a nicer section of Philadelphia. I graduated from high school in June 1969, and in July I went into the Marine Corps. It worked out well for me and my brothers, though. Most of them are doing fine today.

□

My parents are first-generation, Italians. My dad is an attorney, my mother is a teacher, very successful people. They were raised in a way that you get up early, you work hard, you mind your own business, and you save your money—next thing, you bought a Cadillac and you lived in the nice end of town, that sort of thing. So I think I had an advanced set of social ideas as I have gone through my life.

When I was four years old, I lived in Jamestown, New York, and one day my mother and I were driving down the street in the middle of town, and we stopped at a traffic light. We were the first car at the light. The fire engine drove in front of us and stopped. They cut the hydrant and laid a line down the street to a building that was on fire. It was a tire store. So we were stopped there by virtue of their firefighting operation. I was standing up on the front seat, watching all this. That was the first connection I had with firefighting, the classic child's image of firefighting that never left. I appreciate that.

□

I grew up in what you would call a low-income neighborhood, a Bill Cosby type of neighborhood. I had an uncle named Charlie. He's dead now, but he was a fireman. When he would smile I would smile, because he was my idol. I was always watching him going off to work, and then I would see him come by on the fire truck, because he worked in the neighborhood. As a matter of fact, my first company was Ladder 6, and he worked at the same company, Ladder 6.

And when I was a small kid he was always saying, "When you grow up, I want you to be a fireman." I would say, "I will." Something that he kind of instilled in me. Whenever I heard sirens I would stop and I'd rush to the corner and just watch them go by, and it would give me some kind of a thrill. I just couldn't wait to be a fireman.

I went to a vocational high school and studied to be a machinist. Nothing spectacular about it. My background, it's a trade background. I played a little basketball and football. I was just a normal kid, nothing spectacular. Then I went into the service for a few years and worked at the Navy Yard as an electrician's helper.

I just had a sister in my immediate family. My mother and father separated when I was about seven, so my immediate family is small, just me, my mother, and my sister. But my mother had a lot of sisters and brothers, so the family itself is very large. We had Sunday dinners in a large house with a lot of people, a lot of love.

I think that sort of environment geared me toward the path I finally ended up taking. With a big family, everybody is always helping out, and I always had a sense of doing something for somebody—a sense of, "What can I do for you? What can I help with?"

When I was a little kid and got into a fight in the street, if I lost, I got beat up twice, because if I got home and my uncles knew I'd lost, I got beat up by them, too. Not Charlie, the younger uncles, they'd beat me good. So I couldn't lose in the street, and I think that's what built up what I have, my attitude about things.

□

All little boys want to grow up and be firemen, but for me it was always different. The first time I ever saw a fireman I knew I was going to do it. I was about four years old, I guess. I can even remember the location. It was back in Chicago in a two-story gray stone house. They had a bad fire, and I stood there watching it, and I was fascinated by the whole thing. I was fascinated by the apparatus. I was mostly fascinated, though, by the men. They were doing something that was terribly important, something everybody respected. It was the tail end of the fire, and they were bringing things out of the house and giving them to the people who lived there. You sensed that this was very, very important.

As a kid I didn't simply run to the fires in the neighborhood. I understood what was happening: that there were engine companies and that there was a ladder truck, there was a squad wagon and a chief's car, and that each one arrived on a certain time schedule.

I gotta tell you one other part. After I got interested, I learned that my father had been heavily influenced by it. This is important because it reflects something about the fire service that most people don't know. When my father was a child in the early 1900s, he lived down at Third and the Bowery in New York. His mother had died, and at various times he was abandoned by his own father, and his grandfather could only take care of him at night. There was nobody to take care of him during the day, and they were going to put him in an orphanage. The firemen of Engine 33 took care of him, and that saved him from going to the orphanage. My father became a buff at 33 Engine in the early 1900s and rode to many of the great fires in Hell's Hundred Acres in lower Manhattan—the Equitable Life fire, Boston Excelsior.

My dad, who died at the age of eighty-eight, had a lifelong love for firemen and a respect for them. In his later years, when he had several heart attacks, it was the fire department rescue companies that took care of him. He always felt good that he was in the hands of firefighters. And all his life, whenever he heard of a firefighter in trouble, he always wanted to do something to help him.

I remember one July fourth weekend in Chicago, a firefighter who had been burned over eighty percent of his body was dying from the poisoning. They didn't have air-conditioning in the hospitals at that time. He needed an air conditioner, and my dad heard about it. The firemen had called me because I was working on a newspaper, and my dad devoted the entire day to try and help me find an air conditioner for that fireman. We found one, and we found an air-conditioning man living out in the suburbs who was willing to come into town and set up the air conditioner in the hospital room. The firemen from Squad 2 and Engine 34, my old stomping ground, met us at the hospital, and we installed the air conditioner, and it really helped save this firefighter's life. Then a four-alarm fire came in right about that time. We all went to the fire, and several of the firemen who had helped install the air conditioner wound up in the same hospital a couple of hours later from heat exhaustion.

So anyhow, my dad taught me this great respect for firefighters, and I started riding the fire trucks when I was about fifteen. And you had to earn it. You had to earn your rides by helping to roll up hose and running errands. They hardly ever do that any more, because everything is real strict and by the book today. In those days, some pages of the book were sometimes turned. It was not uncommon in many of the big city departments for that sort of thing to happen. You stayed outside the building, and you helped pull the hose in the street, helped roll it up afterwards, and ran errands around the firehouse.

One way or another, I have been associated, officially and unofficially, with six different fire departments, because I have had to move as a result of the nature of my work. The Chicago Fire Department was where I was raised. I spent seven years riding with a heavy rescue squad on the West Side of Chicago. That experience helped shape my life, it helped shape my thinking about many things.

I gotta go back. When I was fifteen, sixteen, I used to ride with a rescue squad in the South Side of Chicago, which was an almost totally black slum district. I learned what life was like for a good part of our population, how tough it was. It taught me how lucky I was in the circumstances that I was born in, and in my later years as a reporter, the lessons I had learned as a teenager, riding with Squad 3 out of Fortieth and Dearborn, gave me an advantage other young reporters didn't have.

The firemen were wonderful people. I can remember almost every one of the firemen I have been with on all those companies my entire life. My dad could do the same thing with the people on 33 Engine back in 1911. I can remember the firemen on Engine 70 when I was a kid, and on Squad 3 and of course on Squad 2 on the West Side. That's when I really learned. I can remember everybody on Arlington Engine 1 and the Port Chester Fire and Rescue Company.

□

I suppose I'm special in that my father has been a career firefighter, and he is the deputy chief now, the fire marshal. The department has always been around. I grew up with it. We used to go on picnics with all the other firemen and socialize at family gatherings.

He was hurt quite a few times. They had a bad fire over here in my local, at Thirty-sixth and Chestnut. It was the Normandy Hotel, and my father was hurt and hospitalized for two weeks. He was in an oxygen tent and all. I was ten, and I remember going to the old Pennsylvania General Hospital to see him in the ward there. It was like a big open squad room, and he had plastic all around him. He was burned, and he took a lot of smoke. He had been a heavy smoker, but that's when he quit smoking because the doctor told him if he didn't it was going to kill him.

I always looked up to him, and I thought he was a hero. In fact, I have a newspaper clipping of him helping an old woman off an icy fire escape. They called that fire the Miracle on Thirty-sixth Street because it was in a high rise and it was a real bad fire on an icy night. I mean, the walls were falling down all around.

I never thought to say to him, "Hey, this is a dangerous job. Why don't you try something else?" I knew that's what he wanted to do. I respected his wishes. I felt bad that he was hurt, but I knew that's what he wanted.

□

I always wanted to be a firefighter or a police officer or something like that. My father was a fireman in Baltimore City for about four years, but that was before I was born. I think he was drafted, and then he stayed in the Army. So when I was young and he was in the Army, we traveled all over with him. We went to Texas, California, Colorado, Hawaii, all over. Then after he did his twenty, I guess I was around twelve, we moved back to Baltimore, to East Baltimore.

It was a hard neighborhood then. But life was pretty good. We had a strong mother and father, with seven of us. Everybody graduated from high school, three graduated from college, and two went into the service. I didn't get into too much trouble in the neighborhood. I got into trouble for shooting dice once when I was thirteen. That's about it. I was kind of scared to do anything because I knew my folks would tear me up.

I went into the Army after high school, and after getting out I worked at a pharmaceutical company for three years. But I really wanted to be in the fire department. I liked the trucks, they look nice and they are always kept clean.

I really didn't like school, and I went into the Army because I didn't want to go to college. I didn't have a scholarship anyway, and there were seven of us, and they were paying for the three oldest, so money was tight. I could probably have gotten a grant and gone to a community college, but going into the Army has worked well for me. They will pay for my schooling, and I'm going to school next year to take up fire technology.

I was twenty-five when I saw they were taking applications for the fire department, so I applied, and that was it. When I told my mother, she told me that my father had been in the fire department, and I said, "Is that right?" I guess whenever he had mentioned something about the fire department I never really listened to him.

One guy I grew up with, he's in the fire department, too. Mostly my close friends are doing pretty good. Some of the younger guys, they're not doing so good. I believe it has something to do with drugs. There were always drugs around, but it wasn't like it is now, wide open. You can go anywhere and see drugs in plain sight now. I think most people having single parents has got a lot to do with it, too.

When I was sixteen going on seventeen I started looking at the future, and I knew America wasn't really going to do anything for me. So I did something for myself. I strived. I wanted to succeed in something. I didn't want to be on the corner or get locked up because I didn't have a job. I wanted to work just like my father raised us. I wanted to have a family, too.

I think my family prepared me for the fire department. Because out of the seven of us my folks were always fair and didn't treat any one of us different. One didn't have, the other didn't have. We had to share, and that's the way we were brought up, to stick together and help each other out. My father liked the Army. The only thing he didn't like was picking up and moving every three years, moving here, moving there. All seven of us, back and forth. I failed one year in fourth grade because we had moved from Colorado to Baltimore, and when I got put into school here the lady said the credits didn't have anything to do with their school. My father didn't like that part.

□

I knew I wanted to go into the fire service when I was about ten years old. Even younger than that, actually. I haven't the faintest idea why. I can remember hanging around the local fire station when I was four or five. And when my mother was looking for me, she knew exactly where to go to find me. She just had to run around the corner to the fire station, and there I was.

That was in a small town in the Los Angeles area. At twelve years old I got to where I was basically a fire buff, chasing the fire trucks down the street on my bicycle, that kind of thing. And it just grew and grew and grew, and I decided that's what I wanted to do.

□

When I was eight or nine, I was in the car with my mother, and we came on a car fire. We were there before the fire trucks and had to wait with the traffic. The guys came then, pulled the hose off, and worked as a team. It was something to see. Just the action of it. It fascinated me.

I attended the regular schools in West Virginia, Brook High School in Weirton. I graduated and went on to trade school up in Ohio and learned welding. Then I came back and worked in a steel mill for a while. Then I joined the fire department.

My mother was a sergeant in the Marine Corps, and she's pretty tough to get along with. When she says something, you better do it. My father died when I was seven. And I had two older brothers that she had to raise also. She had to be mother and father at the same time. She had a strong hand. She didn't let anything ever get past her.

She thinks the fire department is great. When I joined, I didn't have much in my life, and then I just took off like a house afire. I'm really involved in the community. I'm involved with my fire training and teaching now. Before, I had small things in my life, but nothing this demanding or this exciting. It gives me a focus for my interests.

□

There weren't any firefighters in the family. I didn't even know what firefighters did. In my neighborhood in New York City, they seemed to be people in a strange-looking building, and I never saw much of them. I had an uncle who was a fireman, but he never talked about it.

The only experience I had with firefighters was when I was ten years old and my aunt was burned in a Christmas Day fire. She died five days later. This was up in Rye, New York. She was my mother's sister, just thirty years old.

I was allowed to visit her in the hospital. I remember the smell. There was no burn center. All they did was wrap her up and drug her. But I'll never forget that smell.

They didn't know if it was a cigarette or something on the stove. But apparently she had gone back in for her cat. They said they had found her on the bed under the bedroom wall that had collapsed on her. I remember reading, years later, in this old box that my mother had, the fire report from an officer on the scene. I guess my mother had asked for a report on how it had happened and why.

And I had forgotten all about that until about a year after I got on the job. My mother reminded me about what had happened—mothers are like that—and she felt that as a young kid I had been very impressed by the whole thing, so I chose the career when the opportunity came up. As far as I remember, I had had no interest in the job at all.

I tell everyone I'm from a broken home. Some of the other women in the department have the same background. My mom and dad split up when I was two. My mother raised me by herself. Parochial school, nuns, this was in Queens. Very hard with a broken home. It was hard for my mother, and it was hard for me being the only child. At that time there weren't very many single mothers. Now I'm married with four children, and that's a novelty. Today it's normal to be divorced.

I used to dream a lot as a kid. It's gonna sound corny. We were poor. I remember when I was nine or ten years old, my mom was painting the kitchen ceiling. It was a very high ceiling, and she did all the work herself. She was only five foot one and about ninety pounds. I remember her scraping and painting the ceiling. And she fell off the ladder and broke her pelvis.

She was laid up for quite a while. She had been working for Union Carbide, and whether it was a long-term thing or not, she was let go. Fired. We were on welfare for a while, and that was a horror. It was the biggest embarrassment there could possibly be, and then there was the idea of making sure no one found out. She was a fighter, my mother, a tough lady. She had been dished out a lot in her lifetime, but she never gave up. She is amazing.

Today she is on Social Security and disability. She still lives alone and prefers it that way. She remarried for a brief period when I was about twelve, but it only lasted a year. It was hard on me, but not because there was this man in the house. That I liked.

You see, my mother and I were two females living in the same house. We became very close. The bonding was extraordinary, especially between a mother and a daughter when there is no man around. You almost start to live your lives through each other. She was very happy when he was around, though, and that was enough. It was contagious. It wasn't what you would think, there was no jealousy. Just seeing her happy was great. So I was very sad when it didn't work out. I had never seen her that happy before.

I didn't see much of my dad when I was a kid, when I needed a great deal of attention. Not until I was much older. He was six-one and an Irishman who was in the Navy in the Second World War. He was very typical. My mother was a little blonde from a traditional family, and she married this man who was completely foreign to anything that she had seen. He was a hard-drinking man. It was a definite problem. I mean, it was ruining his life. Physically. Personally. I remember him picking me up Sundays with stitches and cuts. He stopped drinking the day my son was born. I hope that was why, but it doesn't matter, as long as he did.

My father was a sandhog. They're tunnel workers, doing subway tunnels in New York City, water tunnels. They're like small cities hundreds of feet under the ground. They're so deep in some instances that they have to go into decompression chambers before and after working in the tunnel, and by law they are only allowed to work four hours underground. One of the most common injuries for a sandhog is lung disease, which my father has. He worked on the Holland Tunnel, the tunnel under the East River, the Harlem Bridge, the Second Avenue subway, and a few others. I can't remember them all.

My husband got in the sandhogs too. On that job you get a union card, and then you have to shape up. You don't have a regular spot on a gang. At that time there were black gangs, there were Irish gangs, there were Italian gangs, there were all sorts of gangs. He wasn't sure where he fit in, because he had a beard, and the Irish gang didn't want him because they thought he was a Communist, and the black gang didn't want him because he was white. He said he really didn't make good money until he shaved his beard off, and then he found that he was shaping up.

He lost a finger in the tunnel, and once he had a skull fracture. He had a very bad experience the first time he poured concrete. These tunnels are huge tubes of concrete. One night he didn't have the right boots on, and the concrete got in under his shoes and his pants. When he got home the skin was peeling off his ankles, and his feet were burned by the lime. It was the sort of job where you never really helped the other guy through it. You more or less let things happen. If he was really tough enough for the job, he'd come back. It was that kind of mentality. He went back.

That's what I thought the firehouse was going to be like. That was the only male-oriented job I had come across, the all-male comradery where they go out drinking, partying, and gambling.

I was always a very big kid for my age. I was a tall, gawky girl. I didn't look like a girl, I looked like a boy. My feet were too big for ballet dancing. In high school I was always getting yelled at for being on the gymnastic equipment, where they expected only the boys to be. I taped myself up because I wanted to be on the trampoline.

□

In my younger days here in Midland, Texas, I always respected and looked up to firefighters. They were really neat people because they were there to help you, not to get on you or give you a ticket. But I never gave the fire department much thought. I was a pretty wild kid. I just didn't have any idea about the general direction in which I wanted to go. Since I had no real father figure, I didn't have someone to follow or to teach me.

My dad and mom were divorced. He lived in Mexico, had a saddle shop in Veracruz, leather goods and stuff like that. He still has a big ranch down there, and the last time I talked to him he ran a ship's chandler shop. I have a half brother down there, going to college to become a lawyer. In the summertime, my two brothers and I would spend three months with my daddy in Old Mexico. We were always ready to go down there, and when we were there we were never usually ready to come back.

I quit school when I was in the tenth grade. My brother Rusty and I were real happy-go-lucky, and did pretty much what we wanted. What was I going to do? It was kind of up in the air. I got a full-time job with a surveying crew, then when I was seventeen I went into the Army. The Army wanted me to get my General Equivalency Diploma before I went in, so I did that, and scored well.

I got out of the Army on a medical discharge, because I had had a broken foot before I went in, and it flared up on me. You see, I had gotten into racing motorcycles when I was in Mexico. I won the 125 national championship there, but they wouldn't let me have the title because I wasn't a Mexican national. There were jumps and hills on the racing course. We usually raced for forty minutes plus two laps. Real endurance.

I've had plenty of injuries from it, broken collarbone, torn ligament in my knee, broken thumb, foot, a lot of breaks.

I'm still racing now. I know the chances of getting injured are high, but I've never worried about injury. When we went to the beach in Old Mexico, they had jetties made up of boulders stacked up at the mouth of the river and into the Gulf of Mexico, forming the channel for ships. We would go out on the jetty, dive into the water, and play around the rocks. Our dad found out what we were doing and put a stop to it, because that was the place where barracudas liked to stay. We never worried, we just did it and suffered the consequences later.

My mother did the best she could, she worked as hard as she could to do the best for us. But it's not easy with boys. One time when Rusty and I were teenagers, we got into an argument in my mom's Mustang. I was in the front seat, and he was in the back. I had had enough, and I swung at him, fixing to nail him, and my mom made a mistake. She was trying to say, "You all stop it," and she put her head between us. So instead of Rusty getting it, she got it right in her left eye.

Well, Rusty and I kind of calmed down then. We knew we had made a mistake, and my mom was sitting there crying, and we were both feeling pretty bad. It took a while, but we did a lot of making up.

Another time, when we were younger and living out in the country, we had a lot of boys over and we were going to sleep out. We had gotten a lot of eggs, and we were going to egg cars when they went by. My mom, wondering where we were, was driving down the road looking for us. Just about the time I threw the egg, somebody said, "No." It was too late. It splattered my mom's car. It wasn't easy for her.

My first real contact with firefighting was when my mom got remarried to David McClure. He was a policeman, and then he went over into the fire department. I was never that close to him. He was just our stepdad, and that's how we looked at him. We came around to the fire station once in a while. We get along a lot better now since he and my mom divorced.

She remarried David Poe later, after we were all pretty much on our own, and they're still married to this day. He was running the cattle auction barn over in Big Spring, and they live there.

After the Army I still wasn't interested in the fire department. I worked and went to college part-time. I took drafting classes at Howard College trying to get a degree in drafting. I ended up getting hired as a geophysical draftsman for a small company here in Midland.

Really, my main deal in life at the time was that I wanted to be able to afford the things I liked. Like most people, I guess. My grandfather, Casey Jones, was probably the biggest guidance in my life. Through him I saw that whatever I was, I wanted to be happy with my family, and that was more important than the value of money or anything else. I also looked up to my other grandfather. He came up from being a roughneck to one of the high officials in an oil company. He was the money side of our life, and Casey Jones was more or less the human side.

When I was young, I was very fluent in Spanish, but now I speak what they call Tex-Mex, a lot of slang. I can talk with the Spanish-speaking people on the South Side here better than most others can, and that's one of the reasons, when I made driver, they sent me to the station where I'm now assigned. I'm a paramedic driver with the Midland Fire Department out of Station 2 on the South Side, but I still get to fight a lot of fires. It's one of the roughest parts of town and usually has more fires than any other district.

□

I started first with the U.S. Forest Service. I was going to City College at the time, and I was playing football. My main ambition was to become a professional punter. I had some friends who were working as hotshots in the summertime fighting forest fires, and it looked exciting to me. They're a crew of twenty-one people who fight forest fires with chain saws, axes, and shovels. I did that for three years.

My father was a highway patrolman, and my mother was a nurse. My sister became an RN, and my brother has his own carpet business. After college I lived in a couple of ski resorts, then I started looking at the city fire department, and the more I looked the better it seemed to me.

The fire service is pretty much traditional, a lot of old tradition, but there were a lot of progressive ideas and a lot of challenges, and a lot of things that I could relate to, such as getting involved with medical stuff.

□

I was born and raised in the Yorkville section of Manhattan, and my dad and mom were raised in the same place. We lived in a five-story tenement on East Seventy-seventh Street, then moved down the street to another tenement. The bathtub was in the kitchen, fire escapes in the front, a small yard with a clothesline, no washing machines or dryers in those days. Real tenement life.

When I was around twelve, I spotted a car on fire on First Avenue. I pulled the firebox and waited for the apparatus to come. When the fire was out, I talked with the firemen, and they invited me to the firehouse on Sixty-seventh Street. So I've been associated with the fire service since I was twelve years old.

I never got in trouble, never had a police record, no drugs or any of that. My mom and dad both worked, and so I had a grandfather take care of me. I really didn't have much of a family life, and I spent most of my time in the firehouse. The guys on Engine 39 would help me with my homework, and they made sure I'd be at home by nine o'clock. I used to ride my bike down there, and, when it was broken, I'd walk. I was too young to ride the apparatus, and every time an alarm came in I used to run to the fire. Eventually I became a good runner. And after a while I would get a ride back with them.

In summers I would go to camp from the East Side Settlement House, and I used to run cross-country there, three- or four-mile runs. For four years straight I always took first place. I also became a good swimmer, and, as I got older, I was a lifeguard down at the John Jay swimming pool. At Evander Child High School in the Bronx I was on the swim team. I was freestyle All-American for two consecutive years.

In 1960 I joined the U.S. Navy and was a Navy diver. I went into training for the 1964 Olympics in swimming. I wound up going to the Military Olympics in Barcelona in 1963, and four of us got food poisoning and missed the trials for the Olympics.

My dad worked for Farmers Feed on Seventy-sixth Street near the East River, where they used to process grain. He was a big man, around six-three and 230 pounds, but when I was a kid I really felt sorry for him. I used to watch him carry hundred-pound sacks from the factory down to the river, over a ramp, and load them onto barges. They didn't have a conveyor belt, just loaded them on their shoulders and walked them to the barge, then walked back and got another one, back and forth. My dad raised homing pigeons on the tenement roof as a hobby.

My mom used to work at an electrical equipment factory, wiring sockets and things, down on Seventy-second Street. I remember she used to come home at night in tears, and I wondered why until I saw her hands. She had pin holes all over them from the wires that penetrated her fingers.

When I joined the Boys Club of New York on the Lower East Side, my dad used to go to meets with me. I spent many years at the Boys Club. In fact, I became one of the counselors and a lifeguard at their camp on Long Island. It kept me out of trouble. I used to swim in high school from three to six, go home for a quick bite to eat, then jump on the Jerome Avenue subway to the Boys Club and swim until about nine-thirty. And I was still hanging around the firehouse in Manhattan even after we moved to the Bronx. I would take the train down there on weekends and sleep over in the firehouse.

Our apartment in the Bronx was another tenement, but it was much nicer. It wasn't the old railroad flat we'd had in Manhattan, room after room after room, where you had to pass through everybody's room to get to the living room in the front.

In the Bronx I started listening to fire calls on the radio, and one night they had a third alarm over on Broadway and 225th Street. I ran over as I used to do. It was raining and it was cold, and I helped Engine 75 pack some hose in the truck. The lieutenant asked me if I'd like a ride home, and I said sure. They dropped me off in front of my house, and this big old Irish guy, Pat Murphy, said, "Come on down and visit us." I was all excited, because it was a new firehouse. So the next day I went down, and I've been visiting there as a fire buff ever since.

I know it was against the rules and regulations, but they never told me to leave, and I just kept my mouth shut. I used to shine the brass on the old engine, a Mack, and help out around the firehouse. I didn't really consider myself a fire buff. Now I know there are all different kinds. Some just go to fires and stand there, some help the men. Then there are fire buffs who take photographs, which fire departments sometimes use in their training.

I met guys who were like fathers to me, and I was treated with respect. The kids of today don't have the welcome and the warm feeling I had. Some of the guys on the job are moody, and say, "Get out of here, kid." It hurts me.

I'm in a predominantly Puerto Rican area here in Hartford, and I have two Spanish kids come in. I treat them like my own children. They're

Benny Garcia, who's ten, and his seven-year-old brother, Angel Santiago. They live right across the street, and neither one has a father, so I know where they're coming from. I take them to my home in the country, and I feel that if I can contribute a little to their life, maybe in the long run it'll help keep them out of trouble, away from drugs. And they're both doing excellent. Other guys I work with see what I'm doing and are getting involved with the same kids, taking them home, taking them to picnics, taking them to amusement parks. It's a good feeling, it really is. I see a lot of compassion in the city here, a lot of morale, a lot of unity.

I think every kid wants to be a fireman, or maybe a policeman. It's their exposure. You always hear sirens, you always see a policeman if he's directing traffic, not like the milkman who's delivering milk at five in the morning when you don't see him.

I always wanted to be a fireman, and I had it in the back of my head that you could never be a fireman if you had a police record, and that's why I stayed out of trouble. Maybe my social life wasn't that great as a young kid, but I had friends I hung around with. We used to go sleigh riding in Central Park or in Carl Schurz Park. We used to play on the high-rise buildings under construction, play in the ditches, jump off the cranes.

One night, for some reason, I didn't go with my friends, and went to the firehouse instead. A real good friend of mine was killed that night by a hit-and-run car. He jumped off the crane into the street, and a car hit him and kept going. As I think back, it might have been me, if I had been there.

I attribute a lot of my staying out of trouble to hanging around the firehouse.

□

My mother was born in the Bronx, and my father was born in Paterson, New Jersey, and we moved out here to Cleveland in the thirties, when the Erie Railroad came out to Ohio. I was raised mostly in Ohio, but I spent a lot of summers in New York.

I didn't become interested in the fire department until I started dating my wife, Sheila. Her father was a lieutenant in the Cleveland Fire Department. I still had no intention of going into the fire department. I was working for Greyhound, in sales and administration.

Then her father talked me into taking the fire exam, which I did. I didn't do too well on it, because I was going to college at the time and working two jobs, so I couldn't prepare too well. I had no intention of taking the job, but I passed, and it worked out real well for me.

□

I was born and raised in Long Beach, California. My father was a schoolteacher and principal, and my mother was a kindergarten teacher. From elementary school on, my aspiration was to be an airline pilot. But as I went on, it became more and more evident that my math skills were probably not up to that, so I started looking in other areas. I finished high school and had one year of college.

On my father's side of the family, I had a grandfather and two uncles in the fire service, volunteers in Lorain, Ohio, a small town on Lake Erie. I didn't see much of them, but I was cognizant of the fact, by photographs and that kind of thing, and conversations with my dad, that I had relatives in the fire service.

After the year in college, I went into the Navy and was stationed at an air operations base in Japan. It was an air terminal, and the work was loading and unloading aircraft, placing the planes about the flight ramp, and scheduling passengers. Aviation has kind of followed me all along.

Firefighting was never a childhood thing with me. It wasn't until after I got out of the service that I got interested, through a friend. I got to know him when I was in high school, and he became a barber in the local barbershop. I had an after-school job cleaning up the place. Well, this guy, he got on the Long Beach Fire Department, and fed my interest in the fire service. The more I learned, the more it seemed like a pretty fulfilling career, and it had good benefits, you know, security and all the other things that you consider.

Getting into the fire service was a process of about five years for me from when I first started getting interested until it came to fruition. I went about it by going to the different cities around the immediate area that were giving examinations for firefighters. It sounds like five years is a long time, but you have to consider that not every city gives a test every year or every other year.

Meanwhile, continuing the aviation connection, I worked on the assembly line at the Douglas Aircraft Company. Then I went to work for United Airlines on the flight ramp, again a freight/mail/passenger kind of thing.

I have two brothers and a sister. One's a contractor, one's a teacher, and the third is a beautician. No other firefighters in the family.

□

I was raised in Beverly, a small city north of Boston. My father was in the Beverly Fire Department for about twenty-five years before he had a major heart attack and had to retire. As a kid I visited him at the firehouse. That was great, but the big kicker was to go see a ball game at Fenway Park, to see the Red Sox play.

When I was about six years old, and we were in town, I saw a ladder company go by. I think they were one and six, that is, one officer and six firefighters, but to me it looked more like one and twenty on board the rig. I said to myself, "Holy mackerel, this is unbelievable." And I never forgot that, because they just looked like they were having a great time. And later on, my father said, "Look, never mind the small city stuff, go work for Boston if you want to get on the job. You'll be a lot better off."

Being in a firefighter's family, there was the traditional stuff, we can't go here, we can't go there, your father's working. And we have to leave early, so everybody just go out and have a good time. Then it's check-out time because he's got to go to work. Yet, my father never complained about it one bit. I couldn't figure out why, until I got on the job myself and saw what it was about.

I went to a Catholic high school, with nuns, you know, the whole nine yards. They beat you over the derbies, literally and figuratively. Nothing extraordinary at all, just run of the mill. As each year passed, I was just marking time until I'd be able to take the exam. I knew I was going to be a firefighter ever since I saw that ladder company near Fenway Park, everybody hanging off the side or on the turntable and everywhere else.

I did go one year to state college, taking liberal arts for schoolteaching, because you gotta fill your time with something, right? I had a total lack of interest, and I just dropped out after the first year. I said, "The heck with this." And, of course, I was getting closer to age nineteen, when I could take the civil service test. I got a schlemiel job in a bank pushing canceled checks around for a while, a regular slave labor job, and boring.

And I was always listening to the fire calls on the radio. Even back in the old tube radio days, you could get the channel, if you tuned it in just right.

□

I grew up in Dearborn, Michigan, number four in a family of eleven children. It's a marvelous family. We really had a good time, and I was never lonely. We're still all very close.

I was never very excited about fires or fire trucks. Law enforcement meant more to me, and I was in the Dearborn police reserves for ten years before I moved out to Pinckney and became a firefighter. I was also on their pistol team. My father was in the police reserves with me, and we used to compete quite a bit. Every Sunday we'd go down and shoot at the range, and I went to different matches throughout the state of Michigan.

I liked working with the community I lived in. When I moved out to Pinckney, I thought of joining the police force. But it was a lot smaller than Dearborn's, and they only had three or four police officers at a time.

Then one day the whole family was outside playing when we heard some screeching and a loud noise on the next street back of our house. I knew that someone had gotten hurt, so I asked my husband to go in and call the fire department and the police, while I went to see what happened. I found a gentleman who had flipped over in his truck, and he had severe head injuries. From my CPR training and the medical classes I had attended in the reserves, I knew what to do. So I did mouth-to-mouth CPR, and my husband did, too, until the police and the fire department got there and took over.

I just sort of stood back and watched how the police and the firemen and the ambulance crew united into one group, and it was amazing how they all blended in together. And that's when I decided this was something I wanted to do. I wanted to be able to respond to the community in any kind of crisis, and to be a firefighter.

I think that anybody in a large family learns to get along with people. Because when you have thirteen people in a house, you've got to learn to share. To take what's given to you, and even to share part of that with somebody else.

In my parents' house we were safety-conscious, but we never really talked about "stop, drop, and roll" and things like that. We were always told how to use the stove properly, and we weren't allowed to use it until we were old enough to see over the top of it. That was a rule. And we could never cook when my parents weren't home, no matter how old we were. So we all had a consciousness of fire. Safety was one of the rules that you had to have in a large family.

□

My dad is a firefighter. When I was at school, all the kids used to talk about how much their dads worked. It was really ironic because I didn't even know if my dad worked. He never really brought the job home, never talked about it, and he would get the whole summer off and spend it with us camping up north. It was great because I learned to hunt and fish, and we still do a lot of that. He got the summers off by making a lot of tour changes with other guys.

He's an All-American dad. He was always easy to talk to, didn't get upset with us kids. I've got one brother, who's on the police force, and three sisters, who are married. But nothing any of us did really fazed him. He was always calm. My mother was the emotional type. She doesn't like the fire department, and she didn't want me to go on the job.

My dad worked two jobs all the time, bartending and doing carpentry and stuff like that, and he's one of our union leaders. He sent us to Catholic schools, and the month after I got out of high school I fell into the greatest job in the world. I put my application in to the Detroit Fire Department. I went to the community college and worked at my girlfriend's father's funeral home. I took my EMT, went through all the tests, and trained really hard—and the February after I got out of high school I was on the job in the fire department. I was only eighteen years old.

I always wanted to be a firefighter. The job, it's like a high I get on adrenaline. I get pumped. It's the excitement that really gets me. I played at the Silver Dome for the Catholic League championship, and the place was filled with thirty thousand people screaming and yelling, and when I was running out for a pass, the adrenaline was shooting through me. That's what the fire department is like.

Because of the requirement that we live in Detroit, my brother and I bought what's called a hut house for a thousand dollars, two doors down from our mom's place. It's not the greatest neighborhood in the world, but it's okay.

□

I was born and raised in Buffalo. My father was a firefighter with the Buffalo Fire Department, and my brother, Harvey, recently retired from it. And strangely, my mother was sort of a fire buff in her own way, always interested in my Dad's work. From the time we were small kids, we were fascinated with firefighting. We used to chase the rigs whenever they came into the neighborhood, and if there was a multiple alarm and my mother was available, she used to drive us to the fires to watch.

Harvey is almost four years older than me, and when I was smaller he used to pull the bicycle and take me along. Harvey went into the Navy before me, then when I went into the Navy and wherever we'd go, I'd generally stop in a firehouse and see how they ran it. When I got out I wasn't old enough to take the exam Harvey took, and when he got appointed I used to go over and hang around his station.

When my father was a fireman, every other Sunday they worked a twenty-four-hour day, on the old eighty-four-hour system we had here. And I used to take his supper over to him. My mother would pack it up, and I would pedal on my bicycle or run over with it. We lived just a few blocks from the firehouse. That was the one chance I had to get into the firehouse. He didn't want me hanging around there, but when I took him his supper, I could wait until he finished, to take the dishes back. It was a thrill for me to take that over every other Sunday.

Dad really wasn't a fire buff. He had two other brothers in the job, and I had two other uncles in the department, my aunts' husbands. So there was a lot of the family in the fire department. None of them got to be bosses— they were pretty much just firefighters, though I had a cousin who ended up as a deputy commissioner.

My father never got injured very badly. Oh, he got cuts and burns, never anything serious. He may have been hospitalized in the earlier years, but not that I remember. He was in the department for forty-three years. He came in as a horse driver. He drove the horse-drawn hose car for a while, then switched to the old steamer, Engine 13. You see, when his dad came over from Ireland, he was a drayman, a horse driver, and he taught his whole family how to drive. That's how come two of them went into the fire department as horse drivers, which was a separate list at the time. They weren't really firefighters. Then my father switched over to firefighter, and when they eliminated the driver's job, my uncle automatically became a firefighter.

It may seem strange that my grandfather, after coming from a cold, wet country like Ireland, decided to settle in Buffalo. I think it's the old deal. The immigrants came up the Erie Canal, and they probably had some relatives or friends here. Buffalo was a strongly Irish town at the end of the Erie Canal. Every winter I look back, and I wonder why they came. I don't think they were too intelligent, let's put it that way.

□

When I was a little kid, like everybody else, I was fascinated by the engines, the noise, the excitement of firefighting. I grew up in Detroit, in a bad part of town. There was a lot of racial tension, because we were in a black area and we were one of the few white families living on the street. My family is scattered all over the place. I've got a sister in L.A., a couple of sisters who live quite a ways from here, and a brother who is God knows where right now.

I work in the fleet service department of Northwest Airlines. I used to work for McCloud Steel, and I got laid off from there, and I got a couple of jobs after that. McCloud called me back, and they laid me off again. When they called me back the next time, I said, "The heck with this." So I came to Northwest. The fleet service department cleans the planes for their turnaround flights.

I like the job real well. On the midnight shift, it's pretty laid back. The planes are in for the night, and they're not going to go out again until the morning. So if I work on a 747, a Tokyo flight that they have going out of here now, I've got all night to clean it.

I'm really from Detroit, but one of my wife's relations had a house out here in Romulus that needed a lot of work. So I bought the house from him. We got an excellent price, and it has about two acres of land. I've been working on the house for three or four years, and I'm still working on it. I've completely redone the whole thing, inside and out. All the major stuff is done, but there's still carpeting, moldings, stuff like that.

When I found out that Romulus had a volunteer fire department, I figured I'd better step in the door, because they might get into full-time someday. That's what I want, full-time firefighting.

□

I was born and raised right here in Fallon, Nevada. For six or seven years my mother was ill, and I was farmed out to a family out of town. So I was raised on a farm during that time, did all the farm chores, milked cows by hand, ran teams. Everything was done with horses. There were no tractors or anything. Mowers, rigs, wagons, anything you did that required any hauling was done with teams of horses. When you're raised around it, you become familiar with the stock and know how to handle it and talk to it and pet it and so forth. It was hard work, but it was a case of survival. I mean, you had your jobs to do, even though you were a little kid, and they had to be done.

We didn't have balers in those days, back in the twenties and thirties—we shocked the hay. It was raked into big piles, and when the piles were dry, a guy came along with a pitchfork and hand-lifted it onto a wagon. It's an old-fashioned way, but that's the way it was in those days.

I was raised during the Depression. At that time I was living with my mother in town. I lost my dad when I was about two years old. My mother came home one day, and she said, "Well, the banks closed today." I think I was about eleven or twelve, and it didn't mean anything to me. I didn't have any money, so what's a bank, you know? My mother was making eighty dollars a month as chief operator for the phone company. That's what we lived on.

During high school, I worked all the jobs I could find, so I was pretty much self-supporting except for my board and room. In those days they had a lot of small ranches outside of town, and you could raise a family on forty acres. Today you're lucky if you can raise them on 400 acres, you know? And it would be hard to buy a 400-acre farm today.

I had moved into town, and in the summertime I slept on a screened-in porch, because they didn't have air conditioners then. One night there was a fire in one of the large construction companies. Fallon had just gotten a new 500-gallon-per-minute Ford pumper truck. All I could hear all night long was the screaming of that Ford engine, and this thing was clear on the other side of town. It scared the devil out of me. In fact, I even went in and woke my mother up to console me.

I never went near the fire or anything. This huge shop burned down, and they had a lot of fifty-gallon drums of oil blow up. I had never been around anything like that before, probably the biggest fire Fallon had ever experienced. And it was a tremendous loss to the community, because the company had employed forty or fifty local people, and the fire put them out of business temporarily.

There's a tremendous cross section of personalities in the volunteer fire department, a lot of business people and a lot of service people, so the community is well aware of what goes on down here at the fire department.

When I got out of high school, I wanted to be an accountant. Then the war broke out, and I volunteered for the service and I was turned down. I would create a hardship for my mother, they said. Then I was drafted twice and was still turned down. So I went to work for a construction contractor developing airstrips, grading and paving, constructing roads around the state of Nevada.

Then I went into business for myself, started out with a service station, then a bar and gambling place for three years, then I was a franchised new car dealer for about twenty-one years—Pontiac, Buick, and General Motors trucks.

I think my motivation in joining the volunteer fire department was the fact that I was afraid of fire, going back to that night when I listened to that fire truck run all night long, when it just ran chills up and down my back. I didn't even want to go look at the fire, I was just flat scared, period. So I figured, well, the only way I was going to overcome that fear was to get involved, get right in the middle of it, and learn something about it.

And besides, I was pretty service-oriented at the time. I belonged to several service clubs and was involved with a lot of things going on in the community, and the fire service was just another one.

□

I come from a very white-collar background. I descend from two generations of Milwaukee public school teachers. It was always the expectation in my family that I would go to college for four years and wind up becoming a doctor or a lawyer, something like that. I was a bookish kind of person. I read a great deal and wasn't terribly physically inclined. I wasn't heavily into sports or anything like that.

My family moved out of the Midwest when I was very young. We lived in Iowa and Montana, and we finally moved to Oregon just before I went into junior high school. My dad was a school principal. When I went to the University of Oregon, the notion of service was very strong. It was a very idealistic period, at least for me. There was the Vietnam War, civil rights, and all kinds of issues. There were student protests all over the country.

I was never involved in any kind of violence. I am philosophically opposed to violence of any kind. I was in a couple of marches and demonstrations and that kind of thing. I was not a complete pacifist. I was in the draft rolls, I went through the lottery twice, but my number never came up. If I had been called I would have gone. I never thought of going to Canada. But at the same time, I was definitely against the war. I have a strong philosophical position against war. This was probably a result of peer pressure when I first went to the university. The rhetoric was, if you're not part of the solution, you're part of the problem. There was tremendous emphasis on getting involved in community service.

I was majoring in public health. I had dropped out of college for a year and was working for the public health department. I was interested in emergency medical care, and I was in the middle of classes for getting my certificate as an emergency medical technician. I thought perhaps public ambulance work was what I wanted to get into. Then, ironically enough, the thing that drew my attention to the firefighting service was the book *Report from Engine Co. 82.* That was the one single thing that got me the most interested.

There was a firehouse, Engine Company 3, that was stationed right across the street from the University of Oregon campus. I became the classic fire buff and probably drove the guys in the station nuts, because I kept dropping by and visiting. Before long I was paying my coffee dues once a month, just like everybody else. I got to hang out at the station. I'd take my books down there when the dorms would get too noisy. I read all the magazines, and when I turned twenty-one, I applied to three different departments and was lucky enough to get called by the Eugene department. So it was college that pushed me into the fire service.

My parents are not really snobbish people, but their attitude was that firefighting was very blue-collar. You go to college, get a degree, wear a tie, stay clean, and don't get involved in that kind of stuff. When I first announced I was going to drop out of school to become a firefighter, my parents were shocked. My mother felt my life would be in mortal danger. She began looking at the daily fire reports in the local paper, and she realized that for every working fire there were several hundred false alarms, little calls and trash fires. My dad had his reservations, but he found out that the son of one of his schoolteachers had gotten a degree from a prestigious college in Salem and had then joined the Salem Fire Department. He had a degree in biology, but he was in the fire department, was making good money, and really enjoyed what he was doing. So I think in the end my parents were satisfied.

But then my brother decided he wanted to be a cop, and all hell broke loose.

I think my parents respected my strong sense of wanting to do something that was service-oriented, as opposed to going for a profit or going for an MBA or something like that.

□

When I was seven my father was killed at a fire. He was a battalion chief at the time. Everybody respected him, and I'm so proud of that fact. I'll never fill his shoes, but I'll sure try. My brother Ray and I used to go to the firehouse with my father. Ray is now a captain in the fire department.

I'm a third-generation fireman. My grandfather was a captain. I never knew him, but he was still on the job when he died of a stomach ailment. He had his hand crushed at a fire in the stockyards, but he was able to go back to work. My uncle was a battalion chief in the same house as my brother. He's retired now, but his three sons, my cousins, are firemen. My father-in-law is deputy district chief, and his two sons, my brothers-in-law, are firemen. My sister's husband, another brother-in-law, is a fireman. There's a lot of hose and a lot of smoke at weddings, let me tell you.

From age seven on, I'd be at the firehouse. Fire fans weren't allowed to go into the building, but I was sort of accepted as one of the firemen. I was able to go in and go to work. I was injured a few times, but I covered it up by saying I'd done it at home. That's basically where I got my background. This went on for several years until a fire fan fell off a truck and was killed. Fire Commissioner Quinn stopped all unauthorized people from riding fire apparatus, and I had to go down and get a special letter from him giving me permission.

When I was in grammar school and high school, I wasn't looking forward to college or anything. My goal was to be a fireman. And the first test that came along, I took it. We had to wait a few years before we would be called. I took my emergency medical technician course, and I applied to get on the city ambulances, which are part of the Chicago Fire Department. I figured if I wasn't going to be a fireman I could be the next best thing. So I was an EMT, and I was assigned to the firehouse where my father had been a lieutenant. The ambulance in that house was the busiest in the city, and I went there because I wanted to get experience. I was there about nine months before I got called to become a firefighter.

□

It was a very normal thing for me to become a firefighter. I wanted to be one so bad I just wished that I could be done with high school, with all of the crap, and have it over with. When you're a fourteen-year-old and you're going down and riding with squads, all the other things—high school football games, dances, and stuff like that—are anticlimactic. I was seeing what real men do. And when I got a little older, I was actually doing a man's job. I was strong for a high school kid, and when I would go to the firehouse they'd let me work as a firefighter.

That was in a suburb of Chicago. I see these jokers getting off the train. You ask a kid in school, "What does your dad do for a living?" They say, "I don't know, he goes to some office." Well, I knew what my old man did for a living. I knew why we were eating and why we had a roof over our heads. It's because my old man was busting his backside as a fireman on the West Side of Chicago, freezing in the wintertime and having rocks thrown at him in the summertime. I knew what he was doing.

Other people, they take the train and they commute back and forth to the city, and I thought to myself, "That's not for me. I want to do something that's important, that's vital. If these jokers did not go to work, nobody would miss them." Of course, now that I'm a little bit more mature, I realize everybody's job is just as important. I don't think firemen are supermen, by any means. At the time, I thought, "Hey, firemen are gutsy, and they're doing an important job, and people's lives depend upon them being there." Other jobs are not like that, and the police did not appeal to me. I didn't want to be a doctor, because you had to go to school for too long.

Anyhow, I was working for this town Mapleville, waiting to get called by the Chicago Fire Department. I was still single, going with my future wife, and her dad was a big mucky-muck at the Chicago Bridge and Iron

Company. Well, he ended up coming to Coral Gables, which is the headquarters of their Latin American and Caribbean operation.

I came down on vacation, and I took the fire test here for the hell of it. I didn't even know if I wanted the job, and I didn't think I could get it. Well, for the first time in something like six years, they took guys right off the top of the list without being concerned with minorities. So as a result, we got a bunch of guys who were schoolteachers, guys with engineering degrees, all kinds of real sharp guys in our class.

□

When I got out of the military, I had the opportunity to get into the trucking industry. I was in it for ten years. I started out as an assistant to a dispatcher and worked up to operations manager. I trained people coming into the industry. I was doing pretty good, and I enjoyed it. The problem was that there was no real job security, and though the pay was good I was putting in too many hours. I was missing a lot of time with my family. I had to do it, though, because I needed the job.

Then I heard that the fire department was giving a test. Up to that point, I'd actually thought about becoming a policeman. I was an MP in the military, and I thought maybe it would be a good field to get into. So I went down to City Hall and filled out the fire department application. I didn't do it reluctantly, I just did it with a little bit of skepticism. I said to my wife, "Oh, I don't really think anything is going to come of this, because I don't think I'm going to make it."

I knew that the cutoff age was thirty-six years, and at the time I was thirty-five, and I thought I really had to get in on this first class, otherwise I'm not going to make it. So they scheduled the test, and I studied hard for it while I was still doing trucking. And I was fortunate to have the ten-point veteran's preference, so that added ten points to whatever score I got on the test. But I was concerned because so many people had taken the test.

My sister called and told me, "Twenty-six thousand people took the test, so your chances of getting on are small." That depressed me, but I felt I'd done good because I did study hard and the test wasn't that difficult. So my brother called me the next day and said, "Six thousand people walked out halfway through the test." So that lowered the odds. I thought, well, twenty thousand, that's starting to sound better all the time.

I kept calling, and some months later I was notified that I had aced the test, I was number six on the list. I was ecstatic, I thought, now I've got to be in the first class. As it turned out, I was. And from then on, everything has been running smoothly. Everything has been great.

□

Guys from our volunteer fire department on Long Island were taking tests for the Washington, D.C., fire department, they were taking tests all over the place. I know some who went to Florida, a couple of guys who went to Texas, some right above us in New England. But I was still in New York, and I didn't want to uproot my family. For me it was just the way it went down. The New York City test came at the right time, and after eight years of the phone company, I left right away and never went back. In the interim, I switched to the truck company at the volunteer fire department, which further tuned my skills as a firefighter. When I went into New York, I was appointed to Engine 74 on the West Side of Manhattan, which wasn't so busy by any standard. It was just the way it went down.

□

I think people become volunteer firefighters for the same reason people become career firefighters. It is true that in the small towns the fire department has a social status as well. It's part of the social life. Political as well, in some places. But I think that the hard core of firefighting volunteers become volunteers for the one reason, the love of firefighting.

Now you are going to say, "Why would anyone love firefighting?" I mean, it's a rotten, dirty job. The answer is, it's the challenge of the thing, the excitement, the sense of accomplishment when you do it right, the pride that you feel for yourself and for your company. It's the comradeship.

I started out on the City News Bureau in Chicago as a police reporter, and then I went to the Chicago *American*. I was on the Chicago *American* for six years. In that time I went to India as a Fulbright Scholar, and I stayed over there as a foreign correspondent and also covered the Middle East. I came back and went overseas frequently. Cuban revolution, things like that. And gradually advanced in journalism. But all this time, in all of my off time from the newspaper, I was always at Squad 2 and Engine 34 being a fireman, at night or on the weekends.

And when I came to New York as the political news editor of *Newsweek* magazine, we lived in the suburban town of Rye. There I joined the Port Chester Volunteer Fire Department, assigned to the Fire Patrol and Rescue Company. That was one of the great five years of my life, working with a really great bunch of guys. We were a busy company, and we had some heavy-duty firefighting, because Port Chester was an old town and parts of it were a kind of miniature South Bronx.

Previous to that, I had been a volunteer in Arlington, Virginia, so I understood the difference between a big city fire department and an unpaid volunteer company.

□

When I first got out of school I went into the Navy for two years and then got a job in the post office. I wasn't married at the time. I was a single boy, and I just really loved the fire department, and that was what I wanted to do. So I put in for the fire department in both Baltimore City and Baltimore County. Baltimore City came in just about a week or two before the county, and that's where I really wanted to go because I had heard that that was where the fire service was. I took a $4,000 cut in pay to come in here.

I really didn't have a lot of experience in the city. I didn't know anybody. I was a country boy. I had heard of it and talked to a few people, and I knew that was where the fires were, and that was where I wanted to go. When I came out of the academy, I was assigned to Ford Avenue, Truck 19, which is an exceptionally slow house. I stayed there six months, which was the rule at the time. I made up my mind that if I wasn't transferred out of there in six months I was leaving the city and going back to the county. I had come here for the fire service, and there was none down there at all. It was a nice, clean residential area where they just didn't have any fires. I wanted to get where the action was.

□

The Aldine Volunteer Fire Department was out collecting on a street corner, raising funds. And I asked the chief, who was at the intersection at that time, "How do you become a fireman?" And he told me to come down on a business meeting night, that's how you join the service. You have to go through certain training schedules, and you're put on ninety-day probation to see if you're really interested.

We're not in Houston, we are Harris County firefighters, volunteer organizations that protect the county around the city and bordering Intercontinental Airport, roughly sixty-three square miles. Right now Aldine has twenty-two members.

I'm an electrician by trade, and when I became a firefighter the majority of my work was in the downtown Houston area wiring the high rises. So I had a feel for construction.

In my spare time I was heavy into T-ball, doing volunteer work, teaching little kids how to do it. It's for ages four to six years. You put a tee at home plate and put a baseball on top of it, and they just hit the ball. There's no pitching, but they learn the basics of baseball.

I joined the fire department because I believe in the individual in American society, individuals helping each other. Not that it really impressed me, as it does a lot of people, to get out there and run on the fire trucks. It was getting down there and helping people who are in need of help—vehicles in accidents, house fires, where folks are in trouble. To help them out is something I want to do. When everybody sticks together, it has results. It's a team effort: let's get this fire out, it's what we're here for.

We can always use more members. There are numerous jobs at a fire scene, and the more people there are, the more efficiently the job gets done.

□

One of my best friends joined, and he was telling me about it. And I was kind of hesitant because it sounded really scary. Then he invited me over one evening to look over the trucks and talk to some of the members. And the closer I got, the more intrigued I was, and the more I thought to myself, it's just not as scary as it looks. So I gave it a shot, and here I am today.

□

When I was a freshman at Colgate, in Hamilton, New York, I was a fireman there. Hamilton has a very active volunteer fire department. So firefighting continued to intrigue me when I got home that summer in Brainard. A good friend of mine from the Bronx came up to Albany with the Carey administration. He was a city slicker, and he bought this small farm up on the hill while he was working in Albany. He joined the volunteer fire company, and he cosigned an application for me. That's the Tri Village Volunteer Fire Department in Old Chatham. They welcomed me with open arms.

□

I wanted to get involved early. At that time the only way to get into the fire business was by first getting into forestry, because of the eighteen-year age limit. Through my skiing activities, I met a couple of guys who worked for the Forest Service and found out how to get in and what to do. So I went through that formality. Incidentally, in recognition of what we mostly do, they recently changed the name to State Department of Forestry and Fire Protection. It's primarily a wildland fire organization. We also run a lot of structural fire departments under contract to various agencies.

It doesn't take any special schooling prior to getting on the job. It's kind of like many city fire departments: you put in an application, you get hired, and then they send you to school while you're on the job. Maybe you go through an academy, that kind of thing.

□

I knew a lot about the fire department from my father, but I didn't plan to go in. I went into the Marine Corps and worked security for three years, guarding the naval bases and the armored trucks and this and that, both in the Philippines and here. And when I came out of the service I continued working in security. I worked for a bank, then for a private security company, and then on two different naval bases.

It wasn't like all of my life I wanted to be a fireman. In fact, I was trying to be a policeman. While I was working security I went to college, to a school for criminal justice. My two brothers were taking the civil service test to be firemen, but they hadn't been in the service. They said, "Why don't you take it? You have a better chance than we do because of the extra points." Veterans get ten extra points.

So I took the test, and I scored 99.71, and with the ten points it was 109.71. That made me eightieth on the list. I missed the first class and made the second. The difference of one point is probably two or three hundred people. And they only take fifty at a time. My brothers didn't make it.

My father was proud, but he never pushed it. He always said to do what you want to do. I knew he liked being a firefighter, so I was curious as to what he liked about it, what was so good about it. That's the way I kind of backed into the job.

□

The Philadelphia Fire Department was closed to everyone except veterans, and I was too young to be a veteran. Departments in southern New Jersey such as Atlantic City or Trenton, weren't hiring at the time. The jobs weren't available. I think I liked just about every aspect of the fire service from a very young age, and I was fortunate to get the volunteer experience in Cherry Hill, near Camden in New Jersey. I was an active firefighter and also in the fire marshal's office. I worked up to captain before leaving. In the fire marshal's office, we did fire prevention and put on public information programs. We assisted the county arson investigators and frequently made calls to determine the fire cause situation ourselves. I was unpaid for many years, and when I was finally hired, the salary was small.

I never did have the opportunity to take the New York City test. They have long lists, and a recent one was held up in court for quite a while, because of the women, I think. Maybe someday I'll still get to take that test. It's a dream I have, to work in New York.

Still, I was very fortunate to have a friend who moved here to Charlotte. Most cities in the Northeast were still in that recession, they were either laying off or not hiring at all. My friend was working here in the motion picture industry, and he saw the openings to get on the job here. This is a fairly large department, I believe it's the largest fire department between Washington and Atlanta.

I applied through the mail. My friend got an application and forwarded it to me. I filled it out and returned it with a résumé. I went through the selection process and was hired. When I got here I saw the city, a quickly growing city where they were hiring a lot.

□

When I graduated from high school in Albuquerque, I went to the University of California at Davis. I was a student firefighter there, before I transferred to Arizona State University. When I was twenty I took the test for the Phoenix Fire Department, and I was hired right away.

I think I had a fairly good perception of what firefighters did. The part of the business that always attracted me was fire operations. I don't know exactly why. Maybe it was the combination of the fact that it was a military, well-organized kind of thing, and yet it was exciting, and it was obviously a helpful kind of thing, too. I guess all of us are still attracted to fire operations.

□

Once I decided that my ambition to be an airline pilot was out the window due to my poor math skills, and I focused on firefighting, I figured, well, there's nothing like the hometown fire department. Long Beach, of course. I think it's the dream of everybody who considers the fire service to get on the hometown team. And that almost came to pass. I was on their list for two years, and I would have been hired, but at that time minority recruitment was a big factor on the West Coast. I didn't get a job because the open slots were filled from the minority list.

Well, I figured that it was unfortunate that this was the way it went in the city of Long Beach, but I knew that if I pursued it long enough I'd eventually succeed somewhere. And I tested in a number of cities in the county of Los Angeles—Seal Beach, Santa Fe Springs, Whittier, and L.A. County itself—in the five years it took me to get on the city of Los Angeles.

It was ironic that the city of Los Angeles was the last place I tested, and it was the one I got on. You run into the same people at these different tests, and the word of mouth was that Los Angeles was absolutely the toughest place to get on. Which made me reluctant to take the examination. Finally I said, I've been everywhere else, this is one place I haven't been, so why don't I give it a shot.

The initial step is to file what they call an interest card with the city personnel department for the fire department examination. Then at some point down the road they notify you by mail when and where to appear for the written examination. After you take that, the second phase is the physical agility test. Next, they have the medical examination, then last would be the oral interview. At some point after that you're notified how you're placed on the list and when you're to start at the fire academy.

The notification of my standing on the list was probably the ultimate high. Great elation, excitement. I probably jumped six feet off the ground. Having been down the road for so long and finally having the least likely prospect come to fruition made it all that much sweeter.

□

After I submitted my application at Fire Hall, I had to go through a six-month probation, where you attend the meetings and you can go to the fires, but you can't participate. I did a lot of training in those six months, I read everything I could get my hands on and asked a lot of questions. At the end of the six months, I was voted in as a regular member in the apprentice stage.

I'm the only woman ever to be on the men's unit of Hamburg's Fire Department. They have a women's auxiliary that they use on occasion, when, let's say, there's a really large fire or an unusually low response, or if it's a daytime fire or medical emergency. But no, I'm on the men's unit.

I didn't do it for the accomplishment, I did it more for myself. I was really excited about this. I thought it would be a wonderful opportunity to get to know the community better.

My husband was very proud of me. He's been very supportive. Having lived with me as long as he has, he understands that I'm not your normal woman.

□

You had to be twenty-one to get appointed in Boston, and I couldn't wait. I wanted to start taking the test. After the written exam they have the strength test, and at the very end of that they had a hundred-yard swimming test. They've since eliminated that, but back then you had to pass it or else you were out of luck, even if you passed all the other stuff.

So not being a great swimmer, to say the least, I was not doing too well. You only get three chances at it, and if you don't make it you have to start all over again. So I'm down to my last try, and everybody else goes four laps in the pool in about three and a half minutes, and they're done. The instructor just stands there watching me, and about twenty minutes later I finally pull up at the end. I managed to stay afloat without drinking the whole pool. Nothing much has surpassed that day in my life. I practically flew out of the pool.

That was it, the longest swim I've ever swum in my life. I thought I had just climbed Mount Everest without a rope. And that was how it got started.

□

I was sitting around one day between jobs, and I saw that they were having a test for the Midland Fire Department, and I said, "What the heck, I might as well." So I went ahead and took the written test, and then came the physical. I had real trouble carrying the dummy and doing the hose drag.

I was athletic enough, but I was real slender. I only weighed 117 pounds. As a matter of fact, when I went into the service earlier, I had to be weighed three times to make the weight for my height. I had to go away twice and eat a lot of bananas and drink everything I could, then come back and be weighed. I actually ended up a pound over. As soon as they finished weighing me, I took off to the bathroom, because I was about to blow up like a grenade.

When Robbie and I got married, I weighed around 130 pounds. Neither of us knew much about the dangers of fighting fires, it just looked like a good regular job, real secure, with a good future.

So I ended up sixth on the list. That was in September, and I wasn't hired until the following February. I kept pestering them a lot, waiting and hoping. I went to work for a financial service as a collector, then I worked for the city's meter department, replacing water meters, and finally the call came.

One of the stipulations at that time was that we had to become an emergency medical technician. I had a pretty hard-nosed captain, Bobby Collins. He taught me a lot, but he was a militaristic type person, and since I was pretty much still a maverick, we had our clashes. I was twenty-three and still hardheaded.

□

They were recruiting for the Hartford Fire Department, so about eighteen of us from the New York City Fire Patrol went up to take the test. They were recruiting nationwide. I liked the fire patrol, but I wanted to be a real fireman. I wanted to be on the line. I wanted to be a truck man. I wanted to be up on roofs and everything else. So I took the test, and I had the honor of joining the Hartford Fire Department in 1967.

I went up. They said, you're appointed, you're in an engine company downtown. I had been spoken for even before I got on the department. By a lieutenant downtown. But I wanted to go where the action was, and that was in the north end of Hartford, a poor area like the South Bronx. So I spent a couple of months at this engine company, and I said the heck with this, I don't want to die in a no-action company. I respected the lieutenant, he was a good egg, but I wasn't happy.

So I flew out to California at my own expense, went out to Coronado, and I was going to join the Navy demolition team, the Seals. I always kept myself in shape, running, swimming, working out. I was doing 800 push-ups a day. I got out there, and guys I knew said, what are you, crazy? And I said, no, I want action, and they weren't giving me what I wanted.

So I passed all the Navy Seal tests, and I flew back to Hartford, and three days later I got my transfer to the North End truck company, Ladder 3. I think they got wind I was going to leave. Ladder 3 was the busiest truck company in New England outside of Boston. I spent fourteen years there.

□

As soon as I got out of high school, I put in my application to the Detroit Fire Department. The written exam was ridiculously easy. It was just to see if you could read. The physical exam was something else. I knew it was very demanding because my brother had gone through it three years earlier. I was a short, stocky kid, only five-eight. But I knew how to train, and I trained harder than anybody else. All I did was run stairs.

I did well on the tests, but there were about twelve hundred people taking the test, and I was kind of downhearted. I heard the results the same day I was taking my final exam for my EMT classes up at McComb. I was flying high, I was ecstatic, it was a lifelong dream come true for me.

But it was scary, too. My dad had never talked to me about the job until I put my application in. Then he was telling me, it's the most dangerous job in the world, you've got to watch yourself, every day you go to work you could get killed.

I know that now.

□

We had a grass fire in our backyard, and my wife got to talking to a couple of the firefighters out there. She had heard me talking about wanting to join the volunteer fire department. And one of the firemen said, "Yeah, we're looking for a couple of guys here." It just kind of went from there.

I put in an application at City Hall, and about a week later they called me. There wasn't any kind of written test. I took the physical, and a small oral test there with the captain. The first thing he asked me was how my driving record was. He wanted to know if I had points on my license or any kind of bad record. If I did, there would have been almost no kind of chance of my getting on.

To me it was a chance to serve the community.

□

I think just being around firefighters got me. It's like being a sports fan, being there and watching: you get to know more about it and you have more admiration of the good ones. The firefighting process is like a well-oiled machine going to work. I got fascinated watching it and wanted to be a part of it.

I was just so happy to go in there, and I always wanted to do the very best I could, to keep it that way. When I was a kid, I thought the world of the department. I want to hold up my end of it.

□

I got heavily involved in the fire department the first fifteen years or so, I made all the calls. Then my business got bigger and I got tied down. I was elected chief in 1967, then in 1973 there was an opening here, and I approached the city dads, the commissioners, and said I would take the job as a paid officer. I had some backing from the state fire marshal's office, they needed somebody here that they could always contact. And it worked out pretty good.

What makes people come in here as volunteers when I'm the only one being paid, I don't have a pat answer to that. I don't know if what we do here would work in any other place. We don't take every Tom, Dick, and Harry that comes through the door. We don't overload the department. We've had thirty-one people for sixty-some years, and we hold that level. If a guy retires, he's out, he doesn't have to come back, we don't need him back.

We've developed a prestige in the community, whereby, boy, if you belong to that fire department, you're really "in." I've had people say, "You guys are a bunch of prima donnas." I say, "Yes, we have to be. If you belong to our fire department, you earn it." It isn't easy to get in, but once you're in, boy, you better produce, or you're out. Because you got to get along with thirty other people, and if you don't pull your share, brother, they'd make it so hard on you, you don't *want* to be around.

We've always had a waiting list, people waiting to get in. And that's good. When a guy comes in, the first thing I check out is how old he is and where he lives and so forth, because there are some limiting factors. I say, when you turn this application in, you're gonna become a number. Your name may not come up for two or three years down the line. The department controls all that by vote. And they look at them pretty hard from the standpoint of: are they local residents, how long have they lived here, and are they gonna *continue* to live here. Once they take them in, they want to get twenty years from them. By the time they got a damn good fireman, he's getting ready to get out!

We don't have the turnover. We don't have them come in and stay six months, a year, two years, and then they're gone. That doesn't happen here.

□

I can still remember the day the Eugene Fire Department called me. I was so happy. That was the place I wanted to work. I had just taken the fire exam in Salem, where I had gone to high school and where my parents still lived. I really didn't want to go back there. I was back in Eugene about a week, when somebody from the city personnel department called, saying, "I've been trying to get hold of you for days. Where have you been? We want you to come in and talk to us."

The exam process consisted of an initial interview with a personnel staff member, covering pretty general stuff like, "Why do you want to be a firefighter? Why do you think you're qualified for this work? Do you get along well with people?" Then there was an interview with one of the department's chief officers that was a lot more specific.

If you passed the interview, you were given a physical agility examination, where you ran a dash of I'm not sure how many hundred yards, you had to walk a balance beam and climb a fifty-foot ladder up to the department's drill tower. Once on top of the tower, you had to lift a hose bundle. That was 150 feet of inch-and-a-half hose tied into a bundle, with a rope tied to it that went up over a hose roll at the top of the drill tower. You had to pull that up, hand over hand, to the top, and then set it back down again. You wore a doughnut roll like a backpack for a couple of sessions and had to climb a ladder to the third floor and back down. You had to take a twenty-four-foot ladder off the side of a pumper, set it down, then put it back on. All of this was timed.

Then there was a mechanical aptitude test, where you had a series of nuts and bolts you had to assemble. That was the exam at the time.

It was funny because the hose bundle pull was the thing I was most concerned about. I had been running for a long time and felt good about my heart, lungs, and legs, but having been a student, I wasn't pumping iron, and my arms weren't real strong. I had a summer job managing a gymnasium for the Salem parks department. We had a rope that went up to the ceiling, and the test for the fire department then was a rope climb, so I spent the whole summer climbing the rope and did it with no problem.

Then I returned to Eugene, and my friends in the fire department said, "They changed the test. There's no longer a rope climb. Now you've got to pull a bundle up, hand over hand."

Anyway, I wound up passing the test without any trouble, and came to work a few weeks after that.

Chapter Two

TRAINING AND FIRST FIRE

WHEN I GOT CALLED FOR THE FIREMAN'S JOB, I WAS SENT TO the fire department training school to learn all the things you have to know to be a professional firefighter.

The training school confronts you with a lot of tough situations. They put you in really heavy smoke without masks, so you get a sense of what it's like to be in a terribly hostile environment, one that's like claws around your neck, just squeezing and squeezing. You get an understanding of what it's like to work in complete darkness, where you're totally blind. This is what it's like to be in a burning building, you learn.

You're also taught many other things. You learn how to use the equipment, the fire trucks, the Halligan tool (it's a pry bar with a fork on one end and a point and adz on the other), the axes, the claw tools, and hooks. You're taught how to use hoses and nozzles, how to stretch hose, hump hose, pack hose. You learn the science of fire. You learn how fire travels. You learn the various kinds of building construction. You know what kind of windows to expect in different buildings, and you know how to deal with those windows and whether to break them or not.

In a way, it's like studying to be a lawyer or a doctor. In law school, the student studies law books, goes through mock trials, and says, "Hey, I really know what I'm doing." Then he finds it's a lot different when he's in an actual courtroom. The medical student studies chemistry, physiology, anatomy, and how to use a scalpel. But once he gets into an actual operating room, it's different—suddenly people's lives are at stake. It's no longer an academic confrontation. It's right now.

It's the same thing with a firefighter. You learn all these things in training school so that when you are out in the field in an emergency situation,

51

you know where to go and what to do, so that your actions will be effective.

Here I was, a trained firefighter. I got assigned to a firehouse in Queens. The men I worked with there were great guys, what we call stand-up guys. They had fast lips, they could get around any situation with their mouths when they couldn't do it with their dukes. You meet all kinds of personalities in a firehouse. They're all fundamentally good guys who care about other people. That, in my opinion, is what sets them apart. That's not to say that you have a room full of Francis of Assisi types figuring out how they're going to help the poor. But in an emergency situation they care about what happens to people.

I got to the firehouse, met these guys. Then, of course, the alarm started ringing. So I went through a few alarms. Maybe it was a false alarm, a garbage pail on fire, a car accident, maybe somebody went out to get a paper and left the soup on the stove. All kinds of things can happen.

I remember the first fire. Not really a great fire, but there were a couple of things that happened that day that stick in my memory. The area outside the firehouse is called the apron. When the fire trucks are coming out, two firemen are out there stopping traffic. In those days two firemen rode on the back step of the fire engine. We don't do that anymore because it's unsafe.

I remember being on the back of the rig, it's two in the afternoon and I'm putting on my coat, with one arm in the D-ring hanging there like a subway strap. The truck is stopped momentarily, waiting for the traffic to halt. I look up, and who walks by but a priest from St. Mary's parish up by Queens Boulevard. He looks over, and he blesses me and the guy beside me on the back of the truck. Now, the other guy may be an atheist for all I know, but I have this priest blessing me, so I make the sign of the cross, a conditioned response like a dog salivating to a stimulus.

We get going, and I'm thinking, "What's going on here? I'm just doing my job, and this priest is blessing me on the sidewalks of the city of New York." I guess in his head he's saying, these guys have a tremendously tough job and they might be in a bit of trouble, so I'll bless them. But at that point I don't want anybody reminding me that I might be in trouble. All I know is that I've been blessed, and that we are going to this alarm.

From blocks away I could smell the wood burning. It has a particular smell, not like a car fire, for instance, which has a heavy smell of plastic and rubber. This was a two-story frame building in a row of houses typical of that area of Queens, generally lived in by working-class people. It could have been Archie Bunker's house, because they filmed the introductory sequence to that TV show in this neighborhood.

The first thing I thought of, what every firefighter thinks of, was: "is there anybody inside, how bad is the fire, and what is the immediate thing to do?" One of the saving things about being a trooper in a war is that there is leadership you can rely on, and in the fire department we have a lieutenant or a captain on every truck. I was probably with the captain, Captain Finnegan, because I was a probationary firefighter, and they always put a probie with the captain so the captain can keep an eye on him and assess his performance. The captain has to make reports and decide whether he wants to keep him or transfer him after six months.

I'm in an engine company, and the captain says, "Okay, stretch a two-and-a-half-inch line." This tells us it's a serious fire, because for a small fire you stretch a smaller line. This was the way we were trained. So we stretch the hose into the building, and I'm still thinking that I'm probably in better shape than the others because I was blessed. The ladder company arrives, and they immediately go in and do a search. I don't remember anybody being caught in the fire, maybe somebody was, but it didn't matter to me at the time. I had my job to do.

We're on our stomachs, crawling into this fire, and I'm humping, pulling, this gargantuan snake of a hose filled with water. Fifty feet of it weighs ninety pounds when it's dry, so you can imagine how much it weighs when it's filled with water. There is black, dense smoke, and we can't see an inch in front of us. There's a red glow in the background, and we're pushing toward it. Without masks. Making it a "snotty" fire, that's one where for every square inch of smoke you ingest a square inch of something else comes out through your eyes, nose, and mouth.

The red glow is in the back of the building, and we learn later that the fire has gone out through the back windows and is shooting up to the afternoon sky. We're on our stomachs, the guy on the nozzle, myself, and the captain behind me, advancing slowly into the fire. Then all of a sudden, this big guy, another firefighter, comes in and jumps on top of the hose, he grabs it from the hands of our nozzle man, and he runs with it in a crouch toward the red glow. Apparently we're not moving fast enough for him for some reason.

None of us have smoke masks or SCBAs [self-contained breathing apparatus], so we're all choking. Then we start cursing, "Hey, what the hell is this guy doing?" And our nozzle man goes running after the guy, following the string of hose that's dancing in front of him. This big guy pulls up maybe fifteen feet, throws himself on the floor, opens the nozzle, and hits the ceiling. The red glow darkens to blackness. He has stopped the fire. It's amazing, you can have a whole big room on fire, and a two-and-a-half inch hose will put it out in twelve seconds.

My captain was really mad. He said, "What the hell are you doing?"

And the guy said, "Listen, I got the job done, right?"

Well, the captain let it go. I didn't say anything because I was new on the job. But I felt that this was our line and our hose, and our territory had been infringed on. Later I heard about the old-time firefighters in New York back in the nineteenth century, when territory was the main thing and there was competition between one firehouse and another. When an alarm came, they'd send one firefighter ahead with a barrel while they got the horses and everything else ready, and he'd slip the barrel over the fire hydrant. And if another gang tried to use it, he'd fight them off. They'd have big fistfights over this hydrant, because the first team to get the water would have control over the fire. But at that first fire of mine I just knew that somehow we should have put out the fire, particularly, I suppose, in view of the fact that I was well protected by the blessing.

What I learned is that it is your job to control the nozzle, and that every fire is a personal confrontation. This is your job, and you have to go in there and put the fire out, and a lot of people are watching you to be assured that the fire is being put out.

Firefighting is a highly coordinated job. You don't begin ventilating a building, for instance, opening windows or doors or breaking windows, until there is water in the hose and the water is shooting out of it. Then you operate in a mathematically correct way. What you're doing is creating pressure inside the room, and the pressure has to have some way of being released, so you break some windows. This is called ventilation. Otherwise, you have the energy of the fire and the energy of the water shooting from the hose, and you have nowhere for all this energy to go. It will just blow back at you toward the door you came in, where there's oxygen. That is what creates flashover fires, when the fire and heat search for oxygen and the fire flashes as it consumes the oxygen.

I carried that lesson with me for the rest of my life. The hose is your job, and you have to do the job. If you don't do it and somebody else does, that's hard to live with.

Dennis Smith

□

Four months out of the fire academy, I had had a lot of garbage runs, you know, smoke scares and pots of food. Then one day we had a fire in an attic, and we had the old service masks, just a canister and a face piece. I was climbing through the attic, and the flap of my coat kept coming down over the intake hole of my mask. It was cutting my air off, and the only air I was getting was the air that I was breathing out. I was hyperventilating.

The next thing I knew, I was lying on my side, and I thought, "What the hell is going on here?" I was lying on a rafter, and I just rolled over and fell through the plasterboard into a closet. There were no injuries or anything.

Looking back on it, I thought, "Hey, I could have died up there." I could have been pinned or whatever and never come out.

After that, three of us were on top of a house extension, it was a summer kitchen, and we were pulling some boards down when the whole thing collapsed. Fire and the rot of the old timbers brought it down.

I didn't know I was injured until I took about four steps and my leg went out that way. Both the leg and the ankle were broken. They sent me to Mercy Hospital, that's where they used to send us, and the hospital sent me home. To let the swelling go down, they said.

The department infirmary was on Eighth Street at the time, and the doctor told me to come in on Saturday and he would put it in a cast. The guy was a boozer, and I looked at him that morning, and he had half a jacket on. I looked down, and he had two different shoes on, a brown wingtip and a black one. And I said, "Oh, shit."

When he was wrapping the foot, I kept telling him he was wrapping it too tight. He said he had to go play golf. He said, "If your toes turn blue, come back in." Well, I got home, and they turned black on me. So I went to the hospital, and they took that cast off and put another one on.

I was out of work seven months that time. I had to go for whirlpool treatments, and one day the leg was in the whirlpool and the technician came in and said he had to take the hospital rig to a fire, so he left. The temperature gauge on the side climbed up in the red, and I was like, "What's going on here?"

I wound up with blisters on my leg from that. If it had been too hot to start with, I couldn't have put my leg in it. But it was like, you know, if you're sitting in a warm tub you can stand the water getting hotter and hotter. The guy, being in a rush to get to the fire, didn't adjust the temperature right.

So you could say I was in a job that was dangerous, and I was surrounded by people who were dangerous, too.

□

In the U.S. Forest Service, when I first started, the training was all done at the station level. The old-time captains and engineers teach you as you go along. Then, as you advance in the ranks, they begin to send you to specialized schools on fire behavior and safety and all kinds of things. It's an ongoing process. Then, when I switched to the California Department of Forestry, it was pretty much the same program, although as part of the probationary term you have to go to a six-week academy for engineers. Driving, pumping, hydraulics, ladders, hose, fire behavior tactics, everything compacted into a six-week school.

Then the same thing when you come back to your unit, it's an ongoing training thing at the local level. Plus schools, they send guys to the more sophisticated schools with other agencies. And now, of course, like everybody else, we're sending people to the National Fire Academy too.

I was fortunate when I first came to work, we went to several rather small fires, and I was able to kind of gradually build up to the tough ones. That doesn't always happen. I've seen some guys come on the job, and right off the bat they're put on some monsters, some hairy deals. That tends to scare some of them off. They decide this is not what they really want, and they go back to being a bookkeeper or something. But in my case I was able to kind of wade into it and go from the little easy stuff into the big bad stuff. That way I gradually became aware of what was going on and conscious of the difficulties of the job and the safety problems.

When I came back from the Army, the first thing they sent me to was a fire weather class. All I knew was that on a hot, dry day, things burn better, and when the wind blows they burn still better. I had never been taught the effect of weather on fire behavior. In the class, this guy's going on about wind and dry weather, and humidity, and the causes and effects of all those things, and methods I had never heard of before. It was almost funny, because every once in a while all of us in the class would go, "Oh, no wonder. Now I understand why the fire did that."

Earlier there had been a lightning-caused forest fire that kind of startled me. It was a small fire, and five of us walked into it with our tools. There was no doubt in my mind that, with a little bit of backup, it would only take us a few minutes to put the fire out. Well, so much for predicting the behavior of fire—that fire wound up taking 5,000 acres.

We were there for over an hour before anybody else showed up. We didn't realize that there were a lot of other fires going on, and that was why backup troops weren't available. Anyway, we attacked the head end of the fire, the direction it was moving, and we made pretty good progress, only to realize that we were suddenly on the back side of the fire—the front end of the fire was on the other side now, going the other way. It dashed around us, and finally it blew out at the canyon, and we couldn't stop it.

I never did understand totally what had happened, until I went to this weather class and the guy explained it.

□

I was a training officer in the Canal Zone for almost two years when the Boulder, Colorado, Fire Department advertised for a drillmaster, and they hired me. They were looking for somebody from the outside because of the training fire that occurred there in January 1982, which killed two firefighters and injured two others. That changed the department. It was a very powerful, emotional experience, because it is a small, closely knit outfit.

It was a smoke training exercise, there was no intention of having a fire there. They used a small shed that was going to be demolished for a smoke-in. A hopeless structure. For example, they had put up cardboard walls, and it had a low-density combustible fiberboard ceiling. And there was probably a fine layer of carbon from previous burns. This was the third exercise of the morning.

There was a flashover.

Since this was only a "smoke exercise," they weren't prepared for firefighting. This was a case of their intentions outrunning their idea of what the potential was in that situation. So they weren't hooked up to a hydrant, and there was nobody by the pump panel. They were generating the smoke by burning tires, a series of fires in this long shed. They were advancing a booster line to simulate hose line advancement, but they weren't in there to extinguish fires.

I don't know if it was an oxygen flashover, or, more likely, the presence of all that combustible material getting heated up and liberating its gases to the point where everything ignited simultaneously, the walls, the ceilings, everything.

There were four people inside. Two died. Two made it out, the company officer and the officer who was putting on the drill. The company officer suffered extensive burns and spent considerable time in a burn ward in Denver. The officer putting on the drill wasn't a regular training officer, he was just somebody who'd volunteered to conduct the drill.

I have to commend the Boulder Fire Department for wanting to get the details out. They commissioned an investigator who flew out here, and his report was published nationwide. This was to let other people know what had happened. The real tragedy was that people were only looking at the individual circumstances and not at the overall aspect of this question of potential versus intentions.

□

To be honest with you, a collapsed building was never a thought that entered my mind. I always thought that firefighters were firefighters, and that's all they did. I never really gave a lot of thought to even interior firefighting until I actually got into the job and realized, as I was training and going through fire school, that there is a lot more to this job than people know. I certainly never realized that it is as involved as it is. There's something different every day. And when we got the collapsed building, that was far above anything I might have imagined.

□

When I was in high school, I was riding with the Chicago Fire Department, and we went to a four-story brownstone apartment building that had a fire in a store on the first floor. Back then the firemen weren't using masks. I watched those firemen go into smoke that was so thick it was like heavy drapery, and I saw them carry out those little kids, some of them down ladders and some out the front door. What an experience, to see somebody's life actually being saved. After that, I knew that this was what I wanted to do.

To me the things kids did in school, football games and all that, was kid stuff. When I became a volunteer firefighter in Wheaton, which is a suburb of Chicago, I felt I was a man at eighteen. I wasn't just an observer like I was in Chicago, I was a full-fledged volunteer fireman, and there the volunteers were paid on call, that is, for the time they put in a fire call. They paid for my fire science degree. I remember making $2,500 that year. That was a good buck in 1973, when I was still living at home.

I lost my teeth and just about lost my lip driving to a fire one winter night. You know, you put a blue light on your car and drive like mad. The whole volunteer concept is insane. Guys, and it's usually young guys, getting in their cars, driving like maniacs so they don't miss the apparatus leaving the station. I see it all over the country. I see it on vacations when I go to other towns. They drive like maniacs.

That's what I was doing when I almost smashed into another fireman racing to the same fire. I overreacted and slammed on the brakes, spun around on the icy road and smashed into a telephone pole. My face went into the steering wheel, and a piece went through my lip here. I was hospitalized for a week. I felt very foolish. The department paid my medical bills, but they didn't reimburse me for the car.

But the system is crazy. I used to sleep with socks on every night and a T-shirt, with bunker pants right by my bed. And I'd have a big piece of cardboard over the windshield of my car so it wouldn't get frosted up. When the radio call would come in in the middle of the night, I'd hop into my clothes, get in the car, start it up, and race to the fire station. But for me, it was a good deal because I was eighteen, and they were paying for me to take fire science classes at a junior college.

I became a full-time firefighter in the neighboring suburb of Mapleville, which gave me some experience. I thought I was hot stuff when I came down to Dade County, because I had had icicles on my helmet in Chicago. A lot of fellows were coming down from New York City at that time. They were more mature than me, they kept their mouths shut going through the fire college, which is our four-month-long academy. I found out I wasn't such a hotshot.

I was assigned to a relatively slow fire station in the southernmost part of the county. I didn't fit in. I don't drive a pickup truck, and I don't listen to country-and-western music. They're great guys, but I'm not one of their people, and I didn't fit in at all. They looked at me a little strange when I was studying fire engineering at the station. I wanted to go out and drill. I think I'm starting to sound pompous.

The first fire was a typical old, what we call a Dade County pine wood frame house, one-story with a huge attic and a porch in front built up on concrete block piers. This was in a poor black neighborhood. This Dade County pine is coated with resin, resistant to just about any kind of insect, and it'll last forever. You don't have to paint it or anything. But if you ever see one of these houses burn, you can hear it, it sounds like shotgun shells going off. Pop, bam, bam, bam. And what it is, it's these resins boiling off, adding to the fuel load, and these things burn unbelievably hot. I've fought wood frame fires up north, but they were just regular pine. These suckers here are unbelievable for the speed and the heat of the fire.

We were attacking the fire, I remember, with a couple of inch-and-a-half lines, and the fire was laughing at us. I was starting to find out that this was no joke. The academy was tough, too. I thought I knew a lot about firefighting from my experience, but I found out that Dade County has certain ways of doing things, and I figured I better just keep my mouth shut and learn their way. It was no piece of cake. It was tough for me, both physically and mentally.

I tell people that the firefighter earns his pay in an environment that is very hot, very poisonous, and without being able to use his sense of sight. So he has to follow some kind of search pattern—first of all, to get his own self out, and second, to save somebody's life and get that person back out.

Another thing, you're only staying in the building and being of use as long as that supply of air stays on your back. That is why staying in shape is vitally important. Experience. The more you work with a breathing apparatus, the more relaxed you are going to be with it, the more confidence you are going to have with it. And stamina is the name of the game. I work out an hour a day, every day of the month. I do calisthenics, push-ups, sit-ups, pull-ups, and running. I gave up lifting weights about a year ago, because I think it's only cosmetic.

The average citizen gets his opinion of firefighters from what he sees on the news. But the news media don't come to the little house fire and show the man crawling in smoke so thick he can't see his hand in front of his face, doing his job without worrying that the fire may be burning over his head or kick back over him.

□

I'll never forget, it was the third day of fire school, and you know how little things stick in your mind. About four of us were raising up a fifty-foot ladder. It was a windy day, and we were getting the ladder up when it started to fall. There were some guys standing around, and everybody instinctively ran to the ladder and grabbed it to keep it from falling.

There was a lieutenant there, who said, "You know what, there was one guy who ran away. And he should have kept going right out that gate, because firemen don't run away."

Firemen don't run away. All my life I've been that way. A good fireman instinctively knows what to do, and one of the things is this: a fireman doesn't run away. That is some kind of pride I have, and I get it from being a fireman.

□

I was in the Army and stationed in Arlington, Virginia. I joined the Arlington Volunteer Fire Department and was on Engine Company 1. But I hadn't had what I call the "moment of truth."

In firefighting, I think you get into it by degrees. Everybody has his own motives. For most of us, it's the excitement, the challenge, all the things that go with the fire department, the apparatus and everything. But you still don't know what it is until you get your first working fire where you have to lay yourself on the line. I don't want to overdramatize it, but from the time I was fifteen I had been going to fires and pulling hose, but it wasn't until I had been on the Arlington Fire Department for a few months that I had my "moment of truth."

Then we got a fire that not only was a working fire, but there supposedly were people trapped. It was about three in the morning, and it was one of those times when you instinctively knew, by the way the alarm came in, that you were going to have a working fire. When we turned into the street we were still four blocks away, and you could smell the smoke. We pulled up, and there was a lady standing out in front in her nightgown, screaming that her daughter was up in the bedroom, and the house was heavily involved in smoke, and some flame was showing.

This other guy and I stepped off the back of the engine, and we pulled off the booster line. Archie Hughes was a wonderful guy and a great friend; he became a career firefighter, rose to captain, and was later killed in a fire. Anyhow, Archie and I started up the stairs with the booster line, and we hit that wall of heat. We didn't use masks much in those days. We carried a couple of MSA demand masks and a couple of Scott air packs, but we normally didn't wear them. We only wore them when we thought there was a gas condition. Anyhow, we started up the stairs and hit that wall of heat and smoke, and we thought this girl was trapped in the bedroom.

I remember the feeling of "I can't make it." I had this great desire to back away and get out of there. The only thing that prevented me from fleeing was the fact that I would be shamed in front of Archie. He later confessed to me that the only thing that stopped him from fleeing was the fact that he would be shamed in front of me.

So we continued up the stairs, got to the landing on the second floor, and crawled into the bedroom trying to find this girl. Now the fire was starting to drip down the walls. We couldn't find her, and then it got real hot. All we had was the booster line. I remember yelling at our captain to bring a big line up. It got so hot that we finally had to start backing out. We just got to the stairs when a flashover occurred, and everything around us took off in fire. We dove head first down the stairs, just as the rest of the company was coming up with a two-and-a-half-inch line.

We crawled out onto the street. I don't remember much at that point. I sort of woke up, and Archie and I were sitting on the back step of the pumper, and they had inhalators on us. They wanted to take us to the hospital, and I wouldn't go because I was convinced that if I ever lay down on that stretcher I would never get up again. I also was convinced that I wasn't cut out to be a fireman, because I knew how close I had come to running away.

So we sat there for a while, and the fire was knocked down. It turned out the girl never was there, she was staying at a friend's house that weekend. Her mother had forgotten. That didn't matter, really. I've been to many fires since when that sort of thing has occurred.

The company was up on the roof overhauling, and I remember standing there and thinking to myself, "In the morning, I'm going to resign. I'm not going to be a fireman because I know how close I came."

I got home around five in the morning, got to sleep, and I guess it was around eight o'clock when the alarm went off again. I jumped out of bed, got into my bunkers, headed for the fire. It was a working fire in a basement, a couch, and we went, pulled the couch out. All of a sudden I realized that I was okay, that I wasn't that much afraid. I guess it was kind of like when you're thrown from a horse, you get back on.

So I had overcome that first obstacle. Then, as the years go on, you get deeper and deeper involved, and you go through various stages until finally you reach the point when, without knowing it, you have made a total commitment to being a fireman.

One of the things about the fire service that is perhaps the most satisfying of all is knowing that, as long as you have the equipment and the manpower you need, you can face any challenge that is thrown at you, because of the constant repetition of the procedures—the training you go through, the experience that builds up, the teamwork that's there. Because when you get into a fire situation, especially one where a life is involved, the adrenaline flows, and it's very easy to do the wrong thing. The only thing that prevents you from doing the wrong thing, and forces you to do the right thing, is that disciplined training experience, plus the motivation.

I think that those are the ingredients for success in anything you do in life. It's especially true in the fire service. The motivation and the desire and willingness to be a firefighter, the training you go through, the discipline imposed on you, the discipline from your officers, the discipline you impose on yourself to be a part of this team, and finally—and most important of all—the experience. And by following the prescribed procedures, those seemingly routine things that have been drilled into you, when you do it enough, in that crucial situation you will do the right thing. It becomes almost instinct.

I've also come to believe that fear is a pretty good thing for a firefighter to have. The more you know, the more you're afraid, because there are things you should be afraid of. What you do is to discipline yourself to cope with your fear. And when you reach the stage of experience when you make that fear work for you, you will then know the dangers you should be looking for—the signs of a possible backdraft situation, the buildup you know is going to lead to a flashover, the signs of a weakness in a structure that could lead to a collapse.

Now, that's smart firefighting, and you do those things only after you have had some close calls and learned that there is good reason to be afraid of certain things. For me, personally, I have always been terrified of electricity. I always look out for live wires.

□

There are a lot of strict requirements in the company, professional liability being what it is these days. We're trying to weed out those who don't come to work, those who don't come to training, who don't know what's going on or how to use the new equipment. When you get someone with a new air pack who trained on an old, outdated model the last time he went to fire school ten years ago and hasn't attended an update since, he goes into a fire situation and doesn't know how to use the equipment. They have to take time out and go to the state fire school for thirteen consecutive weeks.

The way it works in most of the upstate counties is that the fire chiefs, when they have a lot of new guys, put in requests for courses on the essentials of firemanship. The instructor comes to the firehouse every Tuesday night for thirteen weeks. We tell the guys they have to take it. It's interesting to see guys leave the company for various personal reasons and then come back strong five years later. They retrain themselves, go back through fire school. I certainly will end up doing that when I get out of medical school.

I learned most of my firefighting in Hamilton, New York, when I was at Colgate. I had a beeper for four years. Back in Old Chatham, we did maybe one brush fire the summer that I joined. Then I went off to Colgate and started doing large interior attacks. It was my job during a structure fire to get on the engine, put the masks on the people, then get up to the structure, pull the hose line, and make the initial attack and the initial knockdown. Four or five of us young guys worked a lot together, and we would switch around. We trusted each other completely.

Not like an earlier time when I came back to Old Chatham from school on Christmas vacation and we fought a structure fire. I didn't know where we kept the air packs on the engine, that's how unfamiliar I was with my own company at that time. It was a kind of nightmare—what every paid fireman thinks volunteer firemen are like. I took an inch-and-a-half into the house. The others doused both ends of the house with two-and-a-halfs, blowing water at smoke, not able to see the fire. When I crawled in with the inch-and-a-half and tried to fight the fire, I got hit in the head by the fogs and streams from the idiots at the windows.

Then my air tank went dry. I was about two rooms into the structure, and I was out of air. It was the old grab-the-hose-and-follow-it-back-out. This was an old mask that had no alarm on it. It was unbelievable, because the Hamilton company was on the cutting edge of having the best breathing apparatus. So from that summer on I got very involved in the company, getting our breathing apparatus up to date, so when the new standards came out we were right with it.

There is a lot of tunnel vision in the fire service. When you're young, all you see is that doorway and that flame, and you want to go right through it. But when you're a chief, you stand back and look at the big picture, you see what's in store for the enforcement of the building and when the building is geared up for an early collapse. I suppose there are times when you could feel guilty for not going in or for backing down.

Once I became a medic in the Hamilton Fire Department, I felt I had a very serious commitment to the people and to the village. Then, when the beeper rang during class, I was right out the door. Back home after leaving Colgate, there was a bad accident on the thruway that runs through our district. Basically, a truck driver was cut in half, and it was kind of rough getting him out and dealing with how badly mutilated his body was. The Tri-Village chief, at the accident, asked me, "Are you going to be around for long?" I said, "Yes." He asked if I wanted to be the assistant chief. I said, "Yeah, I'd like that." I guess they all felt strongly about my experience at Hamilton. I did some drills and I did some training, and apparently I was fairly good at it. So I became the training officer to the company.

There are rituals that take place inside of a burning room, like religious rites of passage. I would never give a nozzle to someone who is a rookie or a probie who really doesn't know what he's doing. He could spray all the way down the hall and he hasn't even seen the fire yet. You have to find it. It's like, "God, where's the fire? I feel a little heat on this side of my ear, let's go down this way."

You're always going to remember the first guy who ever takes you in, you know, when it turns out to be your fire, and it's your judgment, listening to the crackling, watching the fire, to be able to track it down. You know when you've done it right, but it was good that you had that guy right with you. At least that's the way it is in the volunteer service, where the buddy system is ironclad.

□

I was lucky enough to make a rescue after eight or nine months in the volunteers. Luck is a factor because, first, you have to be at a fire where somebody needs to be rescued. Then you have to be at the right place at that fire. You have to have enough knowledge to know how to do it and then be lucky enough to successfully pull it off. You can't plan it. I don't believe in fate per se, but I think there are certain things in the cards.

I was fairly young. I was on a pumper, and we were the third or fourth pumper there. The truck company was pretty heavily engaged, and there were a number of people on the fire escapes. Freeport is basically a bedroom community. You know, little private dwellings. All of a sudden, we had an apartment house fire, which was taxing. It was a five-story building, and the fire was in the cellar, so the whole building was at risk.

My pumper pulled up, and another fellow and I reported to the chief. "What do you want us to do?"

He said, "I've got a report that there's a baby in that apartment." A baby, right. It happens so often it seems to be a cliché.

So we went up the hallway, it was pretty smoky, and we came to two doors. I had a feeling that the baby was to the right. The other guy said, "I'll go straight." I went into the room at the right, it wasn't extremely hot, but it was smoky. On my first search I didn't find anybody, but I figured I better do it again. The second time around, I found the baby lying on the floor between a night table and a bed, I guess he rolled off the bed or something, I'm not sure. He had on a little green-and-white-striped shirt and Pampers.

Right then, when I took him out, I knew that the rewarding feeling was similar to putting a fire out, only more so.

Shortly after probie school, I was assigned to Engine Company 74 on the Upper West Side of Manhattan. There I was fortunate enough to be involved in my first New York City rescue. You make your own luck in many instances. It was very unusual for a probie in an engine company to be put into a search with an officer. We were at a false alarm when the dispatcher asked us if we were available. The battalion chief gave us the go-ahead, and we were first at the fire by a good five minutes. It was a high-rise apartment building.

Being a gung-ho probie, I had gotten completely geared up for the false alarm. I had a mask on and everything. The other guys, because it was a hot summer night and this was a known false alarm box, had taken their time about getting dressed. People at the apartment were screaming that there was a baby trapped. Another baby, right. People leave them behind like old bathrobes. The lieutenant, seeing I was the only guy dressed, pointed at me and said, "Let's go."

We went up the elevator part of the way, then ran up the stairs to the hallway leading to the fire apartment. The door was open, and the smoke was nearly to the floor. It was hot. We went in the direction of the heat. Again it was another one of those, he went to the left, and I went to the right, and I found this little girl on the floor. She was conscious, and I removed her to the street and took her to the hospital.

The sad part was that there was another child in the apartment, the lady's nephew. A guy, I think he was from Truck 13, went in off the aerial ladder, got in the window, cut himself on the glass, and made a real spectacular rescue of the child. The kid was badly burned, and he didn't make it. It was just one of those things again. You just go along doing your job, and there you are.

It was unusual for me to be there, because the truck company is in charge of forcible entry, going in and searching for victims, and they work more or less independently. Whereas in an engine company the people work together in one group to fight the fire. It was not so much aggressiveness on my part, it was my "gung-ho-ness." I was serious about every aspect of the job, even cleaning the brass, and every time we went out the door, I wanted to be fully prepared. And it paid off.

Sure, putting out a fire is satisfying, there's nothing like it except making a grab, rescuing somebody. But even in a busy area, some companies don't make one grab a year. While a nozzle man in a busy area is going to put out three, four fires a night. There's a lot to be said for that. That's an enjoyable part of it, too.

□

I was a volunteer firefighter for seven years with the Cherry Hill Fire Department in New Jersey before I came to Charlotte. There we had an eight-week basic firefighter course. We also attended the Delaware State Fire College for firemanship two through four programs. New Jersey also had schools, and some of the guys went to the Philadelphia Training Academy. We just went out and found schools around our area and went out of our way to attend most of them. They have a rather good fire science program at Camden County Community College, taught largely by officers of the Philadelphia and Camden fire departments, a two-year course. I would like very much to pursue a four-year degree, but it's going to have to be on a correspondence level.

I was fortunate to have started at a very young age in a quite active fire department and had experience in just about every aspect of the fire service.

The Garden State Racetrack fire was probably the biggest fire that I will ever see. I was on the first ladder, second alarm. This involved the grandstands, not like the one five years earlier in downtown Cherry Hill, where all the horses died. At Garden State, out of eight thousand people in the stands at the time, two spectators and a fire policeman died.

The scene was utter chaos. Conditions were deteriorating rapidly. The building was just being taken. It was beyond anything we could ever control. There was a downwind, the fire created more wind, all the characteristics of a conflagration. The thing was made completely out of wood. It was the first time ever that the Philadelphia Fire Department responded across the river.

Our truck company did a lot of repositioning. We set up our aerial ladder and the ladder pipe at the end of the grandstand, then the fire got hotter and hotter and we had to back out. It was amazing, the progress the fire made. It was self-propagating, and we repositioned three times. Rescues were made from ladders, a lot of people were rescued.

It was like Yankee Stadium burning, except that we didn't have the exposure we would have had at Yankee Stadium. It was pretty much an isolated structure. Our company was at the scene at least thirty-six hours, but others were there a good three or four days. It taught me that fire fighting would never be an easy job.

I was a part-paid firefighter by the time Charlotte telephoned me. They called me at work and told me I had passed the written examination but that I had to come down for the agility exam. I did that, then they called and told me I was hired. So I packed and left home, came down here, passed the physical, and started with the fire department. I started with recruitment training. I wasn't an officer anymore.

The training was sixteen weeks long. It was fun in the beginning, but it became a little tedious, because I was already an emergency medical technician.

The camaraderie started there. From my experience I was able to help many people along, and I got some satisfaction out of that. Many of us still work together, and I made lifelong friends there.

On a typical day, we would start by running several miles and then do a series of, let's say, eight exercises, moving from one to the other. Then it would be classroom sessions. Then, in the afternoon, drill tower training, more classroom sessions, or actual fire simulation. What was nice about it was that the school hours were eight to four, Monday through Friday. So that on weekends I could ride on one of the busier engines or trucks in town.

I had to retake emergency medical service training here as part of the program. We have to maintain our EMT status by taking a new test every two years. We put in hours, do a full day of practical work, and then we take the test. It's an ongoing process.

□

To be a member of our department, you have to take a West Virginia Section One course, that's just basic firemanship; you know, this is a hose, this is a ladder. We have field instructors who are certified to teach these courses, and they come to your station when there are enough students. Also we require that you take a basic first aid course, have a CPR card, and go through six months of probationary time. You also have to go through a SCBA class before you can even put on an air pack and go inside a burning building.

After six months you take a chief's test. That can be a little bit of everything you've learned, and he tests you personally. It's a little scary, because he has the authority, he lets you know who's boss, but he also works with you. Then he recommends you to the voting membership.

Our department sends members to other schools, to the National Fire Academy down in Emmitsburg, which puts on different training seminars.

The department pays for tuition, gas mileage, and rooms. The members take their own weekends, and go down on their own.

The second Tuesday of every month, we have a business meeting, every other Tuesday of the month is drill night, three hours of drills. Members are required to attend one third of these meetings. Right now I'm an instructor, so I have to be there a lot of Tuesday nights. And I help instruct the junior firefighters. We have twenty of them, ranging in age from fourteen to eighteen. They're allowed to do everything except go inside a burning building.

I didn't attend college, but I did attend a trade school. I always liked to work with my hands.

Being an unmarried firefighter, I travel around a lot. I'm an assistant instructor, and every Tuesday night I'm out teaching other fire departments. As an assistant, I'm still unpaid. In some places the training gets stale, just a repetition of classes with nothing new. So a head instructor and some of us younger guys are trying new ideas to motivate the younger volunteers, like actually having them throw a ladder against a building instead of just standing in front of the class and talking.

I was in one firefighting class where the instructor turned off the oxygen on us. That was supposed to see how fast we could react to the situation and get out. We thought it was an unsafe maneuver, but we couldn't persuade the instructors to change.

You want to teach recruits, not scare them out of the fire service.

□

The first time I was in a dangerous situation was back in the sixties. I was on Truck 13. We had a tough job on Pratt Street, a three-story dwelling. When we pulled up, there was heavy smoke and fire on the first floor, which was a storefront. Fire was blowing out and up, and each window had people in it. We put ladders up to the sides of the windows and started to get the people out. A couple of the people lunged at us while we were still coming up the ladder. One fell on the guy who was our driver at the time. He just stuck out his arm and caught the girl right across the belly. It was just his brute strength that held her. He got her down, and we pulled a couple more out. Some had gone back into the building.

In those days we were using all-service air masks. I had the mask on, and the chief said, "Get in, get in." The ladder is here, and the window is to the right about three feet. Okay, get in. Sure. But I've got to look this situation over because I'm going to have to jump from this ladder to the window, and there was no way of rolling over because we still had some fire.

When I leaped over to the windowsill, I was dangling from it. Somehow, unbeknownst to me, the nipple with the filter on the top of my air canister was lifted up, so I had no filter whatsoever. I went in and crawled around, found a young boy, and brought him to the window to one of the guys.

I was taking on smoke, and I didn't realize why. I checked the face piece, and it seemed okay. It baffled me that I was taking in the smoke, and the smoke was getting heavier. I went back a second time and found some older guy, who was in the back room, and I dragged him out. By then, I was so dizzy I didn't know what I was doing. I got out to the ladder, and as soon as I took the mask off and the cold air hit me, I collapsed right there.

The next thing I knew, I was in the hospital, lying right next to one of the guys we had rescued. I heard the doctor say, "Give me a scalpel, I have to do a tracheotomy." I immediately started breathing well. I mean, I was pumping up in panic. I thought there was no way in hell that he was going to cut my throat for a tracheotomy. So he did the tracheotomy on one of the victims we had pulled out. The fellow lived, by the way.

But I didn't know how bad I was. I knew they had brought me in because I was overcome by smoke. I sure in hell didn't want no trache done on me, so I started breathing like a new machine.

That was the first time that I thought this job might be a little difficult.

□

My fire training at that time was right at the fire station. We had one station that was supposed to be the training academy. We just called it the training department. It was only eight weeks long. Now they have a regular school, a regular academy. Basically, it prepared me for the job. It gave me probably 25 percent of the knowledge I needed just to get on the truck and respond to a fire.

Working in the fire station was different. I had just come back from Vietnam, and I was still getting over the trauma of that. There were some practical jokes, like guys would shut the hot water off while you were taking a shower, or short-sheet your bed, little things like that. It was all in fun.

To learn about firefighting, I asked a lot of questions. I followed the people I thought were competent and asked them. The problem here in the South is that we don't get much work. So we don't have a lot of experience, even the senior people.

I'll tell you where I got a lot of my experience was up in New York City. My friend Steve Carter and I have been up there five times, riding with Truck 27 in the Bronx. I followed the truckies, followed the roof man to the roof. I watched what they did and how they operated. I'd question them. We couldn't believe the hospitality that we got.

Going to New York City and watching those men work, you get a little bit more knowledge. Sometimes knowledge kind of scares you.

We visited other companies, and everybody treated us unbelievably. I wish we in Florida could treat firemen the same way. It was like a family.

The first time I was in a dangerous situation, I was only on the job probably about a year, and I got turned around inside of a closet. That scared me. I don't know how I got turned around, a lot of it was from inexperience and not really knowing what I was doing. Because I was ignorant of the job when I first came on. All I could think about was running out of air.

It was a big closet, about ten by ten. The ironic thing was that I was right by the door all the time. I didn't panic, or maybe I wasn't in there long enough to panic. It was black, I was on my hands and knees, trying to find my way out, couldn't see anything. Even with the flashlight on, I couldn't see anything.

I know when I was in Vietnam and I got myself in a couple of bad situations, I was really scared. I don't think I was so much scared of dying, I was much more scared of being captured. But on the firefighting job, I think I was afraid of dying. And it seems like the older you get, the more concerned you are. But when you're young, you're kind of foolish, maybe.

□

My first firehouse turned out to be the same engine company my father had been in, Engine 26 in the northwest corner of Buffalo. A relatively quiet house. When he got sick and had to retire, that created the vacancy the commissioner appointed me to fill. It was nice of him, he didn't have to do it. I actually took my father's locker and everything else. My father was proud to see both my brother and me in the fire department, although he never pushed us to it.

It was a great thrill to walk in the door of that firehouse as a fireman for the first time. I don't know if I even touched the pavement. It was the realization of a lifelong dream.

Neither my brother, Harvey, nor I had dreamt of being an officer. But after a while, through the encouragement of other officers, we got to studying, and we studied together all the time. The tough part of our studies was the laws and ordinances. They were so boring with all that legal terminology. Half the time we memorized them and really didn't know what they meant. The interesting part, of course, was the firefighting tactics and all the fire hazards. Even the building construction information was interesting, I thought. At least it pertained to the job.

But exactly how many feet a fire escape ladder must be from the ground and how many pounds a certain beam must support, that was dull. It's all necessary stuff, of course. Over the years the questions come up, and you do remember it, even if you have to look it up to be sure.

The tests are a sort of elimination contest, and winning involves a combination of two things. You have to do a lot of studying, and you have to be lucky. I don't care who you are, they can always ask you about things you don't know. A lot of fellows do all the work and still don't make it. My brother ended up a battalion chief, and I made it to division chief.

As I said, I never expected to be an officer, and this is just frosting on the cake all the way.

□

I really feel that if firefighting is what somebody really wants to do and they take the time to get the proper training, anybody can do it. You've gotta want to do it.

I've had 240 hours of training, plus I went to the National Fire Academy. I've been there about ten times for different classes. I paid for everything myself, because the classes at the academy are taught by the best-trained people in the fire field. I feel that the more knowledge I get, the safer my life is going to be. I know that bookwork can't always help you in an actual fire situation. You have to have the experience. But hopefully my book learning, my training, plus now the experience I've had will get me out of a lot of bad situations—or prevent me from getting into one.

It took anywhere from nine to twelve hours to get to the academy, depending on the weather. I'd leave about five Friday morning and return about four in the morning on Sunday. I've taken public fire education, firefighter safety and survival, volunteer fire service management, initial company tactical operation, fire service suppression—that's increasing personal effectiveness—and fire service supervision—that's increasing team effectiveness.

I've also taken a class over at Eastern on investigating the juvenile arsonist. I'm a juvenile counselor now in both Livingston and Washtenaw counties. I love that. The kids really open their arms to me. It's a wonderful feeling.

These are children who have actually set fires, and the parents bring them to me. A lot of the parents say things like, "Scare them, and tell them never to do this again." But when I sit down with these kids and talk to them, they understand where I'm coming from. They know I'm a firefighter and that what they did was wrong, but they can trust me and talk to me about it. We've had a real good record with these kids not repeating fires.

There was a mentally retarded boy who was playing with a lighter on his bed, and he set his mattress on fire. He was an eighteen-year-old who, when he was five, had fallen off a curb and gotten hit by a car. Some people wanted the police to talk to the boy and shake him up by telling him, "You'll get arrested if you do this again." It was one of the police officers who asked me to handle this child, who had a six-year-old mentality. So I talked to him and had a real good session with him.

Nine months later I was involved with the Kiwanis Club, taking handicapped kids to Tiger Stadium for one of the games. And this boy was one of the kids in the group. I went up to him and said, "Hi, Carl, do you remember me?" And he said, "Yes." Then he said, "I don't play with lighters anymore." And I was just so tickled, to think that he would remember all those months later. And his mom was grateful for how I handled the situation.

In your original training class, when you go into an actual burn for the first time, you get scared. You think, "What in the heck am I doing? Why am I doing this?" But I had great confidence in my instructors. I trusted them completely, because I felt they weren't going to take a class of twenty people into a burning building and endanger their lives. The neatest part for me was having the breathing apparatus on. I'd never had anything over my face like that. That was exciting. I would challenge myself to see how little air I could use in the training sessions. I got to the point where I would just relax, and it doesn't bother me to have the mask on.

I've come a long way since then, but I think anybody would be foolish to say they weren't scared. I still am, at times. At some fires I feel that that darn thing is a lot smarter than I am. It's a constant game. It's like I say, "Okay, who's going to be smarter this time, you or me? Who's going to win this fight?"

You have to treat fire with respect. Because if you don't, that's when you get hurt.

□

You get sworn in in the morning, they give you the badge, and they say, "Take a hike out to the firehouse you're assigned to and see the captain." This sounds archaic, but I didn't even own an automobile. So I had to take the subway and a bus out to this single-engine company that did a grand total of about eight hundred runs a year. Now picture this: I'm twenty-two, and I introduce myself to the captain. He used to be a state trooper, and he just stands there, and growls at me, "Huh, look what they send me! You're too young. Go home."

I'm shocked. I'm saying to myself, Wait a minute, you don't understand. I swam the hundred yards and everything. I just practically conquered the world to get out here, and this is what happens.

Then I went to drill school, which in my case was four weeks, Monday through Friday. Then you spent Saturday nights in the firehouse. I thought the training was great. The most difficult thing for me was the Pompier ladder, the scaling ladder. The fire department doesn't use them anymore, but they were used as a training exercise in teamwork and building confidence in your buddy. I didn't have a lot of upper body strength, because I was skinny. That was a pretty good challenge, raising that Pomp from floor to floor on the outside of the building, because there was no way I was going to let go of that ladder, have it drop or slip.

The rest of it was just practice, you know, running lines, dogging the ladders. I was never permitted to handle the nozzle, just be a spectator. I just couldn't wait to get there every day, it was more fun than anything else. They were trying to tell us, watch out for this, watch out for that. But I didn't pay too much attention because I was pretty high off the ground, thinking, "Wow, here I am!"

The instructors did their best. They came from the busy sections of the city, and a lot of them were bent and broken from always being in the busy companies. That was partially the reason why they were there. They were trying to convey to us in four weeks what they had learned in over thirty years. It was always interesting to listen to them, but we just couldn't envision it until we actually hit the firehouse and started experiencing it.

The captain didn't put me in his group. Instead, he put me with a lieutenant. I can't say it was because he didn't want me, just that it was where the opening was. I was in that engine company for fourteen months, because they wouldn't let a probie transfer in the first year. But it wasn't busy enough for me. What are you going to do in eight hundred runs a year? It drove me bananas.

On my first run we go to a car accident, and on the way back we stop in a parking lot next to a supermarket. And I think, "Wow, he must have found another fire or something." And then I look beyond the fire trucks. I can't believe this! The lieutenant is rummaging through the charitable donation box looking for a pair of shoes! This was difficult to take. The image of the heroic firefighter was slightly diminished, but what are we gonna do, right?

That company was only good for relocating on multiple alarms, they were practically never first due at decent fires. And, anyway, I went like three months before we got a good job. It was a fourth alarm, in a church. All we did was double up with another engine company, dragging a two-and-a-half up to the choir loft, and the fire was pretty much knocked down by the time we got up there. I was disappointed. I realized I had to be on the first alarm to see any action.

Those fourteen months were difficult. I didn't even want to sleep during the night tour. I used to volunteer to take the other guys' night watches, because I couldn't sleep anyway. I'd say to myself, "We only went out once last night. Give me a break, will ya? This is ridiculous."

I finally got a transfer to Engine 33 in the Back Bay section, a kind of mixed area. There's politics in the fire department. You had to know somebody really well to get transferred to where you wanted to go. And I didn't know anybody. The fact that my dad was a firefighter didn't mean a thing. Too bad about that, 'cause firefighters are the greatest. I could ramble on about the politics, but that's another story.

□

In those days our training school was in a real old building, and we did our outdoor training, our ladder work, at Municipal Stadium on the lakefront, where the Browns used to play. It was a six-week school. We run a much more extensive training school now.

I was a cadet for seven years at my first station, which was a long time. My father-in-law tried to take care of me by sending me to a station that wasn't very busy. We didn't take many men into the department in those days, and not many guys retired. So I had to wait. It was a good learning experience. I took a promotion exam, but I didn't do too well, because my wife had a child right before the exam and I was baby-sitting rather than studying. In those days, getting promoted was no big deal. I enjoyed what I was doing. But then you get to the point where you figure, hey, I want to improve myself.

The first job we had was about three hours after I came to work. It was a mattress fire on the third floor of an apartment house. It was scary, smoky. You couldn't see. I remember that most.

I think the first really serious fire was the one at the Theatrical Grill in downtown Cleveland, which turned out to be an all-nighter. Shortly after that, we had an apartment house fire at West Thirty-eighth and Clinton. It was seven o'clock on a winter morning. We took like 117 people out of the building over ladders and down stairways.

I was scared as all hell when I saw so many people in real trouble, scared about doing things right. Fortunately, we had a couple of old-timers there who were pretty sharp. We carried fifty-five-foot ladders at that time. I always think about it. Under the standard now, we carry forty-foot ladders. In that particular fire, if we didn't have a fifty-five-foot ladder, we would have lost another five people. We used the fifty-five-foot ladder, with a twelve-foot jack ladder, to get people off the sixth floor of the building. There was no access for an aerial on that side. Things just happened so fast, I didn't then realize the magnitude of it. I just worked hard.

Fortunately, this apartment house had balconies on the side. The fire was pretty well involved when we got there. I remember putting a lot of ladders up. It was very icy. We put that fifty-five up with four men. One of them was the captain. It was a wooden ladder that weighed about 350 pounds. Normally you use five men, and some books talk about six. Putting that ladder up under good conditions was a difficult task. This was a cold, icy morning in December. Even putting a thirty-three-footer up was tough at that time. But, we were able to get that ladder up, somehow, 'cause you muster up extra strength when you have no choice.

Over the years I still think about that fire. The guys did a super job.

□

When I was in the Navy, I learned a lot of rope stuff, so when I would come back on leave to Engines 33 and 75 I would make the apparatus fancy. I would braid the handrails with rope, so the guys' hands wouldn't get cold in the winter. Then, when I got out of the service, New York City was looking for fire patrolmen, so I joined the New York City Fire Patrol. That's the only existing salvage company in the country, and it's run by the New York Board of Fire Underwriters. It goes back to 1837.

The fire patrol is not associated with the fire department, but it is hooked up with the fire department's alarm circuit, and when an alarm comes in, they respond at the same time as the firefighters. The patrol's main job is to protect merchandise insured by the insurance companies. We would spread canvas covers over the goods and push water out of the building even while the firefighters were fighting the fire. Fire patrolmen are experts in forcible entry, probably better than the truck companies, because the firemen concentrate on the fire floor and above, whereas the fire patrol concentrates on everything below the fire floor. So if there was a fire on the eighteenth floor, we would open the seventeenth, sixteenth, fifteenth, all the way down to where we could stop the water. We came across every type of door imaginable, and we forced them. We did more door forcing than the fire department because that's what we had to do—stop the water.

I was assigned to Fire Patrol 1, on West Thirtieth Street. Years ago they used to have ten fire patrol houses and four hundred men. Today there are three patrol houses and about ninety men left in them. The patrol was very careful about the type of people it hired, because it couldn't have people going in there and ripping off things like furs, jewelry, and cameras. If anything was missing, you'd have a big investigation. Not only that, you'd involve the fire department, because after the fire was knocked down on the fire floor, the patrol had to go in and push the water out. So we had to be very careful with what we did and how we touched things.

One night we had a special call to a fire at the St. George Hotel in Brooklyn. When we didn't have work for ourselves to do, we often assisted the fire department, helped stretch a line or force doors. It was a real cold and windy night. The temperature was eight or nine degrees. Cold enough, anyway, to make ice with your breath.

There was an elderly woman in a window on the twelfth floor of the hotel, and Ladder 119 was raising a 144-foot aerial to try to rescue her. Two guys went up the last extension of the ladder, and, believe me, in that cold wind it was hairy. At the top, the ladder is only about 12 inches wide, not much room when you're swinging twelve stories above the ground. The woman was on the windowsill, and I remember that she had a shoe box in one hand and a cat in the other. The ladder was at its max, and they were still three feet short of the twelfth floor. And the whole floor behind the woman was on fire. The guys were talking to the woman, telling her to stay.

The next thing, the room lit up, and out she went, on fire. I don't think she had a chance to jump at them. I think that when the room went up, it pushed her right out.

My captain and I were on the eleventh floor. We saw the whole thing, and we watched her right down to the pavement. Later on you always think about what you could have done. They could have lowered a line and pulled up a scaling ladder, using it to go one more floor. That's what I imagined, because I had seen a rescue at Fifty-third and Madison, where two guys from Ladder 2, Neal Cox and a guy named O'Neill, went from the raised aerial two floors with a scaling ladder and made a rescue. A scaling ladder is one with a long hook on the end of it that you can hook over the windowsill above you. Anyway, that went through my mind. But those guys had their hands full, and both of them got department medals for trying to get to her.

The firefighters respected the fire patrol because they used us when they needed us. I remember at a hotel fire, there was no truck company in, and the fire patrol did all the forcible entry and the ventilation until the truck company got there. We didn't have masks, and we took a beating. I remember coming back and being sick for three days.

I took the fire department test in 1968. This was my big chance. I was going to be a New York City fireman. In June 1969 I received my letter that I was going to be appointed. I was so happy because I had prepared myself for it. I went to the Delahanty Institute to study for the written part, and I also worked out for the physical. The list had two and a half years to go, and there was no way I was not going to get in the department. In fact, I even bought a house in Maybrook, outside of Goshen, New York. I had two captains in the Bronx just waiting for me to come. They knew me and wanted me in their particular companies.

The letter said I was going to be appointed on July 1, but a month before that the sky fell in, and life changed drastically. In June I got this other letter saying they were going to freeze the list because of cutbacks and minority hiring. It was a real blow. They actually froze the list for two and a half years and let it die. I was devastated. Here I had my house, and I was all ready to go, and then boom. When I got on the Hartford Fire Department, I commuted for three years from Goshen, New York, to Hartford, Connecticut, and I never was late or missed a day's work.

It wasn't just the minorities, the crunch came when Commissioner O'Hagen went crazy and closed fifty companies. I don't know what they had in mind. They were going from fourteen thousand men, and they were shooting for eight thousand firemen in a city of eight million. It was ludicrous. It was the time of the riots in the South Bronx, and I remember going over to 31 Truck and 82 Engine and the company would be out at a fire, and the next company would catch a job. Then the next company came, and they'd catch one. Companies from different parts of the city were relocating to the next fire, the next fire, the next fire. And then as that area became burned out, it became prairie land, and the fires shifted to the next area. The same thing.

I never accepted it until about a year ago. I had so much hate . . .

□

We had a rookie school, and you're supposed to have all your hours certified by the state, but I was already out in the field. Our training chief waited until he had enough rookies to form a class. Then we would go to rookie school for eight hours, from eight to five, and after that, if you were on a shift, you went back to your station and worked the rest of your shift. We all got a lot of overtime, and that didn't bother us.

As part of the class, we were driving through downtown in a rescue vehicle with sliding panels like a bread truck. One of the guys whistled at a girl, and the chief bawled us out, my first lesson in fire department discipline. We were also given the job of testing all the hoses in the whole fire department, so you can imagine the water fights we got into.

The department's hiring procedures were good as far as the written and physical tests were concerned, but the oral interview wasn't that much. There are people in our department who shouldn't be there, shouldn't have gotten past the oral interview.

One of the toughest fires I ever had was one of the first. I was on the job for maybe a month, and I was still looking for my initiation to come. Then less than two blocks away from our station there was a gas leak under a house, and it exploded. A man was sitting on the commode in his bathroom, and he lit a match to light the gas heater there. The explosion blew out three walls of the house, and part of the roof collapsed. The guy got burns on his rear end, legs and feet, but the mother and baby in another room just had some plasterboard fall on them.

We heard the bang, and we went. My job initially was to do the pumping, but we were on a replacement engine, and it had a different mechanism for charging the line. I didn't know where it was. My captain was standing out there with no water, and he had to run back and turn the knob.

So then we went ahead and got the fire out, except for a fire under the house. Roy Wallace had cut a hole in the floor, eight by twenty inches, and told me to go under there. I told him, "You're crazy. I'm not going under there. This place is ready to fall." I thought he was kidding with me. When I found out he wasn't, I ended up underneath the house, lying on my back in water and mud, and trying to spray water on the fire.

When I came out from under there, of course, I was all messed up. I got ridiculed by some of the men and got a bad rep with the captain for not going straight in. Anyhow, it was really something else.

□

In the Forest Service, there was no training school. We trained on the job over the course of one summer, in the mountains back of Santa Barbara. We walked at least eight hundred miles, mostly at a forty-five-degree angle, fighting brush fires. We did an hour of calisthenics every day, including a twenty-foot rope climb without using your feet. It's very hot there in the summer. We were always learning things, always sweating.

The first forest fire we had was real hard and lasted a few days. We ran out of water and had to pace ourselves. The mountains don't have a lot of tall trees, mostly scrub oak, various kinds of brush, and dry grass. A fire will burn sixteen and a half times faster uphill than down. It preheats, spreads, has a convection column that will carry embers clear across a canyon and start a fire on the other side. It darkens the sky, and it's just a big hellstorm that can cover hundreds and thousands of acres.

When we get trapped by the fire, we have aluminum shields we use. They fold into a packet about eighteen inches long, three inches thick, and about eight inches wide that we wear around our waist. Unfolded, it looks like a big baked potato about six feet long and comes to a triangular top like a tent. You lie inside it, and in each corner there's a strap. You hold the straps down with your feet and your hands, and you dig a hole where your face will go and fill it with water, if you have any, and put a wet cloth over your face. You usually face the fire, as it's making headway toward you, because the wind is going to be blowing from the fire toward you. That way, you can put your head down and hold the thing down with your hands more securely. Facing the other way, you have more of a chance of taking heated gases into the tent.

In my first forest fire, there were about three hundred of us in a big field that formed a natural firebreak. We expected a wind change that would change the direction of the fire, and we couldn't run away from it. So we gathered there and waited for the fire to pass over. We didn't have to use the shields on that occasion, but when the fire passed over it involved some big electric towers and there were lots of explosions. It was a pretty awakening experience. I didn't know what was going to happen, because it was the first time I had ever been in that situation. That time, we were protected by the clearing.

But when you use the aluminum shield, the heat from outside isn't usually the main problem. The shield will sustain a pretty good temperature, but you could have a burning tree fall on you.

In the Santa Barbara Fire Department, I've taken a lot of classes and furthered my education as much as I can. I'm an emergency medical technician, and most of our calls are medical, having to do with accidents and heart attacks. We deal with human emotions. It's given me an opportunity to pursue my medical education. In our drills we learn a lot about hazardous materials, different aspects of fighting fire, ventilation.

I have an AA from City College, and they equate our first year in the fire department to about twelve units of college. We have to know all the eight hundred streets in town, learn our rules and regulations, how to use our equipment safely. We have ongoing classes and can sign up for classes offered by the state. For instance, I recently came back from a heavy rope rescue class, bringing people up cliffs and across rivers, dealing with earthquake type emergencies, how to shore up a building that's falling down. It's a real concentrated time for us.

□

There was no training in the volunteer fire department at that time. I learned to run a pumper by myself, by being an observer, and then, on off hours, I'd go over to the station and practice on my own. The first time I ever got into the truck, of course I got my butt chewed up by the old-timers, because that was *their* job. That was a prestige job in those days.

My business was only a block from the fire station, so I was one of the first ones there on calls, and when I felt confident with that damn pumper I'd jump in the seat and have it sitting outside when those guys showed up. Some of them didn't like that. They wouldn't tell you anything. Same way with the breathing apparatus.

At the Fireman's Association summer meeting, which we had every year in June, we used to have hose-laying contests—two hundred feet of two-and-a-halfs and a Siamese arrangement of two one-and-a-halfs, a hundred feet long. And they timed you from when they said "Go" until water came out of both inch-and-a-half nozzles. We practiced over here every night for six weeks, because there was a particular town in the county that kept walking away with the prize. We were bound and determined that we were going to beat those guys, and we had that thing down pat. Make and break, set that up, and really get her going.

Then we went over to the conference, ready for this contest, and they gave us an old, beat-up ex-forestry truck that our engineer had never seen before. And he messed up the connection to the hydrant, so we got a little screwed up there. Then we got going, and after it was over, there was a big battle over the timers. Anyhow, we ended up losing. And then the fight was on. With fists. My guys were mad, and those guys thought we tried to cheat them. And one thing led to another. I'm strictly a lover, not a fighter, so I had to laugh.

When I'm in charge at a fire scene, the guys I send in to make a search are the ones that attend all the training sessions, because I know they're not going to panic or anything like that. I never send in just one man, I'll generally send two and a captain to be their eyes and ears and guide. We practice that way.

I got an old building where we practice our firefighting tactics with live fire. We get a little bit more of it each time. It'll probably take us three or four more months before that thing finally goes to ground. Great training for these guys.

The state has a training program, but in recent years it hasn't been able to fund enough instructors. So they are trying to develop self-training programs, by training somebody from each fire department to become the instructor for that particular department. And this works out pretty good, because that's exactly what I'm doing, following my own training plans. We do ours in the evenings, Monday through Friday, and the guys get their certificate, and so on. I enjoy doing it.

□

I went to college in bits and pieces. I took some fire science work at the community college. I went back to the University of Oregon for a term to get a degree in public administration. The trouble was, I was an officer of our union, a local of the International Association of Firefighters, while most of the professors were management-oriented. We had serious ideological clashes about management relations, and finally I just didn't go back to school. I've had some misgivings about that.

The fire service did two things for me, really. I provided a service, and yet, for a young man who was looking for some excitement, it provided that, too.

Our fire department has changed. When I joined in 1975, it was a very conservative kind of environment. The music in the firehouses was mostly country and western. Not too long ago, I remember getting back from an alarm at two in the morning, and the guys in the day room were watching MTV. I was thirty-three years old and the oldest guy on the crew. It just shows you how things have changed.

When I first joined, there was this generational thing. The hair code was a major issue. A lot of social stuff spilled over into the fire service. A guy who came on probation with me had a mustache. The battalion chief told him, "You know, we've never had anyone with a mustache make it through probation." I'm not sure if this guy was naive or was jacking the chief around, but his response was, "Oh, you mean I'll be the first."

We had four weeks of basic training, eight to five, Monday through Friday. We were the first group to use the International Fire Service Training Association material. We were assigned homework each night, and the next morning there would be a quiz. If you failed any of the quizzes, you were out of the program. There were also classes on mechanical proficiency and on the use and maintenance of breathing apparatus.

At that time you could join the department and be a firefighter, period. Now the program goes for seven weeks and includes emergency medical training and learning how to drive the vehicles.

They didn't have a very good burn facility in our department for training purposes, so they had buildings scheduled for destruction, and they would burn them. They would actually give us a live fire and put us in a real fire situation. As it turned out, buildings to burn were in short supply, so my class did not actually get a chance to be in a burning building. As a result, the first actual fire that I went to was a real fire.

I was assigned to our downtown station. On my second or third shift, we had a fire in the middle of the night. It was a modular classroom set up behind a grade school. I was in the second-due engine. We used to do a lot more blitz attacks, where the first company would pull a line and go in without masks, and then the second company would lay a line from a hydrant and mask up.

We were second in, and the lieutenant said to me, "Just get a mask on and hang on to my coat. Just follow me. Whatever you do, keep track of where the line is, because if you get lost and go sideways, the line is the only way you have to get back out." I remember crawling in there with the old mask that had a full face piece and an eyehole on either side. I couldn't see a damn thing, the room was filled with smoke. I remember thinking, "These people are crazy." It was just nuts. And yet, I followed right in, took a turn on the nozzle, and got out.

□

In those days, in the late fifties, we didn't get much training, just two weeks at the training towers. It's interesting that we had about 220 firefighters who did around two thousand alarms a year. This year we have 1,100 people in the fire department, and we are going on over a hundred thousand alarms. Big changes, obviously.

I was twenty years old, so I was a baby in the fire department, and in a very middle-class kind of way. I had worked in construction in the summers when I was going to college, I was a hod carrier when I came into the fire department. So I was used to construction guys, who were strong characters. They wanted you to be tired at the end of the day. I went to Oklahoma State University for three semesters and graduated with a degree in fire protection technology, which is what they called it in those days.

If you look at the Phoenix Fire Department today, we are probably just a typical fire department. Thirty years ago, it was inhabited by a lot of very good leaders. They had been in the Second World War, they had been through the tail end of the Depression, and they had tattoos.

They were tough guys—good leaders, guys who had a strong set of values. If you got out of line, they kicked your ass. They didn't know about participatory management, they hadn't been screwed up in graduate school. They were street guys, and these are the people I look back on, who raised me.

□

My first fire was a taxpayer, a group of one-story stores. It was a pullbox alarm, and we were first due in. I had the nozzle. The fire was in the ceiling and the walls, and it had gotten a little bit into the floor, but it was mostly smoke.

Danger never entered my mind. I remember thinking through the whole thing, "Don't fall. Pace yourself." I was very conscious of not making a mistake. The danger, the hell with the danger, I didn't want to look stupid. I didn't want to be pointed out. I mean, this was my first. This was my proving ground. "Don't make a fool of yourself."

It's still like that. I'm disappointed when I'm given control of the door, because inevitably somebody says, "How come you're outside, and not inside?" Sometimes I take it too seriously; they could be teasing, but I get my back up a little bit. That's my main concern—to be a professional and to do it right, to stop and think about what I'm doing.

Having the nozzle in that first fire was wonderful. Just the exhilaration and the high afterwards. My feet didn't touch the ground. Of course, nobody said, "Wow, you did a good job." It was just a nod or a look, or a small feeling of acceptance.

My officer was my backup man. I fell in love with him. It was like a woman and her obstetrician. I thought, "This is it." I never felt closer to anybody. It's a very close relationship. It's magnetic. It's very magnetic for a woman.

I also remember thinking that this was really hard work, that the guys were right: "I'm not going to be able to do this." You can't see anything. It's claustrophobic, you're moving in, and you don't know where. You're climbing over stuff, and you don't know what it is. There's a lot of noise, a lot of yelling. I remember being scared and doubting whether I was physically able to do this. I was constantly talking to myself: "Don't give up, you've got to keep going."

That was the first. It wasn't seven floors in an occupied building, with people coming down carrying their TV sets. I remember thinking how happy I was. But when I look back on it now, it really wasn't anything.

□

I had been through the EMT experience, and I had learned all the basic firefighting techniques from the local firehouse, where they let me take the pipe and open roofs. My brother was on the truck, and he'd take me on the roof with him. The knowledge I got there was unbelievable. And then, I have twelve relatives of one kind or another who are or have been firemen.

When I went to training school, I probably knew as much as some of the instructors there. But you're in there to learn, so you keep your mouth shut and do as you're told. That's just what I did, and I never had a problem. We were in training school five months, and the last month and a half we would go to school for a day and be assigned to a fire company for a day, wherever they needed us.

I'm a very proud fireman. My wife thinks I'm crazy. I've got pictures all over my wall of my father, my brother, because I like to walk by them and think of me following in my father's and brother's footsteps.

The first time I went to a fire in a special unit, I felt excited, yes, also proud I was here following my father. This is what I always wanted to be. A person could go to college for years and years and never gain the goal they want. And here I am, a couple of years out of high school. I got what I want.

□

Fires with multiple fatalities are hard to deal with. I was at my second station in the course of my probationary period, and there was a structure fire up in the Hollywood Hills. Both floors of this large two-story residence were pretty well involved. There were reports of possible trapped victims, and it was early enough in the morning that there was a good possibility that there were people in there. That made me anxious over their fate.

I was with the engine company, and we attacked the fire with a hose line. It was a real hot, down-and-dirty, nasty kind of fire. We took some pretty good fire going in. On the second floor, we discovered the first couple of fatalities, because we crawled right past them as we were knocking down the fire. They probably died of smoke inhalation, but they were considerably burned in the course of the fire. There were four fatalities in all.

Rookie firefighters were always assigned to help with the body removal. They try to prepare you for this in the academy, but it's something you can't fully comprehend until you've been there. It was a pretty helpless feeling. We rookies were assigned to assist the coroner in putting the victims on the gurney and removing them from the fire scene out to the coroner's van.

I remember having a well of emotions inside me, almost to the point of tears. A lot of questions went through my mind: did we do everything we could have done, was there something we could have done sooner or differently that would have changed the outcome? After mulling over these questions for a period of time, I was pretty satisfied that we had done everything that we could, that this thing had just run its course, and there wasn't much we could have done to change it.

□

I'm not really prejudiced about women being on the job, but let's face it, they are not as strong in upper body strength as men. And you need the upper body strength to be a firefighter. I don't know if they're still going through that affirmative action or what. But there were women up there at that physical agility test. I almost croaked after I took that test, I was huffing and puffing, and I was really in good shape. These women passed it. They put them in the first class, and we had trouble with them. They couldn't do the things that cadets do.

□

My interest in the fire department was very casual. There was an article in the newspaper that the fire exam was going to be open to women for the first time. I don't remember being overly excited about it or thinking it would be something in my future. I had been married about eleven years, and I had three children. I wasn't out there looking for a job. I wasn't competing. I was in nursing school, going for a nursing degree. I was in a very traditional lifestyle. I wasn't out there a single mother looking for a job and trying to raise a family.

My husband, Jerry, and I read the article at the same time. He was sitting there, and I don't know if it was meant as a joke or what, but he said, "Go for it. Give it a try." So it was just, "Okay, I'll give it a try." I was surprised how all of a sudden it snowballed on me. I didn't really make a commitment to it, but every little thing that came up would be a commitment, like I was waiting for the event and I'd see how I felt.

Jerry said, "You'll never know unless you try. You can sit back here and say, well, I could have, or I should have. So give it a shot." In fact, when I filled out the application, he dropped it off personally. I didn't even mail it in. But I remember feeling very uncomfortable about the fact that they were all men. I was even afraid to show up in person. It was very foreign to me.

I went to the practices. They offered practice courses for the physical exam. The animosity was unbelievable. The comments that were made. The fireman giving the class made it plain that this was a man's job he was teaching. There were only about five women in the class, but you could feel the tension. It was quite uncomfortable. Through all those classes and then through the written exam, waiting outside to take the test, the comments, the isolation. Comments like, "Why don't you get a job as a secretary?" "You don't belong here, you're taking the job away from a man who needs it."

These were young fellows, not old diehards. We were around the same age. They were in their twenties. I remember finally getting into the school. I waited an hour and a half to get in. You walk through the door, and they tell you where you're going to sit. My head was down, and I thought, "If I get through this day, it'll be a miracle."

A woman handed me the card from Personnel. She said, "You're the sixth woman. Congratulations. Good luck." That was all I needed, the one positive among twenty or thirty negatives. Just the look on her face. She had counted all of the women, and she told me what number I was, and she wished me luck. I didn't even know if they were allowed to talk to us.

I got a 98 on the written test. It was quite an easy test, as a result of a lawsuit filed on behalf of black firefighters years before. There is still a great deal of resentment when we talk about blacks in the firehouse. Not openly, but there is. The fact that I'm a woman and so much more visible than a man makes them never forget. I'm a constant reminder.

What was bad was that in 1978, when the original physical was given, this whole case was in court. I wasn't notified until 1981 that a new physical was going to be given. Was I interested in taking it? In the meantime I had a fourth child.

I had had a bad pregnancy. I spent almost six months in the hospital with my feet up. So talk about bad physical condition. I thought, "Oh, God, what a challenge this will be." Jennifer, the fourth child, was about six months old when I started running. I had always been a physical person, but the pregnancy really took a lot out of me. I was taking experimental drugs to help with the pregnancy. I aged about ten years in six months, then she was born prematurely. I was exhausted.

It was January 1982 when I got notification that the revised physical would be given in September of that year. A summer training program was set up out at the academy. They gave us a working program of our own to help us get into condition for the training. Getting motivated for that was the hardest. I said, "I have a little baby. I have small children. Do I want this?" I was only thirty-one, but I felt old. Then I said, "Well, you've gone this far. You can't give up. You have to go at least until the test and see how you do."

I ran three days a week. I thought I was doing great. When I got to the academy, I realized I had to work a hundred times harder. I had never lifted weights. I had to start learning how to do that. Not just to lift weights but to apply my body physically, in an aggressive way. I had to do that. It was a struggle, because I had been raised to be a mom. Did I have any business doing something that was so completely different? The kids were great. I have three sons and my husband. They were terrific. They said, "Congratulations, Mom. Now get out there and do it."

The temperature on the day of the physical was ninety-eight degrees. We wore full firefighting gear. We borrowed from firefighters. I remember the coat being ten sizes too big. They couldn't find a pair of boots to fit me, so they put fisherman's boots on me, with ankle weights to simulate the weight of the boots. The ankle weights kept digging into my ankles. Somebody's helmet, a mask.

We had to stand outside for quite a while. My husband was in the parking lot, watching. He got a sunburn that day, from being out there. A few girls took the test before me. They were going in alphabetic order. They hadn't shown up for the practice sessions, and when they were dressing, they said to me, "I've been working out on my own. Do you think I'll pass?"

I said, "Sure. Just pace yourself and go ahead."

I was thinking to myself, "I really don't think any woman is going to pass this test unless she went through the practice." Sure enough, most of them didn't make it past the first part of the test. My husband kept seeing people being carried out, and he was worried. It was very hot, and I remember standing around in the gear waiting for my turn to come, and seeing the expression on my husband's face.

One of the tests was a hose pull. Lugging it up to the sixth floor in a simulated fire duty. Another involved taking an eight- or nine-pound maul and hitting a weighted-down tire from one end of a table to the other to simulate forcible entry. And when you are hitting that against the table, there is quite a bit of resistance, and it makes a lot of noise. Up on the sixth floor. This was toward the end of the test. My husband said that he knew by his watch that I was doing okay. He could hear me all the way downstairs, that I was hitting this sucker down on the table. And I was still breathing. I had paced myself.

We had four minutes and seven seconds to complete it, and I remember stopping and saying to the guy with the stopwatch, "Three fifty-six." I was off by a second. I had counted the seconds the whole test—up the stairs and whatnot. I didn't want to do it in record time, because I didn't know if

I would be able to finish. I just wanted to pass it. I was off by a second. That's how close I was.

I remember just hanging out the window when it was over. I was simply glad I was okay. Then they told me I passed. I was exhilarated.

My husband's mother had died the day before, and I never expected Jerry to come. He did. I'll never forget that. How difficult it was for him to be thinking about something like that. She died of cancer, and she died at home. He had helped to take care of her. She was being waked that night. Even with all that, he was able to be happy for me. I don't think my feet even touched the ground.

I had no idea what an impact the women firefighters would make. We were in the limelight. We were hitting the newspapers so often that I stopped cutting them out. It wasn't a fuss. It was waiting for us to fall on our faces.

Even the day of the physical, I remember the fellows making comments. "You made it through this, but you're never going to make it. You won't make it through probie school." It was always something. "Probie school will weed you women out." Then in probie school, we would climb the ladder with tools. "Well, you did this, but you're never going to make it through the smoke house." After the smoke house, "Well, you're never going to be able to take a two-and-a-half into an old tenement." It was never-ending. "You made it through probie school, but you'll never be able to make it through a rescue." Then, when we got in the firehouse, "You women can't handle the smoke."

Even today, five years later, you still hear it. "Yeah, she's done that, but she's never done this yet."

At probie school, you had to wear navy blue. Needless to say, in the last five years I have thrown out everything I own in navy blue. On the day we were sworn in, the captain came onstage and said, "Listen, now, this is a list of things you have to do." And he passed around a sheet. One of them was a haircut. Ninety percent of the women had to get a haircut. Their hair wasn't short enough. The standard was the male standard for a haircut. The only thing we didn't have to do was shave our beards.

They lined us up and put us in squads. I was thinking, "This is the worst day of my life." I was being screened out. There were fifty women and a hundred men in school. There was this tiny little girl in her mid-twenties who was being yelled at for having the wrong shoes on. She was really just a kid, and she started to cry.

We women had more or less made a pact. "Listen, a couple of rules here. We're not going to cry, especially in front of the men. Ever. Never make excuses, and try not to act so damn feminine. We don't know how to act, but we have to act more like men than women."

Well, fifteen minutes into roll call and this woman starts bawling, and she is right in the front, and we're all standing in the back looking at each other, saying, "Oh, hell, she's crying." You could see her shaking up and down, she was crying so bad.

The officer was trying to set a tone for this first class, saying how rough it was going to be. You could see his eyes, and he doesn't know what the hell to do about this dame standing in the front line shaking so hard, crying. I'll never forget the expression on his face—"What the hell do I do now?"

A few guys came over and took her out. From that moment on, I think the captain felt, "I'm not going to be able to do this the way I have in the past, because things are going to come up that have never come up before." You could see he was trying to ignore the crying, hoping it might stop. But she couldn't stop. She must have cried for five minutes before they took her out. And the women felt, "Oh, God, they're going to take it out on us now, because she cried."

I made lasting friendships with a few of the women. I thought I did with quite a few men, too, until we got out into the field, where the peer pressure or the publicity got to them. Most of them were reluctant to be friendly. I've been embarrassed at jobs more than once by going over to someone and saying hello, and having them turn their back on me when the other guys were going, "You know her?" Now I usually wait for that person to make the move to say hi.

Probationary school was six weeks. I think there were only eight women who graduated with that first class. Forty-two women and about twelve guys didn't make it. I think five women were terminated, three or four quit, and there were a few who stayed and went through another six weeks. Which was hell. I was held an extra week and then was signed.

I later did duty out at the rock, that's the New York Fire Department training center. What I was surprised and glad to see was the professionalism that goes into the training there. More so than when I was there. It was more a hit-or-miss kind of thing.

I was assigned to 61 Engine in the East Bronx, and I figured, "Wow, I've done it. I'm out, and I'm in the firehouse, and I'm not going to have any more problems." There was no way the companies or the women could anticipate what kind of problems might arise. It was like a Martian had dropped from the sky, and the guys were told they had to work with this person. I kept getting the feeling, "You're not going to last. You've gotten this far, but it's only a matter of time before you quit."

With all the publicity and the things the union had said, the guys were angry not only at having me in the company, but they felt they were dumped on by the department. It wasn't that I was a woman. They didn't know what I was yet, because no real woman would want the job. So they really couldn't figure out what I was. I wasn't a man, and I wasn't a woman. I must be a freak.

I was put in with a lieutenant who had a lot of experience. A good fire officer. I think that for a woman in a company, it was a good thing to be in his group. He was a good officer to have for a probie and a woman. Very fair.

The first few days were boring. I had the night shift, and I would stop drinking any fluid after seven in the evening, so I wouldn't have to use the bathroom. They were renovating the bathroom, and it really didn't have a door. There was a urinal on the wall. It was in bad shape for a long time. The shower was out in the middle of the locker room. I was constantly afraid of walking in on somebody. I really wanted to be invisible.

I didn't say anything, and I kept my mouth shut. I was constantly at the sink making coffee. All the probie things. I tried not to have the fact that I was a woman get in the way too much. My high voice annoyed the hell out of them. Some guys, who liked to play steamy films on TV, couldn't watch them anymore. I cramped their style. I think it was much more difficult for them than it was for me. Because there were more of them, and there was just one of me. I kept thinking, "Well, how would I feel?"

I felt that it was up to me to set the tone for the company. The men were the product of their upbringing and the department and all the information that was being given to them. So it was up to me. I put a lot of thought into it. I was real careful about everything I did—the way I walked, the way I talked, the way I got on and off the rig, the little things that the guys wouldn't think of. I tried to lower my voice, so it wouldn't drive them up the wall.

We did eleven runs on my first tour, nothing big, mostly rubbish and cars and false alarms. I thought I would never get used to the alarm coming in, the way my heart was always going into my mouth. The alarm was loud bells. When they went off, I thought, "Jeez." Now I think it's funny when I see probies trying to figure out if it would be easier to keep their boots on when they're off the rig. I remember feeling like that.

The siren was something else. I felt excited. Being on a rig going on a run, I had a sense of pride. I felt very proud, and I felt that I had a lot to live up to.

I feel that I'm a part of the tradition of the New York Fire Department. Someday, maybe in two more generations, they'll realize that the first group of women were not out to prove a point or to start a lawsuit or to be pains. I hope they'll understand that we were just here to do our job and do it well, that we weren't anything to be ashamed of. I don't think that there is any woman on the job who doesn't love it, who doesn't feel emotion for it. Some women quit within the first ten or fifteen months, but I don't think that more of them quit because of the pressure. We've got this far, the sacrifices have been made, and I'm not going to give up. I think they'll look at us that way in the future.

Stretching hose up six or seven stories is a lot of work. There are some buildings that don't have clear stairways the whole way. That, to me, is worse than the fire. It's like an oven, and it's hard work. I'm not kidding myself, I don't think I could take three or four lengths of two-and-a-half-inch line up the stairs without running up and down. Nobody can do that without running and weight lifting. When I got on the job, I was 111 pounds, and now I'm 141. I was very, very skinny, but the more you work out, the more you eat. I hope it's not fat.

The bathroom at the firehouse was a problem. It was humiliating to walk in on a guy taking a leak. No two guys react the same, so I had to take each situation and try to keep it light, not make a big deal out of it, apologize. Still, I found they were getting annoyed. I mean, hell, why should you have to wait forty minutes to get into the bathroom, why don't you have your own? In the beginning, the guys' attitude was, "If you don't like it, leave." Now it's, "Isn't there somebody you can call about this?"

Using the officers' bathroom was not something you would want to do, because then you're showing that you're really different. You're sticking out. "She gets to use the officers' bathroom." But I do walk in on them. It's only happened a couple of times, amazingly. I usually bang on the door or knock before I walk in. They now have a lock on the door. That was something that was just recently put on, which is great.

Before that, when I was in the shower, I would just tell everyone. I would time it so that it wasn't change of tours when everyone was there. If it was after a job, in the middle of the night, I would ask one guy to volunteer to be a stakeout. I got caught getting out of the shower once by a guy. It was never mentioned. He never looked at me crooked or cross-eyed. I was stepping out of the shower. I remember being very embarrassed. But the embarrassment was overlooked because of the way he handled it. He didn't make a big deal out of it. It was forgotten. It was just something that happened.

But there was also a lot of humor. I'll be upstairs, and they'll say, "Are you decent?" I'll say, "Of course not, come on up." After a funeral, we all came back to the firehouse to change our clothes. Now you've got twenty-four guys changing in the locker room. There was no way I was going to wait to get into the bathroom to change my clothes. I went into the locker room, and we all just laughed. There we were, making fun of shorts and knees. The moral is, you make light of it, and you don't take it too seriously. There are really only a couple of guys who take it too seriously and get upset. If it happens, it happens. Just don't take it too hard.

Usually one of the first questions asked by other women not on the job is, "Do you sleep with all of the men?" I've had a move made on me, but not often. I've talked this over with the guys, and they feel that the reason I haven't been bothered is that I just don't send that kind of signal. Of course, when men drink too much, they either love you or hate you. I usually try to get out before something like that happens. I leave before the drinking gets too bad.

At a firehouse working situation, if I think that a guy is even remotely serious, I'll make a joke out of it, so as not to embarrass him by saying "I'm not interested." I just make a joke out of it and send a not-interested signal a different way than telling him aggressively, "I think you ought to back off." But there is a lot of joking around, a lot of giggling going on. It's a good thing there's no tape recorder during roll call. I didn't realize I still had so much adolescence in me.

We never talk about our personal problems, and I've never seen any fistfights. It's all just silliness. The one fear that all human beings have in common is the nightmare that they're in a fire. If some firefighters tend to romanticize it, that's okay. It gets you through it.

After I was burned, it was assumed that I wouldn't go back to full firefighting duty. I don't know if that was because I was a woman, or if they would think that of a guy as well. They thought I'd be scared to go back. I was on light duty, and to me it was very boring. I wanted to go back to my company. I couldn't imagine doing anything else except being in a firehouse. I've had a lot of sadness in the firehouse. I've had death, and I've seen people die. I've had to wash down a street after a fourteen-year-old boy was hit by a train. The pieces of his body were on the street, and I'll never forget that.

I hope I never become indifferent to it. I hope I never stop finding humor and funniness. I hope I never become cold.

I had a guy come into the company, whose father-in-law or uncle had died in a fire at a wedding reception. It was the first time anyone had ever come back and said thank you for what you did. Looking into his eyes, I felt that I knew what he was feeling. He must have understood how we felt, too. There were a lot of tears. The guys made jokes, but he knew they didn't mean it. We all felt the same that night. It amazes me how much genuine feeling these guys have for other people. I don't think I have more respect for any other profession than I have for this one.

You become closer to God in some instances, and you do say, "Thank you," you know, "Thanks for letting me out of that one." You never know. The craziest things happen. You get off the rig, and there's a drunk aiming for you. This isn't even a firefighting situation. You're in the dark about what is in store for you. It's part of the excitement. In a way, your senses are gone. You can really feel close to a supreme being, not just your officer or your backup man. I don't think most people would want to admit it, but you do say thank you.

◻

We had to go through the fire academy for two months, then you go to the engine house for four months to fight fires, and then they finally give you your badge. The first eight hours at the academy, I didn't know what to expect. All we did was fill out papers, insurance and stuff like that. After that, the first half of the day we'd be in class, and after lunch we'd go out and work with the hoses and ladders and so forth.

It was pretty easy to get along with the people, but then again I was only eighteen years old, and everyone else there was about twenty-seven. I had always hung around my older brother and his friends, so I had no problem getting along with those guys. But they didn't know how to come across with me, me being so young.

The four hours of book work was just basic stuff, like the engine carries the hose, the truck carries the ladder, what the truck men use for ventilation, how the engine men put out the fire, the chain of command, stuff like that. Communications, what all the tools are used for and how to use them.

Then, in the afternoon hours, we'd split into three groups. One would be working with hoses, sometimes with foam, different pipes, different nozzles, and practice with all of these. Another group would be on ladders, all the different sorts of ladders, and we even climbed the aerial. And the third group would be working on ropes and knots. Then after an hour we'd switch groups and go to a different instructor.

I was number one in the class, and I don't think my instructor liked that. He was a black guy, and they had a young black lady in the class who had six years of college. They thought she was the ringer. The prize was a jewelry box, but the best part was not just getting the box, but that your name went on a plaque in the academy classroom. So that twenty years from now trainees will see that I was number one in the class.

When I look back at it now, the thing they should have showed us was how to stretch the line for a fire—I only did that once or twice at the academy. That was it. And they made us keep our masks on. But when you're actually in a good dwelling fire, you knock down the fire and you take your mask off. You may take some smoke, but you do that to save some air, in case the upstairs flares up and you've got to go up there. You don't want to go up there with an empty tank, and you don't want to go where there's open flames without a tank, because you'll burn your lungs. So they should have let us go through the smoke house more than one day and without masks, like they used to.

Being first in the class and having a father a fireman, I was able to be appointed to the engine house that I wanted, Engine 27, the busiest in the city. It was a totally different experience. They had told us at the academy that you should stay busy in the firehouse, dust windows, mop, do the dishes, and stuff like that. The first day I was there, a senior firefighter, Frank Garson, showed me around, then I started dusting the windowsill. I had a rag in my hand, and Captain William O'Grady said, "Put down that rag and do some real work."

So I ended up painting the whole engine house. I did that for four months, sometimes painting until one in the morning. Captain O'Grady is the greatest guy in the world, and I think he did that just to see how much I could take. It was a long paint job, but it made me a worker. I was constantly working. And it was a pleasure to go to a fire, because then you got to do something fun for a change.

My first run was a brushfire on the side of the expressway, just little weeds burning. The captain said to use the red line, which is the small hose, but I was so excited I grabbed the red and white CO_2 canister. When I jumped off I hit the canister and set off the CO_2. There I'm squirting these weeds, all excited. The captain is laughing at me. He says, "Joe, we only need the water, not the CO_2. Take it easy, it's only brush." So I was pretty excited on my first run.

My first dwelling fire was about five in the morning, and the place was going. At Engine 27 we're aggressive firefighters, and if it's a good dwelling we usually take two lines in. As a trial man, I would take a single line, and Captain O'Grady would back me up. But the captain wasn't there, and my senior man, Frank Garson, forgot that I was a trial man. He says, "Let's take both lines." So he hooked them up to the water gauge, I grabbed the second line, and we went to the front door.

There were two entrances, one going upstairs and one downstairs, and the place is rolling. He says, "Come on, let's go." And I didn't know what he meant. He went in, and I didn't know what to do. So the squad man, Greg Dust, one of the best firefighters in Detroit, comes up and grabs the pipe. He says, "Give it to me." Well, you never give up the pipe to anybody ever, no matter what, and I say, "No." He says, "Well, let's go."

And so Greg Dust took me in to my first fire. We went upstairs, it was hot, and my adrenaline is flowing. I'm shooting the water all over the place, I even knocked Sergeant Mark Carpenter's helmet off. And we got it out. I was tired after that, because I was so excited.

When you're in there you don't think about the danger. But after you come out, and there are big holes in the floor, the stairs are weak, and half the roof is fallen in, you look and say, "Wow, that's crazy." You're a different person when you go into the fire from the person who looks and critiques the fire afterwards.

Chapter Three

FIREHOUSE LIFE

I HATED DOING THE HOUSEWORK IN THE FIREHOUSE, CLEANING the toilet bowls and washing the windows. I didn't mind cleaning the equipment, polishing the fire trucks, cleaning the hose; I didn't even mind sweeping the floors, washing dishes, and cleaning the kitchen every once in a while—all the day-to-day petty labors required to keep the place where you live cleaner.

But cleaning toilet bowls and washing windows are pretty rotten things to ask a fireman to do, in my view of the world anyway. Even the maid in a Park Avenue apartment doesn't do windows, dammit. I always felt it was crazy to ask people to think well of themselves for their contribution to the society they live in, and to think that their work as firefighters is essential to preserving property and saving lives, and at the same time to expect the firefighter to do work a Park Avenue maid would refuse to do. Not that I diminish Park Avenue maids at all, I've had them in the family.

The answer, of course, is that firefighters have been doing such work for a hundred years, and fire departments are such tradition-bound organizations that no one thinks of breaking tradition by bringing in outside help to do the chores firefighters really shouldn't be doing. The word in the firehouse is that we are all suckers for being involved in a political system that doesn't give a high approval rate to us, except when a guy is badly injured or killed in the line of duty. Then, all of a sudden, it's roses delivered to the room and visits from the mayor and the bosses and the union leaders. But unless you're injured or killed, well then, get in there with the bucket and wash the windows.

Firefighters have a fairly tedious job between alarms. The firehouse has to be maintained, and there has got to be, in every tour of duty, a drill period where training is performed. Then there are inspection duties where

101

you go out and do prefire planning and so on. But even with that, there's a lot of down time in the firehouse, in which people study for promotion, watch television, or read books. Often there's a wise guy there to relieve the tedium, a guy with a mouth that's as fast as the speed of light, who will make the simplest thing—a torn shirt, a sneeze, a disheveled hairdo or an innocent comment—the object of scorn. And the language can be as scatological as an Eddie Murphy monologue. I once heard a firefighter use the dreaded "F word" sixty-three times in commenting on the staleness of the bagels some hapless firefighter brought into the firehouse kitchen. Sixty-three, I swear. I counted.

But put a firefighter in mixed company, and it is like he's dressed in a cassock and surplice and ready to serve Mass. A male firefighter will not curse in front of a woman. I have never worked with a woman firefighter, so I don't know how their speech habits will influence, or be influenced by, the men. Time will tell.

Tedium can also be splattered like dropped mercury when someone spots an open hose being used to clean the tools or the apparatus. But playing around with the water can get out of hand. One day it escalated to the point where the hose was taken off the back of the fire truck and connected to the pumps, and everybody was given a good soaking. A police car happened to stop by, and one of the cops got out and started to approach the firehouse to talk to one of the firefighters, who was related to him. He got hit with a stream of water. Everybody laughed and thought it was much funnier than he thought it was. Anyway, he turned around, went back to his squad car and drove away.

Fifteen minutes passed, during which time the dousing continued because it was a hot summer day in the South Bronx and we were waiting for the next alarm. All of a sudden we heard the siren blaring through the sticky, putrid air. A police car came careening down the old cobblestoned street of Intervale Avenue, at sixty miles an hour. It came skidding to a stop in front of the firehouse, siren still blasting.

Two cops jumped out of the car with their revolvers pulled and held at their shoulders and came running at top speed into the firehouse. Everyone started screaming and ran into the kitchen. One cop named Bobby Ulick said, "Well, I guess I taught you guys a lesson." So everyone relaxed and laughed. The joke was over, so the cop and his partner went out to the front, intending to leave.

But the police car wasn't there. One of the firefighters had sneaked out, gotten into it, drove it two blocks away and parked it on a side street. Then he had come back to the firehouse with the keys in his pocket. Bobby Ulick looks at us, his face a billboard of defeat, and says, "Aw, come on, guys, give me back my police car."

It was that kind of a day—hot, a lot of alarms, a fire here, another fire there, a false alarm here, a false alarm there—and between the alarms, somebody would think of something to escalate the small water competition that was going on. The night crew started to arrive at about five, and one of them was an old-line chauffeur of Ladder 31, a tough guy. He was standing in his civilian clothes in front of the firehouse.

One of the guys on the third floor found a bucket filled with mop water, and he thought it would be a pretty funny thing to throw the contents out the window onto this guy. He didn't stop to think, though, that the mop water was really half ammonia, the only thing that would clean the old wooden floors. And the water, seemingly from the fountain of hell, cascaded down on this guy's head and, of course, went right into his eyes.

The guy, thinking his eyes were being burned by some kind of acid, ran for the hose inside and squirted his eyes with the water. That stopped the playfulness of the day. He wasn't injured, but it takes a hard thing like that to stop hard men from playing hard.

Dennis Smith

□

Firefighters, as a group, are different from other people. It's true of the volunteer fire department I'm involved in and of my New York City unit, Rescue 1. It's the camaraderie, a tightness. I think the thing that brings you together is not the lives you save, it's the fatalities that you see together. Most firemen can handle an adult fatality. But the one that gets everybody is the death of a child. Most firemen are family men, and they relate.

In both the volunteer department and the paid city one, there have been times when I have come home emotionally drained and have actually just sat down and cried, because things were beyond my control. Firemen need that feeling of being in control of a situation. At a fire you're doing something not everybody else is doing—you're going in when everyone else is coming out—but you feel that you have a grip on the situation and you can handle it. It's not bravery, it's a matter of fortitude, a little intelligence, with guts mixed in. And then once in a while it gets you, because you can't handle it.

The only thing worse than a child fatality is a fatality involving a fireman. It's because of the brotherhood that's there. You can share good times with any group of people, but I think it's the bad times that bring people together, because you can't really share it with anybody else. It's only the guys in the room and the feeling, "This is what it's about, this is what we're doing this for."

Some outsiders have the idea that what firemen do at a fire is throw things out the window. My volunteer fire department doesn't do that. Our point of view is not to break anything in the interior unless it's necessary in attacking the fire. Most all cities operate that way. These are people who are leaving their jobs and willing to put their lives on the line, for free, to help their neighbors out, or to fulfill something in their own lives, or whatever their reasons are. But they do it.

Just as in any other job, there are various degrees of success. Not everybody is as good as everybody else in any field. That's why there are superstars in baseball while there are guys in the minor leagues. Not everybody is going to be Hank Aaron. But they're doing it, and doing it successfully throughout the country. For a country that's as under the gun from fire as this country is, we have given it a good fight.

I've been to fires all over New York City, and the thing that amazes me is the blasé attitude of the populace. They will stop and look for a second and then just keep going. Here is somebody's life tragedy being played out on the streets of New York, and they'll just stop for an instant and look. Or watch it on television while they're cooking dinner. There is so much going on here that people get immune. They put walls around themselves. In small town America, everyone would be involved. There are some exceptional good samaritans. When that helicopter went down in the East River, a jogger, who was a teacher, dove head first into cold water to help some people out. Nobody asked him to do it. He was in his mid-fifties. It was a pretty wild maneuver to jump in the water, because the water was moving.

I've had close friends on teams I've been on and business companies I've worked for, and we were kind of like brothers. But it's not like the brother feeling that you get with the firemen. Even if you don't like the guy. I mean, I had an uncle I wasn't too fond of, but he was still related to me, and there was nothing I could do about it. It's like that with the brotherhood in the fire department. They are your brothers. You might not like one of them on a given day, but he is your brother.

It's not the shared danger. There are lots of other jobs where you share danger, or sports like surfing, which I used to do a lot. It's more the things you see, the shared grief, the loss of another fireman, the loss of a child at a fire, the unspeakable things. The things you can't bring home and tell your family. You tell them about the rescues and the funny things, but you can't go home and graphically explain. With other firemen, you don't have to graphically explain, you just look. You just look into each other's eyes after a fire, and you know that he is thinking what you are thinking. Because nobody else on the face of the earth comes across what we come across on a regular basis.

The fireman knows the awful dangers civilians manage to get themselves into, and that's why he is willing to go to the point of killing himself to make a rescue, because he knows how bad it is. I've heard it said that firemen already know what hell is. That could very well be. I wouldn't want my worst enemy to die by means of fire. I myself really don't think about it. You wouldn't be able to do the job you have to do. You get the job done, and you think about it later. You sit around and have a cup of coffee, and you shake your head: "I can't believe I just got myself through that."

One of the great things about a rescue company is that they are handpicked men, and they get unusual incidents to go to. I have been to building collapses, train crashes, plane crashes. Light planes. I haven't gone to a jetliner yet, thank God. I hope I never see one of those. I've been in many successful rescues. At least four people are walking around today because of me personally, which makes me feel great. I've been extremely lucky. I'm lucky to be part of Rescue 1, the best fire company in the world. I'm also lucky to be part of a volunteer company, Truck Company 1 in the Freeport Fire Department. There are tremendous people working there, including three of us from Rescue 1. In all, we have eight professional firemen who spend their spare time being volunteer firemen.

I was lucky to win awards. I used the award money to take my family to Hawaii, which was a lifetime dream of mine, having been a surfer most of my life. I use the word luck, and I don't know another word for it. To make a rescue, you have to be working that day, there has to be a fire your company goes to, there unfortunately has to be somebody trapped, and you have to be in the right position to go get them. Luck stops, though, when you find those few minor obstacles you have to overcome before you can make the rescue.

All the brothers have a common interest, a shared understanding, and that is that we're out there protecting life and property.

□

Firefighters are individuals unto themselves, with a tremendous sense of humor. I think you need it in this type of job. I don't think there is another occupation where a sense of humor is so important. The pranks that are played on one another, the fraternity house atmosphere at times, is necessary to cut both the tension of what it is you actually do when you go to work and the tedium in between.

Sometimes you meet guys in the job who think they know everything, but the job doesn't let them get away with it for very long. There was this kid, one of those people who don't know anything but think they have it all together. He was a probie, a probationary fireman, and he looked like an altar boy just escaped from Mass or something. When you tell him something, he says, "I know that. I know that."

I'm cooking in the firehouse kitchen one day, and my friend Bruce is there peeling potatoes. We had a puppy in the firehouse at the time, and he used to leave little puddles around. Bruce says to me, "Did you know that dog piss burns?" I look around and realize this kid is standing next to me.

I say, "Oh, really?"

He says, "Only when it's fresh."

The probie has been listening with interest. Bruce says, "Come here and take a look." So the kid goes over to see it, not knowing that Bruce had beforehand floated gasoline in it. So Bruce lights it, and there's a ton of smoke on the apparatus floor. When the flames died down, the kid goes, "Wow, that's great." Then we hosed it down.

Later in the afternoon the puppy goes to his spot and leaves a puddle. The night crew is coming in, including the captain and a couple of the senior guys. And here's this probie, standing there throwing lighted matches into this puddle of puppy piss, puzzled because nothing is happening.

□

I'll tell you something. Danny and I have been tight because we work together in the same station. I've never been to Vietnam or anything like that, but they say that when you are close to death and you're with some-body, it makes you closer. Well, I know that since we found that baby in that collapsed building, Danny and Dave and I are a lot closer than we were.

I guess just knowing that you could die, just that fact does something to bring you together. We knew that if something happened we were all going together.

□

I think that firefighters are still highly regarded by the public, but we're not the heroes we used to be. I think the reason is that they know what we're making. Last year I made around thirty-seven thousand dollars with overtime. I went to college for only two years. In how many other jobs can you go to training for four weeks and get a job paying that amount of money?

Some people think about firemen as just sitting around. But for the most part, the public thinks that we're pretty good, especially here in south Florida, because we run the emergency medical service. That is a big plus. I want to get rid of the myth of the guys sitting around playing checkers, and get people to understand that we are actively doing other things. I've had people tell me, "Oh, you work one day, you're off four, you're off five. I saw how much you make in the paper. You guys don't do anything."

To them, firemen are making tremendous salaries—whether we deserve it or not is immaterial to them—firemen have tremendous benefits, tremen-dous time off, which allows them to work second jobs. Plus, they go past the fire station, and they see BMWs and other expensive vehicles in the back of the station. They say, "Look at those damn firemen, man, they're making a tremendous amount of money, and I'm pounding nails and not making anything near them." A lot of it is envy, or at least resentment.

The cops are the heroes now. *Miami Vice* has something to do with it. A lot of the buildings that you see, they paint those pastels on the buildings before they shoot, especially the ones they blow up. I've worked those sets as a fireman. Miami is changed. They call it the Casablanca now. I wouldn't have a cop's job down here. Statistically, more firemen get killed and injured than policemen, but not in south Florida. Here the cops get killed way more often than firemen do. The killers are stealing or looting because they need money to buy drugs. Drug City, Florida.

I really believe that professionalism is the name of the game, and that we have to continue to become more vital to the public. There is a lot of community in us. We care about Dade County. And we have to serve the public in many ways, emergency medical services, for instance. The more we have mandatory sprinklers in buildings, the less manpower and resources a fire department will need, and so we must be community-involved.

I will say one thing, I'm gladder than hell I'm not a paramedic. I tried it for a while, and I didn't like it. I don't begrudge going on a medical call, but I'd prefer fighting a fire.

□

What does it mean to a firefighter to work in a black neighborhood? It means that most firefighters you find there are the most dedicated ones. They have a higher rate of activity, more fire activity, and they are in more danger. And there were times, not so much recently but five or six years ago, when some of the citizens did not appreciate us being there. Now that has changed.

I tell this when I teach the recruits in firefighting. Did you ever notice, when you get a kitchen fire in a nice white neighborhood, they make sure to put themselves up in a Howard Johnson's for a couple of weeks? When they come back, did you ever notice their house? It's nicer than it was before. New curtains, new draperies, new wallpaper, new Formica tabletop. They probably lit the thing to begin with, either intentionally or they were just careless. Probably intentionally. Let's face it, most of our fires are.

What about a poor black person? They haven't got a pot to pee in. When you look at that burned-out hulk, you know they are going to be sleeping in that house tonight. So the harder we work and the more diligent we are in fighting the fires in poor areas, the more those people are going to be materially benefited.

I thank God I was born into a family with good economic means. These people are a lot less fortunate. They didn't ask to be born into a horrible situation, but they were. In a way, it makes you feel good to help people who really need the help. I think that most firefighters who work in those neighborhoods, whether they're churchgoing folks, Christians, or whatever, feel the same way.

□

We've had training and classes on the problem of AIDS and hepatitis B in medical emergency situations, and we take precautionary measures. We're required to wear rubber latex gloves, and if it's a situation that warrants it, we'll put on goggles or glasses to protect our eyes. And we'll even wear a mask or a bandanna to protect our lungs.

I don't recollect that I've ever been exposed to those two things, but I was on the rescue unit where there were a lot of medical emergencies of various types, so I've been exposed to some things. And I've been tested to make sure I haven't contracted those things. I did it on my own. I went in a couple of weeks ago for a personal checkup and a blood test, just to make sure. I think all firefighters should do that from time to time.

Our fire department takes pretty good care of us in that they provide us with nutritional training. They have our physical evaluation every year where they measure our body fat, see how much weight we can push, and have us do a series of push-ups and that sort of thing.

As this AIDS thing becomes more prevalent, if they have any question about it, firemen should check it out. We fill out injury slips or exposure reports when we get hurt or get smoke in our lungs. So we would pursue this new stuff through a doctor. If we have any question that we've been exposed to AIDS, I believe that guys—women, too—should pursue the testing for their own health.

□

The State Department asked me to go to the Soviet Union and several other communist countries to speak about contemporary American literature to the writer's unions, and to the English-speaking clubs of the universities. It was a great trip, because the Russian people are gregarious and full of subtle humor, though, before *glasnost,* the Soviet authority seemed dark and pervasive, like a giant shadow. Consequently, I liked the people and the architecture but felt uncertain about the country.

I kept asking to visit a Moscow fire station, and the authorities kept stonewalling me. Finally, after a week of telephone calls, they agreed to take me to one of their huge centralized fire stations where there are ten or so fire companies. This was pretty unusual, for the fire department is quasimilitary, that is, run by and attached to the army, and they do not normally take Americans to military installations. A *Newsweek* reporter came, but they wouldn't let him in to the station, which was rimmed by a high wall, and he wrote a long story about it in the magazine.

I was taken to a reception hall, where I met a group of pretty congenial officers, a general and some colonels, who ran the Soviet Fire Service. I was pretty impressed, though I just wanted to talk to a few back-step firefighters. I was working at Engine Company 82 at the time, and I wanted to hear what the Russian firefighters felt about false alarms or nuisance fires—if, indeed, they existed in that country.

I sat at the head of a long table and began talking about the problems of fighting fires in a large city, in overcrowded buildings where impoverished people lived, where false alarms were as frequent as changing traffic signals, where my one company would respond to forty calls a day, every day.

I talked a little about the personal challenge of firefighting, the renewed confrontation, never really resolved, one fire after another. The general stood and pointed to a colonel sitting down the table. The colonel stood as the general related with great pride that this man personally had been in more than a hundred fires. "Very good," I said, "congratulations," thinking, but of course not saying, that to us in the South Bronx, a hundred represented not a lifetime's work but a single weekend in July.

Dennis Smith

□

The Hartford Fire Department has been very good to me, good to my family. I have excellent benefits, but there's still a lot I desire. Coming up from New York, you want to see some changes, but every department has its own little ways of doing things, and you can't make the changes. And it hurts.

I remember when I first went up to Hartford, we couldn't even carry a flashlight. Only the chief officers were carrying flashlights. And we had the same problems here that they had in the South Bronx. We had the vacant buildings. We had a lot of frames, these wooden three-deckers. Mostly Spanish and blacks in the area I worked in.

I went through the riots of the sixties. I was in them at the north end. I saw a lot of destruction. They were doing it against their own people. They didn't care who they were destroying, because it was all in their own area. They were putting people out of business, their own people, and it was very sad.

I was never really in a situation where I felt I'd never see my children again. I've learned from experience, and I know my limitations. Many times in a fire you're with somebody and then you're not with somebody. They might have backed out or something happened. But I never really felt I was alone. It's almost like having an angel there with you. I've been in situations where I was alone and I had gone deeper into a fire than I should have. But I never really felt I was alone. It was almost like a tap on the shoulder: this is enough, back.

□

I recently took the lieutenant's test, and I passed the written. Then I had to take the oral. I don't like the oral system. I think it stinks. It's unfair. I was kind of nervous.

The system is tough. You go in there. I'm in there for fifteen minutes, and these three guys are sizing me up in fifteen minutes. They don't know anything about me. They don't know my credibility. They don't know anything from the chief of the department about me. They don't know if I'm an abuser of sick time. They have no idea what my background is. All they do is shoot nine questions at you, and you're nervous, and you've got to answer them. If you don't answer them right, or if they don't like the way you look, I mean, my whole twenty years can be blown down the drain by these three guys.

I would not evaluate a man's career without knowing something about the man. I'm not the only one who feels this way. In my twenty years I've taken maybe thirty-some sick days. I'm a professional firefighter. I do my job. If my chief and the twelve district chiefs had to say thumbs up or thumbs down on me, I know it would be thumbs up with every one of them. I've been through a lot of stuff. I've received burns. I was caught in a backdraft. I've been hospitalized. I received the medal of valor for rescues.

They don't know all this. All they're judging me on is nine questions, and I'm hesitating, I'm nervous. And they could blow my whole life down the drain. It's unfair.

□

There have been sixteen firefighters who have lost their lives in the fifteen years I've been in the department. I attended the funerals whenever I was able to. It's a tough situation, because these guys are family, almost as if they were part of your own personal family. You take the death of a firefighter brother almost as deeply as you would a personal relative.

After the funerals, there are no big station parties. There might be something at a battalion level, but mostly everybody just kind of goes their own way.

As far as firefighters hanging out together is concerned, I don't think it's done as much today as it was in the past. It depends largely on the geographical location of the station. Often you'll work at a station where a lot of the guys live in the same general area; then at the next station you're assigned to, everybody may live in twelve different directions from the station. So it just kind of depends on the station.

I got into photography shortly after I got on the job. It became readily apparent to me that fire scenes were areas of great excitement, and the photographic possibilities were endless. There are continually things going on that the average person doesn't see. When the fire department arrives, you're looking at a very chaotic scene. Then, by the extinguishment of the fire, the rescue of people, and the evacuation of the building, we bring a more normal semblance of order to the scene. These kinds of things can be quite dramatic in a photographic sense, whether it be a rescue or a heavy stream of water being applied to the fire.

□

Buffalo is a wooden frame city. Almost all the houses are wooden frames. In the older neighborhoods, they're on top of each other, just jam-packed in there. So if we have a fire in one, the chances are it'll go to another, unless we are both lucky and hustling.

In my early days, I never realized the heat and the smoke conditions in a fire and the punishment the fellows take in there. And along with that was the damage. You see people's treasures just absolutely destroyed. Again, when you have people burned and killed, it isn't that detached thing it was before you got involved. And seeing the teamwork of the men, it's fantastic.

I moved from a quiet engine company to the downtown district of Buffalo. Down there is where I grew in the job, because of the experience in various types of fire. We got everything from ships to grain elevators to high rises and warehouses, and slum housing. I thought it was great.

The guys are certainly aware of the dangers and are safety-conscious. Once you become an officer, you become even more acutely aware of it. It's a different thing to go diving in yourself, from sending somebody else in there. And as you go higher in rank, you're sending more and more people into danger.

There are times when the responsibility is awesome. But of course, when you get to the scene of the fire, you are methodically thinking of different things, and it really doesn't enter your mind. It's in the back of your mind, but you can't dwell on it.

In Buffalo, the division responds on all working fires where two or more lines are being used. The division is split into four platoons. I'm in charge of the second platoon, and our dispatchers give me a tip-off when they're getting several phone calls or hear reports from a police car. That lets me get a fast start on it. I enjoy going to the fires, but I don't take command unless we go for additional help. I let the battalion chiefs run it, and I just help them. That's an understanding I have with all my chiefs.

I've been to many funerals of friends of mine who were killed. You know that it can happen, you read about it all the time, but when it happens to a firefighter it's just like a person in your family dying, completely unexpected, like possibly in an auto accident. You know it's there, but you kind of think it isn't going to happen to you. And when it does, it's an awful blow.

But I have never had it, the danger, really affect the job. I've never worried about it going to a fire, or worried about myself. When you come back, though, you kind of second-guess everything—should I have done this, what if that happened—and you learn that way.

□

A friend of mine died in that big warehouse fire. He and his boss, Captain Leo, went in there. They both died. Some people said they shouldn't have. Well, they had to go in there because they thought it was occupied. There was so much water upstairs that the weight of it caused the floors to collapse. Three floors went down, and they were smashed inside the rubble, flatter than a pancake. I got to look at that, and thought, "Wow, he was my age." This was right after my own close call.

Before that I had this feeling I would never get hurt, only the older guys get hurt.

I've been to a lot of funerals, but I've never seen anything like this. You've got five thousand firemen there, the best, the strongest, toughest guys in the world, all crying. There were different funeral homes, but at the final funeral home we lined the streets with our brothers, five thousand from all over the country. They all got tears in their eyes. They don't even know this guy from Adam, and they are all crying. It was tough.

□

Most of the guys I came out of the fire academy with, we're pretty close. There's about seven of us. We pretty much hang out together. We go to the gym and play racquetball or basketball, and we invite each other over to our houses for dinner. The morning I was hurt, I was supposed to meet the guys at the gym when I got off work. They were looking for me. When they found out I was in the hospital, they came up there immediately to see how I was.

But my life doesn't really center around the fire department. When I leave the job, I don't want to think fire department or talk fire department, unless I'm studying and reading my books. I'm studying for lieutenant.

But most of the time, when I leave work I like to go to the movies or to somebody's house and socialize.

□

A lot of movie studios are located in Burbank—Disney, NBC, Columbia, Warner Brothers, and a lot of others. When they do filming on the streets in Burbank, it's required that a fireman be on location, so we do a lot of that. It's separate from the job, and the movie company pays for that. They pay the city, and we get it in our regular paychecks. It's equivalent to time and a half. You have no equipment there, just a portable radio. That's about it. We don't get to be stars.

I was an engineer for nine years before I became a captain. I wasn't really excited about being an officer until my eighth or ninth year, when the captain I was working for at the time sort of pushed me.

The responsibility for the lives of others doesn't weigh too heavily on me. I'm very confident in myself and my abilities. I know the guys I work with feel that way, that I know what I'm doing. Most firefighters feel that way. They have a good self-image. They are confident in what they do. It's a macho image.

□

In every fire station it's important for everybody to be able to perform at maximum efficiency at all times. We don't get working fires every day, though lately we've been very busy. We go through a lot of dead periods. And when there's a fire, if the men are not ready to perform, to me it's wasted effort. Because the one time—it may be only once a year—you've got to look good and you can't, then it's letting everybody down.

Sometimes with the people applying for the firefighter job there are problems of drinking and drug abuse. In those cases, I think urinalysis is a better test than the polygraph. We test with both. I'm not much in favor of the polygraph. I think a lot of people are eliminated unnecessarily because of the polygraph. I'm in favor of a good, lengthy background investigation and urinalysis.

We have a lot of young guys in the department. They're not stereotypically troublesome people. Many of them are married, so there is no drinking or drug abuse problem there. Many times it's the older guys who have the problems. These are the guys who had the problem before we hired them. In my own experience, I don't know that this job has caused anybody to become an alcoholic.

Even in a slow company, it's a fundamentally dangerous job. That's what I tell the people at some of the slower houses. These people in our department are gung-ho and very interested. Captain Brady, for instance, has a company of fine people on the outskirts of town. I enjoy working with them.

But that one time you need to perform, the public is counting on you, your officers, and the men you work with to perform. You need to be able to get the job done.

□

People think that firefighters have a pretty soft job. They don't see the guys at three in the morning. They don't see them after one of their fellow firefighters has died or when a child has died in a fire. They don't see the look on the guys after they come off duty, the total exhaustion from fighting a fire. We have a lot of educating to do.

In Cleveland, we don't get very good news coverage. If you do get coverage, it's a major incident where they see apparatus set up and you're pouring water on a building. That's the easy part of firefighting, as far as I'm concerned. If it happens in the middle of the night, you probably won't have anybody there. At three fires this year that I was in charge of, we lost kids, multiple fatalities. Any time they take pictures, it's well after the fact. The first part of the fire is usually the most critical.

In comparing fire departments, I think what the administrators fail to look at is the type of buildings we have. In cities like Scottsdale, Arizona, or Plano, Texas, where they have sprinkler ordinances, they don't have the risks in property and people that older cities have. Even though Cleveland has lost population, all the old buildings are still here.

I discuss the job with my wife, Sheila, a lot. She has always been a great support to me, and she always worried about me going to work. That was on her mind. One year we lost seven guys. There was a fire in a garage where they were repairing a propane truck. A water heater was on the floor, and the truck blew. We lost three guys there. Then we had a fire at a metallurgical factory, where manganese dust collected and blew up, and we lost four guys there. So the fact that you could get killed on the job was pretty evident.

I never really worried about it. I was always safety-conscious. I became interested in the problems of protective clothing because I saw the need for it. When I got promoted, that was always my prime concern. You want to get through your whole career without having any firefighter who works for you getting killed. When something like that happens, it makes you take a look at things and reassess your position.

I think firefighters tend to become overaggressive. I would always rather have that type of a man on my company—a guy I had to hold back. You certainly have to know who your men are and what they can do.

We have difficulty convincing the city managers of the need for minimum manning on the fire trucks. Though we don't have five men on a truck anymore, we feel fortunate that we have been able to maintain four and four, that is, four on a truck and four on an engine. The department has been cut down from twelve hundred men to something like nine hundred ninety. We have had problems where we haven't had enough truck companies to cover the city. The city administration doesn't appreciate truck work. They don't understand the importance of immediate search and ventilation. And if the truck company can't do its job, it makes it really unsafe for the firefighters.

The city was interested in consolidating, closing down stations. So we consolidated three stations into one. About a month later, there was a fire where we lost a lady who ran a restaurant called Mom's Restaurant. She was a celebrity in that area. The people in the community were really upset, and the city responded by reopening a single station, Engine 20. It was our busiest engine company. The consolidated station was a long way from the fire site. It took longer to respond. So the single house was reopened.

There's always a debate about whether you're better to arrive on the fire ground in sixty or so seconds with a single engine company or, say, in three minutes with three companies. It's more expensive to operate single houses, but I doubt that this house will be closed down again. Computers are certainly not right when it comes to a lot of things, because there are many factors they cannot consider.

I can't say the city hasn't cooperated as far as protective clothing goes. I can't think of anything that the present chief or the chief before him didn't push for us at city hall. I think Cleveland was the first major department to use Nomax turnout coats. But then they combined the two busiest battalions into one superbusy battalion. I know the administrators have a lot of demands put on them, and obviously they are trying to save money. Unfortunately, sometimes it takes a disaster for people to see their mistakes. Right now, I'd like to see more manning on the fire companies.

The heavy fire duty makes for better camaraderie. It's not like having an eight-hour job. You live with these people, you work with them, you die with them. It's a special feeling. There's nothing else like it in the world.

In the past, it was a very close-knit group in the firehouse. We did a lot of things together. We had a lot of activities with families, with groups. We would have picnics together. We'd have outings together at each other's houses. There's a different feeling now, though, because things have to be run differently. We have problems with hiring. The Cleveland Fire Department has fired more people in the last six years than we fired in the whole history of the fire department. We have drug abuse and also disciplinary problems.

We've had a problem educating our officers so they understand that we can't handle problems the way we used to. In the old days, we were able to handle a lot of problems at the lower levels, in the engine house. It's impossible to do that anymore in this day and age, what with litigations and access to the media. That's been a big change. We have a serious morale problem, where a lot of members think there's been unequal treatment. When a guy has studied for six months for a promotion, he gets passed over and somebody down the list gets the promotion.

Affirmative action is a different story, because the people who got passed over aren't part of the firefighting force yet. They're applicants, not people you live with. They have been hurt, but it's not as personal a thing. But when you see guys you work with get passed over because some judge mandates it, even though according to our testing procedures they're the best person for the job, it causes a lot of hard feelings. Many houses still have a good feeling of camaraderie, but morale is not what it used to be.

So we are conscious of building morale. I think that one of the things that New York does is let different companies have company logos. Things like that are really good for morale. One company there has Kermit the Frog on the front of the truck, saying, "It's not easy being green." We tried to implement that here. Our squads have it, but the other companies aren't allowed to do that.

My best time in the fire department was when I was a captain and a battalion chief. I was five or six years with Truck 3, the busiest truck company in the city. We had a super group of guys. I worked with a lieutenant who was older than me. His name was Dick Ward, and he was truly a firefighter's firefighter. He would do anything and go any place. We had a dog, a ghetto dog we had taken in. That dog would climb the aerial ladder. He was fantastic. He went to all the fires with us. This was really a close-knit group of guys who really took pride in the job. You could count on any one of them for anything. You like to see that kind of company.

Dick Ward died at fifty-five. He could have retired. He had a heart attack after coming back from a fire in a housing project. That was a very traumatic experience. The man was doing what he wanted to do. He stayed on a busy company until the day he died. He could have gone out to the beach belt, but he didn't want to do that. It seems that our best companies and the closest companies are the ones that are busiest.

We talk about the old days, but despite all our problems today, I would have to say that, out of five hundred new firefighters, you only hear about the bad ones. Hey, 95 percent are conscientious young guys who really want to do the job. And they do do the job. We have problems, but they're different problems. During the time of the riots, you felt there was a good chance you were going to get injured or killed, maybe not even from a fire. We had police officers riding shotgun on the apparatus; we had incidents where our apparatus was shot at, tires were flattened, hoses were cut. The risks were so great it made the troops come that much closer together.

We have had fires where somebody dies, the family is distraught, and they try to blame somebody. And the one they like to blame is the firefighter. We had a fire recently in a West Side apartment house, and two children died. The people complained about response time. Well, when it was all brought out, from the time we received the call until the time the two victims were in the hospital, it was less than fifteen minutes. That includes getting to the scene and taking the victims out of the building. That's a pretty tight time span.

When you lose kids in a fire, you try to be diplomatic, but people get distraught. They don't appreciate what you've done, and you have to understand them. That's one of the tough things.

□

I went to 13 Truck on Carey Street, which was the second busiest in the city. I spent twenty years up there, and I loved it. That's one of the reasons I didn't make lieutenant in that time. I fell in love with the company and the men I worked with. They were great, and we had plenty of action, we were involved in all kinds of fires and rescues. The company had a good name. When you said 13 Truck, people looked up. I really enjoyed that.

Many a time I took the fire department over other personal things that came up. Whether it was a trip with the family or whatever, if the fire department had something to do, I would give up the trip to participate with the department. When it was time for me to go to the National Fire Academy at Emmitsburg, if the family had something planned for that weekend, I tried to talk myself and the family out of it so I could go to Emmitsburg.

There's nothing I really dislike about my job, maybe some of the budgetary problems, that's all. I did shift work all these years, and I like that. I like doing day work and night work, back and forth.

Firemen don't like to show emotion. Rather than show any emotion, you shove everything off with a little humor. Even in tragic situations, in order to protect yourself you kind of bring some humor out. Not that it's funny, not by a long shot. But you can always find a little bit of humor in it. I found that out when I got injured a couple of years ago. It's just to protect the way you think you are supposed to be, I guess.

We're getting more EMS calls these days than fire calls. You get a lot of silly calls with those. I remember one of the calls we had, and this was an emergency call, we brought in a medic unit and an engine company, and we have six guys pulling up with their sirens blowing. Here is a guy standing there, and he's been drinking, and he's seeing pink elephants. It's ridiculous that we are even running on these types of calls. There has to be some way to screen the calls, cut them down or educate the people. That's what I think.

□

It was on Squad 2 in Chicago that I really learned what being a big city fireman was all about, because by that time I had graduated to the point where I was not just a fan who was riding. I was a member of the company and wore a helmet and worked as a fireman. Those experiences never leave you because you were challenged constantly. We had a district that was skid row, slums and heavy industry. We probably had more fires and extra-alarm fires than any other company in the city. Also, we probably took more casualties than any other company, because of the nature of our district and the amount of heavy fire duty we did.

The bond among us was tremendous. One of the things about a fire company, especially a busy, hard-working company, is the bond between you and your brothers on the company. It comes through shared experiences, and one of the great honors of my life is that firefighters I respect would accept me as one of them. That probably is the most gratifying of all —to be accepted as a firefighter by other firefighters.

I think the greatest compliment anybody can ever pay another person is to say simply, "He's a good fireman." Often you will hear firemen talk about someone, and they will finally come down to one sentence, "He's a good fireman." It says everything about a person. It means that the commitment is there, that they have stood the test, that they have been accepted because of what they delivered when it really counted.

That was a tremendous influence on my life. The funny thing is that it has been thirty years now, and we all stay in touch. If today I had a problem or needed help, I could pick up the phone and call one of those guys, and, if need be, they would be on the next plane to wherever I was. I feel the same way about them.

Some of the memorable experiences you have on the fire department are not really spectacular fires. One that will always stand out in my mind was a snotty basement fire, in which we held our ground, and that meant all the difference between saving or not saving the building. There was no life hazard involved, and we didn't have masks in those days. When we first went into that sub-basement we were crouching, then we were down on our knees, and finally we were close to the floor. There was a real bond between the six of us and our officer, Lieutenant Wally Peterson, for having stood our ground. It wasn't a very spectacular fire by most standards, but the fact that all of us stood together really meant something among ourselves.

There's another aspect of the fire life. I mentioned the case of my dad, who was adopted by Engine 33 in New York. I've noticed through the years that fire companies will do that with some unfortunate person. At Engine 34 and Squad 2 in Chicago, we had Art Kelly, who lived in the basement of the firehouse. He was a shell-shocked veteran of World War II, and he couldn't work or do anything, and there was no place for him. So he lived in the basement of the firehouse. He would take care of the furnace and help clean up the firehouse each day, and in return he got food, a warm place to sleep, and some people who cared about him. When he died, it was the firemen who gave him a funeral.

At Engine 5 on the West Side of Chicago, there was a "paisan" who was a dwarf, and apparently his family wouldn't take care of him. But the firemen of Engine 5 did, especially a guy by the name of Bobby Reed. "Paisan" lived his entire life at that firehouse, being taken care of and trying to do things to help the firemen. When he died, it was also the firemen who gave him the funeral.

I've known stories of this happening everywhere. It's sort of a reflection of the kind of people that firemen are.

When the Chicago Fire Department band went to the Rose Bowl one year, they smuggled "Paisan" onto the plane with them. They took him to the Rose Bowl. One of the newspaper columnists complained that some "illegal people" had gone with the band. It was "Paisan," and it was the trip of his life for him.

I'm not saying that all firemen are angels, that's not true. We know better than that. But I'm saying that a majority of the people involved in the fire service are really pretty decent people.

I think government tends to take the fire service for granted, because it causes them the least amount of trouble. Although in recent years the fire service has had its share of turbulence. There was a time when the fire service seemed to be immune from the problems that plagued society. Well, those days are gone forever. Fire departments today have the same problems as the rest of society—drugs, unrest, indiscipline at times. So the fire service is no longer isolated as it once was.

The fire service when I started out as a kid was really a world unto itself, and it operated behind closed doors. They put out fires, and everybody loved the firemen. I think that began to change in the sixties, just as American society began to change. We got involved with all of the social unrest that took place in the country, and personnel coming into the fire department reflected society in general. So the fire service is very different from what it was. It is much more reflective of the society itself.

In the old days, especially in the big cities, the fire service was basically an Irish club, and everybody came predominantly from the same background. The Irish dominated the fire service I grew up in. I would say that seventy-five percent of the people I knew as a kid in the fire department were Irish. It was a very cohesive group. Those days are gone. The fire service today is made up of everybody.

One of the more tragic things at a fire is when people get out of a building and go back in. We had a fire in an auto body shop on a warm spring day. Everybody got out okay, and this one guy went back in to get a leather jacket. He was burned over 90 percent of his body.

I remember a house fire in which a lawyer got out, an intelligent man, an educated man. He got out, and the building was heavily involved in a fire. And he went back in to get some papers or something. He died in the fire.

The things people do are amazing. In Port Chester in the wintertime, we were coming down the street, and the whole side of the house was on fire. A guy was out there waving a blowtorch in one hand, and waving his other hand at us. He had been using the blowtorch to thaw pipes that had frozen. He set his whole house on fire.

□

When I arrived, there was a huge hole in the wall of a brick housing project. The main gas line that fed the whole unit was broken, and gas was pouring all over the place. It was not on fire, but the crews were stretching lines to cover, in case it did blow. They were evacuating the building, getting the people out as fast as possible. My brother Harvey was the chief on the scene, and everybody was uptight, because this was the same platoon that had had the big propane explosion just a short time earlier. Harvey was back only a few weeks from his injuries. The tension was pretty high.

Well, we got the gas company on the scene, and things settled down.

I was standing inside the building by the big hole in the wall. Harvey said, "The rescue company is getting the guy out of the car." I couldn't see any car. I looked at him, and said, "What car?" He looked at me like I was slightly nuts. His hand was on the side of his face, and he pointed a finger up toward the ceiling. I looked and saw the rear end of a car sticking through the fire wall up at the ceiling.

The guy had come barreling through a parking lot, hit an obstacle and gone up in the air, flew through the wall, broke the gas pipe, plowed through the fire wall, and got stuck in the ceiling. I didn't see the rescue company because they were in an adjoining room, digging the guy out. So after all the emotional tension, it ended up that the guy was drunk as a skunk, and he never even got hurt.

The only thing that got hurt in the whole thing was my ego, when I said, "What car?"

□

I remember one day I was detailed over to the battalion chief to be the chief's aide. It was what we called a "tit job," that is, the aide was sucking on the cow and didn't have to be in burning buildings. Guys referred to the aide as a double-dealing, double-clutching, clipboard-carrying apple polisher. This was all in fun, though, because the chief's aide had to be a guy who was fairly experienced and knew what he was doing. He was also the guy who approved vacation switches.

So one summer day when the sidewalks of the South Bronx were steaming heat, there was a job in one of the old tenement buildings, and, like always, hundreds of people crowded the sidewalk. It was my job, after the fire was put out, to talk to the people who had been burned out of their apartments and get all the information from them about the people who lived there and the possessions lost in the fire. If they had the Crown Jewels from the Tower of London stuck in a back closet, I wanted to know about it.

There was one woman sitting on the stoop. She was about twenty-four years old, good-looking, with those wide eyes that seem to convey innocence. I asked her her name. She said, "Famali Jones."

I wrote it down, thinking it was a kind of exotic name. In the black culture there are many exotic names, particularly if they're using African names. I asked her to spell it.

She said, "F-E-M-A-L-E."

Her name was Female Jones, and my first inclination was to laugh. Then it dawned on me that probably when she was born, in the hospital that brought her forth to be one of God's children, the mother had no immediate name to give to the hospital authorities, so they jotted in her sex, thinking, I suppose, that the real name could be inserted sometime in the future.

Well, the real name never got attached, and here the girl child of the Jones family was left with this mark on a piece of paper for the rest of her life. Here she was on a crowded stoop in the South Bronx, beneath her still smoldering apartment, telling me that her name is Female. It could make for a funny story, like the one about Denise and da nephew. It really isn't very funny, though, when you think about it.

Dennis Smith

□

Our station has both an engine and a truck company along with our rescue unit, consisting of John and myself. One hot day, John and I were washing hose in the alley. He squirted me with the hose, and I decided to get even, so I went after the garden hose, and he squirted me again.

One of the guys from Engine 2, named Bill, was visiting us, and he saw the whole episode. Bill went upstairs and filled a garbage can with water, and dumped it on John from the upper deck. Now John decided to play for keeps. He hooked up a three-quarter-inch line to a standpipe at a corner of the building, and he stood there waiting for somebody to come by.

Pretty soon Bill came walking across the parking lot, defying John to squirt him, but Bill had a raincoat on. As he went to squirt Bill, somebody turned the water off. He went and turned it back on, and in his frustration he went to squirt Bill, and he accidentally got the fire engine wet. So now he had to clean off the fire engine.

Later on that night, Bill was back at his station, and John and I went out on a medical call. On our way back from the call, we decided to pay Bill a surprise visit at Station 2. Bill, who is six foot six, was sprawled on his bed, asleep. John and I sneaked into the dorm with a bucket of cold water and dumped it on him. And I'll tell you, I thought he was going to die. I've never heard anybody scream like that. And the guy who was sleeping on a cot next to Bill's was a Spanish guy who thought he was pretty cool. He sprang into the air and was jumping up and down on the bed, swearing in Spanish. He didn't know what had happened, because we were out of there, man.

□

There was this big guy, a kind of wise-guy probie, who weighed around 220. The older guys wanted to set him straight. So Jerry Albert says, "I'll bet I can lift you up with one arm."

The probie says, "You can't do that. That's a lot of bull." And he says, "I'll bet you. What do you want to bet?"

Jerry says, "Ten dollars."

The big probie says, "Okay, you're on." He agrees that Jerry will try to lift him up through the pole hole by means of a rope. So they lower the rope through the pole hole and attach the bowline-on-a-bight to him, a rescue harness knot. Jerry has the other end of the rope upstairs.

Well, it took three other guys to help Jerry, and they lift this heavy probie eight feet off the floor, then they tie the rope to the safety gate. So now here is the probie hanging down the pole hole, eight feet off the ground. So of course, the guys start up the engine, put the booster line on, and completely saturate him with water from the booster tank. He couldn't even take some weight off himself by holding on to the brass pole, because the pole was slippery from the water. So the guy says, "Okay, okay, you proved your point."

When they took him down, Jerry Albert gave him ten dollars, saying, "Here, you won. I didn't actually lift you with one hand." So the guy goes upstairs and changes clothes. He comes down, and they're all in the kitchen talking about it and laughing.

So help me God, the probie says, "Hey, you didn't really do it."

Jerry says, "I was only kidding around, but I bet I could lift you with one arm."

And the probie again says, "That's a lot of bull."

So Jerry bets him ten dollars again, gets the tensky back and puts it into his pocket, and they do the same thing. They leave him hanging eight feet off the ground, and they put the booster line on him again—for the second time within an hour. This time they left him there for about thirty minutes.

The guy had to learn his lesson. Today he's a deputy chief.

It's not easy, though, to become a legend in your own time. Some are cold, as the saying goes, but few are frozen.

There was a legend guy who used to work with us in the firehouse, named Dumpy. I prefer not to use his real name, because I am uncertain of the statute of limitations on the things he did. He had worked downtown in one of the Harlem companies. He was telling the firefighters there that he could take smoke longer than anyone. He put a fifty-gallon drum in the kitchen and started a fire in it. The fifty-gallon drum went on fire, and so, of course, did the kitchen. And the firefighters had to stretch hose, as they would in any other fire, to extinguish to fire. The place was completely demolished.

So they lifted him to the South Bronx. Lifted is a soft word for a punitive transfer. They sent him to the firehouse on Intervale Avenue, which was one of the most punitive places in New York City, because it was an extremely busy firehouse. It delighted a guy like Dumpy no end. The busier the better. Dumpy was an extremely tough-looking guy. He had great pugnacious hands, a pugnacious neck, and a crewcut on a head as hard as a steel helmet.

Dumpy immediately alienated everyone in the firehouse kitchen one night by saying that he had personally put out fifty rooms of fire with an inch-and-a-half line in an abandoned tenement building in Harlem. Everyone took this as another line of firefighter braggadocio. It wasn't until after the first couple of serious fires that the guys found out that Dumpy was indeed a fabulous firefighter. Mostly because he was very, very strong and he was fundamentally suicidal, meaning that there was not a fire environment roaring enough to keep him out.

So Dumpy tried to be as slovenly and as outrageous as he possibly could. He was a little like the Dada artists of the 1920s, when everything they did was meant to outrage. I've heard it said that people today can no longer do outrageous things after the atrocities of World War II. But I will say that Dumpy certainly attempted to be historically outrageous.

One night we were at a fire that completely burned a tenement apartment from one end to the other. We were in the bathroom overhauling, that is, taking down the ceilings and walls to make sure there were no embers still burning there. There was a hamper filled with soiled clothes, now saturated and filthy. Dumpy went through the hamper and found a pair of women's underpants that were in the hefty class, about a size forty-six. Dumpy grabbed them and put them in his mouth, stuffed them fully in his mouth, like a magician. No comment. Just a need to be outrageous.

One night Dumpy called the firehouse and told the guys who answered, "Hey, look, I'm in a lot of trouble, and I need your help."

The firefighter said, "What's the problem?"

"I broke my leg."

The firefighter said, "Well, call an ambulance. Do what any normal person would do."

"No, no, you don't understand," Dumpy said. "I was breaking into an A & P out on Long Island, coming down a sky light on a rope. I was lowering myself down, and I slipped and fell. My leg's broke."

It was around midnight, and the firefighter said, "Where are you?"

"In the store."

"Where?"

"I'm in the A & P now."

"What do you expect us to do?" the firefighter asked. "Come out with the fire engine, and pick you up?"

"Yeah, yeah, that's what I need. I need a ladder. A thirty-five-foot extension ladder. That'll get me out."

So the firefighter said, "Hey, Dumpy, use your brains. There is not a soul in the world connected to this firehouse, except possibly yourself, who would go out with a thirty-five-foot ladder to save someone who broke his leg while in the process of breaking and entering. Is there some other way we can help you?"

"Yeah," Dumpy says. "Call my brother-in-law. Here's his number."

Dumpy didn't show up at the firehouse for another month. When he did, he had a big cast on his leg and a big smile on his face. Nobody mentioned the telephone call or questioned his story that he had busted his leg sliding into second base.

One day Dumpy got a little too smart-lipped and told the captain he was going to chew him up and spit him out like so much spinach. So the captain had him transferred to a firehouse in midtown Manhattan, which had the reputation of having the worst captain in the fire department. Compared to this captain, Attila, Savonarola, and Rasputin were more like Albert Schweitzer. Dumpy was certainly aware of the captain's reputation.

So before reporting there officially, he went down off duty and had the house watchman call the captain down. The captain came down, and Dumpy went and threw his arms around the captain and kissed him hard on the mouth. The captain was caught in a viselike grip and came as close as he ever will in his life to knowing what it was like to be sexually abused. He was stunned.

"You're known to be one of the nicest guys in the department," Dumpy told him. "I just want to let you know how happy I am to be assigned to your distinguished company, here in midtown Manhattan, among the fire department's elite."

Dennis Smith

□

I was the captain of Truck 3 at Station 9, one of the busiest houses in the city, about six thousand runs a year. New cadets were sent to us. We were close-knit, as busy stations usually are, and proud of our performance. We were quick on our feet, too. One day Chief Michaels was inspecting Truck 3, asking questions relative to truck operations, equipment, and rope drills. We felt we had prepared our cadets very well.

Instead of the usual questions, Chief Michaels asked a cadet the location of a small street in our first-in district. "Where's Colfax?" he asked. The cadet, thinking quickly, responded, "I think he's on a day off."

□

Another time I was working overtime at the Fourth Battalion, and on this shift I was definitely earning my pay. The battalion had been to about twelve alarms when we were backing into quarters about two in the morning. We heard gunshots and realized that the bullets were hitting close to us, since mortar was flying off the front of the engine house. This station, which was affectionately known as the Wild Wild West, was living up to its name.

My aide quickly backed the rig into quarters, while we were crouching low. Safely inside, we summoned the gendarmes. They found that the source of the gunfire was the bar across the street, where a "disagreement" was taking place. Since this was long after the riots had cooled and no one was hurt, we all had a good laugh.

Then the police asked, "Who owns the green van? It's a casualty." The window by the driver's seat was shot out, and the bullet lodged in the back of the seat.

Guess whose van it was. When I got home the next day, I had another "fire story" for the kids.

□

Then there was the night some young hoods stole a rig from a fire scene. It was recovered a few days later, minus breathing apparatus and other equipment. Needless to say, a directive came down advising all battalion chiefs to be sure the rigs were locked and the keys removed whenever they were parked out of quarters.

Well, time went by, and no further rigs disappeared until one day when we were having another busy day in the "Flaming Fourth" Battalion and we didn't get around to making our battalion rounds until after ten o'clock. We parked the rig on the platform of Truck 5, a single-company house. The company was eating dinner in the second-floor kitchen when we arrived. A good friend of mine was the officer, so we went up to the kitchen to visit for a few minutes.

When we came down a short while later, the platform was empty. I looked at my aide, and he looked at me. My aide was sweating profusely. We had lost another rig. My aide immediately called the alarm office to have them sound the recall of the rig.

Thank goodness for modern technology. The flashing light and the audible recall inside the chief's car must have frightened the culprits who had "appropriated" it. They must have thought the car was haunted, because it was located shortly thereafter on the Hope Memorial Bridge, with only a few items of clothing missing.

□

I worked for many years with a man named Horace, who was a bodybuilder. He had the most formidable arms in the firehouse, great construction worker fists, and a voice as velvety soft as any high-quality cloth you ever felt. He sang like Billy Eckstein, and no one ever asked him to shut up when he was singing, although the bulges beneath his shirt would preclude the request in any event. Horace was a mild-mannered guy, but he was also a tough piece of work who had spent all his life in the black neighborhoods of New York City, environments that Gainsborough never painted.

One day Horace was playing poker with four or five other guys at an old wooden table in the kitchen of Engine Company 82. Another firefighter, named Billy, walked into the room. Billy had also been seasoned on the streets of the Bronx and was no piece of cake. Unlike Horace, however, he was not an easygoing guy; he always had an edge of hostility at the corners of his mouth and a strange turn of the eye. He was a big guy, bigger than Horace.

Billy had a wooden-handled knife about eight inches long, and he began throwing it into the scarred wood of the table. He started at the far edge of the table and worked his way along the table toward the card players. Thump, the knife would go in, and Billy would pull it out. Thump, again the knife went in, and Billy pulled it out. The knife was coming closer and closer to where Horace was holding his cards.

Finally, Horace looked up at Billy, and I remember his words as clearly as I remember the definitions in the Baltimore Catechism. He said, "You better stop it, Billy, because you're going to cut me. And when you cut me, you're going to say you're sorry."

Billy laughed the kind of laugh you heard from the villain with the cape when tying the blonde to the railroad tracks. He threw the knife into the table several more times, closer and closer to Horace, until finally the knife went right through Horace's hand. Billy quickly pulled out the knife, the hand was bleeding, and Billy yelled, "Horace, I'm sorry, I'm sorry."

Horace got up, took a step, and with the other hand whomped Billy in the jaw, throwing him back ten or fifteen feet onto the kitchen floor. The knife went flying out of Billy's hand, thank God.

Horace very coolly took a handkerchief out of his pocket and wrapped it around the knife wound. He said, "Being sorry isn't enough."

Dennis Smith

□

I love the horseplay that goes on, and I have to confess that many times I have been an instigator in some of the wildest things that have gone on in the firehouses. That's all part of it, the humor. It's a very special kind of humor, and when you tell other people about it, it's hard for them to understand. It's among ourselves, and we understand it completely.

It's true of the practical jokes and even the wisecracks you hear when you are faced with a tough situation. Trying to make it up a smoky stairway, a guy says, "Did you know that this is bad for your health?" It doesn't seem very funny to an outsider. I guess you've got to be there.

One of the first responsibilities of the company that I was on in Port Chester was salvage. If there was no rescue work to be done, then our next job was salvage—spreading covers and getting valuable things out of the building. We were having a lot of tension in one neighborhood, and hostility was being directed at the firefighters. So I said to our company, "Next time we get a fire down there, let's show the people how good we are in saving their belongings. That'll show them that we are really their friends."

A few nights later, at seven o'clock on a hot summer evening, we get an alarm, and the upper floors of a three-story building are going. The ground floor is one of those storefront churches. So we get hold of the minister of the church, and we ask him where all his valuables are. We tell him that we are going in and save everything. So we get the Bible out, get all of the artifacts and religious things that we can find. Anything we can't move is gathered together, and we throw salvage covers over it.

Now the truck is starting to open up with a ladder pipe into the upper floors, and it's only a matter of time before that water starts coming down. At the same time, the smoke starts banking down, and pretty soon we're on our knees trying to scoop up the last valuable things. There is this huge box, and I can't figure out what it is. We try to move it, but we can't make it budge. It's about eight feet long. Finally we throw a salvage cover over it, tuck it in at every point, so no water damage will be inflicted on this thing.

We come staggering out of the place, and guys are leaning over the fence, throwing up from the belt of smoke that we had. They finally get the fire knocked down, and we go back inside to see what this thing was. We lift the salvage cover, and it's a baptismal, an eight-foot tub of water. Can you imagine that? We had covered it to prevent water damage.

There's another night where we got in and the smoke was banking down. Again, it was the upper floors of a building that were involved in fire, and the chief told us to spread our salvage covers on the second floor. So we got the covers and started into the building. We got to the second floor, and there was a guy, his wife and three kids sitting at a table, eating. There wasn't too much smoke in the place, so we told them, "You've got to get out of here, the building's on fire."

The guy starts to argue with me, and I say, "Now you get out of here, or I'm going to call the police and have them move you out." So the guy reluctantly leaves with his wife and kids, and we get everything together and throw the salvage covers. We go outside to get more, and all of a sudden, I look. We're in the building next door.

What happened was that the smoke had banked down and concealed the doorways. I thought we were going in the right doorway, but we were going in the doorway of the building next door. So real quickly we grabbed more covers, went into the fire building, and got things covered up.

I didn't understand why that guy thought I was crazy.

□

The only time I ever saw a life net actually used at a fire was in Chicago, when I was with Squad 2. We had a fire in a flophouse on skid row. We got a dozen people down the interior stairs before the fire cut it off. Then we started taking them down the fire escape and ladders.

Suddenly we heard a commotion, looked up, and saw our lieutenant struggling with a huge drunk on Truck 39's wooden aerial ladder. The lieutenant, Wally Peterson, yelled for us to get the life net. We got it, held it under the ladder, and Wally pushed the drunk off. We caught him in the net, then turned him over to the police to be charged with disorderly conduct.

Lieutenant Bill Gustin
Miami, Florida

Captain Edward Callahan
Plymouth, Massachusetts

Catherine Lohan
Bayside, New York

Alan Simmons
Sun Valley, California

Andre Darden
Pikesville, Maryland

David Crompton
Philadelphia, Pennsylvania

Alan Brunacini
Phoenix, Arizona

Hal Bruno
Chevy Chase, Maryland

William Henderson
Philadelphia, Pennsylvania

Kathryn Raus
Pickney, Michigan

Joe Haig
Detroit, Michigan

Robert S. Hoff
Chicago, Illinois

James Allison
Fallon, Nevada

Captain Tim Birr
Eugene, Oregon

Scott J. Ulshafer
Philadelphia, Pennsylvania

Chief Walter Zimmerer
Chippewa Lake, Ohio

Larry Ford
El Toro, California

Roy G. Gelbhaus
Boulder, Colorado

Lieutenant
William Thompson
Baltimore, Maryland

Paul Hashagen
Freeport, New York

Edward T. Dickinson
Brainard, New York

William Schmitzer
Orlando, Florida

Captain Douglas D. Hickin
Charlotte, North Carolina

Ronald Baker
Baltimore, Maryland

Charles Menchan
Orlando, Florida

Daniel Kish
Romulus, Michigan

Mike Farmer
Houston, Texas

George Pond
Earp, California

Drew Coates
Weirton, West Virginia

Robert A. Latka
Detroit, Michigan

Robert O'Donnell
Midland, Texas

Danny Paulin
Santa Barbara, California

Edward Pospisil
Bolton, Connecticut

Division Chief Jack Supple
Buffalo, New York

I hadn't handled a life net since training school some years before. I tried to quickly remember how the hands were supposed to be positioned, but by that time the drunk was already on his way down. Somehow he survived, and so did my arms.

□

When I first came out of fire school, I was a firefighter. I worked in an engine company, then a truck company, both very busy. When I made captain, I did snorkel. When the spot in the rescue unit opened up, the chief of the fire department called me at home and asked me if I wanted to go there. I said, "Well, yeah." He said, "Be there tomorrow."

There is only one rescue unit in the whole city of Baltimore. They go on second alarms citywide, every major fire and every heavy rescue in automobile accidents and industrial accidents. When we got there, the chiefs relied on us. We had the big stuff, the heavy tools.

Looking back on it, we were always in a dangerous position. You were on the roof, the weakest spot. The truck companies would say, "We're not going to open it, it doesn't look too good." We were like, "Hell, we can do it." And we'd be up there on the roof, and we'd get it open. Inside, when there were people in there, we'd be in there crawling around.

The tools that we carried, over and above what a truck company would have, made us specialists. We would have a net for the people who wanted to jump out. The city had a high-rise team, and we were involved with the planning of that. We had rappelling gear. The guys were in shape and a little more daring.

To stay in shape I played racquetball, did a lot of bicycling. And after I got married, we bought an old house, and after work I would work another eight or nine hours on the house. I put in a cathedral ceiling, and people say, "How the hell did you do it?" I got strength from doing that type of work.

□

Basically, Eugene is a West Coast city, a relatively new city in terms of construction. In 1979 we were able to pass a retroactive sprinkler ordinance for high-rise buildings. Every residential building over seventy-five feet or three stories has to have sprinklers, at least a life safety system in the corridors. So we have only two or three major multiple alarms a year, and most of them are lumberyards or school fires.

Our two major industries are the university and the lumberyards. When the recession hit and interest rates went up and people stopped building, they stopped buying wood, and the mills closed down. That's when our cutbacks came. The city is now trying to diversify its economy.

Our stations have three shifts, A, B, and C, twenty-four hours on and forty-eight off. Each shift is a separate family and develops a really strong shift identity. The shift begins at eight in the morning. They check out the apparatus first thing, lights, siren, fuel, oxygen, air in the SCBA, oil, making sure everything is ready to go. The second step is usually housekeeping, mopping and cleaning and whatnot. Then we may sit in the kitchen for a half hour while the officer goes through memos. We have a pretty regular work schedule, and it's kind of a running joke in the department that a working fire can be a problem, because it screws up the schedule.

We do business inspections, building tours, area tours, prefire plans, classes and drills, maintenance work in the station. These make up our afternoon activity until about four, when most guys have physical fitness programs that they work on. Then dinner, and the evening is a kind of free period, where the guys can study or do whatever they want.

Of course, the routine is punctuated by calls. Last year we ran about seven thousand calls, and most of those were medical calls. The eight hundred or so fire calls were for everything from a Dumpster to a third alarm at the junior high school.

We've got two truck companies, one a tractor-trailer rig with a hundred-foot aerial ladder, and the other a snorkel. The truck companies double in brass as rescue squads. Our engines are pretty much standard. Two engines are telesquirts, with a telescope and a nozzle on the end, which have worked out very well on larger fires in a defensive kind of operation. Several units operate what we call RAVs, our attack vehicles, which are actually 250-gallons-per-minute pumps. Our medic units also carry light extrication equipment, but the crews are all firefighters. They carry turnout suits with them at all times. And, of course, at the airport we have crash fire rescue.

We have two special units. Because of our rivers, we have a water rescue unit, in which all members are trained as scuba divers and have been through water rescue school. In addition, they serve as drivers. And we recently set up our hazardous materials unit, who work regular assignments in the department but are on call as hazmat people when we need them.

We recently had a fire in an old rooming house, which had been abandoned by the owners and had turned into an urban campground for transients. They would literally set up camp in this place, cooking on the floors and whatnot. It was a three-story frame building with some thirty rooms in it. It was just a maze. Several guys went inside, and they found it funny. But they rescued some of the transients, and it was a good rescue.

We're a very professional and very young department. We had a whole generation of people who joined the fire department right after the Second World War and were retiring in this decade. So our current members are quite young, with a lot of young officers. There have been some real changes. Ten years ago we didn't use breathing apparatus as much as we should have. It was something to be shunned. You had more important things to do when you were first in than to take the time to get a mask.

There has been a complete turnaround. We are now wearing masks routinely. We did a training program recently in a rural area. We were setting up a practice fire for rookies in a shed outside the farmhouse, and when we went into the shed we found the remnants of all kinds of hazardous chemicals and pesticides. The stuff is everywhere.

So we are much more conscious about breathing apparatus, and we have become much more concerned about personal safety. I have never seen people back away from a situation where there is a life at risk. But I have seen fires in the last few years that might have been fought offensively in the old days—in large buildings, or buildings which are unsafe, or where a large body of fire is involved. Today we are doing more defensive stuff. And I think that's healthy.

When you fight a fire offensively, you pull up, throw on a mask, take a nozzle into the building, and you don't open up the nozzle until you're right on top of the fire. So you're in a building that can collapse at any moment, and if there are bad calls on strategy, you run the risk of the fire pushing at you.

On the other hand, when you fight a fire defensively, you don't place your personnel in dangerous situations but fight it from outside. As they say, surround and drown. Or, in other words, break out the hot dogs and marshmallows.

□

If most men live lives of quiet desperation, I guess it could be said that firefighters live lives looking for a fast laugh. Their humor is based on seeing life as a series of mishaps or handicaps.

I remember one fire, a multiple-alarm fire in the South Bronx, where a ladder company from Queens was called in to help fight the blaze. Those men from Queens were in the resort areas of the fire department, meaning they were in areas that were not very active with fires or false alarms. To begin with, they were probably shocked to hear they were going to the South Bronx, and when they got there, they were working with firefighters known throughout the department as the elite, frontline troops.

The Queens company was Ladder 144, and one of the six men in the group had a harelip. He talked with an extremely funny harelipped voice, something like a cross between Bugs Bunny and Elmer Fudd. It so happened that this poor afflicted firefighter was carrying the radio in his company. There were about thirty companies working at this fire, and at least one person from each company was carrying a radio in a harness over his shoulder.

The chief, wanting to know where this company from Queens was, called over the radio so that everyone could hear, "Ladder 144 K." So this firefighter responded by saying, in a very high nasal voice, "Lanna one porty pour, to chief. We're working with engine company 82 on the southsen bullvard side of building K."

Well, that's all these firefighters from the other thirty companies had to hear—this strange, high, cartoon-character kind of voice. And immediately every transmission at this multiple alarm fire in the South Bronx, except that of the chief in charge, sounded like the character of Lily Tomlin sitting at a switchboard.

Some firefighters will go to great lengths in search of a laugh. One in particular was a guy named Wally Porr, who worked with me in Ladder 31 up in the South Bronx. I once brought a friend, the head of the Communications Department at New York University, into the firehouse on Intervale Avenue to introduce him to the firefighters on duty. Wally was in the kitchen when my friend and I entered. As I introduced the professor, Wally came running across the floor and shot under the kitchen table. From a crouching position, he shook my friend's hand and said, "Glad to meet you, pal." Thereupon, Wally backed out from under the table and acted as if nothing had happened. No one laughed or paid any attention. It took a little while for my professor friend to find out that the abnormal was normal in the kitchen of Engine 82 and Ladder 31.

Another time we were having a rash of extraordinary multiple-alarm fires. There was a doctor on duty in our firehouse so that when firefighters got hurt, instead of sending them to the hospital, they were brought to the firehouse first to get treated—people who had smoke inhalation, problems with their eyes, cuts, sprains, that kind of thing. The doctor used the officer's room, where there was a desk and a bed. As the firefighters would come in, they would lie on the bed, and the doctor would examine them.

I was talking to the doctor when Wally came into the office. I said, "Wally, I would like you to meet Doctor So-and-so." Wally immediately jumped onto the bed and extended his hand downward, like a water pump. Towering two feet above the doctor's head, he said, "Doctor, it's a tall pleasure to meet you."

It's not that Wally would search for opportunities to make a nuisance of himself, he just recognized that most day-to-day experiences could easily be complicated, fouled up, or simply ruined. He would as soon throw a monkey wrench into the simplest act as eat breakfast, lunch, or dinner.

On a sweltering summer night, there was a rubbish fire on Charlotte Street. It doesn't take much to attract attention in the South Bronx. The arrival of a fire engine, with siren blasting, was like a crust of bread on an anthill. I would guess that a hundred or so people, weary of the confines of their tenement apartments, were leaning out of their windows watching the street show. Some were leaning on pillows placed across the windowsill, while others were simply braced on outstretched palms.

Wally looked up at them, then started running up the street, waving his helmet in his hand and yelling at the top of his voice, "Please close your windows immediately. Please close your windows immediately. You're using up our air."

I found this an extraordinary act, but even more extraordinary was the number of people who immediately stepped back and closed their windows, thus preserving for the firefighters, working on a small rubbish fire, the sanctity of their air.

It goes without saying that Wally was a bit of a head case, though completely secure, without a hint of neurosis. But to the firefighters of the

South Bronx, the only thing that mattered was whether one was a good firefighter or not. And Wally Porr was a good firefighter.

Dennis Smith

□

When I was hired on, I was already an EMT 1. Then in 1981 our department wound up getting into the EMS business. A private company that had provided the service for twenty years went out of business on two and a half hours' notice. We picked up the ball, and we've had it ever since. We've had some pretty drastic cuts in manpower, but right now we have about a hundred thirty people on the line out of the stations, and the majority are EMT-certified to one degree or another, ranging from EMT 1 to paramedic. The folks on our medical units are paramedics, of course.

But everyone has to be a firefighter first.

We have been involved in lots and lots of rescues, but the majority have been car extrications and pretty basic things like that. Our medics are sometimes helicoptered out of town to do rescues. A lot of logging accidents take place outside of our area up in the woods.

We have an arrangement with the local helicopter service, so that if a helicopter rescue is necessary, our paramedics will be picked up by the helicopter, and they will go out and do what is necessary. Then they will transport the patient back. Two of our local hospitals have helipads; one has its helipad right up on the roof, so our paramedics can treat the patient all the way back to the hospital.

We had one rescue where a guy had a giant earth mover roll over on him. The guy was underneath tons and tons of equipment, and Dan Schneider went under there and treated the guy before they moved him. That was a pretty dangerous situation.

□

All the racial and religious prejudices existed. They dominated the fire service in the old days. But they also dominated society. How did I cope with it, having an Italian name and being Jewish by religion? I coped with it the same way I coped with it in society at that time. You had to be tough, you had to learn how to get along, how to get to know people, and how to make them respect you.

I encountered many examples of prejudice in the fire service as a kid, and yet, in the end, they accepted me as an individual if I could pull my weight, and I could. As a kid, I was polite and learned what the rules were in the firehouse. They learned to trust me and to respect me, as I respected them. And so the barriers began to fall.

As a fireman myself, yes, there was prejudice. There was no doubt that certain individuals I knew were prejudiced, some against me. The whole thing came down to what you did out there on the fire ground. What you did there did all the talking for you. If you pulled your weight as a firefighter, and you did what was expected of you, and you did it well, they had to respect you for it. That really is what breaks the barriers.

With blacks, women, and Hispanics coming into the fire service, for some it's the first time a company has had a minority member or a female member. There is a lot of tension, and all sides have to learn to adjust to each other. What is really going to even it out in the end is how they do out on the street. How do they stand up to the test of being a firefighter?

If they stand up and are able to meet the test of the firefighter, they will earn acceptance the same as anybody else has earned acceptance. If they fail, the individual will never be accepted as a firefighter.

□

There is a woman firefighter I have known for some time, whose name will go undisclosed for several reasons, but, most fundamentally, because she wants it that way. She has been a firefighter for about seven or eight years. I met her about five years ago at a convention in Baltimore, and I thought she would be right to interview for this book, because she has worked on a very active fire company in New York. I called her, and she was very considerate, saying she was honored that someone wanted to interview her, but she begged off.

There are not many women firefighters in the New York Fire Department, about thirty of them, and because of recent court cases it appears that no others will be appointed for a very long time. A judge determined that the testing that had been done for women applicants was not the same as that done for normal male applicants. This created a serious problem for women firefighters. Male firefighters resented the fact that the standards, according to their perception of firefighting, were being reduced to permit the appointment of women to the ranks. I suppose there's no doubt that standards were changed, but whether they were lowered, the women firefighters feel, is an issue worth discussing.

Certainly—and this is a generalization—the traditional woman physiologically cannot pass the traditional athletic requirements that go along with the job of firefighting. A woman's pectoral strength, for instance, is significantly below that of a man's in a normal physiological state. Consequently, most women are not able to hang by their arms from a parallel bar for as long a time as a man can. A woman is not able to climb a wall as easily. But she can if she trains to develop specific muscles.

In any event, the thirty-odd women who were previously appointed to the fire department are in a very funny position, because they are not truly part of the New York Fire Department. This, even though they have been working in the firehouses for some years now. They're accepted, they eat at the same table, they hold the nozzle just like everybody else. But still they are regarded, in an X-versus-O way, as separate: these are the women, and these are the men. Firefighters fall into the male category, and that's the way it's supposed to be, according to most New York firefighters.

When I called this woman, she said a lot of very interesting things. She referred to her position as a job, whereas most firefighters don't think of their profession as a job. They'll say, "I'm on the job" or "I'm a firefighter" or I'm in the department," but they generally don't think of their work as "a job." She declined to be interviewed because she had worked very hard to create a harmonious relationship within her fire company, and she didn't want to jeopardize it.

She said that she had given up a lot, personally and emotionally, to keep her job, and that she realized that, because of this Xs and Os division, she was in a fishbowl, and so were all the women firefighters in the city. The unions have not been very supportive of them. Indeed, the unions have led the fight to make the traditionally tough physical requirements uniform for all applicants.

This woman told me that, because of this fishbowl kind of existence, when she goes to a party with a boyfriend she hopes nobody will ask where she works. People come up with bizarre questions, because the publicity surrounding women firefighters has been so overwhelmingly negative. A woman firefighter is something of a curiosity. They ask, "How can you do it?" Everywhere the women have turned, they have met a wall of resistance. The few women in the department tried to organize themselves into a group led by one person, who immediately became an object of scorn and hatred for many male firefighters.

In accepting this woman's decision not to be interviewed, I felt that it was profoundly disappointing that the history of women in the New York Fire Department is now set in stone. It's not a very happy history. Some women, however, have managed to sustain themselves as confident firefighters, as indeed heroic firefighters, who have given perhaps more than anyone had a right to ask of them in the course of their work.

This woman who chose not to be interviewed is a very competent person, respected by most of the people she works with, and I think she wants to keep it that way. She doesn't want publicity. She doesn't want to magnify her position in any way, and she feels that an interview would magnify her position. She doesn't think she is out of the ordinary in any way. She is a hard-working woman who has a relationship in the firehouse where she works that is a viable one, and she wants to keep it.

Dennis Smith

□

Some of the stuff that has gone on regarding women firefighters in New York City has been unnecessary and pigheaded and stupid.

I will fight fires with anyone, male or female, but I have to know that, if that beam comes down and it's my ass pinned to the ground and I'm out of air, that that person can get me out. I don't care what their sex is, but I have to know that they are physically strong enough to do that. A lot of people outside of the fire service don't understand that. They think that this is an all-boys club, and there are no girls allowed. That's not what this is all about.

It's about coming to understand trust. As more and more women career firefighters come into the service, we will learn to trust them, and that attitude will slowly dissipate. A lot of old-time firefighters have this inbred thought of women being different, less strong, and they're afraid that they can't count on the most important thing a firefighter can count on, and that is the other guy going on without a thought. You know, the other guy pulling him up from a roof—if he goes down that hole, he doesn't want the other guy to turn ass and run. He wants him to get his partner out.

□

I'm only at Engine 33 a month, and at that time I'm always an eager beaver because I want to do the best I can and I want to be right at the front. I mean, I'd rather be the pipe man, not the backup man, but they rotate all the jobs, so it's a big letdown when I'm not the pipe man, because that's obviously the best job. Anyway, at that time in the city we had two or three firefighters fall off the apparatus, and if I'm not mistaken, two of the three were killed. And they all happened on false alarms.

In our district, the Back Bay area, we had a notorious number of false alarms coming from down around the combat zone after midnight, and it was obvious that some person or persons were doing this regularly and continuously. The lieutenant comes out and says, "It's a night tour. The chief's got a guy from his house down there, and he wants one guy from here. The deal is, you're getting one firebox each, and you pick up portable radios down in his quarters, and you watch the firebox between midnight and five." He looks at everybody in the group, and he says, "Anybody interested?"

It's November, and it's part of our tour, so it's not extra money. But, I think, why not? I stick my hand up in the air. So he says, "Okay, you got it."

So I go down there and I meet the other guy, and it turns out that they have only one portable radio, not two. So you know who got the radio— the other guy.

I go to my box, and I sit in my car because it's cold, across the street from the box. At two-thirty, this six-foot-three, larger-than-life man comes up to the firebox, and he pulls it. And now, of course, the reality hits me. Uh-oh, wait a minute here, I'm in trouble. Here I am out in the middle of nowhere, I got no radio, and he picks the box I'm at. I can't talk to anybody, what do I do?

I get out of the car, he's disappeared now down the street, so I follow him. He goes four blocks over and across a turnpike, and I can hear the apparatus coming to the box, but from a different direction, so they don't pass me.

He goes across and pulls another box, false alarm, but not the box where the other firefighter is at, a different box. And now they send an engine and truck to this box. I'm afraid to go right up to him, because he's like twice as big as me, and he doesn't look like he's too friendly.

Now he's on the "on" ramp of the expressway, and he sticks out his thumb. He's going to disappear if somebody picks him up. I think of all the other false alarms, and I say, Oh, I don't believe this.

Finally, in the nick of time, the engine company coming to the other box sees me jumping up and down in the middle of the street, about fifty yards away from the ramp. I say to the firemen, "Get the cops! This is him! There he is! We gotta stop him before he gets away!" I jump on the side of the rig, and we drive up to the guy. The captain says, "Hey you, hold it right there, bud." And I'm smiling to myself, saying, all right! Victory!

Then a police car pulls up, and the district chief pulls up at the same time. Everybody stands there for two seconds. Nobody says anything. And the cops say, "Okay, Chief, which one is it?" And the chief goes, "Okay, lock him up, the snake!" And he's pointing at me.

I go, "No, no, Chief, I'm the detail guy. The other guy."

And he goes, "Oh, yeah, right, right. The other guy."

He didn't know who I was, because I'd only been in the district four weeks. I said to myself, oh boy, this is interesting, to say the least.

One time when I was at the Back Bay company, we went to a fire in a run-down hotel. The fire was in one apartment on the sixth floor, and we got word that one of the occupants might still be in the apartment. There were no standpipes or sprinklers, so we stretched a line up the aerial ladder and into an adjacent window. And we picked the right window.

There's a tremendous amount of smoke in there, and everybody's got their masks on, because you couldn't move in there without them. Everybody's moving around trying to make a search as well as stretching the line further in. And I bump into what I believe is the occupant in question. So I think I'm a hotshot, and I put my arms around the guy and drag him struggling out into the hallway.

As soon as I get out there, the body in front of me turns white, and I realize it's the district chief I have in my arms. He turns around, his eyeballs are all red, and the snots hanging from his nose are nine inches long. And he snarls at me, "Are you finished?" And I do the classic moves from Charlie Chaplin, like try to dust him off and straighten him up. "Sorry, Chief, my mistake."

I got transferred quickly to 52 Engine, which was tremendous because there was an engine, a ladder, and a rescue all in the same house. This was in the ghetto with nothing but fires practically every time you worked. We were all young guys. Older guys just didn't go for a place like that. We had a great time driving the officers crazy. The captain of the ladder truck was a very reserved gentleman, a very nice man, and well respected because he was good at his job. But he never swore. His biggest thing, if you were a screwup, was to call you an apple. So we used to have the Apple of the Week award.

I was lieutenant in a ladder company, and we went to a third alarm in another district. The building was plywood from top to bottom, a five-story brick vacant. We threw a forty-foot ground ladder, and we went in a fourth-floor window in the rear. There was nothing but heavy smoke in there, and I couldn't see much of anything. My last words to the guys, as I went in the window, were, "Follow me, men!" And the next thing they saw were my size nine boots going through a hole in the floor.

As I found out later, the fire was on the second and third floors. And I got stuck in the third floor ceiling, hanging upside down. I was caught there, and I couldn't get out, no matter which way I went. I could feel the heat start to get a little closer.

Our engine company was coming down the third-floor hallway with a charged line, but the thing happened so fast that they had no idea that I was already there. They were passing the room I was in because they were on their way to the other end of the hallway, where there was a larger amount of fire.

Suddenly they saw my helmet go by. That caused them to look into the room. So they pulled me out and knocked down the fire around me, so that I didn't spend my last moments groveling like a fish on a hook. I was really lucky, and just sprained my whole back. That was it.

It took me a while to live down the "Follow me, men" slogan. There was a lot of humor in it, and I went along because they were right. The ribbing was good because it was true. What I hadn't known was that there had been a previous fire in the building. And I just went right into the black hole, without realizing that there was no floor there.

It shows you've got to pay attention.

□

It was in downtown Manhattan. A guy was passing by the firehouse with a truckload of monkeys. Real monkeys. And he got in an accident right in front of the firehouse. Just a fender bender, but hard enough to crash open the back door of the truck. And three hundred monkeys jumped out of the truck. Most of them went into the firehouse because of the big open doors there.

The truck driver said, "I'll give you two dollars for every monkey you can get back."

So the captain closed the doors of the firehouse and said, "Every monkey in this firehouse is mine."

Dennis Smith

□

We have got a lot of good women firefighters. I work with them, I train them, I evaluate them. But women, blacks, and Hispanics have a more difficult time breaking into the job. They aren't able to hide it. Why other firefighters make it difficult for them I never truly thought about before. I don't look upon it so much as a class distinction as perhaps the fact that we are the product of who we are and who our parents are. Some people have been brought up where certain things just are accepted, they don't know better. They don't even know if they're being insulting at times.

As an example, today when we have women coming on the job, many people from an older generation still talk in terms of "girl." Perhaps in a secretarial sense—send it out to the girl to type up. That sort of thing has carried over. If a firefighter, in his home life, heard his father talk about taking his timecard over to the "girl," now he becomes a firefighter, and he is accustomed to thinking of the "girl."

On the basis of my experience in Boulder, I am pleased to report that divisiveness does not have to be the rule when it comes to women coming on the job. Departments can in fact move past the awkward stage to one of acceptance and even harmony. However, it requires commitment from the top on down to just be decent with one another, while recognizing that different backgrounds require different training methods and will also yield different sensibilities. It's interesting how, in a Western state like this, older firefighters will look at people coming from a city background and say, "Who ever thought we would have to teach people how to swing an ax?"

As one firefighter put it, "We didn't practice offensive behavior, we practiced defensive behavior."

Yet even when one tries to approach a group with the best of intentions, there can be pitfalls. I once tried an experiment that had the potential to unduly burden smaller-statured firefighters, male or female. I tried to reassure them that the job was not going to be restructured to drive people out. Well, that approach worked well, I believe, with most of the women. But it bothered one greatly. There is the lesson. We are all individuals who should not be stereotyped; we can't afford to think in terms of all the women, all the Asians, all the Jews, Catholics, blacks, Irish, Italians, etc., if we want to see firefighters fulfill their potential.

At the Firehouse Exposition and Muster in Baltimore, I wore a souvenir T-shirt from the first national conference of Fire Service Women, which had been held in Boulder. I was wearing it deliberately to provoke comment and reassure people that the world was not coming to an end. A firefighter from a major city said to his partner, "It takes a different kind of man to wear a shirt like that." I'm only sorry that I wasn't quick-witted enough to say, "Courage takes many different forms."

□

I feel I've got the best of both worlds. I can be in a fire and get grubby and dirty and work right next to these guys, but when I come home and shower up, I can be just as feminine as any other wife.

Any sexual references come after the fire is out. By the time I approach a fire scene, I always have my gear on, and although my size may be a little smaller, the people don't know that underneath all that there's a female. But when the fire's over and we're all taking our gear off and the people do see I'm a female, a lot of times I get some looks, like, "Oh, I didn't know she was a girl."

My department had a house chimney fire, and when it was over and we were taking off our gear, this lady came over to me and said, "My God, you're a girl!"

I said, "Yeah."

She said, "How do you like it?"

I said, "I love being a girl."

"No, no," she said. "How do you like being on the fire department?"

I told her I really enjoyed it. I thought it was a funny scene.

The children are different. For the last three years in fire prevention week, another firefighter and I go to all the different schools—anywhere from preschool up to fifth grade—and teach fire prevention. The children are just tickled that they have a female teaching fire prevention along with a male. Because people aren't used to it.

It's amazing how many children actually remember you. I've had kids come up to me in church, and say, "I remember you. 'Stop, drop, and roll!' "

And I say, "Yeah, you're right." Then I say, "What do you do if you have smoke in your room?"

And they'll tell me, "I stay low, and I crawl."

To me, that's worth every ounce of time I've spent with these kids. If I can just save one of these kids, ever, that's all I can ask. I couldn't want any more.

One Christmas Eve, we came home from my family's party, and we tucked our children in. Just like in the storybook, they were all nestled in bed. And my husband and I were being Santa's helpers, setting out all of Santa's gifts with their name tags on them, when I got a call that we had a house fire. I remember giving him a kiss and just saying, "I'll be back as soon as I can." And I left him sitting among all these toys that weren't put together yet, and all this stuff scattered around, and I went on the house fire.

Thankfully, there was nobody in the house, they were out visiting, but their house was destroyed, a total loss.

I came back home, and it was like magic: everything had been done. And there my husband was sitting, with a little glass of wine for me, and a candle lit, and he made my Christmas really special. In fact, it was Christmas morning by the time I got back. But he didn't complain. It didn't upset him.

There have been a lot of occasions when I've had to leave him. When I went to the fire academy, it was really sort of funny for a husband to drop his wife off when there were eighty or ninety men and a handful of women going to the academy. He said, "The old role of the man leaving the wife for the weekend is over. It's really different in our house."

A couple of times he has tripped over my fire boots by the door. He laughed and said, "Who'd believe me if I ever said, 'Yeah, I came home from work and tripped over my wife's fire boots!' "

He has been really good, very supportive, and he's proud of me, he really is.

□

The best thing to me in a firehouse is the fellowship. We have good rapport, and it's a learning type of situation for me at this point. Sometimes I just sit around and listen to guys with years of experience. That's enlightening because I've learned so much just from listening. Then to follow them on a job and see how they actually attack each situation, that has been even more beneficial to me. Hard workers and a good group of guys, everyone pulls his own weight. There's no coldness, no harshness.

The worst thing is hearing about firemen hurt or killed in the line of duty. Night watches never bother me, because I'm a night owl anyway. Some people don't like those last hours, two-thirty to five. I work straight through the night.

Cleaning is tough. A lot of times we have to do windows and mop floors. When I go home, it's hard to look my wife straight in the face and say, "Hey, I don't do windows." I don't have a leg to stand on, because if I do windows in the firehouse, it means I have to do them at home. But at least we're working in a clean environment.

If the police have people hired to clean the station, it makes sense to me, because they really don't have police who sleep in. But this is like a home to us, this is where we sleep. So it's really like taking care of your own house.

I don't think people realize the amount of work and the strenuous activity that firefighters do. They see the engines or trucks go by, and they think they're going to a fire, and that's the end of it. It doesn't occur to them the work that is involved in pulling a line and going into these fires and rescuing people, breaking windows just to let some smoke out.

They aren't aware of the hazards in the job. When they hear about a firefighter being hurt or killed, they think that it's a dangerous job—but on a general level. They really don't know the specifics and how really dangerous it is. They don't know about the pumping, and putting the engine in pump, and getting the pressure on. All they think is that you just hooked the hose up to a fire hydrant, you pull it toward the fire, and that's the end of it.

They'll see firefighters at the station maybe sitting on a bench or after they raise a flag. They ride by and say, "Oh, what a life." Or, "Oh, that's where my money to Uncle Sam goes."

Most of my experience in the job, thus far, has been in occupied dwellings, no big high rises yet. I get off the engine, and I'm dragging an inch-

and-three-quarter, and my adrenaline gets going. I'm on the tip, and this is my baby, this is my job, I know I'm going to do it. Maybe fifteen years down the road I'll change, but I don't think so. I think this is something that all firefighters feel. If they're on the tip, they know they're going to control this fire one way or the other. Either they're going to put it out or they're going to confine it. It gives you a lot of satisfaction. It really makes you feel it's you against the fire.

You come into battle with this fire, no matter how bad it is. A lot of times it's scary, because you look at a wall of flames and you think, "Wow, here I am armed with this little hose. I don't know if this is going to do the trick." But you know it always works out and you're always able to get the best of it. There's always someone right there with you. You're never alone. If you get too much smoke, everyone knows, and it's okay. Someone will step in and take over, and help you out in some way or other. It's not a question of, "Okay, here's the tip, and you're on your own, and go do it." Being on the tip is an aggressive type of job. You get in there, and you have to confront the fire, and you know you have a lot of help with you. You just do the job.

I got a Heroism Citation, and one of my fellow firefighters was really glad for me. And he congratulated me. But then he said, "That's it. It's downhill from here."

You know, that's the truth. It doesn't matter. You just do everything in routine, and you just kind of do the job as it comes along.

Chapter Four

FIREFIGHTING AND RESCUES

LARRY FITZPATRICK OWNED A BAR, SUSPENDER'S, ON THIRTY-eighth Street. He had several partners, all firefighters. Tom Neary, a friend I had worked with in Ladder 31, was the bartender. It was a great place, and I would stop in there frequently, much as the Amish people pay social calls—for the spirit of community and friendship. There were always firefighters in Larry Fitzpatrick's bar, and every time I would walk in he would say, "Here's another teabag." Larry called everybody he thought worth talking to a "teabag," and it was a compliment of a sort. He was a tough firefighter, squat, almost square with muscles, and strong enough so that he felt very secure in calling anyone anything at all. And he was the kind of guy who made new friends every time he met another firefighter. He worked in Rescue 3, in the Bronx, with Billy O'Meara, a guy I had worked with for years. Billy had been promoted to lieutenant out of Ladder 31.

It was a hot summer night. I had to work the day tour the following morning, and the phone rang just as I was getting into bed. I was living up on Eighty-fourth Street then. A friend called and told me to turn on the radio. Two firefighters had been killed in a Harlem fire, and the names weren't released pending notifications. I called my own firehouse, where the grapevine had carried the news. It was Larry Fitz and a probie.

I drove down to the bar, then. It was early morning, an hour or so past midnight. I was thinking of Larry's children. He had eight of them, and was known as a great father.

Danny Noonan, one of the partners, was there. He was crying, and put his arms around me, connecting, I guess, to the brotherhood of the job. We decided to drive up to the firehouse, just a few blocks from Yankee Stadium, and Danny put a few six-packs into a brown bag. There would be

151

guys off duty there, he knew, and they would appreciate a beer. It was a classy thing, I thought.

We went up to the top floor of Rescue 3. Billy O' was there, and a bunch of firefighters who had driven in as soon as they heard the news. Billy told us they had been on the roof of a five-story tenement. A young firefighter who had been working on the top floor, the fifth, had been separated from his boss, a lieutenant who happened to be Tom Neary, my friend and one of the most decorated men in the department. A back room lit up completely, and Gerry Frisby was caught. He was at a windowsill, yelling, and Rescue 3 heard him. The fire was lapping up the side of the building, licking over the rooftop. Bill Murphy tied his own small, forty-foot, personal rope to a pipe, attached it to his safety harness, and went over the rooftop.

He knew there was not much he could do, because the personal rope could not take the weight of two men. The manuals said it was to be used for escape purposes only, and only in extreme emergencies. But Murphy just wanted to be with Frisby, to reassure him, to calm him, and so he slid down. He wasn't going to let him be alone.

On the roof, Billy O' watched his men secure the ¾-inch 150-foot roof rope to Larry Fitzpatrick. There was no question about who was going to go down to pick up Frisby. Larry Fitz stepped right up, and he went over the roof, six stories above the solid concrete of the backyard below. Billy O' was looking down over the roof parapet. They lowered him down to where Murphy and Frisby were now framed by the fire. "I have him," Larry said to Murphy. Frisby held fast around Larry's neck, and they both became one, a kind of pendulum escaping the fire. Then something happened, no one knew what. It was an imperfect rope. It just snapped, and Fitz and Frisby fell.

It was hard for Billy O' to tell the story, we all knew, but we also knew that it was all in the family. It was the straight stuff, because there's no point in holding back from the family.

A few beers were opened, and the men relaxed a little. There was not much for any of us to do. Rescue 3 would have to prepare for the funeral, and all those official investigations and reports. But now the men just wanted to regain their breath.

Billy O' and I worked for a long time with a man named Ben Cassidy, who had been promoted out of Engine 82, and who was a good friend of

Larry Fitzpatrick. Billy suggested I call him, rather than have him hear the news in the morning from a radio or TV reporter.

I went to the phone to dial his number, and it then struck me. What if he's not home? What would his wife Chickie think about a phone call at three in the morning? What momentary pain would that cause? I wanted to hang up as the phone was answered. I heard her voice, and the first thing I said was "This has nothing to do with Benny." It turns out he was working that night as a covering officer, and had listened to the alarms as they came over the department radio.

Then I thought, who was going to ring the bell of Larry Fitzpatrick's house this sad night? And, what extraordinary pain would the ringing of that bell bring to so many people?

Dennis Smith

□

It was a five-alarm fire, a four-story building that had at one time been a manufacturing plant but now had a bar and a restaurant on the first floor and a menagerie of rooms upstairs. It was a gay bar, and the guy who owned the place was gay. The top three floors were his playground.

The night of the fire he picked up this kid over at the park, took the kid out, wined and dined him. The kid wanted money, but the guy didn't want to pay anything. So the kid beat him up and left him there in the building, left him for dead. He then set the fire to cover his behind.

I was acting battalion chief at the time, and I covered the fire on the second alarm. The first-alarm company got there and found the guy. He was all bloody. They laid him on the sidewalk at the side of the bar, and he kept saying that the boy was still in there. The police sent the dogs in. They found the kid and chewed him up a bit, but the firemen got him out.

The call that came in said they had a small fire on the second floor. Well, the first-alarm chief saw the smoke pumping out of the beams. No fire, but a lot of smoke coming out of the eaves on the fourth floor. He knew he had more than just a small fire, so he called for the second alarm. I was the second chief in and was assigned to the rear of the building. We were back there, and we had master streams in operation. About then the fire was blowing out all of the windows in the back and front and coming through the roof in one corner.

About an hour later the majority of the fire was out, so we shut the big lines down to get inside and do some interior firefighting. I had the company stretch hand lines and inch-and-a-halfs up the aerial ladders and into the windows. I was at the top of the ladder, and there was a guy from 18 Engine, Dick Fucha, who was having trouble with his air mask. He was below me on the ladder. The department had just switched over to a new self-contained air mask, and we were having problems with this one fitting where the face piece connected to the regulator. Fucha didn't have it just right. It kept popping loose on him.

"Well, look," I said, "get your mask straightened out. I'm going to go inside, and when you get done bring your line up and I'll meet you in there. I'll see what we've got to do." So he went back down.

I was on the fourth floor, and I looked into the window with my hand light to see the floor. It was black, all black. I straddled in, leg over windowsill, and had my feet on the floor. Real good sound floor, nice and solid. The darkness was pitch black, as black as it might be inside a collapsed mine shaft. I took two steps, and I started falling.

I just started falling.

Looking back on it when the doctor asked what happened and going back and looking at it after the fire, I figured out what had happened. But here I was, falling in this complete darkness. Halfway down, about thirty feet, I hit something, straddling it. Thirty feet and I stopped short between my legs. That was where I fractured my pelvis in four places. I momentarily stayed in that position, but the momentum of my fall kept me going off there and down another thirty feet. I was now down five stories, and in the basement. I landed on my back in about three feet of water. I landed hard, and I broke my back in two places. The doctor said that the mask on my back was what saved me. Without it I would have been killed.

I had fallen down an elevator shaft. The building was originally a factory where they made automobile tires. The shaft was for one of those huge freight elevators that you could drive a car into, and take it up to the different floors and have the tires changed on it. That window I had climbed into opened into the shaftway. The law says that windows opening into shafts must be barred, and I think it was originally barred, but the guy, when he bought the building, did all this renovation work up there, either on the sly or whatever.

What I was stepping on was a floor that was probably three feet wide with a steel beam around it, and the car would come up and stop at that floor, that's why it was still there. The elevator was caught in the fire and was burned out, like the whole bottom of the car was burned out. The only thing left of the car was the metal frame. It was the beam at the top of the elevator that I straddled and flipped off of at the second floor and fell through the elevator to the bottom, that second thirty feet.

So I was lying in three feet of water. I couldn't stand up, my legs wouldn't move, nothing. I said to myself, calmly, "Well, I'll just lie here." I'm lying there, then I realize I'm being pulled down. My coat is being saturated, and the weight of the coat started pulling me down, and down, and down. Suddenly, my nose is under the water. I was trying to float, but I couldn't because the coat was pulling me down and the boots were full of water and I couldn't stand. I was beginning to drown.

My regular job was captain of the rescue unit, and I knew about scuba and had a lot of water experience. I said, "Keep your cool, keep your cool. Don't panic. Get your coat off."

I was in no pain. I couldn't feel a thing. I was just worried about drowning. I went completely under water then, knowing it was my only chance, unsnapped my coat, got one arm out and got the other arm out. The coat dropped away, the heavy mask canister with it. I thought that would save me. Then I started reaching out, and I touched this wall. It was an unfinished wall, just plain bricks. I put my fingertips in the mortar joints and started pulling my head up. I realized I was in a corner, and I'm like, "There's got to be a way out of here."

So I started going around like this, pulling with my fingertips. I hit another corner, made another turn, and there was a ladder there, a ladder in the wall. "Great," I said, "stay here and wait." The water was still cascading in from the streams, getting deeper and deeper. "Great," I'm saying, "if the water rises, I'll rise with it up the ladder."

The next thing was, the smoke started banking down. I said, "Oh God. I'm going to suffocate." I started coughing, and I got down closer to the water. I was okay, I had this much room at first, and then the smoke was banking down farther and farther. I was down to the water again, my nose just touching it.

Then I could hear the debris falling. The first thing I thought was that Fucha had done the same thing I did. I went back and started feeling around to see if he's there. I heard people hollering up there. I heard Fucha holler in the window that the floor was going and that something was wrong. I still didn't know where I was. I lost my portable radio on the way down. They found that hanging between the second and third floor where a piece of metal was sticking out. I fell and I just missed the metal, but it grabbed the radio and pulled it off my coat. It was hanging there. I lost my helmet, and they later found a piece of it, the plastic eye protection part melted. It had fallen into the fire on the second floor, which was still burning up there.

Like I said, I hear all this debris falling, and I thought it was Fucha, and I went over to look to see if it was. I took a little step and realized that I just couldn't do it, I couldn't stand. So I started calling to see if it was him. Nobody answered.

Then I heard somebody holler, "There he is."

This guy Ed Rittles came down the ladder, and he started to touch me, and I said, "Don't touch me, something is broken."

He hollered, "Throw a rope down here."

I said, "No. Don't tie any rope around me, something is broken and I can't move my legs. I can't feel anything."

So they got the Stokes basket down there, a kind of wire basket moulded to the shape of the body, and they floated me on that, then lifted me up and out. They put me in the medic unit, and I went right to the shock trauma center.

I still don't remember a lot of it. I don't remember blacking out. There are times when I lie at home and I wake up and think, "Oh, that's right, that happened." The first fall, I didn't think that I was going to fall that far, it was only one floor. It's not going to be even twenty feet. It's not going to be that bad. It's not going to be thirty feet. I'm not expecting that I'm going down a shaft, you know, right to the bottom. And when I hit, it felt like I was falling longer than I should have, but it's pitch black and I can't see anything, so I'm not expecting it or anything. It's just falling into the darkness, and then when I hit, it was like, "Christ, oh God."

The beam went right up into my groin. When I started falling, I was worrying about being impaled, about falling into some debris and having a two-by-four go through me. When I hit with my legs apart, the pain was intense through my groin. I was black and blue from my knees to my chest, a dark purple. My privates were swollen the size of grapefruit, because the actual impact was right there. I thought, Hey, this isn't too bad, it's over, I'm still alive. And then I realized that I was falling again.

I still can't see anything. I haven't seen anything yet, no walls. I haven't felt anything other than hitting that piece, and then I'm going again. I didn't know I was in an elevator shaft. I had no perception of depth or how far I had fallen. I could have fallen five feet and hit something and then five more feet and been on the third floor. I had thought it was over, and I was falling again, and I realized, "No. It isn't over yet."

Another thirty feet. That's when I did the complete somersault from straight up and down when I first fell, and the beam catapulted me over, and I was falling back first, and that's when I impacted the water. And then it was like, "Oh damn, where am I now? What's going on?" In my scuba training I knew that when you first go down you're apprehensive and you start breathing faster and you get yourself worked up, and you have to calm yourself down. That's what I was doing.

I was like, "Okay, keep your cool, you know you're not dead, and you can get out of this." And then I started sinking, and I was like, "Oh, God, you're going to drown. You've got to get your coat off." The water was still coming in. I figure there were ten ladder pipes in service and maybe five two-and-a-half-inch hand lines, that's fifteen hoses shooting water in. Coming right down, you could hear it. It was like a waterfall. It's like, okay, I have the coat off and I'm not going to drown because I have the ladder. Then I thought, "God, it's filling up."

But I felt good holding on to the ladder. If the water keeps coming, I'd just float up with it, and I felt secure. Then the smoke started banking back down, and I started getting scared again. It was like you can't breathe, coughing. Like, let's get to the window. But, hell, I can't move. I can't go to a window. And I had no mask. So I got lower and lower, with my mouth and nose just above the water. It's breathable there. It's still pretty thick smoke, but it's not something that I'm not used to. Then like I said, I heard the debris falling.

I didn't know whether anybody knew that I'd fallen. I didn't know whether Fucha had come up the ladder or not. I had told him to come back up, but he could have gone down and had his assignment changed by another officer and just, you know, forgot about me. My relief wasn't due until seven, and this was about four-thirty in the morning. I'm thinking, this is it, this is the way I'm going to die.

Then finally I heard somebody holler, "There he is."

Like I said, there was no pain at that time. They got me in a medic unit, and that's when I started feeling pain. They put the oxygen on me, and I couldn't breathe. I kept ripping it off. The guy would put it on, I would rip it off. I pushed him against the wall in the back of the unit, and I said, "I can't breathe, don't put anything on my face."

The next thing I remember was being in the emergency part of the trauma center, and they cut off all my clothes. They were going back and forth on my vitals, and the pain came. I said, "Please give me something for the pain. It's unbearable. Do something, shoot me, give me something."

They said, "We can't do anything until we assess the damage." So they didn't give me any painkiller.

I started bleeding from my abdomen, and they put a bandage around me. Blood was pouring out, and they wanted to operate right then. Internal injuries. One doctor took the position, "We're going to cut this stomach open and see what's bleeding on the inside."

But another doctor said, "Call over to CAT scan and see if we can get him in there."

The next thing I know, this priest had come in, and he was giving me my last rites. I was like, "You're going to die." I still hadn't realized how severe my injuries were. I'm thinking that the pain is here, it's terrible, but it's not life-threatening. Well, it was.

My wife, Debbie, is out in the hallway, and she's crying. I look, and there's all the guys from the rescue crew out there, and they're lined up and down the hallway. The chiefs are there, and it's like, "Oh, for God's sake. Something's wrong here. They think I'm going to die."

They got me over to the CAT scan, and it came back, and they said, okay, there was some laceration of the kidney and the spleen, but they're not worried about that. What they're worried about is the back. They said, any movement from here on out and you're going to end up severing the spinal cord. And that's how close the fractures were to going right through.

They strapped me down with sandbags all over, and I couldn't move.

To me, it was like ten hours later before they finally gave me morphine. And when they gave me that, I'll tell you, I can see how these guys can go out of here and be junkies. The way that made me feel, I could have got up and walked on air. It was like, God, I know why these guys are junkies and they walk around like they don't have a care in the world. They don't. And that's the way that stuff made me feel.

They kept me in the emergency room, but they kept me well drugged, and they were bringing accident victims in all night. And I'm looking over, and they're cutting people up. It's like I didn't have a care in the world. I felt pretty good until I realized I was looking at my wife, and like I said, she was crying, and she really broke down.

A couple of firemen came in, and it seemed they were choking back tears, and that made me feel bad, even though I felt good that everybody was there and they cared about me and everything.

Debbie told me about the phone call she got from the fire department. She was sound asleep, and the phone rang. She said it was about five or five-thirty in the morning. The guy said, "It's so-and-so from the Baltimore City Fire Department, and your husband has been injured in a fire. He's in the shock trauma center. We're going to come out and pick you up. Do you have any children, or do you need anybody to babysit?"

That fatal phone call. It's what all the wives must think about. The guy didn't tell her how severe the injuries were or what happened, just that I was in the shock trauma center.

They came and picked her up, and she still wasn't really sure how bad it was going to be. Then she saw the guys from the rescue company outside the entrance to the hospital, and she said, "Oh, God, what are they doing here?" And then when she came inside and saw the priest and the commotion, she was like, uh-oh.

I had an I.V. in each arm and a catheter in my nose. I had a catheter coming out my mouth, and they had done a belly tap and I had a hose coming out there to drain my stomach. I'm lying there naked, still black with soot, embers in my hair the size of quarters, you know. She thought that they just wanted her to identify me, that's how bad I looked. I was unconscious at that time, and they told her to go outside and wait. I didn't see her until later.

Well, right away one of my really good friends who is a chief in the Tenth Battalion, Mike Dalton, he came in, and I was worried about my job. I was thinking, "Are they going to pension me for this?" Man, I sure didn't want to lose my job. The chief of the fire department came over, and he said, "Don't worry, we'll have a job for you. You get yourself back to where you can work, and we'll have a job."

So that made me feel real good. I mean, hey, they were going to do something for me, they were going to look out for me.

I'm still not back to work. I'm on administrative leave. My detail is an office duty job until I can get myself back to where I can go back to firefighting. I'll get there.

□

I had been at the hardware store with my wife and daughter, and we were going home, driving through a residential neighborhood. The first thing I noticed was the smell of the smoke. Black smoke was hanging over the street. I saw this lady in the front yard of a one-story frame house, screaming. As I pulled up, I could see the fire pushing out of one window at the front of the house and smoke seeping out of the two side windows.

I got out of my car and ran over to the lady. My wife and daughter followed me but didn't say anything. The lady said her husband was in the house and his name was Jim. I could hear the flames cracking. It was a pretty good fire in the living room and through the window next to the door, not pushing yet. Just bending, like the flames were swaying.

I never stopped. I went to the front door, and when I opened it, I immediately had to go on my stomach because of the smoke. I was wearing just Levi pants and a flannel shirt, because it was January. As I crawled through the front door, the heat was not too bad, but I could see the red glow to my right and up over my head. As I went forward through the room, there was some kind of electrical short or something, and the electric wires behind me started jumping and popping. That kind of concerned me.

I had my mouth right down on the floor, and it was beginning to be hard to breathe. I started coughing. I was getting in deeper and deeper, and there was a faint light to the left of me, and I took that as a way out. I found out later that it was a room and the light was coming in that way. So I was pushing in, and I was right at the point—this is something that has stayed in the back of my mind—I was right at the point where I had to make a decision: "Do I go deeper to the right and see if I can find this man, or do I go to the left and bail out?" I was coughing, and it was really bad, but I went right anyway.

Then I heard the man moan and say, "Help me." I don't really know what I was doing, it was like being desperate, but I started crawling toward him, and I kept crawling, and I heard him continue moaning. If I hadn't heard him calling and moaning, I probably wouldn't have found him, the smoke was too dense. Nothing was visible. I'd get to a chair and tell it was a chair only by feel, that type of thing.

When I got to him, he was lying on the floor. If he had been in a bed or something higher, he might have been dead, I don't know. He had a little bit of air to breathe down there. He said he couldn't walk, he couldn't get up. He was coughing. I knew I couldn't drag him back the way I came, because of the electrical short and the wires popping. You could still hear them popping. The glow was still over my head, and to the right of me the fire was up the wall and working its way across the ceiling. So I started dragging him straight to the left to get him away from that glow.

One thing I did have, I had a vent. The fire had blown out the front window, and it was venting naturally. That helped me. If I hadn't had the vent, things probably would have been different. The fire was bending out that window by the front door and was keeping it kind of confined. It was rolling, though. All the other windows were closed, it being wintertime. There was no smoke venting out, but at least the fire was bending towards that open window. So I kept dragging him as far away from the fire as I could, because the smoke was really getting to me.

Luckily, then I came across a wall, and then I felt a window. I couldn't see, but I could feel the outline of the window, and a little bit of light was coming through. I got hold of a stand or a little table. I took a pretty good breath down on the floor and raised up to knock the window out. I threw the thing at the window, but it was light and I didn't have much force behind it, because all I could think about was getting back down on the floor to get some air. The window didn't break, the thing just kind of bounced off. God, that was a disappointment.

I was choking and things were bad, but I remembered there was a telephone on that stand. So I grabbed the phone and the receiver, all in one hand, and broke the window that way.

By then, I could hear the fire engine coming down the street, and I could hear people. I guess the people heard the breaking glass, and they started coming around to where I was at a side window. They started taking out some of the glass which added oxygen. The fire began to break out again, now towards me. I knew I had to get my head outside that window. I got down then, got a couple of good breaths, pulled on this guy with whatever energy the smoke didn't take from me, and laid him across the window. He was tall but not real heavy, about a hundred sixty pounds, in his mid-fifties. By then, one of the firemen was there, and was I glad to see him. We just kind of threw the man out the window.

Then I tumbled myself out. When I came across the window, the glass went through my shoes and into my feet. Both arms were cut and bleeding. Except for the smoke inhalation, that was it.

My wife said she was very concerned for me, that it seemed like I was in there forever. I don't know exactly how long I was in there, but I don't think it was very long. They say it only takes a few minutes to kill you. My daughter was too young to be worried, but my son was very disappointed that he wasn't there to see it. He had decided to stay home and do his homework.

The newspapers played it up pretty big. I ended up with seven awards, I went to a lot of banquets. The public thinks a lot of firemen, they really do. I got more recognition from the public than I did from my own fire department. Sure, I got a pat on the back from the guys I work with, but one of the upper-echelon people just said, "Well, what's the big deal?" I didn't say anything, but I guess the only thing that matters is that I know it was a little bit hairy.

Not too long after that we went to a fire on Christmas night to a little house over where the lower-middle-class people live. We got there and it was a fire in the bedroom. Christmas night, nobody home. The people had gone visiting, just in the neighborhood, and had left on an electric blanket. It had ignited the room. So, we do our normal procedures. I'm in there searching again, and I find this little dog underneath the bed in one bedroom. The dog had been overcome by smoke. I grabbed the dog and took him out under my arm, put the resuscitator on him and got him breathing.

In the meantime the people returned.

The dog belonged to a little boy who had gotten him earlier that morning for Christmas. I gave the dog to him, and he was just thrilled. His face just lit up, he was so excited about getting his dog back. I turned around then and walked off. There was never anything said. I know you can't compare a human's life to that of a dog, but that meant more to me than pulling that man out of that fire. That was pretty moving to me, just to save that little dog. It really had to do with the dog's relationship to the little boy and with Christmas.

□

The fire was in a two-and-a-half-story frame dwelling. My company was on the second alarm, so when we got there the fire was well involved. I reported to the chief and went through the normal procedures. The whole upper floor, a converted attic, was on fire, and part of the second floor.

We took a two-and-a-half-inch hand line down the left side of the building to the rear kitchen—myself, my pipe man, and my leadoff man. The pipe man is the nozzle man. We take the line in dry to the place where we're going to use it—it's easier to maneuver without the water in the line. We get to the back kitchen, and I pick up my radio to call the pump operator to get water in the line. As it happens when there are so many additional alarms, it gets so busy that the pump operator is swamped with calls, and radio communication is the biggest problem.

First I sent out my lead man, then I went out, and I told the pump operator to put water in the line. I waited a minute to make sure that he did, because sometimes they are so busy they don't always comprehend what's going on. As soon as the two-and-a-half got charged up, I straightened out a couple of kinks and started back along the side of the building. I felt a couple of embers or wood brands dropping, and I just kind of pulled my shoulders up and dropped my head and just kept moving.

Then, bam. Instantly the whole world stopped. It seemed the entire building dropped, and it came right down on me. It was unreal. The whole left side of the building and the roof came down. It just kicked out. I had never heard of this happening before, but since then I have read articles about the collapse of frame buildings and how fast they just kick out.

I straightened up, and I could feel all of my weight pushing back as hard as I could, and there was just no way that I could stop it. Thank the Lord, right where I stood was a tree and a fence that ran down the side of the property. I must have swung around so I was right at the tree, and when the wood and the roof came down it hit the tree and acted like a lean-to. And instead of squashing me flat, it just pushed me down into the tree and wedged me down there.

I was facedown into the roots of the tree, which was about eight or ten inches in diameter. The weight of the falling building just snapped it over, and I was wedged against it. But my arm was up, like half over the fence. I don't know if I had tried to leap over the fence or what, but the arm was pinned separately from the rest of my body. The other guys thought I was dead, for sure. I had to be. It was just unreal, the amount of debris that was piled on top of me. The radio on my hip was caught in an open position. Afterwards the chief said it was the one thing that showed I was still alive. All they could hear was a string of good, rotten words, one after another.

I was in severe pain. Terrible pain. I thought, "This is it, this is the end of the world." My ribs, my side, my arm, everything was hurting but my head. My head wasn't hurting, or if it was I couldn't feel it. "God, I hope they get me out of here," I thought. I was trapped, no way I could move even an inch. I'm a good-sized fellow, and I'm wedged against the tree into the ground. There is all this roof and wood piled on me. Luckily, there was no fire right in that area. The fire was still maybe four or five feet behind me.

I began to think about a secondary collapse. The way it was piled on me and the tree, I thought, "If this son of a gun drops, I mean, that's it." There was no way I could hold any more weight: if it let loose a second time, I would have been gone. For a few minutes I talked to God. "Well, sure, I'm going to die," I told him. I didn't know how badly I had been injured. I just knew I had been hurt so bad it was beyond hurting.

The first guy over to me was a captain in the fire investigation bureau. He called, "Ho, Will, are you okay?" I said, "Yeah, get me out of here." In our job, if you're not dead, you're okay.

The fellow in charge of the rescue company was Alan Thompson. He came over, and naturally everyone wants to help, and all of a sudden you have a mob of people there, and some of the fellows are coming up on top of the stuff that's on top of me. I could feel more pressure. I thought, "Jesus Christ, get off of the collapse."

Everything gets chaotic. I mean I'm pinned under there, and I can picture in my mind everybody running around and everybody trying to help. That's the first thing when one of yours is down. Everybody wants to get in. I've been on a number of rescues of civilians, but when it's one of yours it's just a little bit different. There's a little more adrenaline flowing. Everybody was just disregarding everything else, trying to get in as quickly as possible.

I heard somebody say, "Truck Company, get a saw." And the company answered, "Our saw's down in the shop." I thought, "Oh, crud, here I am trapped, and their saw is down in the shop." A couple of things went through my mind down there. The first thing I thought was, "Oh, God, let me just get back with my family. Just one more shot. Just give me another shot at it."

Finally the Rescue Company sets up the airbags, which were new in the department at the time. They were to stabilize the rest of the building so it wouldn't come down. Now I was concentrating on their methods to get me out. They got a couple of saws going, and they started cutting the fence down to get in to me. I said to Thompson, "Al, Al, hold up a minute. My arm's pinned separately." I just pictured them cutting this fence and grabbing me and pulling me out, and my arm was going to stay there. All I could think of was, "God Almighty, if they pull me out and leave my arm there, I would rather just stay."

It took them about thirty minutes to get everything under control, to get me out. That's how long I was trapped, and I stayed conscious the whole time. I never really screamed. I tried to stay as calm as I could, hoping that would help them in extricating me a little quicker than otherwise. The lieutenant said afterward that I said a couple of things that didn't make sense to him. Maybe I was going out of my head a little bit, I don't know, but that was his terminology. I thought I handled it pretty well.

One of the funny things I thought afterwards was, "Damn, this is my last night in." It was the end of a four-night trick. Then we get two tricks off in a row. We have Kelly days with double Kelly days, and we call them Double Apples or Double Bubbles. It went through my mind, "Goddamn, this is my last night in, and I'm going on a Double Bubble. I have two weeks off, and I'm going to be messed up." It's one of the things I can remember vividly while I was buried.

They had to drag me out. They raised and secured the wood that was lying over me enough so that they could slide me out. Only then could they stabilize me on a backboard. It was a big job because I'm six-two and weigh 240. The guys said afterwards, "God, Will, don't get trapped again. You'll kill us getting you out again." The doctors at the hospital say my size is one of the things that helped save my life. I mean, I'm a big man, and I'm big-boned, and as this stuff came down on me I tightened up to keep it from crushing me.

So they got me out to the ambulance. The two paramedics were excellent. They went over me, and, of course, I was hurting bad, and one of them says, "Will, I'm going to have to give you an I.V. now, and this needle is going to hurt." I thought, "God, I hurt so bad, pal, there is no way that you could hurt me more."

We started off for shock trauma, which is down at the University of Maryland, a good three- or four-mile ride. It would have been much quicker if they had waited for a helicopter to come in from the state police. I'm lying on my side because they knew that I had internal injuries on the right side, so they kept me on the other side because that was the most comfortable position for me to be in. We were going down, and we were bouncing, and I'm saying, "Oh, man, I wish the mayor would have taken care of these potholes." These things were just killing me, each bump.

We get down to shock trauma, where they take you down the back way right next to the Dumpster. The shock trauma team came down. These people are really terrific. One of the male nurses was a friend of mine, and when they opened the back of the ambulance, I can remember him saying, "Hey, Will, what are you doing here?"

I looked up and said, "I just stopped by to say hi, Terry."

Up at shock trauma on the third or fourth floor, they said, "Will, we're going to have to put tubes in your sides, you've got internal bleeding. This is going to hurt." The same thing went through my mind: "I'm hurting so bad now that you can't hurt me." But they could.

They found that I had nine broken ribs, a broken back, and a collapsed lung. The lung was also torn and ripped, evidently from the ribs. They had to put two chest tubes in. Anyway, this fellow Terry said, "Will, do you want us to notify your wife?"

I said, "Oh, God, yeah, you have to do that, but call her on the phone." It's a standard thing in the family. We had talked about death at times, but we put that somehow in good humor. The wife has always been conditioned that when the doorbell rings and you open up and there's a chief standing there, you know you're in a world of trouble. I could just picture in my mind the department sending the battalion chief at three in the morning—the doorbell rings, my wife gets up and sees this white hat standing on the front porch. She would have collapsed.

Luckily they got one of the nurses to call my house. Joann answered the phone. The nurse said, "Mrs. Thompson?" Right away Joann had a sinking feeling, she told me, because both girls were home, and she knew it had to be me. There was no other reason to call at that hour. The nurse said, "This is shock trauma calling. We have your husband in here."

Joann said her knees went weak and she could just feel herself almost going out. The nurse said, "He has chest pains." Which was right, no exaggeration really. Except, of course, you relate chest pains to heart attacks. My wife said, "Chest pains. What the hell is he doing in shock trauma?" She had been around the fire department all her married life, and she knew the terminology.

Joann didn't really know what to do, she didn't want to wake up the girls because she didn't know what the situation was or how serious, so she called my partner, the fellow I'm in the seafood business with. He's also a city firefighter. So he came over and got her.

Meanwhile, the department notified the battalion chief, who knows me personally, to go out to my house and tell my wife. He said there was no way he was going to do that when he didn't know the facts of my situation. When the wife says, "How bad is it?" and you say, "I don't know," well, that's terrible. So he came right over to shock trauma, and they told him what they knew. Well, my wife arrived with my partner, and the chief could cancel his trip.

They let her come up to the unit to see me. She had to put on a gown, mask, everything. She stood there for about five minutes, and I was conscious the whole time, so that really helped considerably. She said, "Are you okay?" And I tried to say something humorous. They had cut my clothes off, and all they had was a towel draped over me. I said, "If I was, I wouldn't be here." I tried to make her feel better, but she knew that as soon as you say shock trauma, right away that gives you a shiver, because this is where they take the worst ones.

The department treated her terrific during this time. Chief O'Connor and Deputy Chief Delamo made a departmental car available to her. They would pick her up and bring her down to see me. They waited, and when she came out they took her right back home. If she had any other problems, all she had to do was call, and they took care of it. And that made me feel good, lying there and knowing that somebody else really cared.

My daughters were upset, too, but not as much. Here's Dad, invincible. All these years had gone by and Dad hadn't had any problems, and all of a sudden, bam, a building is down, and now Dad is down. They were eighteen and nineteen years old. Afterwards, the conversation would be like,

"Why don't you get out, Dad? You've paid your dues. It's getting tough on you. It's a young man's job."

I'll be the first to say that. I was in shock trauma twenty-one days and off the job for eleven months. Then I came back on regular duty, and I've been working ever since. At times, I hurt. Particularly when I'm wearing a mask at a fire. For two days after, my shoulders hurt, my back hurts, my side hurts from wearing the tank and just the general punishment you go through.

But I'm not ready to go out yet.

□

I did a lot of EMS in the Hamilton Fire Department when I was in college. I became a ski patrolman my freshman year, took advanced first aid. I became a fireman the next summer and began the EMT course in the fall. I originally wanted to become an EMT for ski patrol. I was an EMT by the spring of my sophomore year. I took my EMT 2 training in Utica and my paramedic training in Albany.

I remember very well one of the first calls I ever got. It was the first snow of the season, and a couple of kids skipped school and went out riding on a snowmobile. They were crossing a road on this snowmobile, and they got clipped by a VW Rabbit. Two kids, twelve and thirteen. We were called to the scene.

The snowmobile was there, and one of the kids was lying close to it, but the other kid was fifty or sixty feet down the road. There was a trail of blood all the way down to him, and he was DOA. The first kid had a pulse. So we started doing CPR, and at the first chest compression the blood just gushed out. I had seen broken legs, but this was very gruesome. It was a heavy-duty accident. Finally there was no pulse.

At that time we didn't have much cardiac capability, not even a resuscitator. We did the best we could, we put him on a backboard, and got him to the hospital, trying all the time. We couldn't revive him.

I was in the hospital for quite a while, getting our equipment back. I was there when the parents came in, two sets of parents. They had assumed that the kids were in school, they didn't know that the kids had skipped school to go play with a snowmobile. The response of the parents—I got goosebumps, and I felt tingling in the back of my head. They just collapsed. No one appreciates the word grief until they see how parents respond when they find out their child has died.

I remember calling my mother that night just to convey the story to her and to touch base with that part of myself.

□

It was the Standard Oil bulk plant. That's a complex of storage tanks holding fuel for various consignees, part of the delivery setup. They had about a hundred thousand gallons of gasoline and fifteen thousand in diesel fuel. And they had a big warehouse full of greases and oils and other petroleum products.

The bad thing about that plant was that they had horizontal tanks instead of vertical. Most storage tanks hold thirty thousand gallons, and they sit vertically on a concrete pad. So if you have a fire around them, you have a hazardous situation, all right, but nothing you can't handle, because the fire can't really get them hot enough. You can keep them cool. Also, if they're holding a lot of fuel, the fuel will tumble inside the tank, and that will help cool them, too.

In our particular case, the tanks were horizontal, about seven feet off the ground. So what they acted like was a big cooker. And we had a fire under one of them. And, my God, what do you do with something like that? If that tank had ruptured, we would have lost a minimum of twenty firemen. And if it blew toward town, we probably would have had two blocks of instant fire.

The fire had started out as a small, controlled burn of grasses in the yard. When we made the call, there was no fire in the warehouse, though the fire had sneaked underneath the warehouse and gotten involved there. We stripped off panels to get down in there, and I stepped outside to bring a truck around to that side, and, my God, I heard this explosion. I turned around and looked. Right where I had been in that warehouse was solid fire. If I had waited another minute, I'd have been right in that damn thing.

Now we had a fire under a tank, and the hell with the warehouse. We had to keep that tank from rupturing. We had five two-and-a-half-inch lines trained on that one tank, everything we had. I had firemen at both ends of that tank, holding hose lines. And, boy, not one of them broke. They hung right in there. And we were able to keep it from blowing.

□

I've been on quite a few medicals. When the alarm comes in, I drop everything. All my gear's already in my car. Depending on where it's at, I either respond to the scene or to the hall, whichever is closer. Recently we were sitting down to a big family dinner. I had my parents over, and my sister and her husband. We had just sat down to eat when my tones went off. It said there was a man down on the street, only a quarter mile from my house.

So I jumped up from the table and said, "Sorry, guys." And I took off.

When I got to the scene, a man was lying on the front lawn having difficulty breathing, unconscious. Within two minutes he went into full arrest. I was the only one there. The police, fire, and ambulance had not yet responded. So I took it upon myself to do one-man mouth-to-mouth and CPR. I revived him. The oxygen came, and they transported him to the hospital.

I was told that I did make the difference, that this man would not have lived if I had not started CPR on him. That's unusual to have a save, because it doesn't happen in the field very often. If I had waited, or if I had gone to get a truck, which was about four and a half miles away, I never would have made it back in time to save him from possible brain damage, or even to revive him.

He was a young man, like thirty-two, and he had two little children. His wife was so thankful, and that was really neat.

It was quite a bit later that I got back to the family dinner.

□

I was working the night shift at Fire Patrol 1 when the box came in, and we responded at the same time as the fire department. On the Twenty-second Street side of this old loft building was a lamp store, filled with heavy smoke and high heat. We started to go in for our salvage operation, and one of the firefighters said, "Patrol, there's no sense going up there, because the heat is too high." So we backed down.

There was nothing for us to do at that point because the fire hadn't been located yet, just the heavy smoke and high heat. So our officer sent three of us around to the Twenty-third Street side, Pete Pearly, Bob Sampson, and myself. The fire companies came around too, Engine 18 and Ladder 3 and one other.

One of the battalion chiefs told us to force the door of a store on that side of the loft building, a lingerie store. We did that, and the store was clear. No smoke. We came out and went next door to Wonder Drug. The door was already forced, and there were fire companies in the cellar. Royal Fox was one of the lieutenants there. The drugstore was clear. We went down in the cellar to see if there was any salvage operation that we could do. There was nothing. The cellar was clear of smoke. The firemen were pulling ceilings in the back where there was a cinder block partition.

We went back upstairs to the drugstore level and started to check it out. We felt the walls, and the wall in the rear was very hot. But there was no smoke. There was fire in the walls and flooring, but nothing was visible. I learned later that nine successive layers of flooring had been laid there, and that acted as insulation for a time.

As we were going out, a chief's aide was coming in, and we told him what we found. He said, "Yeah, we're bringing a line in." A couple of guys from 18 Engine were bringing the line in, there was a probie and a guy outside the door feeding the line in. I knew the location of these men as I passed them.

We walked out, went next door, and started up the staircase to go above the fire to see if there was anything we could do, and a fellow from 12 Truck said, "Patrol, get out of here, the heat's building up, and it sounded like there were cracks." We took off down the stairs, and the minute we hit the street, the drugstore just lit up. Heavy flames. A pure white flame. Super heat.

Guys were tugging on the line Engine 18 had taken into the basement. We ran over and tried to help, but we couldn't pull it. Guys from Ladder 3 were coming out. Lieutenant Fox was burned on the ears and I don't know where else. Everything happened so fast. Nobody knew what really happened, or who was in there, or if anybody was missing.

I tried to tell some chief that I had an idea of where the men were, but in the excitement he pushed me away, like I was somebody who didn't exist. I didn't realize the building had collapsed. I didn't hear anything, all I saw was the pure white flame coming out. So Bobby Sampson, Pete Pearly, and I went to the store on the other side of the drugstore, which was a camera store, and we went down in the cellar. I knew there was a truck company in the drugstore basement, Ladder 3, and an engine company, I didn't know which. I figured, if they're where I think they are and if they're alive, we can breach this wall and get to them.

There was a wooden partition along that wall, and when we got behind it, we saw that the foundation was built of boulders. We started at it with a pickax, and Chief DiAngelis heard the sounds. He came down, thinking they were tapping noises from the trapped men alive in the cellar next door. He didn't see us at first behind the partition, then we showed ourselves and explained what was going on. Then our own officer came down, and he had me go up and talk to Commissioner Lowery. I drew maps of the drugstore layout and showed where the men might be. We went to the basement next door again and went over it again with Chief DiAngelis. I had no pencil or paper, so I drew my map on a cardboard box with a nail. I really didn't feel that the men were dead at that time. I thought there was hope.

Then the chief said, "All right, everybody get out of here." I started to leave, and he said, "No, Patrol, you stay." The rescue company came down, I remember it was definitely Rescue 2 and maybe another company. I pointed out to them the two places where I thought the men might be. They brought down jackhammers, and they had to rig slings with rope from the beams, so that they could wield the heavy jackhammers against the wall.

When they opened the hole, that's where a couple of the men were. Barry from Ladder 7, I remember seeing him. And Lieutenant Finlan. They were burned, legs and arms. So we found a couple right off the bat. As the night went on, and the next day, they started to pick them out from upstairs, too. There were twelve who died in this fire, the largest in the history of the New York Fire Department at one incident.

I stayed on the scene for two days, just doing what everyone else was, making a chain, passing debris, until all the men were found. I saw a lot of love, a lot of family. There were firemen there from all the boroughs, not just Manhattan. It was like one whole family just came together like bees to a hive. They all took their turn on the line. It was a real sad scene.

To see six firemen carrying out another dead brother in a wire basket and everybody taking their helmets off as the body passed by was sad. Some of them—grown men—were crying even though most of them didn't know the guy. It didn't matter, he was their brother. Like being in battle and seeing one of your comrades go down, you take care of your own. Outsiders don't realize, even my wife doesn't understand the comradeship and the closeness. There's really a family in the fire department.

I saw a fireman's wife outside, crying. Later, after the funerals, she took the time to write me a letter, thanking me. I really think that going through the wall was the quickest way to get to the trapped men. When Chief DiAngelis wrote me up for a department medal, he stated in his report that I had pinpointed exactly where the men were. That made me feel good. I had felt bad initially when I was pushed away by a member of the department. Later on, I saw the reason: it was just the excitement and confusion. I think he was in a state of shock himself.

The ordeal took its toll on me. I went back to the fire patrol house and stayed there for a whole day, sleeping.

At the funeral, the fire patrol was stationed up front, right in front of St. Patrick's Cathedral. I guess that was kind of an honor. To this day, I couldn't say if it was a rainy day or snowy day or what. It was sad to hear the muffled drums and to see the lines and lines of firefighters who came from all over the country. It was a big shock for everyone to see the apparatus carrying the deceased members coming south down Fifth Avenue, first to the Protestant churches, then to St. Patrick's. It was quite an experience.

□

It was a cold night in January. I was home, we had just finished dinner and done the dishes, and I was going to sit down and watch a James Bond movie on TV. At the time I was working two nights a week in Albany training paramedics. I was walking from the kitchen, and I saw headlights on our front lawn. We have a small dirt driveway and a path to the house, but this person didn't see that and drove onto the lawn.

There was a knock on the door, and a woman, standing there, said, "Excuse me, can I use your phone to call the fire department?" She was very calm.

I said, "I'm a fire chief, what seems to be the problem?"

She said, "There's a house down the road that's on fire, and I don't know if there's anybody in there or not." She wasn't a local woman but was only renting a house nearby. She didn't know the name of the road where the fire was. She agreed to take me back there and show me the way.

I threw on a jacket and a pair of sneakers and ran down to my car. I radioed the fire control center at County Dispatch to activate the fire company and have the guys head out our way. In retrospect, I think that was an important move, to get the guys going. They all got there in reasonable speed.

I came around the bend on State Road 66, and all of a sudden the house was right there, only three quarters of a mile from my house. I knew the house and the neighbors who lived there. It was an old, rundown farmhouse, with a ramp in front. When I pulled up, the fire was through a corner of the house and already up through the roof. The whole second floor was going, venting through the roof. I radioed the position. I threw off my coat and sneakers, put on my turnout coat and bumber boots, grabbed my helmet from the back of the car. I went around the house, just to size it up.

I knew I couldn't make entry through the front, because the windows were popping, they were blowing out as I was going around the house. The first thing I thought was, I need water, I've got to have water. There was a creek across the road, with a good six to eight inches of ice on it. We had just gotten a new four-wheel drive pumper, and the only way it could get to the creek was to drive across a cornfield, but I was sure it could make it. I radioed those orders, and I was joined by Sam, my chief. Then Fire Dispatch radioed that they had reports that people were still inside the structure. The house was now a flaming ball, fire was showing all through the front of the house.

Sam and I went running around to the back of the house, which was venting heavy black smoke. We heard murmuring inside, and Sam said, "My God, they're in there."

We both made a run for the back door. He had no turnout gear on, just a helmet. As soon as I hit the door, I crawled. Sam didn't get down quick enough and took it right in the face. He had to back out. There was a good thermofire in there, because as I dropped I felt the temperature go down. It was still breathable on the floor. The whole time I was screaming out to him, and he was screaming in to me, just to keep contact. I had no portable radio, no hose line, nothing.

I was crawling in through the house, as far as I could go. I had my helmet on, with a flashlight strapped to it. But it was hard to see. Suddenly I was crawling right on top of this woman. Her eyes were open, she was just kind of sitting there, and there was a lot of black mucus on her face and coming out of her nostrils. I was dumped on, because in earlier fires the only people I had been asked to go in and get were dead as doornails.

So I grabbed her and dragged her back across the floor to the door, and I got her out to Sam. While I was in there, I sensed there was still someone else in the room, nothing specific, just sensed it. So I said to Sam, "There's someone else in there, and I'm going back in." So Sam took the woman and carried her down the road away from the house, because at that point the flames were banking down and melting the snow by the doorway there.

So I went back in and crawled in the same direction that I had before. I came to a loose stack of firewood, and I was trying to get around it when I looked up and saw this big, big woman standing in a corner, pinned there by the flames, which were now about head level. I reached up for her, and probably because of smoke inhalation she suddenly went down like a load and was out.

So I grabbed her by the scruff of her nightgown behind her head, I cradled her head in my right arm, which is my dominant arm, and I turned to go back out. I didn't have far to go, because this room was a small add-on to the back of the house. But now the whole wall through which I had come, instead of being smoky, was all of a sudden just a wall of orange. It's the orange that firefighters look for when they're chasing smoke, but it was the last thing I wanted to see, because I wanted to get out with this lady. It was so intense I really couldn't figure out what it was. I said, "The door has got to be here."

I felt trapped, and for a second, I thought, "This might be it. This might be the last time." But Sam and I were still yelling to each other, and he knew I was still okay because I was hollering to him from the floor. I yelled, "I got her. I'm coming out."

He said, "Ed, this way. Come this way."

I wasn't particularly gentle with the woman. I think I had her torso airborne, and when I got to the door I had to be basically standing. I didn't crawl out the door. I lunged through the door, the woman and I locked together, going through a wall of flame. I don't think it was a flashover. Sometimes fire just consumes. I'm glad I didn't hit the frame of the door.

When we hit the ground, I bounced away. I was face down on the snow. I can still feel the coolness of that, going from fire into snow.

I lay there, and there was a very heavy feeling in my chest. A girl I used to date was there, with her whole family. She came to me and rolled me over. She said, "Ed." I said, "Kathy." I didn't say anything else to Kathy, because I knew I had to keep going. The women I had rescued were badly hurt, and there was no EMS on the scene yet.

I got up and made my best time over to my car. I grabbed a resuscitator from the back of the car. By that time another emergency medical technician was there, Susan VanEgghen, chief of the local rescue squad. With our two resuscitators, we gave oxygen to both of these ladies. The ambulance was there very quickly after that, and they were off to the Berkshire Medical Center.

Sam almost talked me into going to the hospital. We both had inhaled smoke. And when Sam had gotten hurt, his helmet fell off, and by the time he got back to it, it had burned up. We had trouble with the water and ice, and I really felt I had to stay. From a firefighting tactical standpoint, we had a bad time. We lost a lot of water. The ultimate sin in rural firefighting is to lose water. We ended up losing the house.

The first woman I brought out was a cripple, a paraplegic. She had had multiple sclerosis for years. It was clear, in retrospect, that the other woman was probably her companion. She probably dragged her as far as she could until she became disoriented and trapped. Her legs were burned.

For a couple of days I knew I had gotten it pretty good, a very tight feeling in my chest, like my lungs were made of concrete. But I wasn't burned, I had no long-term effects from it. There was only a hole in the back of my turnout coat.

I got a $3,000 award from *Firehouse* magazine, and I did the natural selfish thing. I went out and bought myself a VCR. I put another thousand toward med school and general expenses. I also felt I should do something to pay back the two fire companies, Tri Village and Hamilton. Hamilton was doing a lot of EMS work because the local ambulance had gone out of business. So I bought them a set of military antishock trousers, which are used to stabilize trauma patients. They can make a big difference, because they were waiting fifteen or twenty minutes sometimes for an ambulance to come into the village.

I didn't know what to get my home company. So what I finally did, I sent them a check for $500 with a note saying it was to be used however the officers wanted to use it. They have been using it to modify tankers to get water more quickly.

□

I had just gotten my EMT verification in the mail, and I was excited about it. Not ten minutes later, I responded to the hall for a medical emergency. I got into the truck, and there were two guys in there with me. They just sat there waiting. I thought of my good news, and I said, "By the way, guys, I just got my EMT verification in the mail." And all of a sudden the truck took off. "That's what we were waiting for," they said. "An EMT."

So we're going down the road, and I'm trying to get my mind prepared, going down the list, oxygen, medical kit, suction. Then everything just started to gel, all my training and all my books, and I knew I was ready. I knew what I had to do in case of a heart attack or any other emergency.

When we got to the scene, I was excited and grabbed all my equipment and walked into the house. There was a gentleman sitting in a chair. This man had been dead for at least twelve hours. Rigor mortis had already set in. My trained eye noticed that the blood had pooled, and I said to myself, "Oh, well, I can't save *this* guy."

One of the guys came up to me later and said, "You did a good job on him, Kathy." And I felt so embarrassed. I had been so excited, and it just didn't happen the way I wanted it to.

I had a case recently where a lady died. She had gone into full arrest, and we responded to the call. We started CPR and gave her oxygen. The whole time we were driving to the hospital, I kept thinking to myself, what a beautiful woman this must have been. She was seventy years old, and her husband, who was following the ambulance, was in his seventies, too. And you could just tell that the two of them had been together for a long time.

I get very personal with these people in my mind. Even though she was not responding to the CPR, I kept her hair out of her face, and I made sure that she was comfortable. And the ride was pretty rough on me, a lot of curves and some bumpy roads. But I felt that if I was going to be the person to be with her in the last few moments of her life, I was going to make sure she was happy and comfortable.

I talked to her in my mind, like mental telepathy, telling her that her husband was right behind us, that he must love her very dearly, and not to worry about anything, that we were doing the best we could. And I touched her face, just rubbing her cheek, and for being as old as she was, she was so soft. I could just imagine what a wonderful woman she must have been in her life.

They continued the CPR in the hospital, but there was no response, and she never came around. But I felt good, I really did. Maybe it's all in my mind, but I felt that I made a difference in her life to her.

I would sure like somebody like me with me when I die. I really would like someone to care. And I hope that I never lose the sense of human touch . . . and care.

□

It was Christmas Day, Christmas before last. I had worked nighttime, eleven to seven, and I had just come home from work. I was having some coffee with my mother, and the radio alarm came in, saying, "Reported structure fire, occupants trapped." I drove to the firehouse, only a couple of miles up the road, and since there was no traffic that early in the morning I was the first one there. I saw the column of black smoke only a few blocks from the station, and I knew it was a bad one. The radio said the police were already there.

I got geared up while Assistant Chief Bonnevich and driver Shumate arrived. So we hopped on the engine and drove to the scene. We saw good-sized flames shooting up in the air toward the street. People told us they had seen people at this bedroom window, but they weren't there anymore. The window was on the second floor, above a garage.

There was a ladder there, and the chief told me to go ahead and use it to get to the window. I climbed up, but fire was coming through the garage door, so I had to jump back down. He went to get an inch-and-a-half to knock that down, and I got another inch-and-a-half to try to make the doorway. Well, I couldn't do that, but he had his fire knocked down, so he said, "Come on, get back up there. Let's try it."

I got up there, the window was already broken by the heat, and I hopped through. The window was so small that, after the fire, the guys said, "I don't know how you fit through there." It was divided into panes by metal strips that you couldn't break unless you had the right tool. So I jumped through there and landed on a bed. And the room was totally black—black like you never experienced, not even when you put tape over your mask for training.

I got low to the floor, staying close to the wall, trying to go over in my mind everything I was trained to do in this situation. My job was to go in, look for victims, and rescue, if possible. I crawled along the wall, felt under the bed with my left hand while keeping my right hand on the wall. I came to the foot of the bed, and I felt something on the floor, real spongy, kind of moist, like Playdough or Silly Putty.

I picked it up, and it was kind of heavy, but I didn't know what it was. I dropped it, and you could hear it thump. Then I picked it up again, and I could feel that it was a person. I had picked up the arm. The bedroom doorway was near there, and she had tried to get out the doorway, but she had dropped right there. I tried to pick her up—talk about dead weight, that was really dead weight. She only weighed about 120 pounds, but she felt like a ton.

I couldn't throw her over my shoulder for a fireman's carry, so I had to bear-hug her with all my strength and drag her back toward the window. And she was slipping away from me. I got another grip, using all my strength, and carried her toward the window, where the bed was. I started to hyperventilate from the excitement and exertion, and I had to take a break. So I set her down on the bed.

I was breathing so heavily that my mask couldn't keep up with me until I could regain my composure and slow my breathing down. I said to myself, "Okay, this is what you're supposed to do. Come on, you can do it." The whole house was involved. The fire had started in the basement and traveled through the whole house. The only rooms not burning at the time were two bedrooms, the one I had entered and the one beside it.

So I regained my composure, got her in a bear hug again, and put her out the window. At first I thought I had thrown her out and she had fallen to the ground. That was all I needed! The smoke was billowing out the window, I couldn't see two feet in front of me. And I thought, "Oh, my God, there's nobody here to help me." I was yelling, and I lifted my face mask to yell louder. My body was so demanding of oxygen that I accidentally took in some hot air and gases.

The woman had been sort of hanging out the window, then all of a sudden she wasn't there.

The truck company had arrived and put up their own ladder, but they couldn't see much better than I could. They just happened to reach out and feel the woman's arms, and they just took her without me even knowing it. So then she wasn't there, and I thought to myself, Well, it's time to get out.

I climbed over the windowsill onto the ladder I had used to get up there. I started to step down, and there was a rung missing. I hadn't seen the fire department ladder, so I was on the wrong ladder. I lost my balance and fell backwards about fifteen feet, landing on the air bottle on my back. They thought I had spinal injuries.

They dragged me up on the sidewalk, cut the air pack straps, put on a cervical collar, and strapped me on a backboard. I don't remember anything until I was on the backboard. I started coming to, and they said my eyes were all glassy and rolled back. Then I started to cough severely, bringing up black mucus. Just one or two breaths of gas and hot air was enough to do that.

I kept asking about the woman, is she okay, is she okay? They said they were doing CPR on her in the next house. They put me in the first ambulance, because they were afraid I had a broken back. They put her in the next one.

I was in a daze. I remember the lights flashing over my head as they wheeled me down the hall at the hospital. Then the doctor and a group of nurses worked on me, getting my clothes off, examining me, drawing blood, hooking up IVs, putting oxygen on me. It was a mass of work being done on me all at once. It was really confusing. I was in the hospital for two days. I had a minor shoulder bruise from landing cockeyed, but basically it was for smoke inhalation.

I still had no fear, I still didn't worry about how bad a situation I had been in. The only time I came to that realization was when a fire chief with about twenty-five years in the service said it was the worst fire he had ever seen, and he couldn't believe that I had gone in there.

I was happy to hear that the woman was still alive, though she had to go to a burn center. But I felt kind of guilty because there were two other people in the house who did perish, her daughter and her husband. I hadn't known they were in there. The woman is now living out of town with the rest of her family. She never came to the firehouse, but I did meet her son, and he thanked me.

I heard that the woman was shock-blind for a while. She was in so much shock that she was blind. She later got her sight back.

I guess God had a plan for me, and I did what he wanted me to do. I feel closer to him. I have no fear of dying if that's how God wants me to go. What I do fear is the day when I'm faced with a really bad fire and I say to myself, hey, that's even too bad for you, there's no way you can go in there. Am I going to go in there and maybe die, or catch myself before I react? I'll be testing myself.

I kept replaying the fire. The guys at the firehouse kept wanting me to tell the story again, what was it like inside. It was like everybody's dream, and they wanted to be part of it. I mean, it's the dream of every fireman to make a successful rescue, to save some human life. And I was lucky enough to have done that.

□

When I first went on the rescue squad, we had the old-fashioned Cadillac ambulances because they were the best for heavy-duty work and would stand up best under the wear and tear a hard-running service was going to give it. Of course, in later years, we have gone for a totally different type of ambulance with the modular unit and have gone into a much more advanced type of emergency medical care with EMTs and paramedics. When I first started out with the fire department, the only thing we could do for somebody who had a heart attack was to give him oxygen or, in the case of first aid, put a tourniquet on if there was severe bleeding and patch them up the best we could.

I can remember a time when there were no ambulances in Chicago, and people would lie in the street for forty-five minutes, waiting for a police paddy wagon to come and pick them up. We have come a long, long way in this country, and the fire service has been the main operator of emergency medical service.

□

We had had a busy day, a fire here, a fire there, and we had done well. Our spirits were high. We were at the dinner table, and we had with us one of the local fire investigators and a retired captain from New York.

An alarm came in for 133 Honeywell Avenue, an older, run-down area in Charlotte with many fires. We were greeted at the street by some frantically waving civilians. They pointed to the rear of the house, screaming, "He's in the back, he's in the back." So I grabbed a Halligan bar and went to the rear of the house, which was two stories in the rear and one story in the front. The people were pointing to the cellar stairs. There were six or eight steps down to the basement. It was a basement fire that had already spread up the interior stairs to the first floor and on up to the attic and roof.

So I descended the cellar stairs and opened the door. The fire had already taken the whole basement, it had flashed over and the entire ceiling was involved. As I opened the door, the fire was licking out and going up the siding of the house. I felt the wind drawn in from the doorway behind my back. The smoke was down low, but the wind cleared the air a bit, and I was able to get down low enough to get under the smoke. At floor level it was fairly clear, and I could see because the fire was so bright.

I could also see that it was a heavily fire-loaded building. The man was more or less a packrat. He cut up his kindling wood down there with a chain saw. So there were stacks of wood and motor vehicle parts, a conglomeration of junk. Also a large bed.

The victim was over by the stairway, about twenty-five feet in, lying facedown. Later investigation showed that he was filling his gasoline-powered chain saw near a large potbelly stove. There was probably a vapor explosion and a flash fire. I was by myself, and the hose line had not yet been stretched to cover me.

The man was unconscious and severely burned. His clothes had apparently fused to his body. He was a big man weighing 250 pounds. I weigh 150, so it was a lot of work to get him out of there. By the time I had dragged him to the doorway at the bottom of the outside steps, he was completely naked, because the flash fire had turned his clothes into part of his skin. I didn't know if he was dead or alive, just that he was a dead weight.

I was able to get him out the door, and I closed the door behind us. I got him as high up the steps as I could, then couldn't go any further. It took three other men to get him up. I stayed with him and performed first aid. I turned him over and opened his air passages. I looked for a pulse, and, much to my surprise, I found one. He wasn't breathing real great, so we assisted his breathing with oxygen and began treating for burns. We wrapped him in burn sheets and wet him down. On the way to the hospital, from my understanding, he was sitting up and talking. I felt good about that. Unfortunately, his burns were too severe. He only lived about four days before he died.

At the time, I had about ten years' experience. School is great and training classes also, but experience is the teacher. So observing the conditions and mentally adding up the risks, I had elected to go in. I don't know how long I was in there. I was struggling with him so much I just wanted to get out. I was able to do that. You just have to concentrate on what you're doing.

I had seen his injuries, and in the back of my mind I was surprised that he had lived the night. So when I saw the obituary four days later, I was saddened, but I had done everything I could do. That's one way I get by these things. As long as I've done all I can do, it's out of my hands. It helps me cope with losses like that.

□

It was a fire in a high school at two o'clock on a Monday morning, and one of our rescue crews was coming back from the hospital, where they had a job. They smelled smoke. They drove all around looking for the fire, but they just couldn't find it. The trouble was that this school, like many buildings in South Florida, was completely windowless, for reasons of vandalism and air-conditioning. So they couldn't see the fire.

At six in the morning we got the run. This fire had been burning in a windowless structure for twelve hours. We felt the door, and it was hotter than hell itself. We stretched our preconnected line, a long stretch, and we put it into position. Then we forced open the door and felt the air rush in. Right there, I knew that was the closest we had ever come to blowing ourselves to kingdom come. Why that building didn't backdraft, I don't know.

We crawled in with the line, and the smoke was real black, almost to the floor. We were in the library learning center. I got close to the wall, and there was a telephone on one of the desks, just above the level of our heads. It was melted to a blob. Now our ears were burning, really tingling, because we weren't using helmets with earflaps and we didn't have any ventilation.

We went a long way in, thinking, cover your ears, cover them up and push the line along. By this time everything was in a smoldering state and picking up. We stretched that thing, we must have stretched it a hundred feet. This other guy and I were up front, and the rest of the guys were twenty or thirty feet back. We cracked that line, and the water upset the thermal balance. The steam came down, and we couldn't see a damn thing.

The steam rolled down, and I told the guy, "I got to leave, I'm burning up." He didn't get the burns I did. I said, "I got to go, I'm burning up."

I turned around and tried to follow the hose line out, but it was all tangled around a chair we had knocked over on the way in. It was behind a receptionist's desk, and I remember going there. In retrospect you say, "Feel the male and the female of the coupling, and you know you're heading in the right direction." When you're burning up, you don't feel anything. I started to stand up, and I was telling myself to get back down. This was the closest I have ever come to losing control of myself because I was burning up.

I finally did get outside. To be honest, I had left that guy on the line. I had told him, "Come on, come on, come on." He came out a minute later and was okay.

They worked on me in the emergency room at the hospital, and they put ice packs on my ears. They were second-degree burns. Why we didn't kill ourselves by forcing that door and letting that air in, I don't know. I think it was just God saying, "Hey, it's not your time to get killed."

There are always other times, though. Like, we had a fire in another one of those Dade County pine houses, where a lady and a baby were trapped inside. So the guys pulled the line, they were good firemen, but they were attacking the fire at the front. It's hard to make yourself go around back of the fire when the fire's in the front. I said, "Hey, Eddie, if there is anybody alive, they're in the back of the house. Go there."

Well, anyway, the firemen went in the back and found the lady while I was getting my self-contained mask on. They came out and they were burned. They were helping the lady, but the baby was still in there because I could hear it crying. I went in with a line. The fire was one of those where it was burning up over your head. I intentionally didn't open the line, because I knew that steam would come down and I wouldn't be able to see the kid. Also, I would steam the hell out of myself.

This time I did have my earflaps down. I could hear the baby crying, and I said, "Oh, man." I jumped through doorways, and I melted the eye shield on my helmet. I never did find the baby. It was in the back bathroom, and for some reason the sound wasn't right. I went way past the baby, and another guy came in and got it.

So I got burned, and I didn't get the baby. That was the first experience in which I heard a baby crying, and I thought, "Well, you just better stay in here, and you just better suffer until you find that baby."

I didn't make the rescue, but I do feel that by ordering the guys around to the back, I really saved those people. So I feel good about that.

◻

I'm going through EMT right now. I was an ECA, that's emergency care attendant. With that I could run first aid for the fire department. There are widespread deaths from vehicle accidents in the Houston area. We have a lot of busy intersections, and we also have people who go out and party, and they get on the roads and bring death with them.

I have handled a lot of situations. We had a baby born on one run. It was pretty exciting, even though I've done it with my wife. We were called out to a trailer, and the lady was having good contractions. She was in the third stage of delivery. So, in the ambulance, I assisted a paramedic and we delivered the child. We set him up on the mother's stomach so that the two of them could be pretty comfortable together, for the hospital was maybe seven miles away.

◻

We responded to a fire at the Howard Johnson hotel on West Colonial Drive. On arriving at the scene, we saw a small amount of black smoke coming from the seventh floor, and guests were out on the balconies waving for help. Our company, Engine 1, entered the lobby just as Rescue 2 brought down a lady who was pretty charred. This was the first time that the seriousness of the fire dawned on us.

We went to the fifth floor and took a line up to the seventh. There we searched and found about five occupants whom we helped to exit the fire. It appeared to be a racing fire that wasn't involved with the structure so much as with the carpets and wall coverings, a flash fire that raced down the corridor. No fires were visible, but there was a lot of heat and smoke. They had a lot of plastics, and the smoke was black and thick, like flowing oil. If you held your hand in front of your face, you couldn't see it, the smoke was that bad. The exit lights couldn't be seen from more than three feet away.

We could hear people talking, and we could hear people screaming. People were trying to find their way out. They were helpless. We led some of them back into their rooms and out onto their balconies. Others we led to the fire escape that came down through the entire building.

Then, as our air pipes were running low, we came across a man in one of the rooms. He was wedged under a vanity or dresser of some type. He appeared to be dead, so Lieutenant Murray took his self-contained and gave the guy some air. We saw his lips move a little, so we knew he was alive. Our next thought was to rescue him.

The exit we wanted to take him to was about seventy-five feet away. When we tried to remove him from under the vanity, it was quite a tug. We realized that he had been burned through his clothing, and his skin was stuck to the carpet. We managed to pull the guy up and drag him down the floor. He was a large individual, weighing about 300 pounds.

We started the three-man carry and got him down the hallway about fifty feet from the exit, when we ran out of air. Our oxygen supplies ran out simultaneously because we had all entered the building at the same time. We had to leave him there and go to the exit area ourselves to get air. When we got out into the fresh air in the exit, we decided that we didn't have time to get replacement air packs, we had to go back and rescue the guy immediately. It was his only chance, now or never. So we took off our air packs, got a good breath of air, and went back in to try to drag him another fifty feet.

I helped drag the guy to maybe twenty feet from the exit. I knew the smoke was filled with PVC, and I knew it was very toxic. So what I did was hold my breath while we were dragging him, until I couldn't hold it anymore. I told Lieutenant Murray and Welch that I had to leave. I dove out of the exit, but not before I did breathe in some of it, and I went through the coughing and the spit and that stuff.

Walter Murray and Welch succeeded in dragging the guy the rest of the way out. A relief crew was there to resuscitate him.

Welch and Murray were taken to the hospital for smoke inhalation. Since then, Welch has retired from the department for respiratory problems, and Lieutenant Murray is still on the job. So it affected one firefighter enough to end his career. I didn't take nearly as much smoke as they did, but it had some effects on me. I have sore throats and a skin problem, but all in all, I don't think it had too much of a lasting effect.

The victim's name was General. That's all I know, we called him The General. What his real name was, I have no idea. I never got to talk to him, but he sent us some letters, saying that he was grateful for what we had done. I think he was an ex-general, and, as far as I know, he is alive and well.

If you weren't spiritual before, this job would probably make you that way. It has made me appreciate life, believe me. If you asked if I would do it again, I would probably tell you no, because it was real hell. But I know I would do it again.

After that, going on fires, it isn't the fire I worry about, it's finding somebody in that same position again. I think that bothers me more than anything else. Because that stuck with me for a long time. To see an individual I rescued, see him that close to death, it really bothered me for a long time.

□

When you're young and ambitious in the volunteer service, you leave your beeper open so you can hear neighboring companies going out. We heard a neighboring fire company get a report of a house fire at about four-thirty in the morning. It was a bitterly cold night, maybe ten or twelve below zero. We knew that the location was very close to our district. Their chief got to the site, but we heard his men radio him from the station saying that their bay doors were frozen shut. They had washed their truck the night before, and the water had frozen the doors to the concrete.

The chief said it was a farmhouse, heavily involved, and there were kids trapped in it. We're sitting there, saying, "Dammit, call us. We got a full crew in the station, and we're ready to go." They did call us.

We got out there, and the house was cooking. There was heavy smoke coming out of the windows; since the fire hadn't gone through the roof, it was bending out all of the windows. This was the first time any of us young guys had a situation where we knew someone was trapped. We started stretching an inch-and-a-half because that's what we always did, and our chief said, "The hell with the inch-and-a-half. The kids are trapped up there, and we've got to get up." None of the guys from the other department had air packs on, and we were all masked up.

They pointed to the back of the house, which wasn't so involved with flames. The kids' bedroom was there. We put a ladder up to the little roof over one of the side doors and went up. I looked inside the window, and the whole quarter of the house was going, trapping the kids. These were farm kids, and they had already been up doing their chores. Now they couldn't get out.

We tried to get in this window. I could see down the hall, I could see a crib. It was at the point where the flame is so intense that you can see again, when it's really lit up, before you deal the water. I tried to get in the window and I got blown right back. I kept trying to reach for the crib, and I kept getting burned back, because the whole damn fire was venting this way. Two other guys were trying the next window, meeting the same thing —getting blown back. There was just heat coming at us. I lost my helmet, my New Yorker, in there.

Then our bells went off, and we were called down.

I was so mad, I said, "Dammit, we couldn't get to them, we couldn't get to them."

And one of the guys I had never given much of a thought to slammed me against the side of a wall, and said, "That's it. It's done." Apparently I was sufficiently obnoxious about my frustration that somebody felt it necessary to snap me back. Meanwhile, a booster line, a high-pressure beam gun, was working on the fire.

I had to change air packs because the face piece on my mask was burned so that I couldn't see out of it. We went back up and made an entrance through the second window. We knew it was too late in the fire for the kids to be alive. I went in and started searching the room. The far corner of it had burned through to the first floor. I started crawling and found one of the kids practically underneath the window. It turned out to be a fourteen-year-old girl.

I took off a glove and felt for a pulse, but I could see by the way everything was burned there that there was nothing I could do and I should just report it. She had probably gotten to the window and opened it, and then probably got sucked back in. The room had flashed. I don't know why it flashed.

I searched further, and I came across a lot of stuffed toys, and there was a little girl with a ponytail, all charred and black and very brittle. I remember reaching out to that. It was the little girl's room I was in. Further on, across the hallway, there was a body strewn there, with a nose falling down across the face. It was absolutely gruesome. I came back and reported the fatalities to the chief.

You think about scenarios. The older sister must have gone into the little girl's room to try to save her and gotten trapped and just passed away. The chief and I were standing in that room, waiting for the medical examiner to come and talking about it. The little girl was the child of a poor farm family, but she had books and toys and stuffed dolls and everything she could want. It was striking.

The parents got out, and they were an absolute mess, the thought of their kids trapped upstairs and them getting out because their bedroom was downstairs. But the worst thing for them must have been the knowledge that the fire had started in a faultily installed wood stove, which they had twice been warned about by the fire company when they had been there earlier on less serious fires.

The most striking thing is, I was glad I was the one who had failed, and not someone else. Because up until then I had been a young snot who really thought he could knock the hell out of any fire. I had been in real hot fires and gone through it and really had done my job, and I would have sworn that I could have gone through anything to have gotten to the kids. That is just not the way it is.

The thing is, you think you're invincible, that you can get through any smoke or anything. I mean, the fire was horrible, four kids died in it, but I feel better knowing it was me. If it had been one of my fellow firefighters, I might have said, "He should have gotten through that window." But I know it was physically impossible to get through, and I don't feel guilty about not being able to do it. I did everything I could, and I know I did.

I went up to the house a couple of days later. I wanted to find my fire helmet, which was still in there somewhere. There was a lot of clutter all around. I looked up and saw my helmet inside the crib that I had been trying to reach into. I took it back, cleaned it up, and repainted it white.

□

Those timber fires are rather spooky, and they move something terrible. I was home in the evening and got the call by telephone to go to a fire in north central California, on the west slope of the Sierras, somewhere near Yosemite Park. I had time to pack things like extra socks and get my gear together, drive to an airport, meet other people, get on the plane, and fly for an hour or two. Then we were taken by bus to the base camp for the fire.

I was what they then called a sector boss with a fifty-man crew of hand laborers, in this case Indian fellows from Arizona or New Mexico. The overall strategy in fighting such a large forest fire is planned by someone else, and we're given a particular sector of the fire and told what to do and where to go, though the tactics are left to us.

This particular incident was at night in a piece of country I had never seen before, very steep and rocky, lots of big trees, three and four feet in diameter. We weren't able to see the country before it got dark, so we had no idea how the terrain lay or what we were dealing with. That was spooky, literally working in the dark. We were given papers telling the extent of the fire and weather conditions, and a map of the area giving us some idea of where we were going and where other crews were supposed to be working. This was at a five- or six-thousand-foot elevation.

We were to work our way down a slope, cutting a fire line about eight feet wide by removing all the brush on the ground around the trees to keep the trees from going. At the same time there were supposed to be crews coming up from the bottom. We were working solely with hand tools, no chain saws or mechanized equipment. And down the hill we went. We could see the fire a mile or so below us. That's not really a good tactic, to be coming downhill with fire below you.

I saw that the information we had been given didn't fit, it wasn't quite right. We were having an awful time, so finally I got the crew together and explained our position. I told them to stay in the burned-out area, which was fairly safe, and not to go into the green stuff, where the fire might run onto them. I left them there with one of our supervisors, then took two other fellows and two of the crewmen, and we started walking down toward this other fire to see what was going on. We had radios, but only between ourselves; we had no radio communication with the rest of the firefighters worth a darn.

We were walking into a pocket of fire. It was burning not only below us and off to one side, but also way beyond the far side of where our line was supposed to be, so we were walking into a U-shaped cone of fire. When we got close enough, we figured out that this was not part of the main fire but a new fire, ignited by the other but separated by some distance. And the only way to protect ourselves was to move down there and attack that second fire to keep it from spreading up the hill at us.

And that took us the rest of the night, cutting and clearing to stop it, keeping ourselves on the edge of the burn, the separation line from what's already burned and what hasn't burned, so that if the fire went wrong, we could immediately run into the burned-out area and get away from it.

In a situation like that, you concentrate on what to do, how to get yourself out of the mess and not take unnecessary chances, gather information as you go along so that you have at least one of two choices—to abandon your position and get back to a good safe place, or pull off into the burn area and let the fire go by you. You don't have any other choice.

Several days before that incident, we were at a large brush fire in southern California. We were given a crew of about forty Mexican nationals, fruit pickers out of the Bakersfield area. These guys had very little experience and a minimum of training. The Forest Service flew us up onto a mountain, and we were to back up another crew by working in one direction while they were working in another.

The fire had burned from the top of the mountain on down. We started from a good safe point, what we refer to as an anchor point. They started working east and we started west, away from each other, to cut fire lines through the brush and get below that fire to keep it from continuing on down into the canyon bottom.

I soon discovered that this crew didn't know how to cut brush in a speedy and efficient manner, and I actually had to train them as we went, show them what to do and what not to do. They weren't building a good, safe line. Meanwhile, the other foreman and myself were watching the other end of the fire and saw that it was getting down the mountain a long way ahead of the other crew. That occurs because of rolling things, for burning debris will roll down the mountain and start the brush down there. Then the fire comes rushing back up at you.

The further we got, the more we realized that our position was becoming precarious, and we looked around for a place to get out of there. One way was to retreat into the burned-out area, but even that wasn't real safe, because if the fire came up from below us, we were going to be in trouble from the heat. We had to do something, either totally retreat to where we had started or get over to the top of a ridge and be flown out by helicopter.

I got on the radio and called the supervisor for that whole sector, explained that we had to get out of there or we were going to be hurt, certainly from the heat and smoke if not the fire. He told me to find a place to land a helicopter, and if he couldn't get something moving in five minutes he would call back, and then we would have to start walking out of there just as fast as we could.

The Mexican leader of the crew wanted to go into a burned-out area. I explained to him about three times that it wasn't a safe area. It had been burned out, but not cleanly enough, and if the fire came roaring through there again, it would reburn; we would be sitting right in dead grass, and we'd have been in bad shape. The man was very determined, and we began to have a heated argument. Finally I had to talk to his crew about their choices, whether to follow us or follow their own leader. I laid it out, what I thought could happen. They decided they wanted to go with us, figuring, I guess, that we had the experience.

The boss radioed that he had two helicopters, and did we have a place. I described the ridge top. Then we had to get there by walking through the green, which was not the best plan in the world, but it was the only quick way to cut across the mountain away from the fire coming up from below us and get to the ridge top. There we quickly built a heliport by cutting away the brush and making a forty-foot clearing. It took us about ten minutes. Then the helicopters started flying in, each taking two guys at a time down the mountain. So they were able to get us out.

Before I left, I took this Mexican crew leader and showed him the spot he had wanted us to retreat to. I said, "You watch that spot." And while we were still on the helicopter ridge, we watched the fire make a long run up the mountain, going right through where we would have been standing.

His eyes got as big as saucers. He shook my hand and almost gave me a hug and a kiss and said he was very pleased that he hadn't forced the issue.

□

I was in a double house, stationed on Engine 5, but that day I was moved to Ladder 6, because I had a transfer in to get on the ladder. I like ladder work. It's probably the most dangerous job in firefighting, and the real purpose of it is to go in and look for anyone trapped in a fire. You're more or less on your own, you're not with the rest of the men, and you don't have the benefit of the hose line. I was assigned the SCBA (self-contained breathing apparatus) that day.

We got the call to a fire in a three-story dwelling. We were second in. Another engine and ladder company was ahead of us. When I got off the truck, I was all prepared to go in the building.

It was a strange fire, actually—a kerosene heater, which was overfilled. It had been knocked over, and the kerosene went between the floor and the wall down into the basement from the first floor and was ignited by the hot water heater. So the fire ran up the walls to the upper floors, and the flames were coming out the third-floor windows when I got there. As I say, I had my air pack on.

I went around to the back alley before the other guys. The first company was still trying to get the ladders up in this narrow alley. I went up some steps to the kitchen door and kicked it open. A couple of guys were already in there on the floor. They didn't have packs, so they were taking a beating from the smoke.

One of their ladder guys also had a pack, so his chief put him on a hose, and he said to me, "Go down to the basement with this guy and give him a hand with the tip." Engine or ladder man, it didn't matter to him. He saw we both had packs, and it was pretty smoky. I helped this guy drag the line, and we both went down to the basement from the kitchen very quickly, because it was like a chimney.

It was getting real hot, and the fire flashed over us. He hit it with water and knocked it down. There was a small window next to the steps, and he was trying to fog the smoke out the window. The heat was coming toward us the whole time.

Then apparently somebody saw how bad it was getting and called, "Everybody out of the basement." There were only the two of us there. I didn't hear it. The guy on the tip supposedly did and told me he was leaving. Again, I didn't hear him. He closed down the hose, and all of a sudden he was gone. I learned later that he went out the window. He had to take the pack off to fit through the window, it was so narrow. I didn't know he had left.

So the water was stopped, and I was alone in the basement. I couldn't go back up the steps to the kitchen, because when he shut down the water the fire had flashed over again and set fire to the stairs. You see, the water wasn't really putting the fire out, but it was keeping the heat away from us. Now it was getting very hot. It was very dark, it was smoky, I couldn't see. I was down on my stomach on the basement floor, looking for the back door I knew was there, but I couldn't see it. I was probably only ten feet from it the whole time.

I became a little disoriented, but I didn't panic. I had been in basement fires before, and I knew you shouldn't panic. I thought, "Now, how did I get into this situation. I don't have any water. I don't have anyone with me." I could see that the fire had engulfed the kitchen steps and I couldn't make it up there. I knew there was a back door there somewhere, but the people had been remodeling the basement, and I had to feel my way through a lot of debris. There was paneling against one wall, and I thought that might have been the door. I slid on it like a slide and fell to the floor.

I sat there for a second, and said, "I gotta compose myself, or I'm going to be in trouble here in a minute." I thought to myself, I've been through a lot in my life. I probably should have been dead eight times over. "Well," I said to myself, "I haven't come this far to die in this person's basement. This can't happen to me. I'm going to survive. I'm not going to die in this guy's basement because he was overfilling his kerosene heater." I got mad then. I remember. I said, "Dammit, I'm not staying in here. I've got to get out."

So what I had to do was raise my mask and holler for help. If I hadn't done that, they wouldn't have found me, because they didn't know I was in there. This guy didn't tell them I was still down there, and my lieutenant hadn't ordered me to go down there; he thought I was on one of the upper floors. It was the chief of the other company who had sent me down there.

They heard my hollering, and they were saying, "Come this way. This way." I would put my mask back on and walk toward their voices. I couldn't see anything, so I was going by their voices. But they couldn't hear me with my mask on. They didn't know where the hell I was. It was getting harder and harder. It was very hot down there. I burned my ears, and I still had my helmet on. I knew if I didn't get to that door soon, I wouldn't make it, so I just kept going.

I pushed things out of the way, and finally, after what seemed like an eternity, I had my hand stretched out like a blind man, and somebody grabbed my hand, and they pulled me out. One of my boots came off, and my helmet fell off. They never found my helmet, it had melted away, and the only thing left of my boot was the sole.

There are points that I don't recall. I didn't actually black out, but I think it was my mind acting it out for me. I don't recall exactly how I got to that back door. I was just glad to feel someone's hand. I was kissing the floor, and the gentleman who grabbed my hand was in the doorway. He couldn't advance any further. In fact, he was on the ground, and somebody had hold of his legs.

I didn't realize I was saved until I was in the rescue squad actually. I was on my way to the hospital, and I was holding the oxygen mask over my face, and I started crying. It finally hit me that I had almost died. I don't normally cry. I believed I was going to be all right. I knew I was hurt, but I also knew I was going to make it.

The first night in the hospital was hell. I had a tube going down my mouth into my lungs. It had a balloon-type thing at the end of it to keep the air passages open. Everything in there was swelling, and I would have choked otherwise. And they were pulling a lot of things out of my lungs and throat, big pieces of black stuff. I didn't know I had taken that much smoke, I had thought it was mostly heat.

They gave me morphine, but I was conscious when they were putting that thing down my throat. It makes you gag. They refused to give me more morphine, saying they had given me enough already. When I wanted to say something I had to write it down, because I couldn't speak. So the first night I was going in and out of consciousness. I kept writing down, "If you don't take this tube out of my throat, I'm going to pull it out myself."

I was a terrible patient that first night. I was in intensive care, and the orderlies, nurses, and doctors were at the desk fifteen feet from me, drinking soda. My mouth was so dry, I wanted some water, and they wouldn't give it to me. They'd say, "Okay, we'll get you something," thinking I'd go to sleep and forget. I would wake up an hour later, and nothing would be there. I threw my pencil at them one time to get their attention. Then I threw the clipboard. I was a bad patient.

My father was there within an hour. He's a fireman, too, and he heard the call come on the fire radio. He knew, before he was told, that I was in trouble. He heard the call for the rescue squad, and he said, "I knew it was you." The commissioner came, and so did a couple of guys I work with and my wife and my mother. Everyone showed a lot of concern, and everyone was as nice as could be. It meant a lot to me. Because if I was just left there with the doctors and nurses, I would have snapped. It's good to see friendly faces.

The next day I was more relaxed. I didn't fight the tube, I just tried to make the best of it. Then I felt lucky. I felt glad to be alive.

I was released from the hospital a week later, and after a few days at home, I was mad. Angry that I got hurt when I shouldn't have been hurt, that my whole life had changed. I don't like changes. I'm used to going to work, and now I had to stay home. I wanted to get out of the house and couldn't. I was miserable as hell, I was climbing the walls.

I took a lot of it out on my wife, Norma Jean. She had had a back operation less than a year earlier and was bedridden. Then she had had a premature baby, and my son was in intensive care for two months. He had just gotten out of the hospital and weighed only 2½ pounds. So she was dealing with her back, and the baby was home on a monitor and she was worrying about him breathing, then I came home and she worried about me breathing. So her back was forgotten for a time, and now it's in terrible shape.

I was miserable even to the kids. I was jumpy all the time. I was physically hurt, and I was still spitting up things. My ears were burned, and the doctors told me I would need glasses, because my corneas were burned. I became depressed, and I was mad. The only ones to take it out on were my wife and kids. I feel bad for them now, but they understood. Norma Jean was great. She had a lot of patience with me.

□

We were asleep, and the alarm came at about 5:55 on a Sunday morning. My company, Engine 22, was first in. It was a one-family row house, two floors and a basement. It started as a fire in the basement and had spread to the first floor. I was the nozzle man.

We knocked down the floor fire on the first floor, then we tried to find the entrance to the basement. We stumbled around in the living room because there was so much furniture in it and we couldn't see in the smoky darkness. The family had redone the basement, and instead of opening a door and going down steps to the basement, you had to open the door and walk about eight feet before you came to the steps. We didn't know that at the time. It's an unusual arrangement for that kind of house. Anyway, we couldn't find the basement.

It started getting real hot in there, and everything started cracking. The lieutenant, John Killian, said, "Too hot. Let's get out of here." Before we could make a move, the floor collapsed and knocked us down. The fire just took off, and we were trapped in there. I was slightly unconscious for a while, then I had to pause for a little while to get my senses together, because I was burned on my forehead. Lieutenant Killian was in worse trouble. He was dazed.

I had to get him out of there. I grabbed him under the arms and started to lead him toward the back door, but we stumbled over the furniture, and we tripped and fell. So I grabbed him by the hand, and my glove came off. The next thing I knew, my hand was badly burned. Then I started dragging him along the floor, and the next thing I knew, I was stuck. My air mask had stuck on a table or chair or something. I was stuck, and I couldn't move.

It was real scary. It was like being in hell, really. I thought, "Lord, don't let me die like this. I deserve a chance." I thought about my wife, Corinne. We were only married a year. I said, "Wow, I'm going to leave my wife right now, and my family." The way it happened, it was unbelievable. I was totally stunned. I didn't believe I would be in a situation like that.

I was lucky I had my turnout pants on. Sometimes I was in the habit of not wearing them. But it was a little cold out, so I put them on. If it weren't for them, my legs would have been badly burned, because my whole outfit was black charcoal.

From my training and previous experience in other fires, I knew we had to get out of there. I tried as hard as I could to get us out, but every time I tried to move, somehow I was getting weaker and weaker. I thought it was hopeless. Then my air bottle ran out of oxygen. I thought I was going to die of suffocation. I was just hoping I wouldn't burn to death. But the fire didn't seem like it was coming toward us anymore. I could hardly breathe in my air mask, and I had too much smoke in my chest. Just then, the other guys managed to get back in there and pull us out.

At the hospital they put a tube down into my lungs. They could hardly get it down there, my throat was so swollen. It had been burned by the heat. They were shoving it down there, and I was scared. They finally got it down. I don't remember much of my first three days in the hospital. A lot of people said they came up to see me, but I don't remember who.

I asked somebody if everybody had made it out of the fire all right, and they said no. I saw the other two firefighters who were hurt, but I didn't see Lieutenant Killian. I kind of figured he had died.

After the third or fourth day, everything started hurting real bad. My hand. My face. I was in a lot of pain. It took me a while to get over that. The first day was hardest for Corinne. She was really hurt to see me, but she tried to hold it back. Afterwards, she didn't want me coming back to the department, but I told her that that was what I wanted to do. So she respects that, and she supports me.

I was in therapy for a year and a half for my hand, using grips and putty. Then I went to this physical therapy center and did all sorts of other things, exercising every day, working with my hand to build things. Today my hand is not as good as it was, but it's okay.

The department was excellent, supportive in every way. Everybody came up to see me, even guys I didn't know. It seemed like the whole fire department was at the hospital. Anything I wanted or needed, they got me. They treated me excellently.

I was off the job for about five and a half months, then I was put on light duty for about a year. Now I'm back on the job full-time. I've had a couple of falls since then, but everything is pretty cool. I'm not anxious, I just go with the flow, and do the job. I talk about the fire when somebody asks, but I don't really like talking about it.

About the hand, they grafted skin onto it, two sections of skin from my thigh. They put me out, so I don't know all the details of that operation. The cold affects it; it stiffens up and my fingers feel numb. The hand is much bigger than the other one. The fingers are still swollen. They're flexible, but they can't hold anything too long. It gets heavy, then I have to let it go.

I'm lucky to be alive, right?

□

A child was caught in one of the rooms. The main fire was on the second floor of this apartment building, and there were women and kids downstairs screaming at us. We used every length of hose in the bed, it was a long stretch, because we had to go around a courtyard and up the stairs. The fire was coming around the cracks of the door to the second-floor doorway. I remember thinking, "This is it, this is where the stuff hits the fan."

We had to knock down the fire before the guys from the truck could get in to search. I was on the nozzle, and we crawled through the doorway, and suddenly I had excruciating pain in my knees. The heat went right through my boots. We first hit the doorway with the line, then the hallway and the ceiling. The heat was extraordinary. We didn't do it scientifically, we went in very, very fast because there was somebody in there.

Halfway down the hall, I screamed, "My knees are burning." My officer said, "The hell with your knees. My knees are burning, too. Move in." I said to myself, "He's right." It was the most fire I had ever seen, it was from wall to wall and ceiling to floor. There was all sorts of junk on the floor—a baby carriage frame, a shopping cart. The metal was glowing. It was blocking our way. I said, "We've got to pass this stuff out." I couldn't move around it, and I couldn't climb over it. The guy behind me thought I said, "I'm going to pass out."

Realizing that communications were down, I handed the line over to the backup, grabbed the shopping cart, stood up, and threw it back down the hall. The man at the door claimed it came flying out the door and caused an injury to his family jewels. When I lifted the shopping cart, just for that split second, I got second-degree burns on my fingers.

I got back down and grabbed for the line, and they gave it back to me. I realized that this must be really bad, because you never get the line back. We went on, and I was thinking, "This is it. My sanity is gone. Nobody can stand this much pain. I can't give in to it." Then I told myself, "You don't feel it." A lot of guys don't feel it when they're burned. I did. I felt the whole thing, the whole time. I was making a conscious effort not to pay attention to it. I just kept moving. I had visions that I wasn't going to have any knees left, they were just going to be gone.

Afterwards I really didn't think I did that good a job. I was disappointed in myself. While I was throwing that stuff out, it must have looked like I was backing out. Maybe I could have climbed over that stuff. I felt I was too slow. I should have moved in a lot faster. And then, when I got outside, my knees were killing me.

I found out the rescue had been made by a die-hard fireman I know, Vinnie, the salt of the earth. He always has a puss on his face. He had gone up the fire escape and into one of the back windows and found a kid in the bathroom, a three- or four-year-old boy who was in the next bed to me in the emergency room at Jacoby Hospital. Rosy pink cheeks, he looked like he was half Puerto Rican and half Irish. Really beautiful-looking child.

They were taking him to the air chamber on City Island, a decompression chamber for smoke inhalation victims.

Anyhow, after the fire was out, we went back up with the hose, and I remember I had trouble walking upstairs because of my knees. The truck really took most of the line up. I wasn't doing much of anything. I was dragging. I didn't say anything about my knees. I kept thinking it wasn't as bad as I thought it was. I was making too much of it, and everybody else must be just as sore. I did say to somebody, "Boy, my knees are really killing me." And he said, "Yeah. Well, okay."

I got back to quarters, and my lieutenant said, "You don't look so good. Are you sure you had the right gloves on?" He was worried about my hands. I told him it wasn't my hands, it was my knees. He said, "Well, all of our knees hurt a little." I said, "No. They really hurt." This was about forty-five minutes after getting back. He said, "All right, let me see."

I pulled up my pants, and my knees looked like a couple of golf ball blisters. I said, "Holy God." I had pulled some of the skin off. The chief took me to Jacoby. I was dirty. They put on a sulfa drug, which is supposed to be a miracle drug for burns. They determined I had second-degree burns. At the burn center a few days later, they determined that the burns were third-degree.

The doctor at the burn center said it was the most common kind he treats there at New York Hospital. Burned knees. From kneeling on a hot surface. It seems that each time I knelt, I was burning the knees deeper and deeper. The doctor said I had cellulitis, which is a bad infection. "You have to be admitted right now. You're going to have to go on intravenous for six or seven days. Then you're going to have grafting."

I was shocked. I had to call my husband and tell him and the family. That was very hard. I spent thirty-three days there, on and off. I've had three surgical grafts since then. I don't think the guys who haven't been in that situation know how painful it is. The burn is just the beginning. After that is when all the pain starts.

Being in the burn center with other firefighters, there is a lot of camaraderie there. You're all in the same boat. There were two others there, one with knees and the other had a hot cinder down his boot and he grabbed it with his hand. I thought I was in hell. I woke up in this icy room, and I was in a room full of men. God is punishing me, I thought. It was like a MASH unit. What an education.

The skin grafts came from my hips and pelvis. Supposedly it wouldn't show so much there. My dad said to me, "Boy, Kathy, you've some stretch marks on those hips." I said, "Dad, they're not stretch marks. They're just warped donor sites." Because I was a firefighter, they took deeper sections of skin, because I was going to be back on my knees.

One of the guys was a probie. His recovery was going to be a lot longer than mine. You're lying in bed, half naked, but we tried to make the best of it. We became very close. When we were separated at one point, we came to see each other on crutches or in a wheelchair. His wife has had a baby since. I remember feeling very close to him. We shared the experience of the job.

□

It was nine o'clock in the morning, and I was just going out to shop for food, because I was cooking that day. The alert came in that there was a fire in an occupied dwelling. I always wear my Nomex hood because I don't want to get burned up. It's really ironic that that day the hood had fallen off, and I just didn't put it back on.

We pulled up to the place, and Captain O'Grady and Lieutenant Bovich yelled for a ladder. It sounded like there was somebody trapped on the second floor, because there was a lot of screaming going on. One woman, who looked like she was burned, was screaming the most. I grabbed the twenty-foot free beam and ran to the side of the house. But the woman was screaming that her baby was in there on the first floor. "In the crib," she said. "It's in the crib."

So Lieutenant Bovich got on his knees under the first-floor window, and I jumped on his back. I tried to get in the window sideways, but my big fat butt wouldn't let me do that. So I had to go in straight, diving head first. There was a bunch of junk in there. The people had just moved in the day before. It was a small room, maybe ten by ten. I could feel my ears burning. I remember kneeling at the crib, looking over my shoulder at the window. Then it got terribly hot. That's the last thing I remember.

Captain Kevin Ketchen, senior man at Engine 27, dove in after me, lugged me to the window, and they pulled me out. I must have gone into respiratory arrest, because Captain O'Grady was beating on me. Then the squad came, scooped me up, and took me to the hospital. I was in that room only about a minute all told.

What was weird about that fire, was that my dad, who had been in the department for twenty-five years, was driving to the union office when he saw the smoke, and he figured that his kid was at that fire. Then he said, "nah, I've seen him work," so he passed up the exit to go there. But something made him turn back at the next exit. He pulled up in front of the house, and he saw a guy lying there, and they were working on him. Chief Ed Smith said to Dad, "That's your boy."

So Dad rode in the squad with me. I remember waking up in the squad, and Dad was straddling me. They were trying to give me oxygen, and I didn't want it. I didn't know what was going on. I was burned up bad, but I didn't know that. I felt like there was a ton of ice on my face. I remember trying to kick my boots off, and it was all pain. I knew then I was hurt. Then I blacked out again.

They were wheeling me in, I remember that. They cut my clothes off. Ronnie Winchester, a guy I went to Hawaii with, was there. I said, "I loused up, I loused up, I loused up." Then I asked him what I looked like. Ron's eyes were bulging, they were bigger than I've ever seen, bigger than plates. He said, "Don't worry about it, Joe. You just lost your suntan." He didn't want to tell me.

I don't really remember much of being in the hospital. I remember a bunch of firemen coming to see me. I was only in for two days because of the danger of infection; you get more infection in the hospital than you would at home. I had second- and third-degree burns on my entire face, ears, and left hand.

They did an experiment on me because I was so young, only nineteen. They did this biobrane. It's like a skin that they put on a leg burn, a thigh burn, or an arm burn. They put that on my face, and it saved years of reconstructive surgery. Aside from that, all I've had to do was get eyelid surgery, because the fire burned through my eyelids. So they took skin from my neck over my left clavicle and redid my eyelids for me. I still need a little bit more nose work and then some eye surgery, and that's it.

They did laser surgery on my eyeballs. I had burned corneas, stuff like that, and I had a lot of edema. My biggest problem, though, is photophobia, sensitivity to light. But the best thing they did was let me go home and let my family take care of me. My sister did. My mom was so busted up she couldn't even be in the room with me. And my dad, who's not a big drinker, took it really hard and started drinking a lot. I stayed at my mom's for a month while they took care of me.

The smartest thing I did was, I never looked into a mirror. I didn't have the slightest idea how badly I was burned up. And all my running mates, they'd bring the rigs by, and they'd spend time with me—that really meant a lot to me—to see me, the monster man. I mean, I was horrible-looking. My captain took it hard, because he'd never had a son on the job, and I was young enough to be his son. Lieutenant Bovich took it hard, too.

What happened at the fire was, there was a mother, she had about five kids with different fathers, and she was in bed with some live-in boyfriend. The baby was in bed with them. The other kids were playing with matches under the dining room table, and the house took off. She and the guy jumped through the window and left the baby in the bed. Then they told us the baby was in that crib. The baby was obviously dead.

They ended up suing our arson squad, because Arson reported it as kids playing with matches. They weren't worried about their baby. If I had a tragedy like that and my child died like that, I'd definitely not want to dwell on it, I'd want to get it behind me and end it.

Kevin got some minor burns on his neck and burned the tops of his ears, because that room was going when he pulled me out. It flashed over, and flames burst out the window. And he went in there. He's a little black guy, real shy, doesn't talk loud at all. He won the Medal of Valor, the highest award you can win in the Detroit Fire Department, for pulling me out of that fire. If anyone ever says anything bad about him, I'll fight to the death for that man. He saved my life.

That biobrane, to me, is the greatest thing since sliced bread, because I would be Mr. Scar. I would just be totally scarred. It's evident from where it didn't take, at the corners of my mouth and my lips. My lips always peel now, they're always dry. I've got scars at the corners of my mouth, over my upper lip, right on my nose, on the ends of my nostrils, and under my chin, where the biobrane didn't take. But biobrane is the best thing that ever happened to me. Lieutenant Bovich wants to get in touch with the doctor who did it, a young, aggressive plastic surgeon, but he went down to New Orleans, and it's hard to get in touch with him.

The burn center I went to was Detroit Receiving. I was supposed to go to their clinic, not the burn unit, but I went up there anyway, and the nurses were A-one. When I went in for the eyelid surgery, they sewed my eyes shut for six days, and that was the worst part of it. I was super-depressed then. The nurses understood.

The firefighters were pretty serious about the whole thing, but the first day I came home the doctor put this net over my head to hold the biobrane mask on so it wouldn't fall off. Captain O'Grady laughed and said I looked like a ham. That kind of broke the ice for the other guys. They took pictures of me every day, and they wanted to use one of them for a Burn Tournament poster for the burn center, but it was too hideous. The caption was going to say, "They never ask what happened to the firefighter who tried to save the baby." It was just too horrible.

It takes a year for your skin to heal up. But I was going stir crazy. I was bored, lethargic, gaining weight. I just wanted to get back to work. I told the doctor I would wear my Nomex hood all the time, so I went back to work after less than nine months. I would have gone back sooner if I didn't have such trouble with my eyesight. I still wear sunglasses outside. It's going to be a long time before that clears up.

My goal is to become a good fireman. The skin is really sensitive. I wear my Nomex hood, and I still get the tops of my ears a little bit fried, and my face blisters up. I had a good one last night and got burned a little. But I've stayed on duty because it's not that burned, just a little blistered. I've got to work for a guy tomorrow, and I don't want to screw up his work release.

That dive I took into that room wasn't so good. For one thing, my mask was knocked off, and I kind of busted my nose, and my left cheek was swollen up pretty bad, so I must have hit something. My helmet must have come off, too, because I had burns on top of my head. But the helmet is still living. It looks like a good squad helmet. It's all black.

◻

When the alarm came in at nine-thirty that Wednesday morning, we were in a class about the enhanced 911 system. All we knew was it was a baby trapped down a well. We were all told to go back to our stations and wait. Only our captain, Dave Felice, was taken out there, possibly because he's a small-boned man, yet real aggressive at whatever he does.

We just got bits and pieces of what was going on out there during the rest of the day and through the night. We kept calling the dispatcher and asking if they needed relief people, and they never would let us go over there. I got to bed at the station at about two A.M. and got up at seven, so I had five hours' sleep. Thursday was supposed to be my day off, when I was going to take care of our youngest child. But my wife, Robbie, got him ready and took him to the sitter's.

The more I thought about the baby in the well, the more I thought I should be out there: I'm skinny, and they're going down holes, and I can fit down holes. So I loaded up and told the dispatcher they probably needed a paramedic, and he agreed. I just went over there on my own. You could say I volunteered myself. This was about eight-thirty Thursday morning.

I had to park two blocks away because of all the cars and trucks. There were a couple of hundred people there, trying to help. The news people were starting to come in. The well was in the backyard of a house in the middle of the block. Steve Forbes was already there, standing by the air cascade system they were using to send oxygen down to the trapped baby. The battalion chief and the EMS chief and everybody else were listening to the microphone they had lowered down the well.

I saw the hole they had drilled down the day before, about five and a half feet from the well, and they were sending guys down there to drill horizontally across to the well. The well itself was just a metal casing sticking up about two or three inches above the ground. It was about eight inches in diameter. They had a yellow tent over it like workers use over manholes in the streets. A fire captain was guarding the air hose, a real Mr. By-the-book type guy, who just broke out and started jumping all over anyone who came close to it. Actually, he did a good job.

Police officers Andy Glascott and Officer Maney did all the monitoring of the hole.

The baby in the well was Jessica McClure. Her parents lived out in the country, and this well was in the backyard of her sister's house, where she was operating an unlicensed day care center. There were five or six kids in the backyard when Jessica went down the well. The older kids were playing by themselves, and the younger kids were playing by themselves.

There was supposed to be a rock over the hole, and I saw some big rocks near there. Then we heard that there was a potted plant sitting on it, and I observed a bucket with what looked like a cactus plant in it that had been turned over and pushed out of the way.

They couldn't tell exactly how far down the well the baby had fallen, because the other small children threw stuff in after her, foliage from the yard. So we could only see down eighteen feet and lower the mike that far. They were afraid to disturb the plant material, for fear they would make more stuff fall on Jessica. They had lowered flashlights, and when I looked down I saw the lights shining on the green foliage stuff. I listened at the mike and could hear her moaning.

That was the last time I looked down the well, but I kept going back and checking with the officers on what they were hearing. Supposedly the night before she had slept for about three hours because they didn't hear noises from her in that time.

I don't know why the kids threw the stuff down the well after her. They were so young they didn't know the gravity of the situation. Perhaps they were just being playful. There was a story that two older kids put the baby in there, or she might have been pushed. But from the position in which I found her, I feel that she stepped in with one foot, lost her balance, and went down, because one foot was down and one was up.

My captain, Dave Felice, had twice been down digging and had worked for a day and a night, and he had been ordered to go home because he looked exhausted. He could have kept going, he's in excellent condition, but they felt they had to order him to leave. Chief Roberts of the fire department and Chief Richard Checks of the police department were pretty much in control of the whole operation. The drilling engineer, Mr. Lilly, was in charge of the digging. And Captain Carl Rogers was a coordinator.

There was talk that the first person to reach the baby should take her out. But because there might have been serious injuries to the baby's neck and back, we thought it should be a paramedic. We talked to the doctors there, Dr. Best and Dr. Klinnock, and Dr. Best talked to the chiefs for us, and it was agreed it would be a paramedic who would bring the baby out. The only exception would be if, when they broke through to her, she just kind of grabbed somebody and she looked good and healthy, then they could bring her out. We had the smallest backboard all ready, cut down still further in size.

The hole they drilled straight down was about thirty inches wide, a pretty good-sized shaft, big enough for two small, skinny guys like Steve and myself to stand in it side by side. The tunnel they were digging across to the well was much narrower, but some pretty big guys were doing the drilling. One guy had a forty-six-inch chest, so we figured we shouldn't have any trouble at all.

They were digging through hard rock to a point in the well below where the baby was wedged, then coming up vertically beside her, and a window between the two was being chopped out to get to her. They put a sort of bubble or inflated air bag below her to protect her from the drilling.

It wasn't until one o'clock on Friday that the drillers told us they were ready for us to go down. We went over to the hole. Any time we moved toward it, the media went crazy, thinking the rescue was coming up. But the chiefs made us go back to the ambulance. We were brought over to Chief Checks' motor home for a last conference, Steve and myself and this other guy, Bill Martin, who was a rapeller, a rope man.

Then we went down. I went in first. I was real apprehensive. I don't go into caves a lot. I've been in tight places, but usually by choice, not by need. I'm real cautious, aggressive but cautious. I try to evaluate everything before I do it. Mr. Lilly was still in the hole. He took the bubble out and talked to me for a minute. Then I went into the tunnel. I had no room at all. I had to decide whether to go on my stomach or my back. My shoulders were pressed on both sides. I had to position the light so it would shine up into the well. I got my first look at her. But I couldn't touch her. To get my arm in there, I had to crawl back out and start back in with my arm ahead of me.

The width of the tunnel was probably fifteen to sixteen inches, and its height was no more than twelve to fourteen inches. I had no headroom. When my head was at the back of the tunnel was the only time I could see up into the well. I got scratches all over my forearm and elbow forcing my arm up into the well. I thought, "Oh, God, how am I going to do this?"

All I saw dangling down was her left foot. So first off, I started an evaluation of her physically. How is she doing? What can she move? What can't she move? People had told us they thought she was horizontal in some kind of widening of the well shaft. So I couldn't just start pulling, because I was afraid I would snap her back or her neck. They had said I could reach her. But reaching up with my right arm, I could feel her left leg and her buttocks, and that was it. I couldn't reach any higher or find her right leg or anything else. She was conscious. Not crying, but moaning.

I got her to move her left foot for me. She did that. I told her to move her upper body, and I could feel her move somewhat. It looked like she was trying. Her mother had told us that Jessica's nickname was "Juicy," so that's what I was calling her. I told her to push as hard as she could with her right foot, and it seemed that she went up a little bit. I communicated all this to the doctor by the phone line they had down there.

They gave me a wedge made of a two-by-four and a round piece of plywood on top, supposedly to push her up and feel around her. I was able to push her no more than three inches. It sounded like she was throwing up. I told her to turn her head to the side and spit it up. I didn't want her strangling on her own throw-up.

I determined that we couldn't get her out right then. I didn't know what position she was in, and I didn't have enough room. So I told her we'd be back. To me, on God's green earth, that's the hardest thing I ever did in my life, leave that little girl in the well that first time. I came back out.

We went into conference, and all the chiefs and doctors were there. And every time I would get close to talking about having to leave her there, I would get teary-eyed, and my voice would crack. The doctors took this as a sign of emotional instability or whatever. It was the first time I had been in a situation like that, and with me, the first time I go into something, as a paramedic or firefighter, I always get real emotional.

When we got out of the hole, Steve Forbes was first, and his face was so solemn that people thought it meant that the baby was dead.

This big water drill had been there since early in the morning, but they hadn't put it in use because Mr. Lilly thought it was too dangerous. They had flown it from Memphis to Houston on a United Parcel 747. It took a plane that size to carry it. I told Chief Roberts I needed more room in the tunnel, that the baby's butt was at least forty inches from the top of the tunnel, that we had to go faster than we had been going. So Chief Roberts and Chief Checks insisted that Mr. Lilly use the water drill. So they took it down there, and they really did a good job with it.

Meanwhile, the doctors were talking to the chief, expressing their concern about whether I was emotionally and physically able to go back down in. He took me aside. He said, "We don't need any macho trips. There's no shame. If you can't go down in, just tell me, just be honest with me." I told him, "Chief, I can go down one more time. If we don't get her out this time, there is no way I can go down again. I would be mentally, emotionally, and physically wiped out."

So he understood that, and he backed me. Assistant Chief Dean Williams backed me. Evidently Chief Checks did, too. And Ray Sprague, the EMS chief, really backed me. He said I was the one to do it. They had confidence in me. We had plenty of guys in the department who were willing to go down, so they really had to feel good about me or they wouldn't have let me.

We went down a second time. I'm not really sure of the time, I know it was still daylight, six-thirty or seven. We had done a lot of sitting around, waiting. Everybody was saying, this is our last chance. Nobody said it to me personally, but the word was, if we had to break bones, break bones. Whatever we had to do to get her out. Bill Martin, the rope man, came up with a device I could lift her with, a tripod pole maybe an inch wide, with tape on the top. He was the guy who did all the rigging in the hole. He helped us a lot.

Down in the tunnel, Mr. Lilly said, "This is it, Robert. This is the best it's going to get." They had chipped away with the water drill and give me some headroom and more shoulder room. So he went to the surface, and Steve came down with the stuff we thought we were going to need. I had the tripod pole with me. I went into the hole and talked to Jessica. I tried to lift her with the tripod pole, and it was too short. So Steve got Bill Martin on the phone, and he found me a longer tripod pole. This one had a rubber stopper on the tip of it.

I tried to push the baby with it, and I couldn't move her at all. I was lying there trying to figure out what to do. Looking at the tripod pole, I saw that the other end of it had a rubberized point that couldn't hurt anybody. So I used it as a probe to see if I could figure out the position of her body. I poked it up the wall of the well shaft along her spine. I knew if I encountered anything solid, that would give me some indication of what body part was where. I ran it up along her spine past her head, and air rushed down at me from the well above her. That meant she was in a vertical position. Her back was straight up and down.

I did the same thing with the pole at the side of the shaft where the right leg should be. It went all the way up, and air rushed through again. So I knew her right foot was up by her head somewhere. I went all the way around her body with the pole. Then I knew that she wasn't in any crevice or bubble-shaped position. The metal casing I had seen at the top of the well didn't go very far down, and the rest of the well was lined with a sticky petroleum-type substance. It was like glue or tar. I had it all over my hands. If you got into the stuff, you just stuck to it.

So then I knew she wasn't lying down and I could pull on her without breaking her back or injuring anything. I talked to Dr. Klinnock and the female pediatrician, Dr. Reese, and I called for the K-Y jelly. They sent down some baby forceps that they use at childbirth, but they were useless in this tunnel. Earlier I had tried to use goggles to keep stuff from falling in my eyes, but they fogged up immediately. It was real warm and humid down there. I was down there close to an hour and a half. All activity above the hole had totally ceased.

Steve opened the K-Y jelly and gave it to me, but there was a seal that had to be broken, so I had to throw it back to him to break that. This whole time he was doing great. He was having to deal with those at the top on the phone, and he was having to deal with me, because when I wanted something I wanted it two seconds ago, not later. And his legs were cramping real bad at the same time, and I didn't know it. I smeared the K-Y jelly over the walls of the well all the way up to the baby's buttocks. Now I needed paper towels because I've got this stuff all over the place. I told Steve that if the paper towels hit him on the head and knocked him out, I was going to kill him. My attempt at a joke.

Now came the pulling time. I was totally confident. I felt we were going to get her out, no matter what it took. And I wasn't going to come out of that hole without her, unless they came and dragged me out.

She had on snap-on pants. They had come undone from the left leg, and I was using them to pull on. She was stuck to the walls, and she was crying and whining. I would pull as hard as I could, and she would tense up; then as soon as she would relax, I would pull again. The first couple of inches were the hardest to get her to move. They were really pressuring us from the top. I had Steve tell them we had moved her a quarter of an inch, to get them to leave us alone for a while.

I was pulling as hard as I could, and she kept tensing up. Both of my arms were exhausted. My right arm went numb two or three times. Once I got her started in the K-Y jelly, I was able to move her a half inch at a time, and she would tense up again. I knew she was coming down. Steve got the backboard ready. When I got her all the way into the K-Y jelly, I had no more problems.

I got her out of the hole and turned over on my stomach. I reached for the backboard, but there wasn't room for it, because her right leg was beside the right side of her head. All the time I was telling her to stay calm, that we were going to get her out, we weren't going to leave her again. When I got her in the K-Y jelly, she was quieter, because it wasn't hurting her anymore.

She didn't say a word. Of course, she was only eighteen months old. She made different sounds, but nothing I could understand. She knew someone was there trying to help her.

I couldn't get her out on the board, so I pulled her onto my right arm, supporting her back and neck. The light hit her left pupil and she reacted, which was great. It was a good sign. I pulled her right leg in far enough so I could get her on the backboard. Steve was getting stuff out of the way, and while I was waiting, I said something like "Great" or "Fantastic." I said it too loud, and she jumped a little bit. To me that was a good sign, too. But all she was doing was lying on the board, just looking around, real relaxed.

I slipped her out, supporting her with my legs, and Steve wrapped her waist to her chest. We used a Velcro strap across her chest to make sure she stayed on the board. Steve put a towel on her neck, because the cervical collar was too small. I took white surgical tape and went all around the board and around the towel. Her hands were welded to her temples by the sticky substance. We left her right hand where it was. We didn't try to straighten out any limbs. We finished getting her strapped. Then Steve stood in the shaft holding her. I secured her to him with seat belt straps. I secured them both to the tether line of the backboard, and I attached him to the main cable of the rig. So he went up with her.

The only thing that fell down from her was a pair of toy binoculars and a few twigs. When I first got her, there was a big twig between her right arm and her chest. I thought it was embedded, but when I moved her arm I saw that it wasn't, so I threw it out of the way. Nothing else, none of the green stuff.

I heard them yell and scream up top, everybody was just ecstatic. I was yelling, too. Nobody could hear me, but I didn't care. I was totally calm. As a matter of fact, I was totally exhausted, mentally and emotionally. I was light-headed, I was having a hard time focusing. I just felt I needed oxygen.

So I was trying to get stuff together, and the chief said, "Come out now." He meant *now,* and he said it a couple of times. So I said, "The heck with this stuff." They brought me out, and I shook the chief's hand. He's a big man, and I just laid my head on his shoulder for a minute.

I did see little Jessica and her parents at the hospital. She looked a lot different, a lot better. She looked somewhat swollen, and I hadn't realized that mark on her forehead was such a bad scrape.

They planted a tree in that backyard that will live as long as she does. And we're going to put a plaque on that backboard and put it in our museum. It was great to be part of it.

The next time I might not be so lucky. I know that the job I do is well worth all the time and all the nonsense we go through, and the good times and the bad times. If I end up dying of cancer because of the smoke, or if I end up dying in a fire, I never think about that. I know it can happen, but that's my job, and I love doing it. I've thought in the past about switching, but this guy's going to be there until they run me off. Until I can't do it anymore.

□

We were working night shift at Engine 13. I sometimes work on my model fire engines, but that night I had gone over to have dinner with the captain of Engine 1, who was going to retire. I had just returned to the firehouse when the alarm came in. The speaker in the apparatus was not very clear, so I didn't hear about the propane tank until later. All of a sudden Engine 13's crew came running out of the kitchen like a football team, and the second alarm came in. With that, I knew that my older brother, Harvey, who was battalion chief, was there.

We had quite a bit of snow on the street, and driving there was slow going. On the way over, I heard Harvey, I knew it was his voice, asking for a third alarm and all the ambulances that were available. I now knew there was an explosion, but I didn't know the extent.

When I pulled in there, the scene was one of utter desolation, it was like a sea of bricks and a fire of low intensity. The nearby buildings were just starting to catch. People were hobbling all over the place. All the firemen there were on rescue. Knowing that help was coming, I told the battalion to make sure the engine company stretched lines. I didn't want them all going on rescue work, which there was a natural tendency for them to do.

I looked and saw our rigs completely smashed. It was a sickening sight.

The aerial ladder of Truck 5 had been blown across the street about thirty feet. It was crushed. The whole middle of the truck was flat down on the street, the tiller sticking up in the air like a sinking ship. Bricks were all over Engine 32, one engine caved in, and there were men lying all over the place. It was just mind-boggling. We had the fire spreading in four different directions, so I called for more help.

Two members of Rescue 1 brought Harvey over, just so I could see him. He was all bandaged and bloody. All he kept saying to me was, "I'm all right. I'm all right." I said, "You're going to the hospital." And he said, "Oh, yeah." They said, "We'll see he goes right away." So now I was the chief in charge.

Harvey had a broken collarbone and a dislocated shoulder, and I didn't know it at the time, but he had a five-inch wooden stake driven into the side of his throat and resting against the carotid artery. I didn't know it, because they had bandaged right over it, deciding rightly that they shouldn't try to remove it at the scene. They had bandaged his whole face and neck, and he looked like a mummy, all bloody.

Of course, it was a shock to me to see my only brother like that, but I had the idea in my head that he was going to be all right. The fellows had control of the situation, and they were taking him to the hospital, so I didn't really dwell on it. There was so much going on that I had to turn to the fire.

I knew some of our men had died, they were lying all over the place, and there had to be people under the sea of bricks and rubble. And there were people in the nearby house fires who were hollering.

I went to a fifth alarm and then got an additional two engines and two trucks, because I knew the first alarm was wiped out. I didn't know how badly, but they were gone. By the time I put one company to work there was another one there looking for assignment. The rubble was starting to burn near Ladder 5, and all I could think of was, if there was anyone underneath it and still alive, I didn't want them to burn to death. I thought that would be a horrible thing. So I had the first lines keep the fire away from the rigs.

It ended up that they weren't under the truck, they were under Engine 32. It was like looking for someone under water, you had no idea where to start in the tremendous confusion. Some of the victims had already been taken to various hospitals in police cars and private cars, and it took us quite a while to get an accurate head count, to find out who was missing. We finally broke it down that the entire crew of Ladder 5 were dead, all five of them.

It was several hours before I found out what had happened. The building was a four-story warehouse, and they had a huge propane tank on the fourth floor, a five-hundred-gallon tank, I believe. It was completely illegal to have it in the building at all. One of the workers was moving the tank with a lift truck near the elevator shaft. It fell off the truck, the valve broke, and the liquid propane poured down the elevator shaft. The entire building got to the explosive stage at once.

The workers ran out of the place and were out in front when Harvey arrived. They told him they had a propane tank that had burst. He assumed it was a twenty-gallon job or something like that. He asked them how big it was, and they said, "About as big as your car." He said that was the last thing that he remembers. That's when the propane hit the wood stove on the first floor and blew the whole warehouse to pieces, totally destroyed it. It's too bad that it didn't blow sooner, we wouldn't have had any problems. On the other hand, if it had blown later, we would have had more men killed.

There wasn't much left of the building, there was so much open fire, we kind of dismissed the possibility of more explosions in the warehouse. But some of the nearby houses had shifted and broken some of the natural gas lines into the houses. That got ignited. We also had a large frame church burning behind the warehouse, which probably in itself would have been a third alarm, and for quite a while we had just one engine company working a turret on it.

There were about nine or ten houses that were heavily damaged, and there were innumerable houses that got damage and window breakage for miles around the area. It was a tremendous sight. Once we got enough help in there to work on all the perimeters of the fire and hold it, then it was several more hours, I would say after midnight, when Commissioner Fred Langdon said they had the final count of casualties. It was the five members of Ladder 5 and two civilians. Then I got his permission to replace every company at the scene, because the weather was bitterly cold and the men were physically shot and emotionally shocked.

I stayed until all the companies were replaced, then I went back to quarters and had a bowl of hot soup. Then I went to the hospital for the second time that night. By this time Harvey had been operated on and they said he was all right, so I didn't even go in to see him. The first time I had gone, he was still in the emergency room along with some of our fellows who were burned, so I had a chance to talk to them. I also had the very unpleasant task of identifying one of the bodies.

The chaplains and the commissioner and his deputy went to each individual's house to notify the family of the deaths. They did the same thing with the injured. They brought their wives in and met them at the hospital. It was complete chaos there.

The families were very cooperative. They realized that nothing could have been done to avert the tragedy. The companies had pulled up, just as you do on every box you go on, to find out what was going on. The five men of the ladder company had gotten off the truck and were standing together across the street from the building, waiting for orders. And Engine 32 had pulled in, and they were on the back of their rig getting masks on in case they were needed.

We've had people say they shouldn't have been that close. Well, nobody had any idea what was going on. The members of Engine 32 were just blown into snowbanks, except for one who, along with my brother, was blown into the chief's car. The members of Engine 1 were also blown into snowbanks and, other than burns, were not hurt badly at all. But Ladder 5's crew just ended up being buried by all the debris. They were not blown away like the other fellows. In fact, one of the men from Engine 1 was talking to one of the men from Ladder 5, and he was blown about sixty feet into a snowbank, and the man beside him was buried under the bricks and killed.

The two who were blown into the chief's car were badly injured. Harvey was one of them. The other, named McAndrews, is now out on disability pension, at age thirty-two. He was very badly smashed up, a lot of broken bones. It was the second to last night on the job for the captain of Engine 1, and he was going to get out, and the driver said to him, "Why don't you stay in the rig, Cap, there's nothing going to be doing here." Well, the bricks caved in the roof of the cab and they both received some bad lacerations, but it came out okay in the end.

I always knew it could happen at any time. I felt that after all the fires I have been on, all the years I have put in, I had never had a man killed in a fire, whether I was in charge or just working at it. And it just caught up with me. Fate caught up with me.

I went to all the wakes. They varied from some of the wives sobbing uncontrollably to others more or less accepting it. The younger wives seemed to take it harder. The families themselves were good to us. They even helped to console us. We're all family.

Harvey was in the hospital for about three weeks and out of the job for about five months. He lost his hearing. He had to get hearing aids. He's getting there. He says he has no real bad aftereffects from it.

We had the funerals for the five men on New Year's Eve, and it was bitter cold. Oh, God, it was a cold day. And we had thousands of men who came from all over the country. It hit every one of us in the department emotionally, to think that on New Year's Eve, on a bitter cold day, all those guys would come up. It was just amazing, and it really helped.

The case of the illegal usage of the propane tank is still in litigation. It's been kicked around. The grand jury indicted them, but then they played a little game. The one guy got immunity to testify against the others, then he claimed he was the one who put the tank in there. One of those things.

□

In these California brush fires, there are two basic types of situations. There's the situation where you're busting your behind the entire time you're on the fire line. And the reverse situation, where you're in a ready reserve area and end up doing nothing. They're not the type of thing, like in urban areas, where a fire department comes running in, Johnny-on-the-spot, and puts the fire out. The fire service in California is at the whim of the weather.

These things are very difficult to combat, because you're often fighting a fire fueled by chaparral or other brush that hasn't burned through for over a hundred years. The fuel load is tremendous and often in inaccessible areas, so that the firefighters don't become so much involved in the actual extinguishment attempt as in protecting structures. You might have ten or fifteen companies assigned to one block in a hillside area to prevent the homes from going on fire.

I remember several fires where we were doing just that. We were up on the roof wetting down in preparation for a fire sweeping through or using heavy stream application onto the brush areas surrounding the homes. But usually, when the fire comes through, it's almost as if your efforts were totally fruitless. The area becomes so intense that it's necessary for you to seek shelter inside the home. That's the only way you can get away from it. There's nothing that hiding under the fire truck is going to do for you. You just have to drop the hose line and run.

A few years ago, I was assigned to Engine 15 in south central Los Angeles, and we were dispatched to a major brush fire in Mandeville Canyon, along with four other engine companies, to form a brush strike team. On arrival, we were given the assignment to protect a particular home on a street in the immediate area. The fire was some distance away but was expected to hit our area after dark. I knew we were in for a long night. I expected this fire to be like others I had been on: long hours of nothing, punctuated by moments of sheer terror.

We laid out the hoses and prepared the residence by removing combustibles from the outside of the home. We closed all the windows and made sure the doors were all unlocked and the lights were on, in case this became our refuge when the fire swept through the heavy brush surrounding the house. I remembered previous situations, spending hours soaking the home and everything around it only to have the hot, dry Santa Ana winds and the winds from the fire turning everything bone dry in seconds.

In this case, we were almost immediately engulfed in a hailstorm of burning embers blown by the fifty-mile-an-hour winds. We stood our ground, soaking the wood-shake shingle roof with an inch-and-a-half line, when the captain gave the order to drop the hose line and get inside the house. It was the only place that offered us any safety from the heavy smoke and the furious ember-laden winds. We had three lines around the home. We dropped them, and we all congregated in the main hallway of the house. I was relieved that no one had suffered much more than the usual heavy dose of smoke and a few burns from the flying embers.

We were in there only three or four minutes when the fire engulfed the whole surrounding area. The hallway was positioned in such a way that we could see out through the large number of glass patio doors in the back. You don't want to be close to the windows or that number of glass doors, when you've got that kind of superheated wind blowing around. We were still able to see, but from a distance from the windows.

The idea, of course, is that the fire will move swiftly past in the force of the wind. The thought certainly occurred to us that the fire could take the building, too. It's always a distinct possibility. Given the two choices of being outside in the furious winds and the embers that are blowing around and chunks of tree branches and everything that's carried by these tremendous winds, being in the house is probably the better of the two choices.

Besides, it was tremendously hard to breathe out there. We weren't using anything more than bandannas across our faces, because the breathing apparatus in this type of environment is more restrictive than it is helpful, so you don't use it. You just resort to the old brushfire standby, the bandanna over the nose and face. It's still difficult to breathe, not only because of the heavy smoke, but the hot, dry winds, of themselves, make it difficult.

It was nighttime, and the scene through the patio doors was spectacular, like millions of fireflies, though they were really embers blown by the tremendous wind. They were more like balls of hail—fireballs of hail going past.

As soon as the fire sweeps through your area, that's when you spring back into action, retrieve your hose line, and start putting out the roof fires or whatever else may have become ignited. It's a scary situation. When you're in the house, you're praying like hell that the house doesn't burn down. In this case, when we went outside we were greatly relieved to see only a few small wisps of smoke coming off the roof, and we doused them.

This is not such an exceptional thing. Hundreds of other guys out here have been in the same situation.

□

So I became an EMT. I was worried about it. Blood and stuff really bothered me if it was somebody else's, but not when it was mine. At the hospital, as long as I had a full stomach, I could watch everything except the initial cutting open of a person, even at an autopsy. I would have to look away. Once they're open, it doesn't bother me. After I found out I could handle blood, I went ahead and became a paramedic.

We had two nurses teaching the EMT class. The first night they gave us a whole list of medical terms. One was "blood pressure." Until that day, I never knew what blood pressure was. So I asked, and a lot of the guys in the class laughed at me, but I found out what I wanted to know. The fire department gave me a direction that I was really enjoying. I was headstrong, real hyper. I tried to do everything. Every time I had a chore to do, or a fire to do, I tried to do everything as fast as I could.

The worst one before I really got into paramedic was a two-year-old baby. The mother was fixing to take an older child in a station wagon to some kind of meeting. She was also close to nine months pregnant. The father, who was a preacher, was in the house, and the two-year-old was supposed to stay there. The mother got in the car and didn't notice that the baby had gotten out of the house and was standing behind the car. She backed down the drive, hit the baby, and a wheel went right over the little girl's head.

The father ran out and did CPR and mouth-to-mouth on the baby, and got her going again. We got there just before the ambulance crew, and we helped them. You couldn't really tell if the baby's head was deformed, but she was bleeding from her nose, mouth, and ears. It was just real sad. One paramedic was pretty freaked.

They couldn't get the neurosurgeon to come to Midland to work on the baby, so they transported her to Odessa, and that's where she died. That affected me for a long time. That was before I had any children. It really gave me doubts as to whether I wanted to be a paramedic or not.

They took the mother with them in the front of the ambulance. They were worried about her as well as the baby, because she was freaking. She totally lost everything, which I would, too. Any normal mother would have, after running over her own child.

The father kept his composure. At first, the accident was called in as a 1050, a car wreck. And the father had blood around his mouth and on his nose when we arrived, and I thought there had been some type of car wreck. I didn't know until later that he had done CPR on the child. He also did his best with his wife. At the hospital, of course, she had to be sedated and all that.

I really care a lot about people—whether it's putting out their fires, trying to save their lives, or getting a baby out of a well.

□

There were no windows in the building. This was at three in the morning on December 31 in an industrial section of Cleveland. A pretty cold night. We weren't on the box. Battalion 1 had the fire. The battalion chief, Paul

Wilke, made a triple two on it, a second alarm, and we go on all triple twos.

The building wasn't venting well, the smoke was really stratified and down on the ground. When we came up there, we couldn't even see the building, the smoke was so heavy. Truck 1 was up on the roof, ventilating it. I talked to Chief Wilke, and I recognized the type of construction. My first concern was about the men on the roof. It was an open bar joint, metal deck roof. The first thing I did was get them off there, because I didn't think it was worth risking them.

The fire was fairly serious in the stock and office areas. We had two companies in on the lines. Seeing the situation we had and the need for more manpower, we called for a third alarm and had the companies report to a staging area. Due to the reduction in battalions, on the third alarm we didn't get a chief, which made safety a problem, as far as I was concerned. I made a call for another battalion chief, so we could split the fire up. My normal procedure—and I'm very adamant about this—is to sector the fire because, I don't care who you are, I don't think you can run the whole fire by yourself.

At that time we got a call on the walkie-talkie from a firefighter, who said he was lost in the building. We organized the search team, and the fire itself became of secondary importance. The smoke was really heavy even though we had a good ventilation hole in the roof. It was tough to open up the sides of the building, and we had companies working on that. There were railroad tracks and an embankment that made it very difficult to get to the back of the building.

It took us approximately seven minutes to find this firefighter, a five-year veteran on Engine 22 named Dan. He had been to quite a few fires on a very busy engine company, so I don't know what caused him to do what he did. He was the nozzle man on the line, and there were two others on the line with him. One of the men went back to get a hook, and the second man exhausted his air tank and he ran out to change his tank, leaving Dan alone for the moment.

He was only about twenty-five feet into the building, and for some reason he left the line. There was a backup line laid out, but nobody was aware that this firefighter had left the line. We tried to give him instructions on the walkie-talkie, but we couldn't get any response back from him.

The building was approximately 150 by 200 feet with about twenty aisles and racks blocking overhead doors in the back of the building.

We finally found him when we saw the light of his flashlight. He had gotten into a dead end aisle. It was really difficult to find him, and naturally it seemed like an eternity. We brought him out, gave him CPR and oxygen, and transported him to the hospital, where they worked on him for over an hour. He never came back.

The fire had been pretty well knocked, but the building was loaded with smoke. There was a lot of electrical insulation that had burned. And he ran out of air. There's about twenty minutes of air in a tank. He ran out.

I was very depressed after that fire, from having lost a firefighter and talking to his wife. She was distraught, naturally. Since I was in charge of the fire, I thought it was my job to talk to the woman. So early in the morning, after a couple of news conferences, I went out to her house with a couple of other firefighters from his company, and we consoled her as best we could. She was completely broken up. It was hard for her to grasp the permanence of her loss.

I never blamed myself personally for the death, but it makes you want to reexamine and look deeper and see what can be done to prevent a recurrence. In that type of fire, there are some things you can control and some things that you can't control. The possibility of a firefighter getting seriously injured or killed is always a clear and present danger. We tend to become complacent when we go for a long period of time without casualties, and we like to think it's because we've run the fires well and the men are knowledgeable and well trained. Actually, there's a certain amount of luck involved, if you look back and think of the many close calls where a few seconds made the difference.

I remember one fire where we had a very good, experienced lieutenant in charge of our company. We were fairly new guys on the job and didn't realize the seriousness of some of our actions. We were probably 150 feet into a hundred-year-old mercantile building on West Sixth Street, and the lieutenant said, "Back out of here, we have to get out of here." There was the lieutenant, myself, and two other guys. As soon as we got out the door, the whole first floor went into the basement.

You wonder how that man knew that. He knew that the situation was bad, he had that sense. I always remembered that. It made me want to become more proficient, to learn more from experience and studying. It caused me to do a lot of studying.

I was pretty depressed for a week or so. The wake and the funeral were fresh in my mind, and I went over and over and over that fire to determine what I could have done differently to prevent it. My wife and family were completely understanding and supportive.

□

The fire happened about two in the afternoon, a quiet Saturday. The Red Sox were on television. In fact, the TV cameras shot across the outfield and picked up the smoke rising from the fire. It was the old Vendome Hotel, which had two wings, one about five or six stories high and the other six or seven stories, with a penthouse with a bay window on the top floor. Originally, it was a very grand hotel, but it was under renovation for several months at that time. It was going to be restored. The only thing open was a restaurant on the ground floor.

There were four alarms. There was very little fire to be seen, but a tremendous amount of smoke. We did an aggressive interior attack. There were all kinds of plywood partitions the workmen had put up to make temporary hallways. So the windows weren't much help, and ventilation was poor. We went at it, and we thought it was a tough fight but a good fight, and we managed to knock this thing down. Some of the fire was in the coping and parts of the cockloft, and not too accessible.

At about five o'clock we were relieved by the night tour. We had our line up to the top floor, and the relief guys came in and they found us. Oh, yeah, here you are. Okay, we're around the corner with the pumper. Okay, everybody's here, we're going to take off, see you later. The fire was pretty much knocked down, so we left.

The station was only six blocks away, so we walked back. There were a million sirens going, and the firehouse was empty. One guy, who was late coming in for the night tour, was there. I said, "What happened?" He said, "The Vendome collapsed!" And we went, "Holy God, it can't! The fire is out! It can't!" Being young and on the job just short of two years, I was in a total state of shock. I just couldn't believe this. How could it happen?

So we ran back. We were only gone about fifteen minutes. The whole back end of the building had collapsed from the top floor down to the basement. The pile of rubble was in a pyramid shape, about three stories high. Our ladder company, Ladder 15, was in the back alley, and they had their stick up, their aerial ladder, and the entire rig was just crushed to a pulp. The whole scene looked like pictures of a bad earthquake. Just mountains of bricks.

And nobody knew, especially with the change of tours and all the running and milling around, who had been inside the building and who hadn't. There were innumerable roll calls, trying to figure it out. And then we started on it, brick by brick.

Some of the guys were right there on top of the mountain, because they had been on the top floor. The top of the heap was apparently the way it worked out: the higher up you were, the easier it was, so to speak, even though they had to ride down seven floors. So our lieutenant from the night tour was found almost immediately, badly injured, also another of our firefighters from the night tour, Alan Falk. After that, with the piles of cement and brick, you just knew it was hopeless.

We went from the top piece by piece, brick by brick, piece of cement by piece of cement, still watching to make sure the other two sides of the interior walls didn't collapse on us. They got the last guy out about one in the morning. Somewhere around eleven o'clock, I just took my helmet and fire coat off, and I just walked away. I walked away like I was a zombie. I guess that's exactly what I was. It was a way of saying, without actually saying it, "I can't handle this anymore, I'm leaving." I don't know how to explain it, it's like I was hypnotized.

Unfortunately, I can never forget seeing the guy from our company. His helmet was all crushed up. And all you can say to yourself is, there but for a couple of minutes . . . or if somebody had called and said, "I'm going to be late, will you hang in there for me?" . . .

I literally fell apart, because I was saying to myself, this isn't what the job is supposed to be like. It was not a good time at all because I didn't really know how to deal with it.

I later found out that the fire was not the major cause of the collapse. The contractors had removed a good portion of the fire wall down in the basement, and with a duct had penetrated the remaining wall right next to a lone bearing column. And it turned out that this one column was the only thing that was holding up the entire section of the building.

So I walked away, and I walked back to the firehouse, and there was a relocated company there from some other part of the city. They said, "We got people calling here." Then I realized I hadn't called anybody at home. I'd never thought of it. I called my wife, Linda. I didn't have much to say. She said everybody had been calling and all that stuff.

The day of the funeral was a cold, rainy day, driving rain. At Holy Cross Cathedral in the South End. I had never seen so many firefighters in one place before. Because one of the guys was from our company, we got seats inside, up front. Seeing everybody lined up outside, it was starting to sink in—okay, this job isn't all fun. You've heard stories of other guys getting killed on the job, but nothing has the impact of the guy being in your own company and you being there. And it never stopped raining once, the whole time, and nobody said a heck of a lot afterwards. But you could tell everybody was thinking the same thing.

□

In same ways it's worse with EMS, because of the blood factor. In fires, people are burned and they look awful. In EMS, you have the blood factor and severed limbs. And sometimes the trauma and the violence. We see quite a bit of violence. At times we are there before the police arrive in violent situations. Our response times are so quick that we sometimes get there in the heat of the battle, when the shooting is still going on. We have to be very aware and cautious. That can be stressful.

We have some old neighborhoods that are low-income areas, where the crime rate is high, arson is high. These are mostly single-family homes, no tenements. And Charlotte is a city that has a lot of handguns, consequently a good bit of shooting. One summer we had ten or eleven homicides near Engine 13, where I worked. Sometimes we had two in a night.

We provide basic life support until the paramedics get there. You're concerned for your patient, you're concerned for yourself. You're surrounded by people. You look for an area of refuge. You advance cautiously. It's a hectic, hyper type of situation.

We went to one nightclub on Wilkinson Boulevard where we had five people who were shot. When we arrived there were only two, but three more were subsequently shot while we were there, right near where we were operating. Captain Kennedy was a seasoned veteran who had seen a lot of things, but he was upset after that incident. We all were. I had never seen him sit down in a chair, put his feet up, and smoke a cigarette. He didn't talk. The whole company was kind of lethargic after it was over.

It was the emotional stress, dealing with gunshot wounds in a large crowd without much police protection. There was so much going on. We went from one victim to the next to the next. We just followed the trail, logistically getting the equipment there.

One person did all the shooting. Apparently it was the result of a rivalry between high school football teams. The neighborhoods here are very involved in their high schools, which is good. They are very proud of their sports teams, which is good. Until it ends up in a shooting, which is not good.

Not too long ago they had a big drug shoot-out. An automatic weapon was used, several hundred rounds were shot, and eight or nine people were transported to the hospital.

To get back to the blood factor, I'm not concerned with AIDS nearly as much as I am with hepatitis. We try to take the precautions of wearing gloves and cleaning up very well afterwards. We keep a mental list of known cases, and we wear masks as well as rubber gloves when we deal with these people, whether they have hepatitis, tuberculosis, or AIDS. We wear paper masks, like surgical masks.

The city is also providing us with hepatitis vaccinations now, which I think is a great thing. It's an expensive series of three shots, about a hundred dollars per man, but they realize the need for us to have that kind of protection.

You don't get blood on your person every day, but the big problem is, the blood spurts. So we take those precautions not to come into contact with the blood. And maybe they'll cure these things some day. You've just got to keep going. You have to say to yourself, "When the alarm comes, I'm going to be ready."

◻

Danny Brook and I were paramedics in Rescue 7. We were in the firehouse. It was a quiet day, and I forget if we were watching TV or working out with weights, and I was thinking about a date I had that night. And we got a call for a collapsed building.

When we got to the collapsed building, the company had already gotten out a few people who were on the first floor. It was a three-story building that had collapsed down to street level. No fire, it just collapsed.

They had electric wires down, and you could smell the gas leaking. Chief Mahoney said, "Watch out for the live wires."

There was a woman there in front running around hysterically, saying, "My baby is still in the building."

So I ran up to the collapse, where there was a crowd. Somebody handed me a little kid. So I took the kid and ran down to the squad where this woman was, and I said, "Here's your baby." The kid was about four years old. She said, "No, that's not my baby. My baby is about two." So I ran over to Chief Mahoney. "Chief, there's another kid in there."

There was a lot of confusion and hysteria, people running around. By that time we had looked over everything that we could, without seeing the baby. The whole building was mostly in the basement, and it was still pretty unstable. The first floor was a store, so you had freezers and refrigerators and a lot of heavy stuff that fell. So there were a lot of air pockets down in the basement.

We looked and looked through every hole, and we couldn't find anything, and we couldn't hear anything. Finally there was one small hole that hadn't been explored. I said, "Chief Mahoney should send in a few small men to find out if anything's in there." So we immediately shot right into the hole. Once inside, we had to crawl like snakes from one air pocket to another. There wasn't a lot of room, and you could see that things were barely held up by just a few things. All it took was for something to shift, and the rest of the stuff would come down on us. The electric wires were outside, and we could smell the gas.

We were in there for three or four minutes when Dave Crompton asked if we needed a hand, and we said, "Yeah." We were moving stuff around, and Dave came and helped us do that. I remember telling Danny, "Danny, be careful." He's a little impulsive, and I thought I'd better slow him down a little bit. I was saying, "Danny, be careful. Don't move stuff too fast." If he pulled the wrong thing, everything was going to come down.

So we looked and looked, we crawled and looked some more.

I remember saying to Danny, "Danny, it's time to go." We had been there long enough. I didn't hear anybody, I didn't see anybody. And if there was somebody, he wasn't alive anymore.

He said, "But I'm not leaving here, because there's somebody in here, and I couldn't live with myself."

This sticks in my mind because we all knew that this was a little black kid we were looking for, and Danny is white, and Dave is white, too. So I said, "Okay, let's look some more." He was looking maybe harder than I was.

Then there was a little door that had fallen on a bunch of debris, and the kid was under that door. We didn't realize it. As a matter of fact, a couple of times we were nearly on that door. Then we started digging around the edge of the door, which let air under it, and when the kid got the air, he started crying in a muffled way. I sat right there and said, "We have him. We have him."

I got Dave to get the Halligan. When he handed it to me, I used it to pry up the edge of the door. He looked under, and said, "I can see him. I can see his leg." Then Danny reached under the edge of the door and pulled the kid out by his leg. He handed him to me, I gave him to Dave, and Dave passed him out of the hole.

I said, "Well, now let's get the hell out of here." Afterwards, it was funny and it was gratifying, but the whole time we were in there, it was very scary. You could smell the gas, and I knew there were live wires outside. And the debris was still shifting down, and at any time it could have finished collapsing. And there was so much stuff over us, I knew that once it came down on us, there was nobody that could have gotten us out of there. Fortunately, it all worked out for the best.

The child had only minor scratches. It was just his day, that's all. He fell into a pile of dirt, there were heavy things around him, the door fell on top of him, and everything else fell on top of the door. As a matter of fact, it was the refrigerators and freezers that fell from the first floor that really saved this kid, because when the thing fell, this heavy stuff was support for everything that fell on top of it. He fell into a safe pocket, that's what was lucky. I don't think he was conscious at first. Maybe all the moving around stimulated him and woke him up.

If we had left him, he would have died, I'm sure of that. That stuff on the door put pressure on him, and he would have slowly suffocated. When we dug dirt from around the door, what we were doing was giving him air. That's when he came to and started crying. We didn't hear anything until we got the weight off the door.

□

It was about nine-thirty in the evening. I was getting ready to go to my job at midnight. The phone call said it was an explosion. There were some fuel storage tanks in the area, and I thought it might be one of them. I drove to the station, and some of the guys were already getting the engines out. I told them I'd go on ahead to the site in my own car. We arrived there together, and the guys hooked the engine to a hydrant.

I didn't know it was a plane crash until we got there. The only thing that was really identifiable as part of a plane was the front part of it, the cockpit area. I saw an EST on the side, and I knew it was one of ours. I work for Northwest Airlines. I was kind of shocked. I didn't know what to expect. I grabbed a fire hat off the engine, and I ran down to the scene itself, not knowing that I stopped only four or five feet from the little girl who was the sole survivor of the crash.

I had the line, and I put the nozzle on and was spraying the whole area. The water came down like an easy rain. It wasn't like a major fire, like from fuel. I just found little hot spots. Actually, all it was was bodies burning, as far as I could see, the little bits of clothing that was left on them. It was dark, but I could see about a dozen bodies that were recognizable as people. I didn't really know how many were scattered all over the place. I didn't see that until daybreak.

I felt I was in kind of a helpless situation, just knowing that nobody was going to survive. I had never seen anything like that before.

I was standing there hosing the area down in a fog spray, and I didn't hear anything. Then I thought I heard the moaning, and I shut the water off to make sure I wasn't hearing things. It's possible that the water squirted on the little girl and revived her. Anyway, I heard what sounded like moaning. All I could see was a pile of rubble with a few bodies here and there, but mostly rubble.

I called my partner over, and I pointed to the spot where I thought the moaning was coming from. I thought it was a man. I could see a guy right there. I thought it was him. Well, my partner, John Thied, started moving things around, and I took the hose and went off, thinking that maybe somebody would survive, though it wasn't likely.

John heard the moaning, then it quit and he didn't hear it. He checked the bodies for any sign of life. He moved things aside to get to some of them. There wasn't much light there, and everything was black and charred. Meanwhile, I put out the rest of the fires on the bodies.

John moved aside a charred airplane seat. Then he heard the moaning again and saw that it was coming from the seat he had put aside. It was upside down, and he pulled it up, and there was the little girl strapped in it. He called our EMT over, and he did a quick survey of her body to see if there were any broken bones. Then they cut her out of the seat belt, put her on a backboard, and rushed her to the hospital.

There was some controversy about whether she was on the plane or a passenger in a car that was on the ground. About four or five hundred feet away was a Blazer. The thing was on fire from bumper to bumper when we got there, and there was somebody inside it. They thought she might have been a passenger in that car. They didn't listen to us. It was an airplane seat that she was strapped into.

Her mother was there, too. The little girl was facedown on top of her mother. The report was that the mother was trying to shield her from the flames. Nobody could hold onto something in that kind of impact. It may have been a freak thing that she landed on top of her mother. We didn't want to debate anybody on that point, so we just left it at that.

I was there for twenty-two hours. This was in our station area, so we were more or less a standby unit until everything was pretty much cleared up. I did a lot of walking. I couldn't sit still. I couldn't sleep, that's for sure, because of the smell and the things running through my mind. We had a command post with a catering van and a Red Cross wagon, giving out coffee and food. I walked back and forth to there quite a bit, but I really couldn't eat.

I don't know how you describe a lot of burning bodies. We knew enough not to touch anything until the FAA and the other people got there in the morning. They came in and went over some of the bodies, covering them up.

All the other three Romulus stations were there, plus the airport fire department and other fire departments from other communities. We were scattered all over the place, squirting down the whole area. We weren't specifically prepared for anything like this, but everybody kept their cool, saw what they had to do, and did it. We didn't think about the plane crash until later. Everybody there did a heck of a job. We knew this sort of thing would probably happen someday, we just didn't know where or when.

It was the EMTs and the coroners who put the corpses in body bags, and then we took the body bags and put them in the coroner's van, which took them to the temporary morgue. The smell there was unbearable. They had lain there all night, and then in the morning the sun started hitting them. Some bodies were pretty much intact, just burned real bad. But they could tell if they were male or female. But others, all they had was just parts, like a hand or a foot or a leg. The parts were lying all over the place.

My wife had called my company that I wouldn't be to work that night because of the plane crash. They marked it down as leave without pay. I think that in all the commotion, they weren't thinking. I had to put in a grievance to get my pay. It was hard for me to talk about what I saw. I work on those planes. Getting back on them again, I could relate to everything that was splattered all over the ground there. It kind of threw me off there for a little bit. I had recurring memories of what I did at the scene.

I think the thing brought all the guys in the department closer together, since we were all in it together. They have a counseling team for this kind of traumatic situation. We had a guy come in about two weeks after the crash, a cop with thirty years behind him. He met with us to get us to talk about it. Most of the guys really didn't want to say anything, because you don't want to talk to them if you don't know them personally. The guy had good intentions, but unless it was somebody like your pastor, it was kind of hard to open up to him. He said it himself: he had thought he had seen it all, until he came to the crash. He said, "I guess I didn't see everything."

I guess there are guys who are still having a hard time with it.

□

In California we have what we call the Santa Ana winds, usually in August and September, where the winds come off the desert and bring a real dry heat all the way across to the coast. I had my six-month probationary test coming up, and I was studying all the time. I was with Engine 4 in the north part of the city.

This particular afternoon a young guy was flying a kite southeast of town and the kite caught on some high wires, causing an arc that jumped to the heavy brush and started a fire. So they dispatched the Forest Service and every nearby unit, leaving us to protect our part of the city. We looked out our back door and watched the fire grow, we listened to the radio traffic, and finally we were dispatched.

On the way to the fire, I was sitting in the jump seat behind the driver.

Going down Foothill Road, I noticed our exhaust was shooting sparks out into the brush. I let the captain know, and thought, "Wouldn't it be ironic if our fire truck started a fire."

The fire was in a hilly area, with roads winding around and up and down the hills, an awkward place to fight a fire. Our assignment was to go up this narrow little road called Sycamore Vista. The second house on the left was on fire. A policeman lived there with his wife and two children. We couldn't do much about the house. All we could do was make sure they got out. We did that. Then we went up to the next house. There were houses all over the place beginning to burn.

With some difficulty we backed into the driveway next door. I was with Captain Jim Embersby and Engineer Dave Stanley. There was a Chevy pickup in the driveway and a great big eucalyptus tree in the back. We pulled off a 150-foot preconnect and went to fight the fire. The house was on the side of a bank. The lower part of the bank was covered with brush, and that was all burning. The upper part of the bank was also covered with brush, and it was burning, and the big eucalyptus tree was on fire. I noticed the house was preheating, and white smoke was beginning to pump out of it. There wasn't really any fire yet, but I knew it was about to burst.

A very unusual thing happened to me at that point. I had been in forest fires before, and you normally have 21 percent oxygen in the air. But here the fire was so widespread around us that it was consuming the oxygen in the air and we couldn't breathe. We had bandannas on our faces, but they were just filtering the smoke, not giving us oxygen. The captain and Dave Stanley went across the lawn toward the house, and I lost track of them. I went back to the rig and grabbed a Scott air pack, and just about at that time the engine sucked an ember down the air intake, which burned the engine out, killed the pump, and prevented us from having any water. The hose in back of the truck was totally burned out, and I think the tires were, too.

The three of us were in an open air oven. We had fire above us, below us and to the sides. We were in a little spot right in the middle of the backyard. I figured there were other people in the same situation or worse, and that we were basically on our own. Funny, but my main concern during this whole time was passing my probationary test. I was dedicated!

So after I rejoined the other two, we all got into our fire tents. I think it was a miracle that we happened to be in a spot where there was a pocket of breathable air. I believe the Lord sent an angel down to protect us. There was so much fire around us. We shared the Scott pack, but it really wasn't that important. One of the things that helped me was something I learned in the Forest Service, which is, always carry some chewing gum with you. It helps keep some of the moisture in your mouth, otherwise you get real dry, then you get smoke and embers in your eyes and it's real uncomfortable.

We lay beneath our tents then for about forty minutes and listened to the fire popping all around us. We also listened to the radio traffic to see if anybody had any emergencies as bad as we had, and in fact they didn't. So we called for some help, for someone to come up to us. And Engine 1 and Squad 1 did try to come up to us. The driver of the engine got out, but the fire was so hot that he had to get right back in the engine. It was impossible for them to come through with hose lines and rescue us, because there was just too much fire and heat.

Usually brush fires pass over fairly quickly, but there was a lot of heavy brush which burned for a longer while, and, of course, there were all the buildings on fire around us. I noticed afterwards that the windshield of the pickup truck was just a clump of glass. It had melted.

While we were lying in our tents, we communicated with each other. We had the option of either staying where we were or taking a chance on running out through the brush and getting away. The captain convinced us that our best bet was to stay there, and so we did. There were other fire companies in similar situations, but their engines hadn't burned out, so that when they opened up the nozzle and water came out, they could put their faces close to the nozzle and breathe the cooler air with oxygen in it.

I kept lifting my tent and looking around. The heat only twenty feet from us was probably about 900 degrees, but to me the heat wasn't the problem, it was the lack of oxygen. It was difficult to breathe. And then there was the house. I remember looking at the house one time, and then, about twenty minutes later, the entire house was gone. All that was left was the chimney. It was like jumping from one scene to another in a movie. It was amazing.

While I was lying there, I thought, "If this is it, then this is it." I'm not a quitter, but I knew that we were on our own and that nobody in the whole area could do anything for us. I figured there were probably people in worse situations than we were. I prayed. I have a strong faith, and I believe that the Lord provided a little pocket of oxygen for us to breathe, because the fire consumed everything else. I knew that death was potentially nearby, as it is in a lot of the situations that we see. But I do appreciate life, and we all have a great concern for safety.

Finally, after forty minutes or so, the fire had passed over and settled down a little bit. The guys from the bottom made another attempt to get to us, and they got the pump going, but they were still not able to reach us. The ones who did finally reach us came over the top from the other side of the hill. They knew we were still alive, because we had kept in radio contact and given them updates of our situation.

When we got out, the fire was still going on. I would have stayed and gone through the whole thing, but during this time I had somehow cut my left eye. I don't know how, but I had scratched the cornea pretty good, and it got to the point where it bothered me so bad, I couldn't concentrate, and I couldn't do anything to get relief for it.

So they took me to the hospital, where they cleaned out my eyes, put in some medicine, and packed both of them. Actually they were more concerned about the black in my lungs. I had inhaled some smoke, which is common. So they cleared out the black stuff.

I didn't get to finish the whole fire. It stopped burning a couple of hours later, and that was it. History.

And to think that it all started from a little spark from a guy flying his kite! In all, that fire consumed 270 homes, and I don't think any lives were lost!

□

I was involved in a rescue on Eighty-sixth Street in Manhattan. Captain Wallace, Louie, and I went into a converted brownstone that was on fire. Starting our search, we went down a hallway and came to an apartment whose door was hot to the touch. As I pushed the door open, the sprinklers went off over our heads, and a big blast of smoke and heat came at us. I knew we had a good job ahead of us.

The captain and Louie went straight ahead into a bedroom area, but I thought I heard something from the other end, so I went down that way. As I was crawling down this hallway, I was pretty low because of the heat, I heard my name being called. "Paul. Paul." At first I thought, "Allen Funt, *Candid Camera*. They're tricking me." Then I thought it was one of the guys from the company, maybe the outside vent man had gotten in a window and saw me coming.

Then I realized it was a female voice. I went a little faster down the hall, and I kept hearing my name being called. "Paul. Paul. Paul." I came across a semiconscious woman on the floor at a point where the fire was just starting to roll over near the ceiling and take full possession of the back room.

I shook her and asked, "Who's Paul? Who's Paul?"

She started mumbling.

I said, "Is Paul your boyfriend?"

She said, "Yes."

"Is he here?"

"No."

I said, "Are you sure?"

She said, "He's at work." Then she passed out.

I had a good idea there was no other Paul there except me, so I dragged her out and got her out to the sidewalk. I gave her a little forced air until she came around a little bit and was taken away in the ambulance. Two weeks later she showed up at the firehouse with a cake. I was off that day, but the guys told me the cake was great. I thought it was nice that the woman cared enough to come around and thank the fire department for their efforts.

After I transferred from 25 Truck to Rescue 1 in Manhattan I was quiet, waiting for a chance to prove myself. I was there only a short time when I was involved in a rescue. Again it was one of those left-right deals. I went to the right, and this other guy went to the left. I got lucky. I found an unconscious man, and I had to carry him down seven flights of stairs. I injured my back a little. But I felt I had shown the men on rescue that I could go where they went, and I could accomplish the mission.

Some jobs I remember better than others. One night tour I was working, it happened to be my birthday. We went out at six-thirty in the morning to this job down in the Lower East Side. I had one of the outside ventilation positions, and there was a report of people possibly trapped in these apartments. The truck companies had already made a couple of good rescues. I started working my way up a fire escape, wearing an old Scott mask with the big bottle.

I got up to the fire floor and was at the window of the next apartment, which was now taking off, though the window hadn't vented yet. Since there was only one line going, I didn't want to start venting windows. I wanted to get in from above, so I started up the fire escape to the next floor, which was the fifth, and all of a sudden the window beneath me let go. I was in a wave of heat and smoke shooting up the side of the building above the courtyard.

I began getting a little bit concerned as to whether I was going to get myself out of this predicament I had gotten myself into. I was trying quickly to move past the fire escape ladder, but the Scott mask was making me too bulky to get near the wall. Like trying to get the square peg in the round hole. I climbed up on the railing to try to swing out. The fire was just starting to come out of the window beneath me. It was getting very hot. I was more worried than I have ever been in a fire situation.

All of a sudden I heard a *whoosh* and a slapping noise. I looked down in the courtyard, and there was 55 Engine shooting a line up and shoving the fire back into the window. They knocked it down enough so I could reposition myself, and I scrambled up, looked down, gave them a wave, and jumped into the apartment. I did okay. We searched the building and didn't find anybody else.

Afterwards, I made it a point to go down and thank the officer and the men of 55 Engine for saving my ass on that one. I had been a little bit concerned that I was going to spend my birthday in a hospital, or worse.

□

You see a lot in this profession. There was a truck driver driving this tractor-trailer through Santa Barbara one afternoon, and he crossed the highway divider. He hit a Honda head on and crushed it, also a pickup truck with three construction workers in it.

We didn't even see the girl who was driving the Honda until we got a big tow truck to get the tractor-trailer off her car. She was just jelly. We had to cut her out with the jaws of life. The three construction workers were coming home from work. They didn't make it. They were crushed inside the truck.

The saddest thing is to see an innocent person dying. We had several medical calls recently to a young boy who was extremely sick, and every once in a while he would stop breathing. That was a very painful thing for his parents, and it drew a lot of compassion from the firemen.

You've got to live with these things. When we come back to the station, I talk about these things with one of the guys I work with. But the traditional male machoism keeps some guys from expressing their true feelings or even talking about it. This guy now has a master's degree in psychology. He does seminars in Texas on postincident stress reduction, helping firefighters deal with injuries and deaths, mass deaths like in plane crashes. You go out there and do what you have to do, yet a lot of it sets in and affects you. You've got to learn to overcome it, to release it instead of bottling it up inside. So we're learning to do that.

□

There was a rooming house fire up on Beacon Hill. A flophouse really, an eight-story dump, filled with dozens and dozens of occupants who were less well off than the rest of us. I was lieutenant of our ladder company, and we went as an additional ladder company to the fire, which eventually went to six alarms. There were no fire escapes, and these people were being taken out from the inside.

We consulted with the chief, and he said, "The guy in that window." He's pointing to the seventh floor, where a guy was hanging over the windowsill. Our rig was parked a block away, so I told our guys to swing it around to the other block and see if our stick can reach him from there. In the meantime, I went up the inside stairs to the seventh floor. There was not a large amount of fire to be seen, but the smoke and the heat were boiling.

I found this guy, and he was barely conscious. Besides, he couldn't walk very well because of arthritis or something. I said, "Okay, come on, let's go." And I started to carry him down. I was lucky, he wasn't a heavy guy at all.

We were in the hallway when the smoke and the heat changed instantly. I knew it was going to flash, and we had to get the heck out. At any moment the fire was going to chase us. He was having trouble, so I gave him my mask, and I carried him down the inside stairway.

In the street I put him on the running board on the far side of one of the trucks. Somebody brought over an inhalator, and I was trying to get the guy to take some air. Then I don't remember anything until I woke up in the hospital. They told me afterwards that I just went shish, boom, and that was it.

In the hospital, I heard a woman doctor talking to the others. And I said to myself, "That's it, an angel, I'm all done. This is it, I've bought it." The only reason the department saw fit to write me up for a medal was because I had pulmonary burns, burns down the throat and lungs. But they were not from the fire itself, they were from the heat. The difference is, I wouldn't be sitting here today if they were from the fire itself. Just the smoke and heated gases, that's all.

I don't think it's a great idea to talk about the medal—it was nice, okay —but I'm no different from anybody else.

□

We had a record low of fourteen below zero. Some young boys had gone over to the conservation club and stolen some liquor. They took it to a little shack that was built between two small hills so that the roof was even with the ground. For heat, they had a fifty-gallon drum with some wood in it, and they had a fire in it. One of the kids, about twelve or thirteen, passed out, and they wanted the fire to keep him warm while they went to get some more kids.

By the time they got back, the building was engulfed in flames. We were called on it. We could see the child, we could hear him screaming, and we did everything we could possibly do, but we couldn't get near him. It was like, my God, what can we do? We've got all the water we could possibly want, we've all the help we could possibly want, but we can't get into the shack. It was untouchable.

After the fire was all over, the body had been totally burned, and it was frozen solid, because of the weather outside. And we had to cut a slab of ice with the body right in it and pick it up frozen, and take it to the county morgue.

I remember coming home from that. It was in the middle of the night, probably about four in the morning. And I was devastated. I walked around the house a little bit. I didn't want to wake my husband up, and I went and sat down on my son's bed, and I just looked at him. That's when I started to cry. I thought, what an awful way to die. What an awful thing for any child, or even a parent, to have to go through. I am very sensitive with children's calls. Whether it's a child abuse or a medical or a skateboard accident, my heart goes out a little bit more to those kinds of calls.

□

Nelson Taylor, an older fellow, was a late bloomer like myself. When he finally made lieutenant, they sent him to 8 Engine, which is in a ghetto-type area where you get to do a lot of service. He was on the opposite shift from me at 8 Engine.

He had relieved me that morning, and that evening I was coming in to relieve him. He had a basement fire. There is still controversy over what really happened, but for the sake of argument let's say there was a flash-over and a partial backdraft occurred.

The lieutenant was on the nozzle at the top of the basement stairs, and the pipe man was backing him up. It must have been because the heat was so severe that they were changing positions. He was sucked down the stairs into the basement, and the pipe man got thrown out the door. This hap-pened at four-thirty in the afternoon, and at one in the morning he died at the burn center. He was burned very badly, and his lungs were seared.

That gave me the coldest chill the whole time I was in the fire depart-ment. If our shifts had been reversed, I would have been in the same place he was at. It could have been any of us, whoever had happened to be in charge of the company at the time. Here was another case of one of your own. It happened in the daytime, which seemed more unusual, because most things happen in the nighttime. When I came in to relieve that night, God, it was such a terrible, uneasy feeling.

It was devastating to his family. The husband and father goes to work, and everyone is happy, and all of a sudden he doesn't come home. We had a full departmental funeral for him. It was very chilling and made you cry inwardly.

But firefighters have a way of springing back. I'm still on the job. I'll probably be here for another year, maybe two. Under the new rules, I can get out any time I want. But I think I'll hang around a little while longer.

□

A guy got burned up in his bed. I was a nozzle man on the unit, and we pulled the line into the bedroom, which was fully involved. We climbed across a lot of things. And I stepped in something slippery. I didn't think about it at the time.

When the fire was over and the investigator was on the scene, we found what was left of the body in the bed. The investigator said, "Gee, it appears someone stepped on it." Then I realized that I had stepped on the bloated body of the poor guy.

It really had an effect on me. For about three days after that, I couldn't sleep. I had never been sickened by an incident before, but the fact that I stepped on the guy, and he was in bed, that got to me.

Then something happened that woke me up. At an apartment fire. The fire was upstairs, and when we were taking a tag line up, there was this guy coming down the stairs on crutches. He was one-legged. We went on with our search. I found a dog, which was still alive, and I came across a shoe. I also grabbed a leg, but I was so intent on the rescue, I didn't know if it was part of a body or what.

I came out with the shoe and the leg, and I'll never forget it. This guy says, "There's my leg." So I rescued this guy's leg and his shoe.

I got a little ragging from the guys. I made a pretty picture, sitting there with this guy's leg.

□

We rolled into a big two-and-a-half frame, and we got a report there were people trapped up there. When we pulled in, the fire was coming out three or four windows on the one side. I was the forcible entry man, so I jumped off the truck, and not waiting to put on my Scottpac, I ran in the house and went up the stairs. Another fellow was with me.

I opened the door at the top of the stairwell, and both of us were blown back down the stairs by the pressure of the heat and the heavy black smoke. I ran back to the truck, grabbed the Scott mask and just threw it on. I went back upstairs. There was no line in operation yet. I went in and started crawling around. I went into one of the rooms, and I heard a moan.

I found this man lying there, Mr. Peeples, a big black man, about six-two, weighing about 220. I couldn't see him. All I could do was feel. I could also feel the heat. They still didn't have a line in operation. I didn't know where I was. I didn't know which way to get out, because of the heavy smoke condition. The man was unconscious. I tried to lift him. I couldn't lift him.

I grabbed him, put my arms under him, and started to drag him. I dragged him past the rooms that were on fire. The engine company got water, and they hit the fire from the outside, and they pushed it in. Not knowing where I was going, I had to drag this man through the fire. He got burned, and I got burned. I dragged him out to the second-floor porch. By the time I got him there, he wasn't breathing.

I took off my mask and put it on him; I put it on the bypass to give him a shot of air. He started to come to, then he went out again. One of the guys got there and started to give him mouth-to-mouth. The ambulance people came, they took him. I found out that on the way to the hospital he stopped breathing again. They brought him back. The same thing happened at the hospital.

Later on, I found out that the man had five operations, and he lived. He went down from 220 to 167 pounds. On Medal Day, he was there to present me my award. It made me feel good, because I saved a life.

I saw quite a few people die in the North End. There was one fire where a mother and child died. I wanted to cry, because they were right by the window. Probably in the dark, they didn't know where they were. All they had to do was lift up, and out the window they'd go. After the fire was out and they removed the bodies, you could see their outline on the parquet floor as if somebody took a pencil and drew the figures. Everything around them was soot except where they had lain. It even showed where the little baby's foot was sticking out at the mother's arm.

It always comes back into my mind.

Then there was a fire right down the street from the firehouse. It was a big two-and-a-half-story frame house. We lost three people. Two guys dove out the window. One went head first. The other had one leg. He was a war veteran. We tried our best to save them.

I accept the deaths of the adults more than I do the children. The children get me more than anything. It takes a toll. Sometimes I think of my own children. What would happen if I lost one of them in a fire? I don't know how I would handle it. I really don't.

Later on, there was a fire on Garden Street about six in the morning. I was on the truck company then, Ladder 3. A second-floor fire, heavy smoke, heavy fire upon arrival. A report of two elderly women trapped in the apartment. I went up and made it to the apartment door, but I couldn't get in without a line. The line came in finally and protected me.

I went past the fire to the back bedroom, got the woman, a sixty-year-old black woman. She wasn't breathing. I slung her over my shoulder. They kept the line on the fire until I got back. I got her down to the street. They worked on her, and she lived. I feel fortunate about that. Sometimes you're at the right place at the right time.

□

We had had a relatively quiet day at the squad company, which is like a rescue company. We had a couple of accidents where we had to extricate people from wrecked autos, and a couple of small fire alarms. In the evening we had a few more accidents. At midnight, we went to a fire in a vacant two-and-a-half frame close to our firehouse. We did a lot of overhauling, and they asked us on the radio if we were available for another second-alarm fire, and the chief said, go ahead. So we went right from one fire scene to the next.

This second fire was in a two-and-a-half-story frame connected to a three-story brick building, and there was a two-story brick coach house in the rear of the lot. We forced entry, searched in the one building. We took a second line off an engine company and worked it up to the second floor and attic. It was a cool night, but we were pretty tired, beat, soaking wet, and dirty.

We were in the coach house, which was immediately off an alley, just taking a break. The engine was washing down, and we were pretty much done with the overhauling. We heard civilians hollering in the alley, "Hey, there's a fire down here!" Sure enough, there was a fire in a three-story frame building about five buildings away from where we were, across the alley and on the next street, quite a distance away.

The first fire was definitely arson, gang-related arson. We thought the second one was, too, but a long time later I heard that it was probably started by flying embers from the first fire. The embers had gotten into the gutter and started the attic on fire. But we didn't know that at the time.

We were on the second floor of the coach house, and the engine company we were with had shut the water down and were going to drag the line to the new fire. But what they had was a line that was full of water and extremely heavy to drag. I jumped down the ladder and ran down the alley. The commander who was there heard the people screaming, and he came running, too.

I went through the gate to the back porch and up the stairs to the third floor, which was a peaked-roof attic. At the top of the stairs I saw fire in the midsection of the building. I came back down and told the chief what we had. I said, "We're going to need a line up there." Our rig was parked down the street, and I told my driver by walkie-talkie to bring the rig around the block and to get our hand pumps. These are five-gallon water extinguishers that you have to pump by hand. I said, "Get the pumps and bring them up here." My engineer, for some reason, didn't do that.

The head of the stairwell was in the back of the building, and the attic windows in the front of the building were intact. I was waiting for the hand pump, and I sent my two other guys from the squad to help the engine company drag the heavy line. It took them a few minutes. They had to drag it down the alley, through the gateway, and up the stairs, maybe five or six hundred feet. The lieutenant on the engine company had the pipe, and I was on the landing, and he was coming up the stairs. I said, "As soon as you get water, I'm going for the windows." It was getting charged up, up there. The lieutenant had just enough line to reach the top of the stairs, where he could give the fire a whack.

At last he said he had water, so I went down the right side of the attic. The fire was in the left middle section of the attic. I crawled by it as fast as I could. I got to the two front windows and whacked them out. The lieutenant on the engine company was screaming at me, "We lost the water! I lost the water!" I leaned out the window and hollered down to my engineer, "Get that hand pump up here! We lost the water!" My engineer was just staring at me.

I turned around to go back, and the whole attic lit up, it was a ball of fire. I just put my head down and crawled as fast as I could. I knew where the stairs were, and I followed the same route down the same side I had come. But there was this little partition wall sticking out, and I hit it, causing me to roll toward the fire. I lost my helmet, and hot embers flowed by my head. I screamed at the lieutenant, "I'm burning up!" I charged ahead blindly the remaining fifteen feet and dove down the stairs right on top of the lieutenant.

He had just gotten the water back. I felt the mist when I hit the partition, and the water turned to steam because it was so hot up there. I went down the stairs head first. The guys dragged me out of the building. I said, "I'm burning up." I got to my feet and got to the gateway, and just collapsed. The firemen ripped my fire clothes off. I just lay there. I had been soaking wet from the previous fire, and what the heat had done was cook me inside the coat.

The ambulance and the paramedics were there inside of two minutes. I could feel everything burning, my eyes, everything. I couldn't get cool fast enough. They cut my clothes off right on the street. They just took scissors and ripped my clothes, my shirt, my underwear right off me. The stripes on the coat had melted, and the coat looked like the outer layer of black material was skimmed off by the heat. The belt on my pants was rock hard. They soaked me in water, they used every bit of saline solution they had on the ambulance. The two paramedics did a tremendous job. They were fabulous. They helped me immensely. As much pain as I was in, they did what they could for me.

They took me to a hospital a half mile away. I was lying on my stomach, and my eyes started swelling shut. Everything hurt. I kept telling them, "Don't call my wife." It was now about three or four in the morning. The guys from the squad came to the hospital, and I kept telling them, "Don't call my wife. Call my brother Ray." He was a fireman who worked on a different shift from me. They called him, and I lost track of time.

The next thing I knew I was begging the nurse to give me something for the pain. They couldn't pour enough cool solution on me. I looked up, and there was my brother. The people at the hospital decided to fly me to a burn unit. Of the three units in the city, I told them to take me to the Bernard Mitchell Burn Unit, because it was closer to home. The burn unit sent a helicopter, but the hospital didn't have a landing pad. So the night shift of nurses went out and moved their cars, and the helicopter came down between the wires and landed in the parking lot. My eyes were swelling shut, I could hardly see, and I was covered by clean sheets. A nurse started to catheterize me, and I told her not to do it, but she did it anyhow. They shot me with morphine, and I started to calm down.

The helicopter landed, and they wheeled me in. For the next three or four hours I was being debrided, where they pick the burned skin off you. I was burned over 30 percent of my body, second- and third-degree burns on my face, ears, back, arm, buttocks, and legs. Most of it was on my back. I had burns all over my head from hot stuff dropping down. Because I had enough morphine, I was pretty much at ease during the debridement.

My father-in-law, who is a firemen, brought my wife and mother-in-law to the hospital. They told my wife she'd be able to see me in an hour or so. Four hours later, she was still waiting. By that time my head was swollen up like a basketball and my eyes were completely swollen shut. I was burned inside my nostrils and a little in my mouth, and my lips were swollen. They brought me into the room, and my wife thought she was in the wrong room. I heard her say she was there, and then she was gone. She started crying, and she said to her father, "That's not him, that's the wrong room." He said, "No, that's him."

I just didn't look like the same person. I didn't even know she had left the room because I couldn't see her.

That morning my lieutenant came to see me. He came in and squeezed my hand. He said that everything was going to be all right, and I knew in my heart that I was going to be okay, I was going to live. The lieutenant's name was Altman, and he's now deputy commissioner. He said, "If you need anything, or your wife does, don't hesitate to call." That's the kind of guy he is. I kept asking the doctor and nurse, "Can I go back to work? Can I fight fires again?" That was my first thought.

I was in the burn unit eighteen days. Those eighteen days I wouldn't wish on my worst enemy. For four days I couldn't open my eyes, and I never moved out of that bed. After that, they made me get up. I could hardly walk. To sit down and do something simple, like going to the bathroom, was a monumental task. For debridement, they put you in a tub of water as hot as you can stand. This loosens the skin. Just to get out of bed to get in the chair to go down there to get in this tub was unbelievable. They give you shots of morphine before you go down. I didn't think the shots were doing anything for me until after I was released and had to come back every day to get debrided without having shots. They gave me acetominophen, and I was begging for shots.

The physical therapists were real sweethearts, just super people. One of them would give me a towel to bite on and say, "Let's grin and bear it, honey." After I was able to open my eyes, she gave me a mirror and told me to start debriding my own face. She said, "Is there any way you can stick your head under water to loosen the dead skin on your face?" I said, "You got a snorkel?" So with a snorkel, I would stick my head under for fifteen or twenty minutes, then she'd give me the mirror and I'd work on my face while she was working on my back. Then I'd have to stand so she could do my butt and my legs. That went on every day, and I'd come back to my room totally drained.

You become very humble. Extremely humble. My pain was bad, but there were people there who were burned far more than I was. And the thing that made me sick were the kids, little kids. I went home on a Friday night, I was supposed to stay another day or two, but they needed the bed, and it went to a seventeen-month-old baby who had been scalded by its mother. It blows my mind how people could do that to kids. That's what hurts you the most, is the kids. And there was a sixty-five-year-old woman who had been burned over 50 to 60 percent of her body by a heating pad that had somehow caught her bed on fire. Every night she just lay there and moaned so that I never got any sleep.

I had my dressings changed four times a day, and when they pull it off everything that's halfway stuck to it goes with it. Once or twice at night I got a temporary nurse, and I'd tell her, "Oh, I don't have to have mine changed tonight." I buffaloed the nurse, but when it came time to get them changed in the morning, it was twice as bad. So then I kept my mouth shut. Those nurses worked twelve-hour shifts, and they are fabulous people. They went from one room to another. They say the burnout period is two years, but I think a couple of them were there for more than two years. I gained so much respect for them.

The only time I thought I was close to dying was when I hit that partition wall. I thought I'd never see the stairway. I didn't think I was going to get out in time. From the time it flashed over, I don't think I was up there more than a minute. That's how fast that can happen. It made me appreciate my family a whole lot more. And I would rather have been the one who was burned than one of my men, because the guilt it would have given me would have been tremendous.

To this day, I try not to let my guys get ahead of me or get into a dangerous situation. To instill the thought in their heads, I lift my shirt and show them my back. I say, "This is what can happen, so don't get too cocky." You can do a thing a hundred times, but that hundred and first is going to get you. You can't get too cocky. Some guys say, yeah, but you didn't have your mask on. No, my tank was empty from the fire before. I was lying in the hospital bed, and somebody said that one of our chiefs was all bent out of shape because I didn't have a mask on. Well, that chief wasn't at any of those three fires. Somebody else said, "Don't worry about it, nothing is going to be said." I said, "Nothing should be said. I was doing my job." My mask was lying down there somewhere, out of air.

I was off the job ninety days, and I begged the burn doctor to let me go back to work. I was wearing a Job's garment, shorts and a top. It's a pressure garment that compresses the skin to keep it from scarring. When I went home I had open wounds on my back, but the hospital didn't believe in grafting right away. We ruined our bathtub at home. A neighbor gave us a whirlpool, which we put in the tub. I had red iodine on the gauze that dressed the wounds. The stuff stained everything.

When the wounds closed up and I got the pressure garment, I really fought to get back to work, even though I wasn't walking straight, I was bent over a little bit, and I still had to sleep on my stomach. I went to the fire department doctor with the Job's garment on, and he refused to send me back. I thought I'd be smart, and the next time I saw him I didn't wear it. He hemmed and hawed and finally said I could go back to work. I had to wear that pressure garment for another twenty months, I just didn't wear it to the doctor's.

The first day back at the firehouse, the first run we had was a chlorine leak. Chlorine turns the coins in your pocket green. My privates itched, my underarms itched from sweating. The bugles on the collar of my shirt turned green. I thought, "My God, I've got this pressure garment on, I'm sweating as it is, what's it going to do to my skin?" It wasn't that bad, we didn't have to go in where we got too involved, so it worked out okay. But that was my first run back, and I was thinking, "What did I get myself into?"

The day after the fire, the two squad guys who had been with me came to the hospital. My wife said they both broke down and cried. My wife was beat, and they took her out to dinner that night. The guys at the firehouse drove her to and from the hospital. They watched over her. That's when all that brotherly love falls into place. It's the unspoken word. They took care of her. A battalion chief who had been a friend of my father came to the hospital every day, even though he couldn't get in to see me. They restricted visitors because of the danger of infection. He would say to the nurse, "Just tell him I was here." I couldn't ask for better friends. My room was full of cards. My nieces and nephews drew little pictures, stuff that kind of breaks your heart. You find out how much people really think of you.

□

We were at a fire with a neighboring fire company. My guys were up on the roof with them, opening it up. The roof collapsed. There was a big roar. When that roof caved in, my first concern was, where are my guys? Each one on my team has a radio, and I knew where they were at. Everybody was okay.

We were forcing entry in the back door and had a hell of a time with it. I looked up and saw this fireman, he was pitch black and his helmet shield was melted. He was on the coping of a roof next door. There was a ladder there, the guys rolled it over, and I ran up. I said, "Sit in the snow." His fire coat was burning. The guy behind him was yelling, "Roll, roll." He stood up, hopped around, wanting to get down. I guided him down the ladder. I didn't want to touch his ass because his pants were down, and it was all raw skin. We helped him to the ambulance.

We tried to take a line over the roof next door, but we couldn't get near the fire roof because of the heat. When we finally got in, we knew what we were going to find, because there was no possible way anybody could have lived through that. But you have to get them. You have to get all of them. Everybody was exhausted. It was cold. The first thing we found was a child. I'll never forget it. The kid was nice-looking, he had a big smile, but he was just completely burned up. He had roof and tarpaper over him. It's not going to help them, but you bust your back to get them out as fast as you can. You want to show that you tried to help them. That bothers you forever.

Three firefighters were killed in that fire. We found two pretty fast, and we dug and dug looking for the third guy. Finally there was another shift waiting, and Deputy Commissioner Altman told us to get out and let the fresh guys take over.

I went back to the firehouse, took a shower, put my civilian clothes on, and went back to the fire. I wasn't going to leave until they found him. I sat in the command van until they found him. I think he tried to run toward the front of the roof. It took a lot of overhauling to find him. Then I felt a little at ease. They had at least found his body. There was something left of him.

When you go to the funerals and wakes, you look at the little kids, and they have no idea. Someday those little kids will realize what happened, but at that time, at the funerals, they have no real idea. It's sad. I remember being there when I was a boy.

◻

My first fatal fire was a particularly tragic one, in a fraternity house at the University of Oregon. The alarm came in at five-thirty in the morning. I wasn't there on the first-in company, I was called later.

There was a party in the fraternity house, and obviously a lot of alcohol had been consumed. The fire started in a chair. As we later pieced it together, a young man and woman had gone up into a third-floor room. They had a door closed between them and the fire. But the door was giving way very quickly, and the only way out for them was through the window, which was a three-story drop. The fire company had not yet arrived.

The man went out the window and was hanging onto the window ledge. The young woman looked out the window and saw that she couldn't do it. So she panicked. She opened the door and ran right through the point of origin of the fire. And by opening that door, she sealed his situation. He was hanging by his hands when the first-in company got there. There were flames blowing twenty feet out into the night over where he was.

Of course, the young woman got a couple of lungfuls of superheated air, and that was it. We found her about five feet from the fire's point of origin. I was one of the guys who found her, and we had to put her in the bag and carry her down the stairs. When I first began, those things bothered me, then after a while I got to a point where they didn't bother me, and I think that bothers me even more.

What struck me was the sheer stupidity of that whole situation. It just seemed like such a waste. I wound up writing an essay on it that *Newsweek* published as an editorial piece. A sprinkler would have prevented it. The frustration is in seeing the same things happen over and over and over again—the absence of sprinkler systems, smoke detectors that aren't properly maintained, fire doors that are left propped open.

People just never consider themselves to be potential victims of those kinds of situations. It only happens to other guys. And yet, if you're a firefighter, you see those "other guys" day after day after day after day.

◻

The rescue squad handles emergency medical calls, and most of them are not emergencies. You get calls at three or four in the morning for a guy who's drunk or somebody who's sleeping on the street. When anything happens, they call 911, and the police call the rescue squad. Once in a while I've saved people by doing CPR and all that. That made me feel great. I saved a little baby. And I've lost people, too. I've lost more than I've saved. I had a guy who was partially decapitated from an auto accident. It's not easy to carry those memories.

But when you help someone, that makes up for everything that's rough.

There are a lot of abuses of the EMS system. People know what to say to get the rescue squad to come. In fact, the police tell them, "Tell them you've got chest pains, or you're short of breath." And we've got to take it. We can't refuse. You've got to cover your ass, too. If you say the person is all right, then leave, and something happens, then you're in trouble. So you take them to the hospital and let the people in the emergency room worry about them. Sometimes it's like a sport. The police laterals to us and we lateral to the emergency room.

I don't mind the squad, because I've only been on it for two years, so I still have all these ideals in my head about saving humanity and all of that. I don't mind helping in the lower-income areas, in the ghettos, say, because the people are destitute and it means something. We're their only means of aid, so I take that into consideration.

We get a lot of alarms on the campuses, the University of Penn and Drexel. The college kids think it's all a big joke. You respond to an emergency, and you think it's that. You get there, and people are having a party, and they're pulling the boxes. They do a lot of stupid things. I've yet to have a real job there, in fact. It's all been false alarms.

You don't mind even the false alarms, because that's the way it is. But when people laugh at you, "Oh, you guys come here with lights and sirens, and it's only smoke in the room," that's tough. They're college kids, and they don't seem to understand what we're doing. It's all a joke.

There really isn't anything on this job that I dislike. Well, there are some rules imposed on the department that I don't agree with. In fact, I wrote a nasty letter, after I got hurt, about some of the equipment we have to work with. I never sent it, though. But some of the equipment is inferior, especially when you're dealing with lives, not just ours but civilians'. We have Scottpacs with face masks that you can't see out of in the daylight, they're so scratched up. And we've got engines that leak. All the pumps leak, so you have hose lines with power reduced by the amount of the leak. The city should take better care of its fire department.

□

In North Philadelphia, I was rotating from the squad to the engine. I worked engine that night, and I had the tip. We had two first-engine jobs and I was taking a beating, because I really wasn't used to fighting fire that much, since I had been a paramedic for so long. So it was two good jobs, and I had the tip in both. When you fight fire constantly, you grow accustomed to it, but when you rotate, you're in the squad 90 percent of the time.

I think that the most meaningful thing is being both a firefighter and a paramedic and just whipping them all together. There's great satisfaction in fighting a fire. And when you're a paramedic and you get somebody who is having a heart attack, you know that if you don't do the right thing within the next five minutes, this person is going to be down. You feel obligated, you give them the right drug, and they get straightened out. That's meaningful.

The paramedic just does rescue work when there are two men on the squad. If you have three men, that third man rotates out to the engine. What happened was, I had been on a two-man squad for maybe a year, and I was constantly doing paramedic work. Then we got a third man and we started rotating, so that every third week you would go on an engine. When you've been away from breathing smoke for a while, it's a little bit harder.

I got into the paramedics by accident. I was a rookie in a ladder company, and when they needed an EMT, they naturally picked on the rookie. So they made me an EMT, and I worked the rescue squad. An EMT does basic life support, that is, splinting legs, doing CPR if necessary, then running the patient to the hospital. A paramedic goes into heavy life support, he gives IVs, gets into cardiac defibrillation and drug administration, he gets patients to the hospital and contacts the doctor. He has basic command with the doctor and does what is called prehospital care.

I love the system in Philadelphia, where we rotate into the engine. Some paramedics don't like that. When I got into the fire department, being a fireman was something I had always dreamed of doing. Ever since I was a little kid, I loved the horns, I used to watch the engines go by, and my dream was to be one of the guys on the fire truck. I did a lot of jobs. As a matter of fact, I was in my fourth year as a pipefitter's apprentice, and I quit when I was called for the fire department. I loved fighting the fires, and I still love it.

When you're fighting fires, you say, "There's a fire. There's a challenge." You rise to that challenge, you want to beat it. When you do, you feel high. When you're a paramedic, it gets down to you and your partner. You find somebody who is unconscious, you've got to find out what's wrong, figure out the right thing to do, and do it. There's satisfaction in knowing that you're doing something for somebody, you're doing something that's important.

That's the basic line in both jobs. You're doing something important. That's what all firefighters feel about themselves: they feel important. I've done other jobs where I've made more money, but I never felt any sense of worth. It makes me feel good when the kids in the neighborhood come to me when one of them's gotten cut playing football or something. I'm the neighborhood medic, a sort of neighborhood hero. The kids look up to you.

It takes some intelligence to become a paramedic, but we all have to have a certain amount of intelligence to get where we are, the ability to grasp information, retain it, and then apply it. It's not a matter of superior intelligence, just being open to somebody teaching you something. What makes a good fireman is being able to do anything that's put before him. Most of us have another occupation, we're plumbers, carpenters, electricians, whatever. Each one is a jack-of-all-trades. They can do just about anything.

We have deaths too much, too often. I would say maybe 70 percent of the people we treat don't make it. My life peaked when I first became a fireman, I was doing everything I ever wanted to do. Then they made me a paramedic, and I went through a little valley. As a rookie paramedic, I was a little unsure of myself, then I had a few failures, patients who didn't make it.

I remember going home and spending my four days off just sitting in the house, depressed, worried that I didn't do the right thing. Then as time went on, I felt better, I got more confidence in myself. I knew I was doing the right thing, and whatever happened was the will of God, whether it was a save or not.

Being a paramedic is hard mentally, because you have to deal with people at their worst. Sometimes you can change it, you can right it and make things better. But most of the time you can't, so you have to deal with a lot of tragedy. You have to get used to it, and that's where it takes a good partner. If you don't have a good partner, being a paramedic can get real depressing.

The worst things that stick in my mind are crib deaths, babies. Elderly persons have already lived their lives. If they die, at least they have lived their lives. But a dead baby is somebody who didn't even have the chance to talk yet, or see where they're going. What bothers me most is kids. You have to deal with the parents, but after you've been a paramedic for a while, you know who to tune in, and who to tune out. So a lot of times you have to tune a parent out, just to deal with their kid and with the situation. The only thing that really affects me is my particular patient.

I'll do anything the fire department wants me to do. I don't know if I can do anything else that would make me more satisfied. The only thing that they could do for me now is give me more time off and more money. There is no other job I could want. If there's anything else, this is just a personal thing with me, I would like to go fifty-fifty between fireman and paramedic. I would like to do more firefighting. I like to do them both, for they are important in different ways.

□

Norman Newkirk and I were putting gear away on the truck after a high-rise fire of no great consequence, when we heard a report on the radio of a helicopter crash in the East River. It was an afternoon in April. They were sending a full assignment of three engines and two trucks over there. I told Lieutenant Curran of the report and asked, "Do you want us to take it in?" He said, "Tell them we're going. We'll put the scuba equipment on en route."

It was only a five-minute ride away. When we got there, there were many police officers and the firemen from Rescue 4. Some of the men were in the water with cold water survival suits, some just in their uniforms, helping the people who were on the surface of the water. Joe Angelini and I went down the pier to where the helicopter was in the water. It was upside down, and the tail rotor was just visible on the surface. The fuselage dipped downward at a severe angle into the river and was bobbing up and down, with a small rope tied to it to keep it from being swept away.

In the confusion there, I found out that, unlike commercial airliners, shuttle helicopters don't have a passenger list. So they weren't sure of exactly how many people were in there. It was right near a floating dock, so it was relatively easy getting into the water when the lieutenant gave me the go-ahead.

I worked my way underwater to the front of the helicopter and went in. It was laid out like a van-type school bus, with rows of seats four across. I had to twist around to get fully into the helicopter. There were personal items floating around, some seat cushions and other obstructions. I was about ten feet below the surface of the water, wondering if the chopper would sink. I went row by row and didn't find anything. When I reached the back of the helicopter, I remember thinking, "There probably isn't anybody here."

Then I came across a man who was strapped upside down in the seat farthest away from me. He was a fairly heavy man, about 225 pounds. I couldn't lift him enough to release the seat buckle, so I had to take my knife and cut the seat belt. I brought him to the surface, and they started resuscitating him right away. They did get a heartbeat, and they took him to the hospital, but he died two hours later from heart failure. He was a West German businessman who had traveled across the Atlantic, unfortunately to die in the East River. We did everything we could. We did get him going again, and we felt good about that, but it was a little too traumatic for him. He had had a heart attack. I suppose that's why he couldn't get himself out of the seat belt in the first place.

I made another dive down to check the helicopter again, then to the bottom of the river to see if there was anybody else. They took me out and got me to the hospital for ingestion of polluted water and hypothermia from the cold water. It was one of the initial successes in scuba rescue, if you could term it a success. It proved that the scuba team concept in the fire department was an effective one. There were some people against spending any money to equip us.

I was recently involved in two rescues within twenty-six days of each other. Both turned out to be pretty dramatic for me. The first was in a partially demolished hotel on Forty-fourth Street. We arrived with the first engine and the first truck. I had been to the building before, so I was familiar with the layout. I knew that the fire escapes were partially destroyed and unusable. I knew that large portions of the top of the building had been removed in illegal demolition. On this particular job, there were two or three floors of heavy fire in the rear building.

I was helping 54 Engine stretch a line up the stairs when we got a handie-talkie message that there was a victim on the roof. I went up the stairs as quickly as I could and got to the fire floor, which was the fourth. The fire was coming down the hall from the back apartments and starting to vent into the staircase. I told the nozzle man I was going to go up. He advised against it because there was a malfunction in the pumps, and there wasn't going to be any water until the second pumper came through.

Knowing there was a victim trapped on the roof, and knowing the layout of the building, I felt fairly secure, and I continued up the staircase. I was being chased, though, by some pretty hot smoke, real hot, and I just burst out on the roof. A few minutes later there was fire rushing through the doorway I had come through. On the roof I saw Lieutenant Harring, who had done virtually the same thing I did after hearing the report.

We came across twin brothers, twenty-two years old, who were huddled in a corner. They were kind of young bums—homeless people would be a better way to put it. They were living in this partially demolished vacant building. Now there was no way down the interior or down the fire escape in the rear, and the aerial ladder wouldn't reach from the side. We had to bring them to the front, where an aerial was being placed in position.

But much of the roof had been removed, leaving only a bare steel I-beam, which was about eight inches wide and about fifteen feet long, sticking out into nothing seven stories in the air. We saw that we had to walk across the beam to get to the ladder; it was the only way, and we knew it. Conditions were rapidly deteriorating. We now had fire on the roof and in the rear, and smoke was coming up through the demolished lower portions of the top floors in front of us. The smoke was starting to obscure the beam and the ladder, so we had to get there quickly.

I tied a rope to one of the victims, the lieutenant took the other end, went across the beam, and tied it to the aerial ladder. We guided the first guy across the beam to the ladder. I then had to get the second civilian across, but conditions were now so severe there was no time to tie him. I forced him out onto the beam. He did not want to go. I asked him if he could fly. I don't think he got it, because he just gave me a blank look. He was scared. I cussed at him a little bit, urged him, and finally got his butt in gear. Well, I got him across the beam anyway.

When he got to the end of the beam, he grabbed the lieutenant and just froze. He wouldn't do anything we told him. I realized we were in a tight situation, like being on the edge of a diving board seventy feet above the ground. So I had to swing myself around to the aerial ladder, around the lieutenant, who was like a stabilizer, and the victim. Then we hoisted him bodily onto the ladder, for he was like a stiff, and moved him down to the street. All in a day's work, you know?

Well, just twenty-six days later we're in quarters, and a report comes in that a helicopter, another helicopter, has crashed in the river next to the *Intrepid*. The *Intrepid* is a museum that used to be an aircraft carrier for the U.S. Navy. It was only about six blocks away, so we started off immediately, getting into our scuba gear en route. At the scene there was some confusion, a lot of people trying to give us a lot of information quickly.

The biggest obstacle at this point was the vertical drop of about eighteen feet from the dock down to the water. The area next to the *Intrepid* was another berth for large ships, and it was pretty deep. I was lowered by Captain O'Flaherty on a rope, and I swam out to where Ron Driscoll was on one of the rotor blades underwater. The helicopter had settled at an angle on the bottom, in twenty-odd feet of water.

I dove down and swam until I got to the front of the helicopter and found a door, where a part of the canopy had broken apart from the impact. I pulled the door open, and right there was the pilot of the helicopter. I vividly remember him wearing a white shirt. I shook him, and he did not respond. If he had, I would have given him the octopus to let him breathe air underwater. I discounted that possibility as a waste of time. I got his seat belt off him and removed him to the surface as quickly as possible. I turned him over to the four divers and firemen who were there.

I immediately went back down and followed the same route into the helicopter. I was surprised to see that the other seat was empty. But I figured that there had to be somebody in there, because I remembered hearing that there were two people in the copter when it crashed. It was a two-passenger helicopter, a lot smaller than the other one. I swam completely into the helicopter, and in the back I found the passenger, a woman, floating but wedged in with some seating equipment and pieces of broken canopy. I grabbed her, worked her out of the spot, and immediately brought her to the surface and handed her over. I tilted her head back to see if we could clear her airway.

I looked across the water to the eighteen-foot-high pier. They were tying a rope around the first victim, the pilot, and giving him mouth-to-mouth while they were still in the water. They swam the woman over. I had been hyperventilating a little bit, so I took a thirty-second break.

I went back down to search the bottom to make sure there was nobody else, because there were conflicting reports that somebody may have jumped in to help these people. I did that and found nothing. I did a secondary search of the helicopter and found the pilot's headset with his name on it. Not knowing whose helicopter this was at that point, I took the headset to the surface, figuring it might help to identify the helicopter and the people involved.

As it turned out, half of New York City had listened to the helicopter crash, because this was the WNBC traffic helicopter with Jane Dornacker aboard. Jane gave traffic reports and was also an actress who was in *The Right Stuff*. In a way, I'm glad we didn't know what helicopter it was, because we were pumped up enough.

I got up on the dock and saw the firemen and the EMS personnel frantically working on the two victims, with a crowd of police, reporters and cameramen hovering around. It was a strange scene. I remember seeing the pilot, Bill Pate, take his first breath on his own, and it felt like a great weight was lifted off me.

I think firemen work somehow on a feeling of guilt. I don't know how to describe it, really. You do have limited capabilities when you get to these emergency situations. You have your training, you have your tools. But then things go wrong. Things weren't going right for these people. The helicopter not only crashed, it crashed into the water, so besides injuries, now you have to contend with drowning. And somehow we managed to revive Bill Pate, and I felt better as soon as I saw him breathe.

I then started to get a bit emotional. I withdrew from the crowd and for a minute or two just stood by myself and regained my composure. Then I started the round-robin of television interviews. I'll tell you, it's a unique feeling to be interviewed on TV in New York City and then have your mother call you up from Florida to say she saw you on TV. This is a tremendous feeling. It's great to be in a position that you can help people and have such a profound effect on them.

Jane Dornacker, may she rest in peace, despite all the efforts to revive her, was pronounced dead two hours later in the hospital. And I mean, they worked on her, but it was not to be. But Bill Pate has had a tremendous recovery. He must have been in the water eight or nine minutes with no air. He did get some severe shoulder injuries, a lot of broken bones, a broken jaw. He has pretty much recovered. I stay in touch with his family, and they give me progress reports on how he is doing.

Again the scuba had come through and showed how successful it is. If you remember, one of the first and most famous rescues made by fire department scuba teams was in Chicago, when the Chicago firemen got a little boy out from under the ice of a lake after forty-five minutes. His recovery was phenomenal. It's things like that and some of these crashes that give meaning to all the hard work and all the drilling. We can actually save people's lives with scuba. It's not a matter of body recovery anymore, it's an actual rescue operation, and that's how we approach it.

Chapter Five

FAMILY LIFE

THERE ARE SOME THINGS THAT SIMPLY COME WITH THE TERRI-tory, and if you're a firefighter you might as well learn early that there is no point in fighting them. The first thing is that just about everyone wants Christmas and Easter off. It's an American culture state of being, but you're going to have to go to work. Not only because arsonists don't follow the Gregorian calendar, but because the fire department never closes shop. I remember working Christmas or Christmas Eve for six years straight. But at least I had a job to go to, and a steady income, unlike so many others in America who haven't been able to put order and progress in their lives. Certainly, my children were often out of sync with their classmates, but I think they understood that their father worked a job that was different than most. They never complained, and I don't think they ever realized the inconveniences. After all, if I wasn't home Christmas Eve, I would always be home Christmas morning. Unless, of course, there was an especially terrible fire in the Bronx.

Another thing is that in your twenty- or thirty-year career, your vacation period might actually occur in the summer months about half the time. The other half might be spent writing postcards to the wife and kids who will be traveling around in the station wagon visiting relatives, or packed away in the summer rental up at the lake.

Still, my family always loved being a part of a firefighter's family. There were all those company picnics and ball games, those three-day camping trips, times that etch in the memory like shells on a tree trunk, organic interlockings that grow more solid each passing year. The best times, perhaps, were spent playing the bagpipes with the departments' Emerald Society Pipe Band. We would go from parade to parade, competition to competition, always a busload of songs and screaming children and yearning

259

drones. It has always been a great band. We even made the Ed Sullivan show one year. After we played "The Minstrel Boy" Ed Sullivan hushed the audience and told how one of our pipers, Jimmy Corcoran, just the night before had pulled two people from a burning Bronx tenement, and that his photograph was in all the New York newspapers that morning.

It never mattered what we did, or where we were, though, the idea and the reality of service and courage were always with us. Someone in the crowd was always doing a great thing.

Dennis Smith

□

We have one daughter, Brittany. She's fifteen months old. If I hadn't been injured, she wouldn't be here. You see, the night we figure she was conceived, I looked at my work schedule and I would have been at work, and it never would have happened. This was eleven months after I was injured, near the end of my leave. So, in a sense, I was glad to have been injured and to have been home that night.

When I met my wife, Debbie, she was working as a part-time barmaid in a bar in Locust Point. She was working for a shipping company at the time and was doing this at night for the extra money. I stopped at this other bar, Brady's, on my way home, and this girl, who was a friend of mine, said, "Do you want to go out and have a drink?"

I said, "No, I've got to work the day shift tomorrow. I don't want to stay out."

She said, "Ah, come on, just a couple of drinks."

We drove over to the Locust Point bar, and Debbie was working there, and I started talking to her. I asked her to go out to breakfast. A great breakfast, I got home around five-thirty, changed, and went to work at seven. We started dating. I'd pick her up after work and we'd go to breakfast, or she'd come to the firehouse and bring me a sandwich or whatever. We dated a little over a year, then we got engaged and lived together for over eight months, and then we were married.

I was already a captain at the rescue company. I don't think she understood how dangerous it was. I wouldn't talk about it. If I came home and had a close call, I wouldn't say anything. I didn't want her to know what could happen. She thought being a cop was dangerous and that firefighting may be dangerous, but it wasn't going to happen to her husband. I explained what a rescue company did, but she really had no idea what the fire department was about. Now she's a real fire nut, she cuts pictures out of the paper, and she mounted different awards for me on the wall. She'll listen to a scanner once in a while. Yet even today, if I mention a truck company, she'll say, "Is that the one with the hose or the one with the ladders?"

She's not working now, she's staying home with the baby. Little Brittany is fascinated by the golden glitter on my uniform, and she touches it. The kids in the neighborhood say, "Hey, Mr. Baker, did you go to any fires?" I feel good about that. My mother is really proud about me being a captain. My father didn't have a chance to see it. He died before I made lieutenant. I was listening to the home watch, and I heard an ambulance go there for a heart attack. By the time I got to the hospital, he was dead. He would have been proud. I feel good making the promotions that I have.

I wouldn't take a medical disability pension. As soon as I was injured, the guys were saying, "Hey, you've got it made. Get the hell out." I was like, "For what? What the hell am I going to do?" I don't want to go home and sit on my ass for the rest of my life. Why would I leave this job and go work at another job? I like this job. It's been my life, it's been good to me. I enjoy it, and I always look forward to doing it.

I'll keep doing it, if it doesn't kill me. And if it does, I know that my family will be well taken care of. If I were out selling insurance and got killed in a car accident, that company is not going to look out for my family the way the city fire department does. I've made too many friends in here to leave.

My whole life has been screwed up working the weird shifts. I'm having a hard time now, working a five-day week in fire prevention, because for sixteen years I hadn't been doing it. You get used to never being off on a holiday, and it's kind of weird now. I mean, I can tell friends and family that I'll be there Christmas, rather than, "I'm sorry, I gotta work," or "I've gotta leave early, I have to work tonight." I just enjoy the job too much to leave.

When I first went to Rescue, they had a trust fund, set up by some guy years ago, supposedly to give money to victims of fire, also to children and poor people in the area. Well, I talked it over with the lawyer, and because Rescue goes citywide, we could pick anybody in the city. We would go around to different schools and pick children out, talk it over with the teachers, and have a big Christmas party for them. We would bring them over and buy a whole set of clothes, and give them toys and all. We would have a Santa Claus there. A couple of the kids kept stealing coins from our soda machine, and we'd have to smack their hands, but that was okay.

The year I went to the rescue company, they were giving out checks to the parents. I went and delivered the checks, and I looked around, and, hell, they were doing better than I was. You could tell the mother was going to spend the money on herself. She had a color TV, but the kids looked like little ragpickers.

I decided that from then on, we'd get stuff for the kids. We went to the schools, and the teachers know which kids aren't dressed properly and who need more than others. We got the sizes from the parents, and we went out and did the shopping. Clothes were the big things. Our wives would wrap the stuff up, we got turkeys and then a hotel in our district would cook them for us, and the wives would come in and help. They would dress up as elves, and we had a guy come down from the water tower like Santa Claus.

The whole firehouse did this, still do it, the decorations and everything. It made me feel good, knowing that it was these kids' Christmas. I mean, if the kids weren't going to get this, they weren't going to get much.

□

Social life? I've been going with a girl, and it's getting serious, so I have to be thinking about marriage. She hasn't been put through the wringer yet, so she doesn't really know what fire service is like. It's happened with some of my other girlfriends, where I don't show up at all because I'm at a fire. Or we're out someplace and a fire call comes in, and I have to stop the date and go to the fire, because I'm needed.

But our first date was kind of funny. We went out with some friends and their wives, and we were sitting around the house toward the end of the evening, and a fire call came in. I said, "Well, no time like the present to break into the fire service, huh?" And off I went.

I went on the fire call, and she was taken home by some of the other wives. I don't think any woman likes to be left at home in those situations. But the fire department is my first love and always will be my first love. And when duty calls, I have to go.

□

I met my wife in front of the firehouse. She was going to St. Francis Nursing School, and she was walking past the firehouse with groceries, and she dropped them. Like the old handkerchief trick, I guess. One of the guys told me to go out and help her, and that's how I met her. She was from New Britain, and was living at the "Y" at the time. She's Italian, Indian, and French. So I put the groceries inside the firehouse, and I said, "When I get off, I'll bring them over."

So I went over, and we started to date, and we were married. Out of that marriage I have seven children, four boys and three girls, ages sixteen down to five.

My wife, Sue, didn't really know anything about me. She knew that I loved the New York Fire Department, and we had battles because in my time off I would jump in my car and run down to New York to the firehouse. I wasn't spending time with her.

I was on the Hartford Fire Department, but I had applied in New York and had my home in Goshen, New York, to be near there. When I found out that it was all over, that I wasn't getting the New York job, I went into a shell for about three or four months and made it unbearable for Sue. I would come home, and I was like a zombie, I didn't want to be bothered with her. She went through a lot of pain and aggravation. She tried to help me. I just couldn't accept the loss.

I used to come home, maybe kiss her, talk to her for a while, then get in my car and go down to the New York firehouse. I was putting my family aside, and it was taking its toll on my family. Then I had to come to the reality that I wasn't going to get onto the New York Fire Department, and I had to move. Living in Goshen was good for a New York commute, but not for Hartford.

So we bought an old farmhouse twelve miles outside of Hartford. But I still associated myself with the New York Fire Department. I still kept going down. I kept doing the things I was doing before. I got more involved with the people down there. My love for New York was still there.

What I want for my kids, I want them to be safe. I'd like to see them drug-free. I'd like to see them get a good education. I would be happy if one of them followed in my footsteps. My oldest son is already talking about the Navy, talking about the Seal team. They're all talented in their own little way. Some of them draw. One boy is a runner. One writes poetry, stories. He's only ten years old, and his writing is great. I hope I can live to see what their future is going to be.

In the last five years I lost my whole family, my mother, my father, my sister. I have nobody, just my wife and my children. My father and sister died of cancer. My sister left four children. My mom died of a heart attack four months ago. Everything comes down.

But I like what I'm doing. I made two good rescues that really made me feel good. That alone makes everything worth it.

□

I have a girlfriend, she's still in college at Michigan State, so we don't see much of each other. We're planning to get engaged very soon. Other than that, I go trout fishing in the spring and duck hunting in the fall and play basketball in the summer. I also play football and tennis.

In my leave-day job, I work for a funeral home, owned by my girl-friend's dad. I had it in high school. Basically, I do their legwork. I fill out death certificates, chase down doctors and have them sign them, file the death certificates at the different city halls, stuff like that.

Last fall, she and I broke up for a while. I went crazy going to bars—even though I'm underage, I look old enough—picking up the girls, going to Hawaii. Ten of us firemen went to Hawaii. We went crazy. We went to Vegas twice. Those trips were fun, nothing but good times.

Firemen know how to live. Like my mom said, firemen party the hardest and cry the hardest. We just had three firefighters killed here in Detroit, and there were a lot of these great firemen, fearless guys, the strongest men in the world, and you see them crying.

In the next couple of years I want to get my science degree, then get married and bring up a family just like my dad did, and get my time in. Maybe after I retire, go up north, where I love to go, be outdoors, and be a chief on one of those little departments up there.

I have a box of medicine you wouldn't believe for the burns that I got. I needed some bacitracin for my ears, because they bubbled up. The ears got it, because I don't put my Nomex hood all the way on. If you cover yourself completely, you never know when it gets too hot, and you'll be in trouble. But just as we were backing out, the fire flashed over.

My mom doesn't like the dangerous stuff. She gets mad when I talk about it. Because when I get to my dad, I start talking about it, and when I say the "good" fires, she thinks that's horrible. To me, a fire's a good one when the adrenaline is flowing.

□

I didn't get married until just before I made lieutenant. I had been going with the girl for quite a while, from the time I came on the job. Her name is Joyce.

We had a talk before we decided to get married, and I told her that if she was against the fire department we might as well break up, because I couldn't give it up and there was no sense going through life hating me over it. I guess she regards me as some kind of nut, but she has certainly accepted the department, and we've never had a bit of a problem on that score.

When I worked nights, she would do things that she wanted to do, like wash her hair or visit her friends. It's worked out fine. She accepted my idiosyncrasies and adjusted to them.

We don't have any children. My brother, Harvey, has a boy and two girls. The son is not a fire buff. Harvey wanted him to do his own thing. He was in the Air Force in California, and he married a girl from out there, so he's now in California. He has some interest in the firefighting job, but I wouldn't call him a buff by any means. So there are no more relatives on the job. I'm the only Supple left on the BFD.

Joyce and I like to travel very much. We've tried to take some kind of trip every year, and every two or three years we try to make an exotic one. Last May, we went to China, which was her ambition. She's a China buff.

I didn't get to a firehouse in China because we were on a tour. But I was on a street corner near the hotel when a rig came along. By the time I noticed that it was a fire engine, it was going past me. I said, "Aw, nuts." Joyce said, "They're going to get caught by the traffic light at the corner."

So I ran up to the corner, I had my camera out, and I was taking a picture. As I was doing that, I realized I was in a Communist country, do they allow you to take pictures? I saw the officer looking at me with a sort of quizzical look, so, in sign language, I pointed to myself, I pointed to the rig, and he got a big smile on his face and gave me a big thumbs-up signal.

As they went around the corner, he must have said something, because four heads turned and four hands came out with the thumbs-up signal.

I thought that was great. Firemen are firemen, wherever you go.

□

When I was voted into the fire department, even as an apprentice, my kids were very proud of me. It was exciting for them to have a mom who was a firefighter. A lot of their friends would come over to see what I looked like, because they had never seen a girl firefighter. It was cute, a sort of standing joke on the block. When I was going through training, I would have all the kids come over, and I would have them lie in different places in the house and act like they were passed out. And I would pretend that I would come in and save them. They loved it. They decided that this was the neatest house on the block. We had such a good time.

A lot of times I'd let them wear my gear, let them feel what it was like to crawl around with all this stuff on. I feel that all the children on the block have a good sense of fire prevention and fire safety now. If one of them cuts his hand, or burns his hand, or somebody has swallowed something, they call on me first. I have them call the fire department, and I go down and assist. It's been fun, I've really enjoyed it.

We have a monitor in the house, and when the tones go off, everybody stops and one of the kids gets a pencil and paper, writes down the address and the nature of the call. Another of the kids sets my boots up so I can jump right into them. I let them get involved. It's not just "Mom's a firefighter, and everybody's gotta watch."

On several occasions in the wintertime, my husband would go out in his robe and boots and start my car up. He'd warm it up while I was getting my long underwear and gear on. It really does help, it saves time. He does have fears. It scares him at times that I may never come back. He's been my childhood sweetheart since we were fifteen years old, and I've been married to him for sixteen years, so we've shared a good twenty-some years.

This Friday I'll be doing fire prevention for the sixth-graders over at Pinckney School. And my daughter Rebecca's in the fifth grade. She can't wait till I come in, because she told this boy in her class that her mom's a firefighter, and he said, "No way. Your mom can't be a firefighter." So she's really anxious for me to come in and prove that, yes, her mom's a firefighter. And my daughter Sarah, who is six, is in the first grade. I'm also going to the first grade, so she is real excited and keeps telling her teacher every day that I'm coming in.

I went this week, on my own time, to my son's class. That's Sean, who is eight. We weren't scheduled to see his class, but his teacher called and said they were learning about volunteer fire departments and asked me to come in. So I came in with all my gear and showed the kids what a firefighter wears, and explained what happens when they call and how important it is that they give good directions and an address when they call. It was a rewarding half hour. I got a wonderful thank-you note signed by all the kids. That's the kind of thing I think children really need: they need someone who really wants to teach them.

My oldest son, Brian—he's twelve—goes to a private school, St. Paul's in Ann Arbor. He's near genius, that's why we put him in a different school.

I want for my children whatever they want for themselves. I try to teach them that no matter who you are, you can be whatever you want to be. My being a female firefighter has shown the girls that they can be a policeman, a firefighter, drive a tractor, anything. We have our girls cut the lawn with the tractor. My sons cook. This is a house where, to survive, you have to know how to do all these things, whether you're a man or a lady. That's how I was raised. Every week we had a different job to do, so we were very well rounded by the time we left home. Yes, they could be President, if they want.

I did teach them, too, that it's not easy. If you want something, you have to work your butt off for it. It didn't come easy to me, and I know from now till the day I die I will have to work to keep up, with everything in the fire service changing so fast.

My husband and I both work at a heating and cooling company called Gleason and Raus. He's president, and I'm vice president. We started out with only three of us, and now there are seventeen workers and nine trucks. It's an enjoyable business, and what's amazing is that we can go to work and still be together. A lot of people might find that difficult, but I enjoy it. I do the office work with two other girls, and he does the bidding and proposals and blueprints, estimating, things like that.

I think I've done it right, I have no regrets. Just like going into business, this was a dream my husband had, and I knew that if we never tried it, we'd never know if we could make it. So we tried it and made it. If we hadn't, at least we could say, "Hey, we tried."

We helped build our own home. We had both lived in Dearborn all our lives, and we came out here in 1979. It took us six months. My husband and I did all the heating, electrical, and plumbing. I was right by his side. We would just take up a bunch of Pampers and food for the weekend, come down here with the kids, and we'd work on the house.

My most relaxing time is to light candles and listen to some music. To sit down and just talk. To be human beings together. I think that's important. A lot of times when I come back from a fire scene or a medical run, I can't go to sleep. And it's sort of neat, because what I do then is, I clean. I turn the music on low and just go around the house and clean. My husband thinks it's great. He'll get up, look around, and say, "Oh, it was a good run last night, huh?"

We have a small fireplace, and a lot of times it's very relaxing for me to sit in front of it and see a controlled situation, where fire can be beautiful, as opposed to being so deadly in nature. That's a really nice feeling.

We take the kids everywhere we go. We go up north to his parents' cottage, we've been to Pennsylvania. We took them on an airplane for the first time this year. We flew to Florida. We went to Disney World and Epcot Center. It wasn't really long enough, it was only three days, but we all needed to get away from business and the fire service, and just from home, I think.

My husband goes to fire department functions with me. I would never go without him. His name is Brian Senior. He got teased a little bit by the guys when I first joined. At Hamburg Fire Department dances, all the firemen's wives get flowers at the door. So when I came through, of course Brian got the flower. He looked at me and said, "Whoops, here we go!" It's really different for him.

I'm sure a lot of the wives were very concerned when I first joined. But I think they've concluded that it's more difficult for him than it is for them —one woman and forty men.

□

I was married shortly before I got on the department. Being in the fire academy that early on in the marriage was probably a test of whether the marriage was going to work. Her name is Melanie, and she is my rock and my salvation. There were many nights when I came home with tons of homework and assignments, and she gave me a lot of moral support. I'll be forever grateful to her for that.

I don't think she had any sense of what the job was about. She was pretty much caught up in the basic syndrome everybody else has—you play checkers, you slide down the pole, you wash the Dalmatian kind of thing. She's never expressed any fears about the job. A lot of firefighters' wives can name every tool and the specifications of every fire truck, and can tell you all the things that firefighters do on a day-to-day basis. Melanie has never gotten involved to that point. She's just tremendously happy that I was able to have the career I wanted.

She's a preschool teacher. We have two daughters, Jenny, twelve, and Amanda, six. Our lives are different from others in the neighborhood in the hours we work, the situations we're confronted with, the things we see on a daily basis. I spend a normal amount of time with the children, but I also have hobby interests and semibusiness ventures that I attend to.

Free-lance photography, for one, generally in fire-related situations—for a magazine or a newspaper, a publication of some sort. I've done a lot of work for *Firehouse* magazine.

I suspect I'll stay in the job for a minimum of twenty-five years. I can't see myself retiring before that, not with the age of my kids. I've got fifteen years now, and if the next ten are as much fun as the last fifteen, I look forward to it.

My mother and father are both college graduates and working in the professions. I don't know whether they expected me to follow the same course. I think that now they're real pleased that I've been so happy in the career that I chose.

In addition to being a photographer, I'm a helicopter enthusiast. I hesitate to use the term "airport bum," but I do spend some time at airports. Aviation has always been a part of my life. I'm not a pilot, but I have a number of buddies in the helicopter industry, whom I ride with occasionally. They're kind of another second family to me, in addition to the firefighter family and my own family.

Unfortunately, the Los Angeles Fire Department helicopters are out of the way to me. They're at the far north end of the city, and I'm down in Orange County. I flew with the guys a number of times when I was downtown, but I'm a hundred miles away from them now.

In our off hours, Melanie and I do whatever the kids want to do, or rather something that everybody wants to do. Not just to please Mom and Dad and not just to please the kids, but what the family wants to do. We go to amusement parks, the beach, depending on the time of the year. We go to the mountains. We took a trip to Hawaii.

The girls are like their mother in regard to the department. You know, Dad's a fireman, but we don't really know a whole lot about what he does. They certainly could be firefighters, if they want, but I wouldn't encourage them. I'm kind of locked into the point of view—much to the chagrin of some feminists, I'm sure—that firefighting is a man's world.

I would prefer to see them in a more female-oriented kind of work. They might disagree. It's happened.

□

I got married within months of getting appointed to the department. Her name is Linda. She didn't know much about the job, just that I wanted to get into the Boston Fire Department. I think it's difficult for any wife to get used to the idea of her husband living with another family.

I realized immediately, even going to a slow company, that although firefighters are strangers at the outset, they become very close very quickly. It has a tremendous impact on your life, whether you want it to or not. Do I live here, or do I live there? But I live in both places, split equal time. It's not like going to a factory and filling up a cardboard box with something, then putting tape on it and sending it out the shipping door, and you can't wait to get out of there. This is totally the opposite.

Going into the camaraderie of living with the other family in the fire-house is not easy. I guess that wives, when they talk among themselves, feel that the husbands talk about things at the firehouse before they would discuss it at home, whatever the subject. I think a lot of families have trouble dealing with that. It's not easy to say, "Wait a minute, I don't care about the salary, the only reason I took this job was because I want to do it, I like it, and now that I'm doing it I like it even more. So don't crowd my territory, please. If I like being in this family at the firehouse, let me be."

But unless somebody lives there in the firehouse and goes through it, I don't think they can see it. I think that wives sometimes mistakenly believe you're trying to push them aside.

We have four children—Edward Jr., Lisa, Amy, and Michael. They're sixteen, fifteen, eight, and seven. I certainly wouldn't tell them to take this job because their father loves it. I think they're under more pressure than when we were their age. Television and movies have an unbelievable influence on them practically from the day they're born. They're still young.

The oldest guy is interested right now in the sciences and astronomy and outer space and the whole NASA program. Like firefighting, it's a challenge but of something else, where you're taking your life in your hands and going out into the unknown.

All I'd want to tell the kids is, do what you want, as long as you like what you're doing. That's the most I can do, not try to push them in one direction or another, in some kind of vicarious situation where I wish it was me.

□

I was married in 1946 to the high school gal I ran with all the time. Her name is Molly Lou. Her family was one of the original settlers in this valley. She was a little hesitant about the fire department. You know how women are, maybe they've read of some big fire where somebody got hurt, and they go along with that part of it. Then I got involved putting in a lot of hours, and she got pushed out of shape, because she thought that the fire department was competing with our lives . . . which actually it was.

We have two adult children, a daughter named Janine and a son named Duke, after Duke Snyder of the Brooklyn Dodgers. The World Series was on when he was born, and my wife came up with that name, thought it was great. My son never cared about firefighting, and, of course, my daughter never did.

Molly Lou and I are into golfing. She's an excellent golfer, and I'm not a hacker. We enjoy taking off for a few days and play different courses. And we still do quite a bit with our kids. They both live in Reno, so they're not that far away. We've helped them buy houses, do cleanup work and build fences, things like that.

Molly Lou's a pretty fair artist, she does a lot of watercolors, so she's out in the wilds quite a bit taking pictures for her painting, and I go with her. I enjoy that.

Basically, that's about it. I've never had time to develop any hobbies, I was always seventy, eighty hours a week in my business. And since I've been chief here, I put in about nine, ten hours a day. I love it, you know?

□

I got married when I was going to school at Oklahoma State. My first wife, as I call her, and I have had three children—two boys and a girl, in that order. My two sons are both firefighters in Phoenix. One is just about to be promoted to captain, and the other is in the process of taking the engineer's exam. So they are starting to go through the system.

My wife has always been concerned about the danger. I think most wives are. She was a registered nurse and worked in the emergency department and intensive care, so she understood the physical consequences of firefighting. But she has also understood its attraction for me. She says she has lived with "the other woman" for thirty years—the Phoenix Fire Department. Women who are able to maintain their profession both as a vocation and an avocation are basically saints. Which is the way that I would describe her. Just a super human being.

Firefighters pay a unique price in the duty schedules, the danger, and the dedication. And during the first twenty years in the service, I was working at least two jobs, sometimes three. I was going to school, I was teaching school. I got my bachelor's degree in political science, and my master's in public administration. I was head of the Fire Science Department at King's College. I taught three or four fire science classes for ten or twelve years.

So there was my wife, bundling me up to go to work, or getting me ready to go to school, or ready to teach. Between all those activities, she was having babies. With all this, the time you spend together is very important, it is high-quality time.

It is interesting that after your kids have gone through all that and have seen all of it, and their activities have had to take second place to yours, that you discover one day that they have joined the fire department.

In a sense, my kids were raised by firefighters. It's all they have ever seen, so it's probably a very natural thing for these really first-class people to be comfortable figures and role models for my sons. And in my own case, I think of all the education I've gotten and realize that the really important education was from the guys who raised me in the fire department. You appreciate the support the whole thing has given you, and you hope you'll give some of it back to the service.

I never said anything to my sons, I think they decided for themselves. They never showed much interest in the fire service until they were older teenagers. I never bought them toy fire trucks. They used to come down to the station, they knew all of the people, and they listened to the monitor, but they weren't really fire buffs.

They both came on the department, the first exam they took. They both have been active firefighters, and I am proud of that. They are not fire scholars, they are attracted to the firefighting part of it, the service delivery part. They are big, tough kids, and they like fire operations, and I like to think that I see some of myself in that process. So I get to kind of relive all of that.

□

I've never pushed it with my two sons. They knew that I was involved, and it was always around them. I have one son who thought it was interesting, but never chose to get involved, which is perfectly okay. There is no reason why he should.

I have another son who did choose to get involved. He became a volunteer and served on the rescue squad, became a firefighter and an EMT. He is now a professional ski patrolman.

I think that it's one of those things that people have to do for themselves, and you can't inflict it upon anybody else. There has to be a tremendous desire to want to do it.

□

My mother is a hell of a woman, excuse the French. She is a real stickler. She stood behind us through everything. My older brother has been married three times. The third marriage looked like it was going to break up, and she kept trying to keep them together. They have a little two-year-old girl, and I think the ordeal I went through with Jessica McClure helped bring them back together.

I met my wife at a nightclub called Dudes and Dolls. I was twenty and working as a draftsman at Cities Service, and she was an all-district volleyball player for Midland High School trying to get a scholarship to Angelo State University in St. Angelo. The owner of the nightclub was a friend of mine, and I was working the door for him free of charge, checking IDs. I got free drinks and met all the girls.

Robbie wasn't old enough to be in the club, but she was good-looking, so I kind of overlooked the birthdate. I was a real good Western dancer, and Robbie said she knew how to Western dance.

We got on the floor, and I found out real quick she didn't know a thing about Western dancing. So I started teaching her.

We have two boys, the eldest is Casey Shane, he's six years old, fixing to be seven. The youngest is Chance Dillon O'Donnell, he's three. Casey is named after my grandfather on my mother's side, Casey Jones. And when Chance was born, *The Yellow Rose of Texas* was a series on TV, and one of the characters was a cowboy named Chance. We heard it and we liked it. We also liked the name of Dillon because of Matt Dillon, from *Gunsmoke,* and that younger actor named Dillon. We just liked that name. We felt they were real Irish-type names.

My dad was mad at me when Casey was born. My O'Donnell granddad was Roland Earl, Sr., my dad was Roland Earl, Jr., and my older brother was Roland Earl III. I was Robert Edward, and my little brother was Rusty Eugene. My half brother was Ronald Edgar. Every one of us was R.E.O., and my dad was mad because I broke the tradition. But I felt it was my older brother's place, not mine, to continue it.

Besides, I felt closer to my grandfather, Casey Jones, who has done more for me in my life, and he was always taking care of little Casey. Everywhere my granddad went, little Casey went with him.

Both of the kids are great. You couldn't ask for better kids. When they're apart, there's no trouble at all, but you put the two together, it's like mixing a mixture for dynamite or something. They fight, they argue, sometimes they play good together. I guess my brothers and I were somewhat like that, I don't know.

□

I still hang out with firemen. In fact, we're going out tonight. Sometimes my wife, Norma Jean, takes offense, because she's left at home with the kids. She says she's a firehouse widow. She loves me, she knows that's what I want to do, so she supports me. I appreciate that. I've been in the hospital a number of times, so when she got the call that I was in the hospital this time, she wasn't upset. She just came right down, and she was as calm as could be. In fact, one deputy chief said, "Your wife is great. I couldn't believe how well she took this."

I said, "Well, she's been through a lot with me already."

One of the times was when I put my wrist through her car headlight. I was mad at her, that the headlight had gone out. I tried to put it back on, and I punched it twice, and then I used my left palm and it went right through. It severed both arteries and eight out of the ten tendons, and I was thirty seconds from bleeding to death. She got me to the hospital in three and a half minutes. She drove me backwards up a one-way street.

They were going to amputate it and give me a hook. This happened four years ago, and my fingertips are still numb. It takes so long for all those things to grow back together.

I had a motorcycle, and I had three accidents on that. One time I lost control when I was doing sixty miles an hour, and I got up and walked away.

When I was eighteen I was kidding around in the schoolyard where I used to live in West Philly. These other guys were playing basketball, and I never was one for playing basketball, so I was just screwing around. I had just watched a Clint Eastwood movie, and I wanted to make it look like I was hanging myself. I made a hangman's noose in a rope and I tied the other end to the top of the basketball backboard, and I jumped. And I never made it to the ground, because the rope had caught on one of the bars up there. My brother and sister were holding me, and I was purple, and I lost consciousness. In fact, it was a fireman who came from across the street and let me down. He gave me mouth-to-mouth and brought me back.

I was the second oldest out of seven kids. When I almost accidentally hung myself, I was leaning on my motorcycle, and the police pulled up and asked who was in trouble. I ran away, they chased me and put me in the back of the van. They asked me questions like, "Have you ever tried this before?" I tried to explain that it was only a joke and it went bad.

They drove to my house and went to the front door. My mother was in there cooking. She came to the door and saw two policemen there. I was out of view in the van. She said, "What happened to Scott?" She's got seven children, and it was, "What happened to Scott?" She knew it was me right away.

When I was a kid I was hospitalized when I dove through a window, different things like that. Just reckless, stupid things. I wasn't suicidal or anything. I lived life in the fast lane, I guess.

In fact, my wife bought me a tattoo for Father's Day. It's on my back. It's the Grim Reaper, because I figured as long as he's behind me, he'll never catch me. Norma Jean paid for it. She knows I'm like that. I always pull through.

But I've calmed down, and I've learned to appreciate life more. I'm not as reckless. On the job I've always been aggressive, I've been bullheaded and got right in there. Now I'm going to be a little more cautious. Being aggressive is fine, but you also have to be careful. When there is no life at stake, I think it would be foolish to lose my life over material property.

I'm not going to dictate to my children how they should live their lives. I want them to be happy, and I want them to respect their mother and me. We're behind them all the way on education, homework, and cracking the books. Not just me, their mother is always on their case about education and doing the best they can in everything. Sometimes I think we're on their case too much, but it's only for their own good.

We're strict with them, which is the way it should be. I respect discipline. I was in the Marine Corps, and I think that's the way things run easier. You see some kids on the street, and you can tell just by looking at them that their parents don't care. It reflects on the parents.

My own father was the strong, silent type. He didn't have to say anything. He could give you one look, and it would cut right through you. My mother was more of the disciplinarian. She was always hollering and hitting. I was always a brat. I must have been a pain in the neck. I was always questioning their authority. I was always more of a handful than the other children. I have only three children—well, the baby is a baby—but I don't know how they did it with seven.

The baby is a problem. He was premature, and has an illness called apnea. They gave him a sleep study, to see how his breathing is while he's asleep. They have him on caffeine, and it keeps his body going in high gear. It's kind of like revving up a carburetor so it won't stall. So he's up and down every hour, and he's crying and punching the wall, and he's not very happy. He doesn't smile much. He's only four months old, and he'll get off that soon, and he should be able to sleep better, and his mother should be able to sleep better.

I go to work, and that's my escape. She's home with the kids.

□

I got married after I got into the fire department. I met my wife when we were both in the Army. She's still in the Army, but she's getting ready to get out soon. We have one child, a baby girl, two months old.

My wife doesn't like me being in the fire department, and since I got hurt, she is really kind of scared. But she knows that it's what I want to do. I'm sure she wouldn't want our girl to be a firefighter when she grows up. I'd just like her, the baby, to do what she wants to do.

□

When my wife had our first child at the hospital, I went in there and helped deliver it. It was lot of fun, and I assisted. I was trained in Lamaze classes. I was there with our second child also. It's a tremendous feeling to be there, bringing a new individual into the world.

They teach in Lamaze class that it creates a bonding effect between you and the mother, and you and the child. I believe that 100 percent. My kids are real special. And as you grow up as an individual yourself, you see mistakes that you made, and you want to make sure that your child doesn't make those same mistakes. You want the best for your children.

They're too young to have an interest in the fire service. My little boy's only seven. They like going to the station. I just want them to grow up happy, to live a good life and live long, and be happy in what they do. Material things aren't important. It would be nice if Nicholas became a volunteer firefighter, but I'm not sure where the fire service is going in the next twenty or thirty years.

□

I met my wife in 1975, but we didn't get married until 1980. One of the first things that got us acquainted was when I found out that she went to the same oral surgeon that I did. It wasn't just broken teeth, I had shattered my upper jaw, I busted it in a million pieces, and I was all wired up. We didn't meet in the doctor's office, but once we started talking, you know when you first meet somebody, you have to have something to talk about. She had some problems and went to the same doctor, so we started talking about our different ordeals. That's what we talked about.

I was crazy about the fire department, and she knew before we were married that she was going to be second banana to the fire department. I was still going to college, and I was a volunteer fireman in Wheaton, Illinois. When I became a regular fireman, she was going to Illinois State University, and on my days off I would go see her. I went to visit her at Christmas break, took the test for Dade County, and I lived with her and her family while I was in the fire academy. I was on the job in Dade County, out in the field fighting fires for two years, before we got married.

She doesn't tell me she worries about the dangers, but when there are firemen's funerals on TV, she says, "Please don't ever do that to me." I tell her I'm real careful. I am. I'm aggressive, but I'm careful. She knew about the dangers early on. We were just about to get married, we were getting ready for the pictures and the parties and all that crap, when we had a fire in the high school library. This was before we had the Nomex ear flaps on the helmets.

I was on the hose with this other guy. We crawled in. You know you can take the heat before you crack the line. This guy put the nozzle on a narrow fog. If it had been me, I would have put it on a straight stream, because that stuff turns around and the steam comes right back. I was behind him, and the man behind the line takes a worse beating than the man on the nozzle, because they hit the ceiling. Everything was hot as hell. It burned this guy and myself.

So the big worry of everybody at the wedding was whether I was going to look like hell in my wedding pictures. I had these Dumbo ears. When the blisters went down, I still had a lot of scars, but it wasn't so bad. But it was a big concern to her. How the hell was I going to look?

We have one child, a two-year-old boy. He better get all the education that he can, because I think that we're looking at a two-class society—the people that have the education and the wealth, and the people that don't have anything. I don't know where the firefighters are going to fit in, but if firefighters don't continue to increase their skills—and we're heading in the right direction—in areas like hazardous materials and emergency medical, we could easily end up down there with the huddled masses.

My wife knows that the fire department is giving me something no one can give me, including herself. She knows it is giving me a sense of satisfaction and a sense of personal worth. You see some joker win a million-dollar lottery on TV, I don't need that. I want to be comfortable, and I want to be secure, but I don't want a damn Cadillac, I don't want a big boat. I don't want those things. My wife knows it.

If I ever lost this job or became crippled, I don't know what I would do. I would have to go to a psychiatrist and have him tell me that I am worth a damn as a human being, and try to get me interested in something else. But I would have a hell of a time, and my wife realizes that.

□

My wife, Sheila, was happy when I went to the Cleveland Fire Department, because at Greyhound you had no summer vacation, no holidays off. She was a little apprehensive, but happy. We already had four children at the time. We wound up having thirteen, ranging in age from thirty-one to fourteen. There aren't too many big families anymore.

After twenty-five years, when the youngest one was in school, my wife went to college. She's a nurse now. She works full-time as a nurse at Metropolitan General Hospital.

□

I've got five kids altogether, four with my divorced wife and another son with the woman I'm with. He's going to be a fireman for sure, because every time he hears a siren he runs to the window. So for Christmas I bought him a little fire engine set with a dashboard like on a chief's car. It's got the fire extinguisher and the microphone and a little crank that you turn for the siren. And a helmet. It was a funny coincidence. My company is in Battalion 5, and on his helmet was "Battalion 5." I didn't notice it until we opened it up at Christmas.

Basically I divide my time between my family and the force. I spend time with that son and his mother and also with my other kids. Not only that, I've got a lot of little cousins and nieces and nephews and whatever. I spend a lot of time entertaining them, because to them I'm the hero, so I feel obligated to them. I am constantly going around and visiting and just entertaining them any way I can. Playing ball with them, telling them stories. They love to hear fire stories.

That's what I'm doing on my time off, or I like to travel. I've got family down South. In the summertime, I'll just jump on the highway and go to visit my family.

□

My wife has never expressed any feelings of apprehension about the fire service, not out loud, anyway. In a sense, I met my wife through the fire service. She used to spend a lot of her away-from-work time in the mountains in the area where I worked. That's where I met her. She became interested in the forestry fire service and worked two summers as a lookout. So she kind of learned the business and what it was about, understood the training program, and knew lots of the Forest Service people. So she kind of grew up with it at the same time I did.

I think that made a great deal of difference. I'm sure she worries at times when I'm gone, but she's been around the system long enough to know that the guys are not a bunch of dummies out there deliberately trying to get themselves hurt, and that it doesn't happen that often. She knows that I'm a little bit of a fuddy-duddy, that I'm not going to go out there and do something dumb, that I'm a little more conservative than most people, and that I've never really been hurt in this business. So she never really worries about that.

Being away ten or twelve days is not unusual in this business. So the wife raises the kids, paints the house, fixes the washing machine, and gets the car taken care of. The wives become very self-sufficient and independent.

We have three children, all gone from home now. My son is in the Navy, and I have two daughters. The youngest, Carmen, spent a summer as a seasonal firefighter. She's kind of the renegade of the family, very small, five-foot-four. She became more interested in the fire service than the other two. She spent one summer chasing brush fires around Southern California and just totally fell in love with it.

That's what she wanted to be. But unfortunately, at the same time, she also met a young man and fell in love with him. And one thing led to another, and they got married. Now she has a youngster, and her family position doesn't allow her to be in the fire service. She'd like to be. She still talks about it.

□

My wife and I are Catholic, and we're raising our children Catholic. We maintain a Christian life. We like to go bowling. We take the kids, Danielle and David, bowling. I like to ski. My wife doesn't like it too much. We go on trips. We do a lot of things. We like sports, all kinds of sports. I go to the gym three times a week, and I work out. I try to keep in shape, especially now that I'm getting a bit older and I don't feel the vigor that I felt when I was eighteen, so I like to stay on top of things.

It's kind of a young man's job, I see that now. I came on the job when I was thirty-five, and guys with ten or more years on the job are my age. It's an extra effort I have to put forward. Luckily, I have always been in pretty good shape. I went through the Marine Corps with no problem. I'm able to do the job, and I'm in pretty decent shape now, and I just try to maintain that. It keeps me a lot healthier on the job.

Phyllis is thrilled to pieces that I got the job, because in the ten years I worked in trucking, I was away from the house a lot and lost time to spend with the family. Sometimes she worries about the dangers of the job. When I leave for work, I can see it in her face: "Be careful, and come home safe. Keep your eyes open."

□

I read a lot, I keep very busy, it's just the way I am. I work a lot, and I stay home a lot. I do a lot of writing, too. I've got a small sailboat, which I enjoy. I like sailing. There's a pretty large reservoir west of town.

My wife, Holly, had a traditional East Coast kind of upbringing in the suburbs of Philadelphia called the Main Line. She's from Haverford, and she attended the prep school of Bryn Mawr. It's very different from the West Coast upbringing I had. She attended Elmira College in upstate New York. She went there for two years, then decided she wanted to do something entirely different. So she moved out to the West Coast and lived briefly with some cousins in Salem before she moved down to Eugene.

She was working in a tobacco shop named Genesis, and I was smoking a pipe at the time. I would drop by and buy pipe cleaners and tobacco. I found that the cheapest thing I could buy was pipe cleaners. I would go by frequently on my days off and buy pipe cleaners, because it was a chance to strike up a conversation, have a joke or two. Finally, when this one drawer in my apartment was overflowing with pipe cleaners, I figured it was time to ask her out to lunch. Then we got married.

We have a daughter, Meighan, who is four, and a son, Brendan, who was born last April. Holly and I spent a lot of time outdoors before we had the kids. Our area is a great one for that. We did a lot of cross-country skiing and, of course, sailing. We like to go to the coast and go hiking on the beaches and the sand dunes. Oregon is a great place if you're into that.

We've got a couple of guys in the department who are what we call "rock jocks." They are heavily into mountain climbing and that sort of thing. Firefighting is a great job, because it gives them the chance to do that. They are also real good on the job if we get involved in an extreme-angle rescue situation.

The advice I would give my kids is the same advice my dad gave me without being judgmental: "Do whatever you want to do, but just try to be the very best at it. Do the best you can." To him, if I wanted to be a teacher or a firefighter or whatever, as long as I showed some kind of commitment to that line of work and gave it my best shot, that was all that counted.

I don't think I could ask any more of my kids than that.

□

In the beginning my boys were very proud of me, but now they are having a tough time. The eldest, Tommy, is seventeen, and Michael is sixteen. It's a very hard age for boys. They go to an all-boys Catholic high school, and there are no sons of civil servants in their classes. I think it's tough on them.

Michael is an honor student, and he plays football. He is Jack Armstrong, the All-American Boy. His dream is to go to Annapolis.

Tommy is the creator in the family. He amazes me. He is the opposite of Michael, and yet they are more good friends than brothers. They are very close, yet very different. Tommy questions everything. He is very intellectual and creative. He's a good artist, and yet he's a good student. I think he is the most like me, because he is the one that I don't get along with. I also think he's the one who is most threatened by what I do.

Then there's Matthew. He's twelve. I think his dream in life is to own a casino, with a bunch of dancing girls and a quick buck.

Jennifer, who's six, wants to be a firefighter. She never thought about it until she visited the firehouse. She thinks the guys are terrific. I thought it was just a passing thing, but she does have more of an interest than just being inquisitive. There was a made-for-TV movie about a Los Angeles woman who was the first woman firefighter. I believe her name was Cindy

Frohlich. My husband taped it at Jennifer's request. That was about two years ago. That's her favorite film, and God help anyone who tapes over it. She really identifies with it, asking, "Did you feel like that when you had to get your hair cut, Mommy? Were you scared?" Little things like that. I guess the film hit home a little more personally, what it must have been like for a woman—for her—to go through it.

The challenge has been getting through your teenage years. "One day at a time" is the motto in our house. I guess the focus has to be on them now, because it's been on me for such a long time. The past three, four, five years have been very rough on the family. There has been a lot of tension, and it has taken a lot out of the family. Now that my husband and I are making a conscious effort to redirect that attention, things have calmed down a little bit.

The tension of the first few years, then getting injured, the time off, the visits to the hospital have been very rough on the family. Not being home, getting a baby-sitter. Now we're consciously trying to redirect all of that attention back onto the kids and to the family unit.

We're directing our energy to what the kids need and what they want. I'm not studying for lieutenant. I think it's a great job, but in order to become a lieutenant you have to put a lot of time in, and I don't want to take that away from Jenny. She's only six, and she needs a class mother, and she needs someone to go on trips with. This job allows me to do those things. I want to see the kids now, not just be with them but to do it without the drugs and the alcohol, the driving and getting into trouble.

Our kids didn't go to Catholic grammar school, just high school. We took them out of Bayside and sent them to a magnet school in Corona. We bused our children on purpose to send them to a borough school, which was a new project. It was a four-year intermediate school where they were going to be taught computers and a choice of languages, much more math than they were going to see in ordinary life. It wasn't just a concern for morality. The racial mix in this borough school was 33 percent, 33 percent, 33 percent. They were not the majority anymore. They were going to be competing in this school in the way it was going to be when they got out of school. It was more realistic.

□

It was Valentine's Day 1962 when my father was killed. I was seven, and I just happened to be at home with my mother. I was sick and had stayed home from school. My father was a battalion chief at the fire academy. There was a four-alarm fire in a four-story brick veneer building, and my father was dispatched to the fire in place of a chief who was tied up. My ma didn't know that, so when she started getting phone calls asking if my father was at the fire, she said, "I don't think so, because he's at the fire academy today."

My father and another chief, with their two drivers, went into the building to get everybody out because there was danger that the roof would cave in. They got everybody out, and they were just ready to come out themselves when the roof caved in. The other chief was killed, my father was killed, the two drivers survived. The other chief was found wedged under the first-floor doorway. My father's driver rolled onto the roof of the back porch and rolled off onto the ground.

My father and the other driver went all the way down through the floors to the basement. The other driver was floating down there. When they dug him out, all he had was a broken hand. My father was still alive, and he and the driver talked to each other for forty-five minutes. The department had a crane out there to remove the debris, but there was still a lot of fire, and they couldn't get to him. Then there was a secondary collapse, the building shifted slightly, not very much at all, and that was the last the driver heard from my dad. He was crushed.

My uncle, who was a lieutenant in a squad company at the time, came in the commissioner's car and picked up my mother, and she sat at that fire for six hours before they took the building apart and got my father out. They didn't have to tell me, I started getting the drift when they said he was hurt and they came and picked my mom up. They said he was trapped. Then I got the picture, piece by piece, as the rest of the family came home. I sort of knew what was going on.

The next day I went back with my brother, who is a captain on the job now, and we dug through the bricks of what had become a vacant lot. We found one of my father's boots, and I have it hanging in my basement now —the boot he was wearing when he was killed. I also have his helmet.

I have a son who is eight years old. As young as he is, he has an interest in the fire department. He kept asking what happened to my father, and finally I told him. Then, when I got burned and was in the hospital, the first thing he said to my wife was, "I'm never going to see Daddy again. The same thing that happened to his dad happened to him. I'm never going to see him again." That really broke my heart when she came to the hospital and told me that.

□

I grew up in a rural area in an independent family. My father was self-employed, and my mother was, too. The exposure was nothing, I was sheltered. Life was new to me, and when I ventured out into the working world, I had to learn what it was all about. I had taken a lot for granted. Things were a lot worse than I had anticipated or ever been told. I'm speaking of the prejudices I had to learn about when I got into the working world at an early age, probably when I was in the last year of high school, when I was about sixteen.

I was brought up to think that if a person worked hard in this country and you gave it your all, you would excel. Then I learned that color had a lot to do with it. That has stuck with me, and it has affected me. I'm delighted to see that it's playing less of a role today than it ever has before. But there is a lot of improving that still has to be done. I think that people need to let go of the color barrier and look at people for what they are worth.

There are a lot of good talents going to waste, because people look at what's on the surface and never question what's inside.

In the fire department it's kind of like the military. In the heat of action, it all disappears. We thrive on incidents. The more incidents we have, the more relations, the more interactions you'll have between the troops. When things slow down on the job, a few problems start to surface, and prejudice is one of them. You start to see the effects of it.

□

When I married Jane I was a cement finisher. On my time off, I'd always go to the firehouse. At the time her father was a fire lieutenant in that area. But I met Jane through her brothers. I went to high school with them. Also, her father knew my father. We got married shortly before I was called for the city ambulance job, and then, nine months later, I was called to be a fireman.

She had a complete understanding of the fire department. She knew how to accept me coming home tired, or me going out and having a few beers with the guys after being up all night. She knew how to handle it pretty well, until I got injured.

We have two children. Our daughter, Sarah Jane, is ten, and our son, Andy, is eight. Andy goes to the Catholic school a block away from our house. His teacher told the kids, "Bring a picture of someone helping someone." I happened to have a picture of myself when I carried a woman out of a building, and, since there was no ambulance there, I was giving her oxygen. Andy took the picture and gave it to his teacher, saying proudly, "That's my dad." So he's proud of what I do, and I want to keep it that way.

Would I want him to be a fireman? Sure. But I'm not going to press it into his head. I had a pair of fire boots that were given to me when I was seven years old. I saved them for him, and he's got them now. He's got his own fire helmet and his own fire coat. But I'm not going to force it on him.

My daughter is an easygoing, loving person, like my wife. Happy-go-lucky. She likes school.

I'm a God-fearing person. There are certain standards I live by. My wife and I don't go to church every Sunday, but we make our kids go. We try to set an example for them. We're sending them to parochial school, so they can learn religion, discipline, and certain things about life they wouldn't learn at a public school. That's why I work two jobs—to send them to a Catholic school. I don't care if I have to pay, and I'm going to feel the same way about college.

My second job was as a cement finisher, until I got burned. After that, being in the sun a lot wasn't too good for my skin. There was a chief in the department who was retiring. He was fire marshal and safety instructor at a hospital. I'm state-certified as an instructor, so I asked him if he ever needed help to let me know. Two months later he called me and said the job was open. It's a part-time job, and only five minutes from home.

I give monthly classes on fire safety to all the employees. I enjoy giving these classes, and I really get into it. They had taken pictures of me the night I went into the burn center. I got the slides, telling the head nurse at the hospital that the only thing I wanted them for was to teach people what can happen when you get burned. You can feel more confident trying to teach someone something, when you've been there.

Chapter Six

WHAT IT MEANS TO BE A FIREFIGHTER

THERE ARE TIMES, NO DOUBT ABOUT IT, THAT WE ARE KNOCKing our heads against the wall. Like yelling to the sea we scream at politicians about the fire safety of our citizens, and we get in return, like the sea, nothing but white foam. We know that politicians know that sprinkler systems work, that two people or more have never, ever, died in a building that is equipped with an operational sprinkler system. Yet the politicians are in the pockets of the real estate and building construction moguls who know that sprinkler installation increases their costs and diminishes their profits, and so we have hardly any residential sprinkler laws in the country. It is shameful.

But then we live in a crass, statistical world, where the eight thousand or so people who are killed in fires each year are perhaps less important than the drain on our economy that would be created by reduced building profits. Pass along the costs to the consumer? It will never happen in a competitive real estate market. Sprinklers must be mandated by law by enlightened politicians.

Still, our heads beat against the bricks. There are so many serious problems to be solved in the country, and we firefighters are only a one-issue lobby. And our issue is very costly. The problems of drug abuse, AIDS, illiteracy, homelessness are profound domestic challenges and good argument can be made that these issues can take priority over the problem of fire safety. The great difference is, however, that we know the answer to the fire problem. Put sprinklers in all of our shelters and we will save eight thousand lives a year.

Until that happens, America's firefighters will continue to risk their future and their families' futures by running into a burning building where the fire is growing out of control. And they will fight those fires uncomplainingly, knowing all the while that they have been compromised by politicians.

Dennis Smith

□

Our volunteer fire department is only fifteen years old, and we've gone through a tremendous change in the last four years. For one thing, the legislature has enabled us to get away from seeking donations on the streets by helping us set up a tax district and fund ourselves with a property tax of three cents on a hundred-dollar valuation. It let us buy two class A pumpers on a lease option plan and pay for our first station.

We were very, very outdated. We didn't know anything about training. Fire suppression was the "surround and drown" method. We've come a long way from the old method of "just get in there and let's put this fire out." We have two pieces of new equipment plus a small first-out truck that runs the medical, and now we are training close to forty hours a month. And, also, now we're a class one fire district in Harris County.

A Houston fireman, John Coon, joined our fire service three years ago. John has really turned the department around. Not only did the money help, but from his twenty years' experience in the Houston Fire Department he's been able to give us an education, to teach us how to fight fires correctly. He's been tremendous.

Our average monthly rate of response ranges from thirty-five to fifty calls, and more than 50 percent of those calls are EMS assist, the ambulance-type calls. Our volunteer firemen are all first-out medical responders. We don't really run heavy calls. We only have a house fire maybe once a month.

In the early years we really had no protective gear, you had to make what you could, you got maybe a yellow jacket and black pants. You had to scrounge around to get a full set of protective gear. We had poor communication equipment, and at fire scenes there was no coordination. Now we have a good paging system and an elaborate computerized dispatching system that tells you where to go.

Our department is so small, with about thirteen members, that we play dual roles. I'm a district chief in charge of fire suppression, also a first-response medic. And I'm in the prevention inspection department, I do prevention inspections, and I'm also assistant fire marshal. We do fire investigations, and our findings are turned over to the Harris County fire marshal. If he feels a full investigation is needed, they come out and do it. We do the preliminaries. With small departments, you've got to do all the jobs, you've got to cover everything. And it's all volunteers.

There's a lot to be done. You'll hear from your wife, "What are you going down there again for?" There's a lot of business to be done, and if it's not done, the firehouse will shut down, and the only recourse would be to bring in fire services from the city. My regular work is affected. If you get called to a house fire at two or three in the morning and you're there for three or four hours, you're putting your regular job in jeopardy. It's good that the volunteers have a good working understanding with their employers, who realize that these guys are out there serving the community, and kind of let things slide.

What's so hard about the American society's view of firefighters is, when something has happened, whether it's a small or large disaster, they expect you to be there. You should be there, it's your job, why ain't you there? And you see very little in the way of gratitude. But it still does us good to know that we've been able to go in there and accomplish something and save somebody's house or save their lives in a vehicle accident. It does me a world of good just knowing I've been able to help somebody like that.

One thing about the United States, there are many people who really care. If they didn't care, I don't believe you'd have these volunteer fire people in the ambulance service or firefighting service, and all the other people who volunteer in hospitals and other services. There are always going to be people who want to help others.

It's hard to stay in the organization I'm in, for we have a lot of problems with our district board, which governs our spending. We have political problems with them. I was president of the fire department's board for three years, in charge of finances. If you ever wanted something simply to better the department, such as a computer, the answer was always automatically "No." You're doing this for a volunteer service, and you're doing all you can, and after a while you get really frustrated. That's the business aspect of it. As for the fire suppression side of it, the firegrounds run real well.

We've been very fortunate as far as injuries on the job are concerned. In the six years I've been around, the only injury we've had was when a firefighter jumped off the back of a pumper a little early and broke his kneecaps on the tailboard of the truck. No really severe burns or major medical problems. Even in the fifteen-year history of the department, there haven't been any other severe injuries or deaths.

We have had two DOAs at fires and maybe ten more at major accidents. But in the fire service itself, we've been really fortunate.

In starting this volunteer fire department, several men incorporated and charted the area they wished to serve. They sent it up to Harris County, and Harris County said, "This is your area, this is what you'll protect." They only had one or two people who knew a little about fire suppression. They had to go on and learn from there. It was ring the bell and everybody came.

The paid firefighters in the city probably have mixed emotions toward the volunteers. A lot of Houston firefighters respect the volunteers. On the other hand, you're going to have some Houston firefighters who think the volunteers are backwoods types who sit around drinking beer, and when a fire happens they just go there and play around on the fireground, and that's it. There are a lot of misconceptions about how the volunteers really run a fire scene. It's hard for a volunteer company to run an effective fire scene with the city of Houston.

We run mutual aid with Houston. In a larger fire, communications become a problem when you have to work with them and they have to work with you. Recently there was a fire in a bar and grill, and Houston was the first incoming. They staged first. When we got there, we tried as well as we could to take over the scene, because it was in our jurisdiction and our responsibility. We try to work as well as we can with anybody. That's everybody's goal, to work together. But it was not easy to take charge there. Actually, we are number one in mutual aid in the county, because we have a large tanker, and we send it to anybody who needs water.

When I first became a firefighter, we had to assist an outside fire department. The fire was in an area that had been ours, but unknown to me the area had been taken from us and given to another department. We responded to a call in that area. I got there and started asking what was going on, and the fire chief of the other company asked me to leave. I said, "I'm not leaving. This is our area." There were a lot of words exchanged, no scuffling or anything like that. Later on, we worked it out, and this chief and I get along real good now.

□

Right now we have eleven or twelve active members at this station. In all four stations of the Romulus Fire Department, we have maybe fifty or sixty members. Our station has a minipumper and a ladder truck with a fifty-five-foot ladder. The building is an old one, and they're talking about building a new one, but it's just talk, as far as that goes.

Before the big plane crash, we had a smaller one, a commuter plane in which nine people were killed. It was the first time I had seen anything like that. They didn't really call us for an assist like they should have. The airport pretty much had everything under control. We were more or less like a wash-down crew, washing down the foam and things like that.

We're a pretty close-knit group here. You've got to be in this kind of work. It's either somebody is going to have to cover your back or you're going to have to cover somebody else's.

□

I'm a little bit different, I don't hang around the firehouse. When I have to go on a call, I go on a call. When the call's done, I respond back to the hall. I clean up the apparatus, I repack it, I hang hoses, whatever I have to do. I may stay five or ten minutes, and then I excuse myself and go back to my family.

These people in the company are wonderful people, but I do have my family, and they've been very supportive and wonderful to me. And I enjoy being with my family. But I'll go down to the fire hall when nobody's there. I'm supervisor of a truck, and I'll go down and check out my truck from head to toe. I'm responsible for that truck, and if it were to go on a scene and it was short of something, that would be my responsibility. So I make sure it has enough breathing apparatus, it's full of water, flashlights, the whole bit.

I'm a people person, I can mix with people very well. And I listen to them really well. I don't have to tell them anything, I just let them talk. That's what they primarily want in a crisis, when it winds down, to tell their feelings to someone who is knowledgeable. I'm a mother or a sister figure. Not that men couldn't do something like this, but a lot of men don't feel as easy as I do about going up and putting my arms around somebody. Or hugging some little kid who's crying, or wiping the tears away.

I've noticed on a lot of scenes that after I've talked to somebody, I'll get kisses or hugs from these little old ladies. And it's a wonderful feeling. I go away really feeling that I did something. I really made a difference in this person's life today. A lot of times I never see them again, but I really feel I did what I was supposed to do, that was my job, and I feel good about it.

With any house fire, any construction fire, you're always in danger. Fires are never the same. If you start feeling it's going to be just a routine fire, then maybe you better get out and get yourself a desk job, or just not do it for a while. I remember a couple of occasions where we had some large house fires, and they had propane tanks in the garage that we weren't aware of—until one of them blew. Thank goodness nobody got hurt by it, but that's a scary feeling. It almost sounds like a bomb going off right next to you. And you say to yourself, okay, is there going to be another one, what's the deal here? You don't know what to expect.

And you can never let it surround you, never get stuck in the middle. You've always got to have a way out of this stuff.

Being in total darkness doesn't bother me a lot. I've never been claustrophobic, and I seem to have a very good sense of direction. I think that as long as I keep following my training, like always stay to your left or stay to your right, and don't change it. We do that at home with the kids. It's nighttime, and we're in the country, so there are no street lights or any lights at all outside. We'll say, "Okay, the smoke alarm's going off, what are you going to do?" We try to have everybody get it together, think. Before you do anything, think. How are you going to get out of here? Remember where you are. How did you get in there?

I'll tell you, there have been several times I've been just scared to death. But I think that keeping your head together gets you out of a lot of messes.

When you're feeling around in the darkness, the things you feel—you never know if you're going to feel a body. A lot of times your imagination runs away with you, and you think it's a body, or you think it's a child. You always think the worst when you're crawling around in an unknown place. You don't know the house, and before you go in there you size it up and try to get a good idea of the layout, but you never know what people have in their houses—what kind of additions they've put in, like false ceilings or traps in the floor. So you have to be very, very careful.

It's almost like you have to think of it as a game. Not like a fun game, but like an intellectual game. That's what it is.

□

The situation in Weirton is unusual. We have a paid fire department, which runs on all fire calls in the city. Then the city is divided into three fire zones, which are covered by volunteers who assist the paid people. There's Company 1, Company 2, and Weirton Heights. We have the largest zone of all three. We also run mutual aid outside the city limits. Then there's the steel mill, which has its own paid fire department, the Weirton Steel Fire Department, which also runs EMS.

Most of the time when an alarm comes in here on the hill, we beat the city firemen to the scene. They are stationed downtown, and they have a three- or four-mile uphill climb to get here. It's a very hilly area. Lately we've had a rash of arson fires in two-story residential homes. We have an industrial area, but basically it's a residential area. We've been lucky, we haven't had too many hazmat incidents or other kind of catastrophes.

Right now we're going through a pretty tough time with the paid firefighters. Not to say we're cocky, but we've had some training, and we know how some of the situations should be handled. They don't want us to respond in that way. They want to be the ultimate power. They're supposed to tell us, and we're supposed to jump. But we think we know what we're doing and what should be done. They want us to stay back and just hang around. And we're just not that type of fire department.

We're going the political route, through the city manager and the mayor, to see if it can be worked out that way. There's been a lot of bad talk going around, which is not good for either the paid department or us. We don't want to take over and be responsible for our own fires. What we want them to do is to let us handle the situation with them. Let us work with you. Don't shut us out. We're not a bunch of dummies. We've taken the training. I am as well trained as the paid firefighters, though I cannot speak for all our members.

I'm a pump mechanic. I work at the city waste water treatment plant. If it's a small alarm, I don't leave work because the men can handle it. But I have been able to leave for large structural fires. I haven't anything in writing giving permission, but the mayor and other political figures are at the major fire scenes and they get involved. And they haven't said anything to me yet.

Sometimes a run of bad things happens, but then there's always that one time where you get a lot of self-satisfaction and gratitude, and it makes up for everything that was bad earlier. I've never had a thought of quitting.

Sometimes when you go out to fires and the guys don't do what they're supposed to be doing, or don't do it properly, it gets very frustrating. Some of your friends are paid firemen, and when you get on the scene they kind of backstab you. Then you get something that makes you feel great. Even something small, like helping people in a power failure. It doesn't matter how big or small. If it brings happiness to somebody, then that's good enough for me.

When we look bad, like when there's a lot of the public standing around and nothing goes right, that's when I wish I wasn't there. But other than that, I'm glad I'm in the service.

We do things to keep the volunteers interested. We award them T-shirts and hats. We try to give them some incentive to achieve something. We give Fireman of the Year awards at our annual banquet. We give promotions, like junior sergeants and sergeants, to help keep them motivated.

We have a club room at the station that has a pool table, a TV, and a VCR. We try to keep the guys coming around to the firehouse. The trucks can definitely get out faster if the guys are there at the station house. We keep our training film file cabinet open so they can study old fires and training videos. We get *Firehouse* and other magazines at the station. To keep the guys at the station and therefore get the trucks out quicker, they're allowed to wash their cars inside in the wintertime, we have plenty of room. Small things like that.

We have a Squad 30, made up of some of the firemen's wives, and during large structural fires they come out and support us with sandwiches and Gatorade and water and coffee. We have iceboxes, we have pop machines in the firehouse.

I have the responsibility to make sure my men come home safely after every fire. Safety is the number one priority for myself and the men. To me, every fire I go to is a tight situation. We've had major structural calls come in as a Dumpster fire. I never take anything lightly when we go out the door, until we get on the scene and make sure what we got.

□

The greatest unknown in a forest fire is the weather, not knowing what the weather is going to do. Of course, there are times when you can't see the whole fire and you don't know what's coming up out of the canyon bottom at you, or if you're down there you don't know what's coming down on you from up top. Especially at nighttime in unknown country.

Our crews are put into the toughest places. They're expected to go in there and work up to twenty-four hours without relief. They are pretty much self-contained units. They have all their own tools, their own food packs, their own water, and everything. It's very difficult work, time-consuming, and hard on the body after a while, in daytime temperatures of eighty to a hundred degrees. They work long, long hours, using axes and shovels and chain saws, constantly working. And it really tears them down.

So they're really pushing now on physical stamina. These guys have to be in good health and good shape for a lot of different reasons. Because they are just not going to last, and they're not going to get the job done. Then you begin to have medical problems because you're not in good shape.

□

I wasn't a particularly religious person before my injury, and I'm not a fanatic now, but I do attend church a lot more regularly and say prayers more. The only way I can figure it out, the gift of life came through Jesus. I went back and looked at the accident scene, and there is no way I should have lived. I should be dead right now.

Today, I'm on administrative detail, I'm doing a job I really don't want to do, in fire prevention. I give 100 percent while I'm working, but it's not where my heart is at. Riding around a street, going to inspect a building, I'll hear an alarm come in, and I'm like the old firehorse that's pulling a milk wagon. I wander over and want to go to the fireground, I'll stand around and watch, and it's like you want to get in there.

My back is healed enough, and I feel I could do the job. The doctors say they think I can do it, but they're afraid of the way we live in the fire department. It's all uncontrolled. You're on the ladder and you're reaching for somebody—you're on the roof and you're falling—and you grab something. If it were the type of work where you're lifting boxes all day, I mean you can stand there and lift, but fire department lifting is totally different. I mean, you could be on a stairway and the stairway could give out, and the next thing you know a ladder could come down on you.

So right now they don't want me going back into the fires. The chief of the fire department has worked with me, and he could have told me to get the hell out, but he said we'll wait and see. If it comes to the time that the doctors are not going to change their minds, then I'll take a permanent job.

The alternative is to take the pension and get out, do something different. I don't think that I could. I could go out and train myself. I could do contracting work. If I needed to go to school, I'd go to school. No matter what I wanted to do, I could do it, I think. I have no doubt in myself. But at my age—I'm getting up to thirty-eight—they're not hiring people out there. There are no jobs around, really. I could get an insurance job, you know, underwriting or adjustments, but I wouldn't want it.

I like feeling the way I do about myself when I put the uniform on. I get up and come to work, I look forward to coming to work. I look forward to doing my job with the people I work with. I mean, you meet any fireman, you've got something in common with him. I was on night inspection at a restaurant, and a chief from Seattle was there. He introduced himself, and we must have talked for forty-five minutes. Things like that. If I was an insurance salesman and went into a restaurant, nobody would know. And if they did, they wouldn't give a damn.

It's an interesting life.

There are great feelings of satisfaction. One of the rescues I had was a basement fire. I got a man out of there. We were the third engine in, and I was leading off. The radio said there were people trapped down there. I came up and said, "Did you find the people yet?" The guys were like, "No. No." Nobody was going down to look. I was like, "Bull, get your ass in there." I went down and made a search, and on the first search, there he was. I had him up and out and back to where he lived. If I hadn't acted, he probably would have died.

I had one fire where there was a picture in the newspaper of a lieutenant bringing a kid down the ladder, but I had handed the kid out. It was the same thing. Guys were searching in the room, and I just made a turn and went to the other room, and bang, there the kid was in the corner. I went right at him, and there was the guy right on the ladder, and it was perfect. Those types of things.

It's the kind of job where even before you're out of fire school, you know if you want to do this type of work or not. You get people who are afraid of heights, putting a mask on. If you make it through that, it's a rewarding job.

You touch more people's lives than you think just by doing the job, even if it's just going out and pumping a flooded basement, or going out on inspection and showing them about a cord on their car, or smoke detector programs. It touches you to know that you're helping people that way, that it's the purpose of your job, and that your job is to protect the citizens. It's going to make you feel good. If you're doing your job right, you're going to feel good about it.

I miss the excitement, the chance to do the things that make you feel good, making a rescue, cutting somebody out of a car, helping somebody out of a window. Even a vacant building fire, when you put the ashes out and you look back, it makes you feel good that you did it. You pull up, and it's all fire, and you say, "Oh man." And you get in there, and it's out, and you feel good about yourself. I guess it's like a pitcher pitching a no-hitter. I mean, it worked good, everybody feels good, and they're all smiling.

You're out in twenty below at four in the morning, but, "Good job, good job." You get back, and you sit around and have coffee and talk about it. That feeling is great. You go out and inspect a building, and you say, "The guy needs an extinguisher, big deal." Some guys on inspection don't consider themselves part of the fire department, they don't want to have the radio scanner on and hear that noise. It's the way you feel about doing the job. I've always given 100 percent, and I feel good no matter what, if it's a trash fire, a pot of food, whatever. I never shirked my duties, I was always in there, and nobody can say, "He's a bum." I'm always with the people, with the men.

You look back at old pumpers. When I came in, we were still using 1945 Macks. In ten more years they'll look at an old Mack picture and say, "My God, these guys used to stand on the back steps." Riding the truck company, that was the biggest thing, just riding on the side, and when they turned you just turned your head that way. I remember it pulling out, and if you didn't run down the street and jump on it, then that was it. You'd get up there and ride the truck to the fire. But guys trying to do that have fallen and hurt themselves. It's changed now. It's changed for the better because of safety.

You look at what people did, they worked twenty-three hours and had one off; they went home and ate, and came back and put in another twenty-three hours. The only reason those guys did it was because they felt the same way I do. Why else would a person do the job for the money you make? It's because you like it, and because of the tradition.

You look around and see all the firemen dying of cancer. But there is only so much you can do to make the job safe and still do the job. Hopefully, it never gets to the point where you'll be standing on the sidewalk and somebody's house is on fire, and you say, "I'm sorry, ma'am, we have to let it burn down."

It's taken ten years off my life. A guy who came through school with me died of cancer. This guy was thirty-seven years old. I'm an old guy now, still in my thirties. When I came in the department, there were guys in their forties and fifties, and it was like, "Is that old man still in here? When is the old bastard leaving?" I guess I'm the old guy in the department now, even though I'm still young. If I were a banker, I would hope to live to be seventy or eighty, but if a fireman makes it to fifty, he takes his pension, and a month later he's dying of some weird disease.

□

I have two years more to go in medical school, and right now I'm geared toward emergency medicine. I like the immediacy of it, the life-and-death-ness of it and being able to make a big difference quickly. A lot of medical people frown on emergency medicine because they say there is no patient follow-up, you're not following your patient through. But for a lot of people who come through that door in life-and-death situations, you could be the most important medical person in their lives. You are the whole medical profession to them.

It's very important to me to get back into the fire service. I have to be in a field of medicine that will allow me to do that. I sent fourteen applications to medical schools. Medical schools cut 85 percent of the applicants without seeing them. Even if you get interviewed, your chance is 25 percent or less. You wait around, and you go to the mailbox every morning. Rejection, rejection, an interview.

I went to an interview at Dartmouth, which is really where I wanted to go. I sat down with this horse's ass in his office, and he didn't like me from the word go. This was a medical doctor, and he was looking at my records for the first time. He said, "I see you are some kind of Renaissance man," as if that were a derogatory thing.

"I don't think I can let a person like you into this medical school," he said. "When you make a commitment to medicine, you have to drop everything and go after that. I see that you worked as a fireman and as a paramedic all through your entire time at college."

I tried to explain to him that the way I was raised, I learned that you have to have a commitment to your fellow man. I said that when I was in college, sometimes I was the only EMT or paramedic in the village, and that for a couple of people I made a big difference. He had the arrogance to say, "Come on, how many lives did you really save?" The man had no idea of what I was all about.

I got the rejection letter two weeks later.

I'm in the medical school of the State University of New York at Stony Brook. My roommate's father is a fire marshal with twenty-two years' experience in the New York Fire Department. I remember going over to their house, and he started questioning me. "You come up on a house and there is nobody inside. There is fire showing in the front windows. What do you do?"

I said, "You go in, you get behind the fire, and you push it out the windows."

He said, "Oh."

I'm afraid I'm going to have to explain my professional life as an emergency medical man to a whole lot of people.

□

Firefighters seldom curse when talking about the job, because the profession brings out the best in people. We have these noble ideals, and noble ideals are hard to envision when you are in the gutter. We have a purpose in life, and when we start talking about that, I think we watch our language. When we start talking about other things, then maybe we revert to more normal levels of tough talk.

We love risk taking as firefighters. That attracts a lot of us. We are a nation of risk takers, who do not believe in absolute safety. Perhaps it's in our genes from those Europeans who chose to leave an old, established life and embark on a new one at great risk. It shows up in the entrepreneurial spirit we see in our country today.

I think firefighters mature on the job and realize that the reality is different from the image.

□

We work in the darkness of smoke. There's a special point in a firefight when I wonder if I'm going to be able to put the fire out. That was my darkness in the process of growing in this profession. We used to be pretty fast and loose in the way we operated on the fireground. We did things that today you just don't do. We took chances you don't take. We weren't protected the way you are today.

I was a very physical firefighter. I always did things that required a certain amount of strength. I was an athlete when I was going to school, I lifted weights, that sort of thing, and that was part of the process, the physical part of it. It still is. I am still attracted to that part of it. That you put fires out with firefighters, with strength.

Then we started to develop the state-of-the-art envelope for firemen, protect them, communicate with them, and write procedures. But you still dress firefighters up in those goofy suits and you send them out, and you gotta kick ass or the fire kicks ass, and I think that's the part of it that's challenging. That is the part that a lot of us are attracted to. There is a certain fascination with that darkness. You don't move away from it, you move toward it, and that's why firefighting is dangerous, and I think it always will be. There is that special moment where it's you against whatever is behind that darkness—it's where life and death come together—and that is an interesting place for a human being.

I reflect on it a little differently now that I manage people who do that. I don't think you ever really understand it, but you expand your ability to deal with it as, say, a battalion chief. You look at the whole system, but it always comes down to the fact that we operate on the task level, it's just that simple. You still dress those firefighters up, and there they go. You do all the things to help them. You can belt them in and put them inside a cab, and you can communicate with them, and you can give them books to read, and videos to watch. Then you face the enemy, and you face the darkness.

People don't understand firefighters, because they do very special, esoteric things, and they do them in a special way. Firefighting becomes a subculture, and we firefighters tend to hang around with one another, for the darkness is hard to explain to an outsider. It's like trying to describe what ice cream tastes like—it's cold, and it's sweet, and it's peppermint, and it's different eating it. It's hard to describe.

I don't think people really have to understand the details of what you do. They relate to you in a different way, in knowing that you are going to help them and that you are going to come quick. The response I usually get from the general public is that you came quickly and you were skillful and you cared. That's what I want.

You can't get any better than that.

□

Basically, my life is all fire department. I ride motorcycles, and I ski, all activity-related. You gotta keep doing and thinking and using your hands.

There are no two situations alike in firefighting. Always, you go out there, and it won't be the same thing. That's what I like about it.

I hope to keep on serving the volunteer fire department as station captain. I'd like to get more into teaching, though, to pass on the experience and the knowledge I have gained to the younger members. I think the fire service needs new blood in it, and I hope to be the one that puts the little extra push into it.

□

I'm a journalist and a firefighter. Sometimes it's difficult to separate the two. Many of the things I learned growing up in the firehouse were tremendous assets when I became a journalist. The ability to respond quickly to an emergency situation. Journalism deals with a lot of emergency situations. I was heavily influenced by the officers I knew and served under. I learned many things as a fireman that have stood me in good stead as a journalist.

People think of journalism as an intellectual occupation and firefighting as physical. Both are oversimplifications. Good firefighters also have to have an intellect, and for journalists who lead the type of life I have led, a lot of physical stamina comes into the thing. I suppose the fact that in some respects the two are so different is one of the blessings of having a dual life. When I do journalism, it is total immersion in journalism; when I am with the fire department, it is total immersion in the fire department. I have no preference, they are both two of the most essential parts of my life. The third equally important part of my life is my family.

In one volunteer company we had fifty members, but there was a hard core of only ten or fifteen men who were in it for the firefighting. I've noticed this on every volunteer company I have been with, the same ten or fifteen guys you can count on. These are the ones who will take the courses, show up for the drills, and whenever they are available they will never miss a fire. They can have a 100-degree fever, and if that alarm goes off, they are going to drag out of bed and get to the fire. Your bond as a firefighter is always with that hard-core group who are the active firefighters.

A firefighter has great pride in his company, whether he is career or volunteer. Outsiders can't understand that. On Squad 2 in Chicago we always felt we were the best, we could meet any challenge. We called ourselves gladiators. We thought we were invincible. The same thing was true on the volunteer companies that I have been on. We thought that we could meet whatever we had to face, and we always did—a great feeling of accomplishment.

People say it's an unusual hobby. It's not a hobby at all. A great part of my life would be empty if it were not for the fire department. Firefighting is a way of life. You will be in a rotten fire situation—filthy dirty, cold, coated with ice—it's been a long hard night, and yet you feel sorry for the people who have not had that experience. Among firefighters, you feel good about each other and about yourself.

Outsiders can't understand the feeling you get when that bell rings and you know you're gonna go. The tension you feel when a box comes in, when you're not due on the box, but you're due on the second. Waiting to see if they're going to pull the second alarm or not. Everybody gets up and goes to the bathroom, because you don't know if you're going to get another chance. Then all of a sudden there is that feeling of exhilaration when the bell starts ringing, they've pulled the second alarm and you're going. You're going to be challenged. The feeling you get when you're on your way and you look up and see that column of smoke or that glow, and you know you're going to have a working fire.

It isn't that you want something bad to happen to someone else, that's not it at all. It's the feeling that if something's happening, I want to be there. Perhaps the worst feeling of all, the strangest feeling, is the one that you have when you're on your way there, and they tell you on the radio that people are trapped. I call it "rescue fever," and it comes over the whole company. It's a shot of adrenaline. You do things you didn't believe were physically possible. The idea that somebody is trapped in there, and you're going to have to get them. I've always admired what firefighters have been able to do. Sometimes it's also a bit frightening, because it has led people to try to do more than they should have and get themselves into extremely dangerous situations.

The feeling you get when you are in, and the entire building is involved, and you know that it's going to a second or third alarm. There is just your one engine there, you're laying out that one line, and you know that help has been called for but hasn't gotten there yet. There is that state of suspended animation—you're throwing water from that one two-and-a-half-inch line, and it doesn't mean a thing in that volume of fire. Then you start hearing the sirens coming from the other apparatus. You have this confidence that the system is going to work. It may take ten, twenty, thirty companies to do it, but in the end you're going to get the job done.

One of the greatest satisfactions of all is when you're in the trenches, where you have a big fire, and there you are, one company, the five or six of you are right at the point where that fire has to be stopped. There are maybe a hundred guys out there and twenty or thirty pieces of apparatus, you just know when it's your company that has gotten into the right position and you're the ones who made the stop on the fire.

□

When I was in school, I played football at the Silver Dome, and I get the same thrill fighting fires. It's totally overwhelming. Adrenaline flowing superstrength. Everything.

It's the excitement I'm in it for. I like to work on the older guys when they say we're not being paid enough. I laugh at them. I say they're paying us enough. And they get so mad, because they're not in it for the excitement anymore. You get so many fires in Detroit that you get burned out.

We're the arson capital of the world.

□

The Our Lady of Angels school fire was probably the most traumatic experience I ever had as a firefighter. It was my day off from the newspaper. I was with Squad 2, and we were a third-alarm squad on that fire. They jumped it from two to five alarms. As we went in, we could see the column of smoke, and we could see the ambulances and the police vehicles coming away from the fire with the injured.

When we got in, we were ordered to the roof of this U-shaped building. We had to go up an aerial ladder, and in order to get to the ladder we had to run through a crowd of parents, who were running back and forth across the street looking for their children. So we went up to the roof, started opening it up, then we got a three-inch line up there and we were throwing water across a courtyard.

We didn't know at that point what had happened. All this jumping had taken place on the other side of the building. By that time a whole wing of the second floor was fully involved in fire. Fire was coming through the roof. Then they ordered all squad companies to the front of the building. When we came down, a priest came up to us and said that there were seventy-five children inside the building.

At that point, I decided I had to go to work as a reporter. They had plenty of firemen on the scene, but I was the only reporter. So I took off my helmet and went to work as a reporter.

As it turned out, ninety-three children and two nuns were killed in that fire. I was very busy while all of it was going on, but a few days later it got to me. I had seen many horrible things in the past, but never anything quite as horrible as this, because anything that affects children hits you harder. It was a few days later that I really got shook up about what had happened and what I had seen. But when you're young, you're resilient, and you get over it.

The funny thing is, ten years later I woke up one night with a real sweaty nightmare about that fire. I dreamed about a woman I had seen for maybe three seconds. I had run past her to get to the ladder to go up to the roof. If I saw her today, I would still know her. She was wearing curlers in her hair, a scarf over her head, a beige blouse, brown slacks, and she had a look on her face—a look of absolute anguish, looking for her child. I hadn't thought about it at all, and here, ten years later, I wake up in a cold sweat dreaming about this woman. And I couldn't understand why.

So I got up and went into my kids' bedroom to see how they were, and then I realized what it was. My eldest son had just turned eight years old. That was the age—eight, nine, ten—of the children who were killed in that fire. I guess it was, subconsciously, always in my mind. When my own child reached that age, I was so appreciative of having my child that I must have empathized with that woman years later. As a parent I had much more feeling about that fire than I had when I was single.

What is interesting about it is the way things stick in your mind, the psychological impact of what you are seeing without knowing it. Today they have counseling for emergency service people, which we didn't have in those days. Everybody was supposed to be a macho tough guy. The truth is that us macho tough guys were bothered by what we saw and what we had to do at times. Today we have counseling, and we understand that what firefighters do and see has a tremendous impact on them.

Recently, the Chevy Chase Fire Department, where I am on the board, responded to a terrible accident out on the Beltway, in which three young people were killed. We immediately gave that shift the advantage of having some counseling if they needed it. As it turned out, most of them wanted it. So we realize the toll that all of this takes on our people. I think it's very healthy to do that type of thing.

I don't think the people at ABC News, where I work, give much of a thought to my firefighting activity. Most people look on it as a rather strange thing for a person to be doing, but I got used to that years ago. Since it's not something they would want to do, they wonder why anybody would want to do it. They don't know the great experiences that we as firefighters have, the things we share with each other, and the satisfaction that comes from doing it. To me, being a firefighter is an enrichment of my life.

I've never had much enjoyment from watching a fire. It would be a pretty frustrating thing. If I'm in another city and they have a fire, I'll go and observe and try to learn their way of doing things. But there really isn't a lot of satisfaction in simply watching a fire.

□

I don't want to be on an ego trip, but I tell you there is nothing else in the world like firefighting. I have dedicated myself to it, and I've tried to implement a lot of things in the Cleveland Fire Department. As you get higher in rank, obviously, it gives you a better chance to do those things.

I have a large family, and there are always money concerns. You say, "I wish I could afford to pay my kids' way through college completely." I have a number of children who have completed college. I have some in college. I have more than enough credits myself to have graduated, but the credits are just not in the right things. I have a couple of degrees in fire science. I did teaching at Cayuga Community College. I've done a lot of things in the fire department to improve protective clothing and to improve our fire ground tactics to make things safer for firefighters.

Obviously I could have made more money doing something else, but it wouldn't be the same career. After twenty-seven years, if you're doing a job, and you still like going to work and look forward to going to work, then you know it's worthwhile. Money isn't everything, I guess, compared to the special feeling you have being a firefighter.

I have a son now who is going to take the fire exam. He had gone to college for a couple of years, then stopped. It's really hard to postpone gratification. If he wants to be a firefighter, that's great. I know he'll make a living. Hopefully, he'll have equal opportunity and a fair opportunity for promotion. That's one of the sad parts of the fire service. We don't want to eliminate anybody from equal treatment, but I think you end up with reverse discrimination, when other firefighters are entitled to something and don't get it.

A career in the fire service—there's nothing like it.

□

Volunteer firefighting will always be part of my life. It becomes a major headache at times, but I feel good about it. I've got too much invested. I've got about five hundred hours of training alone, and the ranks I've gone through, I can't just say, "That's enough, I want to quit." That's what's nice about the American way: if you're dissatisfied with this fire service, there are a lot of other fire companies that could use your help, especially if you're educated in the fire service.

Operating as a chief at a house fire is a tremendous responsibility. It's something you have to do. I wouldn't mind going in with them, but they know the job's got to be done. They volunteered their time, so the only thing they can do is go in and put the fire out.

Sure, we're volunteers. There are a lot of volunteers, and we work together and get the job done.

□

I don't regret spending my whole professional life in firefighting, not one bit. I honestly can say I have not seen another profession or job that has interested me at all. It's all I have ever wanted to do. When I was drafted into the Army, I tried desperately to get into the fire service within the military, but that turned out to be an impossibility.

I've had other assignments in the job, in fire prevention and even some office-type work I didn't like at all. It was an education and it helped me, but my first love is suppression. And I wanted out of those jobs as fast as I could get out of them to get back on the engine, so to speak. I'm not even interested in promotion above battalion chief level, because that means a desk job. And I want to be on the street.

To quote an old saying from years ago, I hate to see somebody's house burn down, but when it does I want to be there.

□

I enjoy the challenge of the job. You see so many people who dread their jobs. A friend of mine who lives across the street is an engineer. He makes a lot of money, but he's not happy. He envies me. He envies my time off during the week when I'm doing things, or when I'm with my kids. I might not make that much money, but I certainly am happy. I think that's important.

I'm not really looking for promotion. My next step is to be lieutenant, because I'm the driver now. A lieutenant has a tremendous amount of paperwork, and to me, for the additional money you make, it's not worth it. I just enjoy the firefighting end of it.

I think we have the best country in the world, maybe because of going to Vietnam and seeing how those people live. I really learned to love our country back then. We have American flags on our truck, two on the front and one on the back. One of the younger members asked me, "Why do you have all those flags on the truck?" I told him that America is the best country in the world. You should be proud of those flags. They're not there for decoration. They mean something.

□

It can't be the money that keeps me in, I'll tell you that. It can't be the money. It's just that, even after I've been off a week, I still have that desire to get back and get in there. I like the action.

I enjoy getting out there and helping people. A lot of guys don't like to say that. It's not the macho image. But there are so many out there who need some help, it's unreal. Especially in the areas where I've been working. I never worked in the high-class areas, but in my areas it gives you a good feeling to help people who need it. I can go home and say I love life. Very seldom am I down, very seldom. I think that the department has helped.

I would say to a young man coming in that it's going to be a rough road ahead, it's not going to be easy by a long shot. You have to put a lot into it. Of course, the outlook is different now than when I came in, and much to the better. It's tough for old-timers to give up the old macho way with smoke, for instance. That's dumb. I did it, but it's dumb. Now the new guys are oriented to wearing a mask at all times, and this is a great safety feature.

With a young guy coming in now, it's a good job, and you get out of it what you put into it. There are guys that come in strictly for security, and there are guys that come in for the love of the job. There's a twenty-one-year-old fellow coming in now, and that's all he wants—the fire department. Luckily he got up on the list, and he was sweating taking the physical, and he was sweating taking the interview. He finally got appointed, and he's elated.

He called me up at work. "Hey, are there any openings at your house? I want to come and work with you."

I said, "You don't want to come here."

He said, "Yes, I do."

"Well, I'll tell you what," I said. "You couldn't make a better choice if you want to get experience and work with a bunch of guys that are like a top-notch baseball team. It's a team that's always there. If someone has a problem, somebody can look out for you." I love it.

I feel good about my life. I enjoy the department, and with hustling on the side in my other jobs, I have enough money to enjoy the other things in life, vacations, taking trips. If I had stayed with the post office, I would have been a different person. I would wake up in the morning and think, "Do I have a sick day built up yet?" I always wanted to call in sick and get a day off.

In the fire department, when I've been off for a week or two, either sick or on a double bubble, I think, "Boy, I hope I can get back to work soon. I'm ready to go back." A week off, fine, that's enough. I'm ready to get back.

□

I wouldn't do any other job, I enjoy this one too much. I've spent my life preparing for it, and it would be hard for me to find employment doing something else. I don't think I'd want to, I wouldn't be as happy. I'm in for the long haul.

I'm still single, and I'm still young. I'm hoping to advance here as far as I can go, but I still have this desire to work in a very heavy urban area, such as New York, Baltimore, Philadelphia. It's just something that I need personally to do. Here in Charlotte, I've only been a captain a year, and I'm looking forward to getting my own company. I would like to have a shift on the new rescue company that's going to be put into service here in the near future.

I like what I'm doing now because I work with different people all the time and ride different territories. It's good experience. I've been fortunate enough to work in a battalion where most of the people are like me, interested from a very early age, want to do their best, very gung-ho. Professional, very professional.

We do have some firefighters who are more concerned with their sideline jobs and are constant gripers. They come from slower companies, and some take pride in that fact. They don't have to do a lot. And their performance shows on the fireground. When one company looks bad, everybody looks bad, and people's perception of us will go down.

I try to be as professional as I can, because that's the way it should be. We should be good.

□

I found out it's the greatest job in the world. Probably because of the men you work with, the camaraderie. It's like a family, and you're with them as much as you're with your own family. Sometimes more. Where I'm at, the guys keep things light, they don't take things too seriously.

It's a job where you can find a lot of satisfaction, because you can see the results of your work immediately. You know right away that you've helped people. It's not like you're working with papers. People don't always like policemen, but they're always glad to see the firemen. I like helping people.

What makes the job worth the injuries I've had? I can't speak for everyone else. I've always kind of walked a thin line. I've always been—not reckless—but I've always been around danger. I was always in trouble. I wasn't a bad kid, but I was always getting into things. I was the kind of person who would jump into a pool before I'd check if there was water. I've had a lot of things happen to me.

But danger is just part of the job, everyone accepts that. And the benefits outweigh the dangers. I get satisfaction out of this job. I could have died in this fire at the young age of twenty-eight, but that's a risk. I knew the risks when I came on the job, and you just try to be as well prepared as you can. Nobody wants to die. Nobody wants to leave his family. My wife knows that. She also knows that I'm prepared, and it's just part of the job.

I don't want a medical disability. I'd like to put my time in. I've got what they call RADS—reactive airway deficiency syndrome. It's a form of asthma. I asked the doctor, "How long will I have this?"

He said, "Some people get rid of it right away, and some people never get rid of it."

So I'm still taking inhalants and different things. And we'll see what happens the next time I get a smoky job, how I react to it. That's what the doctor said. "The only way you're going to know is if you get another smoke situation. You'll see what happens."

I'd like to work my way up the chain of command. There's nothing wrong with being a fireman for twenty or thirty years. Sometimes you're in a place where you know more than your officer, and you have to swallow it because he's got the rank. That's motivation enough to study. If you feel you can help others and you're a little more on the ball than most people, I think it's your duty to try to attain an officer's rank.

□

I love the job, I really love it. So does everybody in the service. In this day and age, you don't get to do many things that help people out. It's the most gratifying feeling that I know of. I believe it comes from my parents.

My father has been helping people for a long time. He's seventy-seven years old, and he still works six days a week. He's still self-employed as a mechanic. He doesn't need the money, he does it to do people favors. He keeps the shop open because he feels there's a need for his services. It's the motivation that keeps him going.

I believe that I inherited that, to a certain degree, from him.

□

As to the danger, I believe that when it's your time to go, it's your time to go. I'm not looking forward to the day I'm gone, but I just live day to day. I don't dwell on the possibility of this happening, because it breaks your concentration. If you start worrying about every job you go on, you clutter your mind and you cloud your thinking.

You just have to say, "I'm going in there to do my job, and I'm going from this point to that point, and I have these things to do." You have to keep your priorities in order, you know what you have to do, you know what the goal is, and just work to complete that goal. Then afterwards you can say, "That building was shaky, or that fire was really coming up our backs." I mean, you can think about the dangers afterwards, but you can't let that stuff cloud your thinking.

You have to understand that they are there, and you've got to be aware of them. You can't get careless or reckless, you have to be aware of what's going on around you at all times. But don't be so aware of them that you're going to worry about something that really isn't something to worry about. You just go in, do what you have to do, and you're done. I live one day at a time, stay in top health, and do it as it comes along.

Firefighting is a business like any other business, it's a career for me. The only thing to do now is to eventually move up the ladder, advancing to different positions—lieutenant, captain, whatever—set my wheels in motion for my future. I could stay a firefighter for my whole career, there's nothing wrong with that. I could be content with that. I'll plan my future as I move along.

□

Being in the fire department has changed my life. I'm a little more committed to helping people. It's good being in the fire department, it makes you more responsible. I really never thought I would be a family person, but I am now. A lot has to do with the fire department. You're always training, so your mind is steadily working. It's not like a dead end. You've always got to move forward and take one day at a time.

If an accident happens, we have to respond to it, make sure everybody is all right, and do everything we can. If people are upset, you try to calm them down. The job makes you take charge of things.

This one guy I know was disturbed because his lieutenant had gotten killed, and he felt guilty about it. He asked me what did I do to get over it. My heart went out to him. I told him I really didn't do anything, but my family was behind me, and the guys that I work with were behind me 100 percent. But I got the impression that his guys kind of dogged him and blamed him, like he didn't wait and he didn't do enough to save the lieutenant. He was totally upset.

I told him that in my case I felt I did everything I could, but there wasn't much I could have done. So I told him he shouldn't take that weight on himself. When the guys you work with don't believe in you, that could be a problem.

Being a survivor, I don't know if God was telling me to "change your life, young man." I have changed, I've mellowed. He's been excellent to me, God has. That's why I'm here now.

□

I'm doing what I want to do, and there's no better feeling. Even after being hurt, I can't wait to get up and go to work, because I enjoy my job. I love going to the firehouse. A nurse is someone I relate to a fireman, because you're always helping somebody. A fireman should never expect to get a pat on the back, you just give yourself a pat on the back when you do a good job. That makes you feel good. Don't wait for somebody else to pat you on the back. Just do your thing.

When you come home in the morning, you look tired. Your wife and kids don't know what you've been through. But if I've had a busy night on the job, I come home with a smile on my face, because I know I did something good, helped somebody or saved somebody's property.

I grew up in what they call a ghetto firehouse. I worked with black firemen and white firemen; they were all real men, and they taught me so much. Outside of that firehouse, in that neighborhood, it's a cruel world. When people don't have anything, they have nothing to lose. And it's cruel. Life to some of those people means nothing. They kill people, they hurt people, they do a lot of nasty things to people, and it means nothing to them. You see a lot of violence. It makes you a little bit cold and a little bit cruel to the people who are committing the crimes. But it makes you appreciate life a lot more when you go home to your family.

I grew up in that area, in that firehouse, it's part of my life. It's something I'll always cherish. I learned so much about life down there. I look at college-educated persons, and I can see that some of them don't have any street sense. They don't know what it is to be down at the bottom. Growing up there made me think a lot about the basic things in life.

I don't ever want a fancy house, I want a nice house. I want my kids to be well-educated, but I want them to know what goes on out there on the street. I want them to know the real world, so they won't put themselves up on a pedestal. They still have to relate. Everybody is a human being. That's one of the things I learned being there. There's a whole world out there that people don't see, especially people who don't live in a big city.

I studied for over a year, and I'm on the captain's list right now. I take an interest in administration, because I'm interested in the overall good of the fire department. I want to see our job work well. As a supervisor and a company officer, I have a lot of things I have to control. All I want a person to be if he works for me is to be honest and to be a firemen. I run a squad company which is similar to New York's rescue, and it's taken me seven years, but I've built a hell of a company, and I know everyone of my guys personally. But overall, my basic thing is that I still like being a company officer, and I still like fighting fires.

Right now I can't see myself in an administrative position. First of all, I'm too young. Not that I'm naive. I try to cover everything that goes on in the job, but I haven't got that tiger out of me yet. It's still in my tank. As I say, I look forward to going to the firehouse, and if we have a busy day, I come home with a smile on my face.

The pressures on the leadership are tremendous with the changes we've had, women and racial quotas and the aftermath of the strike. We still have the young clashing with the old, the strikers and the nonstrikers. But everybody is pretty much back to normal. I never judge a person by what another person says about him. It's how he deals with me.

I'm on a squad company, and a lot of firemen, I'm told, don't like us because we think we're macho. I don't have that feeling. I'm just there because I enjoy the work and the different types of things you see. For example, yesterday we had a man down an elevator shaft. We had a crane on top of a car. We had a hazardous material spill last night. We do the scuba diving. We're always doing something. Every day I go to work, I learn something different. And you can't go wrong doing that.

I was told when I was burned that I could have gone off on three quarters disability pay. To this day, does my back bother me? Yeah. Do my ears hurt me at a fire? A little bit. Does my face get blotchy? Yeah. Do I have cream in my locker for when my face gets irritated from heat or smoke? I have cream to put on it. Does it bother me? Yeah.

But that's my love, that's my life, second to my family. There's no greater pleasure you can get than if you love your job and you go to work and enjoy yourself. Would I like an administrative job? No.

It wouldn't have been my style to leave the job.

In the back of my mind, am I trying to fulfill something? I don't know.

□

I know what I want to say, but it's hard to get across. I think that with my kids and everything else, I have responsibilities. Being a fireman and being a black fireman, I have to put my best foot forward. I want to leave everybody impressed, that's the way I feel. If anybody else feels malice toward me because I'm black, then that's their problem.

If I ever went down South and got stopped by a white state trooper, and he knew I was a fireman because I've got my emblem or something, I want to leave him impressed with me. When he leaves me, I want him to say, "Well, that's one sharp guy. He seems to be an intelligent guy." That's what I would like to leave with everybody, actually. But especially with the troopers.

It's the only thing I want to do. If I can't do anything else, I want to change people's minds. I know that some people have certain beliefs about the way other people are, or the way they think they should be. It may not be my responsibility, but I would like to change people's minds, if I can, and leave them with a positive attitude toward black firemen.

□

The salary thing has got to be separate, because nobody could continue to do this unless they wanted to. I'll be forty in December, and I see things a lot differently, looking back and looking ahead. I love the job. It's a lifetime challenge because every fire is different, even the same variables move around in different sequences.

We're not paying enough attention to building construction and renovations. And it amazes me that we have young officers coming up quickly through the ranks who have literally little or no fireground experience.

You can't have guys in the companies or battalion who are just strolling along as if it's another day of the week. If I ever get lucky and make district chief, a top priority would be to improve our knowledge of the conditions we work under and what certain types of buildings are going to do *before* the fire, instead of getting there after the fire starts. Not everything is a three-story frame—we call them three-deckers—where you finish yawning and the fire is out.

This is a serious game we're playing. When firefighters seem to be acting up, they're just letting off some steam. It's our way of saying, okay, we're trying to maintain this image that we're supermen but at the same time acknowledging that we're not indestructible or infallible but only human, and this how we say it. Some officers misinterpret the way the guys behave and think they're just clowns or trying to goof off. They're just letting off steam. They do take the job seriously, otherwise no fire would be put out. There is just plain a lot of stress that goes with the job.

I wish we could have a program in all the fire departments, like they do in some parts of Florida, where the media actually go to drill school. I'd like to see the reporters and the mayors of all these cities go down the long hallway trying to make a search, or pulling a line and trying to pull ceilings at the same time. I believe they'd have a different view of firefighters if they could go to two or three jobs in a row, then come out and say, "I didn't quite realize it was like that."

Civilians just don't believe how fast that fire will travel. They leave their kids unattended for a couple of minutes, shoot out the door, and go down to the corner for a second. How quickly it spreads.

Those things hit me nowadays.

□

I've seen the good times, I've seen the bad times. I've gone to jobs, and we didn't wear masks—three days with splitting headaches. I wear my mask now.

The greatest thing that happened to me was when I was sworn into the New York Fire Department as an honorary deputy chief. I'm still associated with the FDNY from when I was a teenage buff. But, of course, I'm happy with the Hartford Fire Department, because they've been good to my family. I work for an excellent chief, John B. Stewart, Jr. He has bought a lot of new apparatus that we've long needed.

I'm proud to be here, and if my health stays with me, I foresee another twenty years with the department.

□

A lot of times I try to put myself in the public's place, as opposed to being a firefighter, and try to think what they're thinking. I think the outside world has to realize the dangers involved in the fire service, along with the mental pressures and the stress. They should know that this firefighter is doing whatever he's doing to save somebody else's life. He's putting his own life on the line, which I know has been said a hundred times over.

We've had different classes in the area on things like hazardous materials. I've attended every class I can. Because you never know. You may not have had a toxic spill in your area or something really dangerous where you've had to evacuate schools. But you're going to. It's going to happen, and somebody's got to have the knowledge and the ability to keep the public together, and help them get out of it.

□

There are several things that have made me angry. What makes me most angry is the needless loss of life to fire. Over the years, as a journalist more than as a firefighter, I became involved in fire safety and fire prevention. I learned as much as I could about it, and I wrote many stories on the subject. What always strikes me, especially at the major disasters, the big multideath fires that I have covered as a reporter or been at as a firefighter, is that in every case the loss of life didn't have to happen.

But they failed to heed the lesson of the past. They failed to pass the fire codes that would prevent this from happening, or they failed to make them retroactive. They failed to put sprinklers in the buildings where you have the potential for a high loss of life—high-rise hotels, office buildings, theaters, nightclubs, nursing homes.

I have been to fires in all of those types of places. I have never been to a major fire disaster in which the loss of life would not have been prevented had the building met the standards we know a building should meet—which is to be protected by automatic sprinklers. There has never been a multideath fire in a building fully protected by a properly installed and operating sprinkler system.

The indifference to fire safety in this country is probably the most depressing thing of all. People look at a fire as bad luck. But the real bad luck was that people were in a place that should have been protected, and that they were in a city or a state that had failed to pass and enforce the laws that would have saved their lives. I see so many cases in which the people who build, own, and operate the buildings have the political influence and the money to block the passage of proper fire codes.

One of the things the fire service has to do through the news media is to create a public opinion that is concerned about fire safety. When that happens, you get results. After a disaster is your best chance to get a retroactive fire code passed that will correct the problem that caused a multideath fire. It's a slow process, but I think we have been making progress in recent years.

Another thing that is tremendously important about the fire service is leadership. Most of the guys I served with who went on to be career officers, some of them top-ranking chiefs of their departments, were dedicated people who came up through the ranks, but who also did all the studying they had to do, and they worked hard to get where they are. I think that modern leadership has an opportunity to overcome so many problems of the past. In the old days we had leaders, chief officers, who were good firemen, but they weren't necessarily good leaders and administrators.

Today, a fire chief has to be much more than a good officer on the fireground. We're starting to see that type of diversity develop now, chiefs who are good all-around leaders. I think that the salvation for the fire service, with all the problems that face us today, has to come from that wiser, more enlightened, more sensitive leadership. Many of the problems we face today wouldn't be there had there been an enlightened leadership that was willing to change with the times, twenty and thirty years ago.

Unfortunately, too many were not.

□

I always knew we were underpaid, but we never knew how much until we saw the figures of what everybody else is making. Granted, in New York the cost of living is higher and the firefighting is a lot more, but the job is still the same. There shouldn't be that much disparity of pay, but there is. Pay and equipment.

Baltimore City is changing, and we're getting a lot more equipment.

After Will Thompson's injury and my injury, we had two lieutenants who died, and the fire department went out and purchased those personal alert devices which give a signal if you're pinned. We never had them before. One of the lieutenants was blown down into a basement and burned, and a floor collapsed under the other one and he fell into the fire. I'm not saying it would have helped them, but it might have helped in Will Thompson's case and my own.

These are little things that they're buying now that they probably never would have bought years ago. It was a big fight with the unions over the air mask. The city wanted to stay with the old filter mask, and the union wanted the self-contained air mask. You have to have something like a union say to the city, "If you can't afford to pay us the money, at least give us the tools and the proper equipment to do the job." But the city holds the salary down, and they hold the equipment down.

You look at the firefighters from Baltimore County, I'm not trying to put them down, but these guys don't get the fires that the people in the city do. They have one-story ranch houses, and they're running around with top-notch gear. You look at the city firemen, and they look like a bunch of ragpickers. It's unreal. The chief of the fire department does the best he can for us, but from there on up nobody gives a damn about the firemen. The mayor doesn't. He sees a fire on TV, and he'll show up and say, "Oh, these firemen are great."

We had a nine-alarm fire a little while ago. The manning and the equipment in the city is so low, they had to get the deluge lines from the county. They're relying on that more and more.

They take some engine companies and truck companies and combine them into one company, called Air Tower Ladders or something like that. When they get to a fire, it's the officer's decision whether it's going to be an engine or a truck, but if he's a truck company he can't be an engine company. They had to get county trucks to come and work on a fire in the city, because they didn't have any truck companies there. I mean, they're trying to save money, and here it is as an expense.

It's the taxpayer who's going to be hurt, and the fireman is breaking his back more.

□

Yes, I think about the possibility of dying in this job. I'm missing five o'clock Mass tonight. When I go to work every day, I'm up for work. It's like a game, I'm up for it. I say my prayers on the way to church or on the way to work, and I ask God to keep me safe and to keep the guys I work with safe. I pray to him that I make the right decisions. I'm not ashamed to say that to anybody. I don't go around handing out religious leaflets, and I'll never talk about it at work, but I don't think a man could extend himself and risk his life in this job without being close to God, because this could be your last day.

What I get from firefighting is the satisfaction of having personal worth.

□

You get suspicious when people tell you that they want to fight fires to serve humanity. Helping people is a by-product. After you are a firefighter for a while, it becomes instinct in any situation to help people, because that is what you have been trained to do. I don't think most of us get involved in the fire department for that motive. We do it because we love the fire department and we love firefighting.

The more time you spend in journalism, the more you realize that there are times when you can be fooled. I'm wary of it. You tend to be skeptical because you know you are capable of being misled. I don't know about firefighters, it depends on what their experience in firefighting has been. I think that firefighters who have been on busy, hard-working companies probably get wiser than those who have been in slower places. A busy fire company is a lot like a combat outfit in the military service. The more you see, the more you learn.

It also shapes your attitude. I've noticed that the busier a fire company is, the happier it is, the fewer discipline problems you have, the closer bond you have between the firemen themselves. The slow companies are where you have the tension and the problems. The more action a fire company gets, the better it gets, the better feeling it has about itself. It's an interesting phenomenon.

There have been times, twice in my life, when I stayed away from the fire department for a period because I had seen more than I could handle. Once when I was around nineteen or twenty, I saw too many things happening that I couldn't cope with. I stayed away for more than a year. If I heard a siren, I actually went in the other direction. It wasn't so much the victims themselves as it was the families. Seeing them shook me up pretty bad, but gradually I got back at it and forced myself to cope with it.

Then, after my first son was born, I became very sensitive to parenthood and my responsibilities to my child. I gave up being a war correspondent at that point and also decided I would stay away from the fire department and stop going to burning buildings. For maybe a year or two, I gave up being active as a firefighter. But I couldn't stay away, and eventually I had to go back because something was missing from my life. I just said the heck with it, there's nothing I can do about it, I want to do this thing, and I've got to do it.

Only a fool would not acknowledge that being a firefighter is a dangerous thing. You have to learn to accept it and to use your head as much as you can. You realize that there are certain situations that you cannot control. Everybody gets hurt at some point. I think all firemen are fugitives from the law of averages. If you go to enough fires, sooner or later you're going to take your share of bumps and bruises.

But I have always loved the actual firefighting. The feeling of being a part of this team and of being challenged. I also love the firehouse, the tension that always exists because the bell could ring at any minute.

Author's Note

My work is different now. I write books, and I edit two magazines for firefighters. It is sedentary work. But I am still firefighting. I don't choke on the smoke any longer, and my eyes are not made blind by the fires' darkness. Yet I still feel each day that I am there side by side with the nation's firefighters, meeting the challenge of the flames, advancing inch by hard-fought inch to an inevitable victory. One thing is certain in our work, and that is fires always die. And where would we be if that were not so? My work at the magazines I publish, or with the two fire safety foundations where I serve as trustee, daily reinforces my belief that while most people respect the work of firefighters, their understanding of the firefighter's profession is inadequate to that respect. Almost every sensible man and woman intuits that it takes a special courage to enter a burning building, but few truly know what actually happens inside of that building. I hope that this book has contributed toward a more popular understanding of what it is like for the firefighter within the whirling darkness of the smoke and the crisping intensity of the heat.

Often I wish that the firefighter would cast modesty to the wind and more loudly and forcefully blow his own horn about his own actions. I know it is not the firefighter's place to color his own courage, though, and within the personal accounts found in these pages are many examples of restrained descriptions of extraordinary actions. The Bible advises us to make our speech to be like apples of gold set in pictures of silver, and it would not do to lecture Americans on courage. Still, when I read of city fathers threatening firefighters, for instance, with ending the traditional pay parity with policemen, or when state legislatures reduce firefighters' health benefits, I want to be marching in the street with a megaphone.

Perhaps, though, the performance of the act of firefighting alone is sufficient, for quiet behavior can scream just as loudly and forcefully as a thousand megaphones.

And so, I leave this book hoping that it will shout the honor of firefighting, knowing that a kind or generous or heroic act done quietly and without assumption can rock the world with the fanfare of a thousand trumpets.

About the Author

Dennis Smith is a retired New York City firefighter, the founder of *Firehouse* magazine and author of twelve books, including *Report from Ground Zero* (March 2002). He serves on the advisory board of the New York Police & Fire Widows' & Children's Benefit Fund, the Congressional Fire Services Institute, and the Foundation for American Firefighters, of which he is chairman. He lives in New York, where he continues his interest in firefighter safety, Irish music, and pencil sketching.